THE LAITY
IN THE
MIDDLE AGES

ANDRÉ VAUCHEZ

THE LAITY

IN THE

MIDDLE AGES

RELIGIOUS BELIEFS
AND
DEVOTIONAL PRACTICES

Edited and Introduced by

DANIEL E. BORNSTEIN

Translated by

MARGERY J. SCHNEIDER

UNIVERSITY OF NOTRE DAME PRESS
Notre Dame and London

Copyright © 1993 by
University of Notre Dame Press
Notre Dame, Indiana 46556
All Rights Reserved

Manufactured in the United States of America

André Vauchez, *Les laïcs du Moyen Age: Pratiques et expériences religieuses,*
© Les Editions du Cerf, Paris, 1987.

Library of Congress Cataloging-in-Publication Data

Vauchez, André.
  [Laïcs au Moyen Age. English]
  The laity in the Middle Ages : religious practices and expe-
riences / André Vauchez ; edited and introduced by Daniel E.
Bornstein ; translated by Margery J. Schneider.
    p. cm.
  Includes bibliographical references and index.
  ISBN 0-268-01297-0 (alk. paper)
  1. Church history—Middle Ages, 600-1500.   2. Laity—
Catholic Church—History.   I. Bornstein, Daniel Ethan,
1950-   . II. Title
BR275.L27V3813 1993
262'.15'0902—dc20   92-53746
                                                        CIP

∞ *The paper used in this publication meets the minimum requirements of the
American National Standard for Information Sciences—Permanence of Paper
for Printed Library Materials, ANSI Z39.48-1984.*

CONTENTS

PREFACE   ix

INTRODUCTION   xv

PART I: THE EMERGENCE OF THE LAITY WITHIN THE CHURCH (ELEVENTH TO THIRTEENTH CENTURIES)

1

THE IDEA OF GOD   3

2

THE MIDDLE AGES OF "THE PEOPLE"   27

3

THE LAITY IN THE FEUDAL CHURCH   39

4

THE CRUSADES: THE MASSES APPEAR ON THE SCENE   45

5

A TWELFTH-CENTURY NOVELTY: THE LAY SAINTS OF URBAN ITALY   51

6

TWO LAYPERSONS IN SEARCH OF PERFECTION: ELZÉAR OF SABRAN AND DELPHINE OF PUIMICHEL   73

PART II: RELIGION IN PRECEPT AND IN PRACTICE

7

LAY BELIEF AROUND 1200: RELIGIOUS MENTALITIES OF THE FEUDAL WORLD   85

8

THE PASTORAL TRANSFORMATION OF THE THIRTEENTH CENTURY   95

9

"Ordo Fraternitatis": CONFRATERNITIES AND LAY PIETY IN THE MIDDLE AGES   107

10

MEDIEVAL PENITENTS   119

11

LITURGY AND FOLK CULTURE IN THE *Golden Legend*   129

12

ANTI-SEMITISM AND POPULAR CANONIZATION: THE CULT OF ST. WERNER   141

13

PATRONAGE OF SAINTS AND CIVIC RELIGION IN THE ITALY OF THE COMMUNES   153

PART III: WOMEN'S CHOICE: HUMAN MARRIAGE OR SPIRITUAL NUPTIALS

14

FEMALE SANCTITY IN THE FRANCISCAN MOVEMENT   171

15

CONJUGAL CHASTITY: A NEW IDEAL IN THE THIRTEENTH CENTURY   185

16

THE VIRGINAL MARRIAGE OF ELZÉAR AND DELPHINE   191

17

A HOLY WOMAN DURING THE HUNDRED YEARS' WAR: JEANNE-MARIE OF MAILLÉ   205

PART IV: THE INSPIRED WORD

18

FEMALE PROPHETS, VISIONARIES, AND MYSTICS IN MEDIEVAL EUROPE   219

19

MYSTICAL SANCTITY AT THE TIME OF THE AVIGNON PAPACY AND THE GREAT SCHISM   231

20

EUCHARISTIC DEVOTION AND MYSTICAL UNION IN LATE-MEDIEVAL FEMALE
SAINTS   237

21

THE REACTION OF THE CHURCH TO LATE-MEDIEVAL MYSTICISM AND
PROPHECY   243

22

JOAN OF ARC AND FEMALE PROPHECY IN THE FOURTEENTH AND FIFTEENTH
CENTURIES   255

CONCLUSION   265

NOTES   271

INDEX   333

PREFACE

ANDRÉ VAUCHEZ is widely known as one of the leading students of medieval religious life. He has written two important books and scores of articles, published two volumes of collected essays, and edited several more books; yet until now, only one of his essays has appeared in English.[1] The present volume is a translation of his most recent collection of essays, *Les laïcs au Moyen Age*, which was published in 1987 and translated into Italian in 1989.[2] Unlike the Italian edition, this translation does not reproduce unchanged the French version: three of the original essays have been dropped, the order of the remaining ones has been rearranged slightly, and one new essay (chapter 5) has been added.[3] The editor and translator have also tried to make the scholarly apparatus as useful and as current as possible, by providing references to English editions of works cited by Vauchez and by adding (in square brackets) exact citations for works mentioned by Vauchez in passing and references to the more important studies that have appeared since the original publication of these essays. The result, we hope, is a coherent and stimulating set of essays that accurately presents to an American public the most recent work of a major French medievalist.

Throughout his career, André Vauchez has focused on the role of religion in society. His early investigations of this subject were dedicated to the mendicant orders: his first essay, "A Campaign of Peacemaking in Lombardy around 1233," was a meticulous demonstration of how certain Dominican and Franciscan friars, by placing themselves at the head of a popular devotional movement, were able to dominate briefly the governments of several Italian cities and enact a series of legislative measures embodying mendicant ideals; his second offered a fresh perspective on ecclesiastical resistance to the novelty of the mendicant orders by examining a number of writings expressing reservations about or outright disbelief in the stigmata of St. Francis of Assisi.[4] But by the early 1970s

Vauchez had already turned his attention to the topic he has made his own: sanctity. A score of incisive articles and a magisterial *thèse d'état* on *La sainteté en Occident aux derniers siècles du Moyen Age* (Rome: Ecole Française de Rome, 1981) have established him as the unrivaled authority on late medieval sanctity.

Sanctity, for Vauchez, is quintessentially social, for people achieve sainthood through the judgments of those around them. Hundreds of such judgments were collected and preserved in the dossiers assembled in the course of papal canonization proceedings, and it is primarily on this body of material that Vauchez has based his studies. These dossiers have been relatively neglected by the Bollandists and others engaged in the traditional task of establishing a reliable life of the saint, for they contain surprisingly little biographical material and what material they do contain is generally fragmentary. It is one of Vauchez's great merits that, by approaching the canonization proceedings with novel questions in mind, he has demonstrated the rich possibilities of this sort of document. His reading of the depositions concerning St. Elizabeth of Hungary clarifies the transition from the ascetic ideals of the twelfth century to the Franciscan exaltation of poverty in the thirteenth; at the same time, it reveals the incapacity of even St. Elizabeth, with her profound empathy for the poor, to question the social structures which engendered poverty.[5] The virtues stressed by those who testified to the sanctity of a series of women connected with the Franciscan order allow Vauchez to trace the progressive spiritualization and interiorization of female holiness in the century following the official recognition of St. Elizabeth's extraordinary charitable activity.[6] Charity, mystical experience, learning, poverty, chastity: the place of each in the constantly shifting complex of late medieval ideals is defined with precision in Vauchez's studies of the canonization proceedings.

Vauchez surveyed the history of medieval spirituality in his first book, a subtle and elegant mapping of the changes from the ritualistic devotions of the Carolingian epoch to the evangelical piety of the twelfth century.[7] His aim was not merely to offer an overview of medieval spirituality, but to redefine the very meaning of the term. Rather than discussing spiritual doctrine and learned piety, he explored the impact of the Christian message on the beliefs and behavior of the populace. He strove to embed the history of spirituality in the social and cultural context of medieval Europe. And in his effort to treat spirituality as the way in which people tried to live their faith in specific historical circumstances, Vauchez was led inevitably to give fresh attention to the role of the laity in religious life.

This concern for the religious history of the Christian people, so profoundly present in his very first book, is also the inspiration for the essays that comprise this volume. Nearly all of them were written in the decade after the publication of *La sainteté en Occident*, and most of them draw on the body of sources—the canonization proceedings and the hagiographical literature—that underlay that work. But in these essays the focus of attention has shifted to the penumbra of devotion on the fringes of officially recognized sanctity. Vauchez looks at holy persons whose sanctity was never recognized by the papacy, objects of popular devotion whose cults remained suspect in the eyes of the ecclesiastical hierarchy, female prophets and visionaries who managed—for a time—to make their voices heard in a masculine world. The recurrent theme is the struggle, never entirely successful, of the Christian laity to carve out for themselves a religious role that would concede some spiritual dignity to the circumstances and concerns of their daily lives: marriage, work, civic life, even war. Vauchez notes the emergence of the ideal of conjugal chastity, which permits married laymen and women to be recognized as saints (chapter 15), and describes the singular efforts of Delphine of Puimichel and Elzéar of Sabran to preserve their virginity within marriage (chapters 6 and 16). He discerns the faint glimmers of a positive revaluation of the world of work, whether the trade practiced be that of the knightly warriors who took part in the crusades (chapter 4) or the merchants and artisans who built the prosperity of the Italian communes (chapter 5). He stresses the lay attachment to religious ideals such as charity and penitence, ideals which can be pursued in the world and for the benefit of the world, and explores the religious self-definition of the civic community (chapter 13). These efforts to establish an authentically lay religiosity are never autonomous; inevitably, they are shaped by the distinctions between clergy and laity and by their sometimes acrimonious debates over the social and religious roles proper to each constituent element of Christian society. But the general thrust is towards the definition of a form of Christian life that is neither sacerdotal nor monastic, but distinctively lay.

Vauchez's approach to this problem owes a great deal to the *Annales* school. His early studies of poverty and charity were inspired by Michel Mollat, and his interest in the reciprocal interpenetration of lay and learned cultures was stimulated by his teacher, Jacques Le Goff. However, an even more powerful influence, in some respects, has been the work of Catholic scholars like Étienne Delaruelle, Gabriel Le Bras, and Gilles Gérard Meersseman, who in the middle of this century began to treat the history of Christianity in social terms, examining religious practice and exploring the relations between belief and behavior. Gabriel Le Bras was an expert in canon law and in the institutional structures of the medieval church, but his interest in the application of those laws and the operation of those structures led him to tramp through the French countryside, visiting thousands of churches and talking to priests and parishioners. Out of these inquiries he crafted path-breaking studies of religious sociology and a history of religious practice; his final book, published posthumously, was a characteristically wide-ranging and passionate exploration of the religious, juridical, and human ties that bind the ecclesiastical institution and the rural agglomeration, the church and the village.[8] Together with Gabriel Le Bras and Herbert Grundmann, Étienne Delaruelle was (according to Vauchez) "one of the principal artisans of the renewal of the religious history of the medieval West"; of them, he was "the first to break the barriers between a history of the Church in which the laity appeared only as the objects of the pastoral solicitude of the clergy and those studies of manifestations of piety which were too often hypnotized by pagan survivals or inclined to peer at things through the small end of opera glasses."[9] Delaruelle, with his sympathetic interest in all forms of religious activity, incorporated detailed information about lay beliefs and practices in his contribution to Fliche and Martin's *Histoire de l'Église*, just as he welcomed lay students to his courses on ecclesiastical history at the Institut Catholique de Toulouse.[10] Vauchez's debt to the work of Gilles Gerard Meersseman, the great historian of lay confraternities, is eloquently acknowledged in his appreciation of and reflection on the three monumental volumes of Meersseman's *Ordo Fraternitatis. Confraternite e pietà dei laici nel medioevo* (chapter 9).[11] As Vauchez notes, the historical studies of Meersseman, like the theology of Yves Congar, were part of the ferment within the Catholic Church that culminated in the Second Vatican Council, from 1962 to 1965. The ecclesiology of Vatican II affirmed for the Catholic church today what scholars like Meersseman, Delaruelle, and Le Bras had been asserting about medieval Christendom: that the Church was the people of God, and not merely a hierarchically structured institution.

André Vauchez, who embarked on a scholarly career in the heady days of Vatican II, has spent much of his career rewriting medieval religious history in keeping with that new, and old, definition of the Church. His work, like that of the persons he studies, is marked by the concerns of the religious context in which it was created, as well as by its intellectual environment. But this is not to say that his work is confessional in the way that some of the finest Catholic scholarship can be.[12] In fact, Vauchez himself would reject the label of "Catholic historian," and define himself simply as a Christian who tries to ply the historian's craft with honesty and integrity.[13] In pursuing his craft, he has had to grapple with some of the most important, and most difficult, issues in medieval history.[14] This volume, for instance, makes an important contribution to ongoing scholarly debates about the nature of popular devotion, the role of religion in civic life, the sociology of religious attitudes and practices, and the relationship between the intersecting spheres of lay and clerical culture. Parts III and IV in particular, with their discussion of how spiritual ideals of chastity shaped the social practice of marriage and how the intimate experiences of female visionaries and mystics impinged on the formal structure of the Church, are a noteworthy addition to the rapidly growing body of literature on women in the Middle Ages. Taken together, these essays demonstrate the diversity of religious experience, which cannot be reduced to the prescribed forms of parochial observances. They also hint at the fresh insights we may expect from Vauchez's continuing exploration of the role of informal powers, such as those of female mysticism and visionary prophecy, within the religious culture of medieval Europe.[15]

Daniel E. Bornstein
Texas A&M University

INTRODUCTION

ONE OF THE FUNDAMENTAL TASKS of the historian is to give their due to those persons or groups who played an important role in the civilization of their day, but were undervalued or forgotten by posterity. In this spirit, for example, some of the best students of the medieval West—Michel Mollat, Bronislaw Geremek, Jacques Le Goff—have rescued from obscurity entire social categories, like the poor and other groups on the fringes of society, or individuals particularly representative of a certain milieu, like William Marshal, whom Georges Duby recently plucked from the ranks of oblivion.[1]

To some extent, the present work seeks to effect the same kind of rehabilitation in the religious history of the Western Middle Ages, more precisely during the period between around 1100 and 1450. Indeed, until a relatively recent date, the history of the Church was too often limited to the history of its hierarchy and its clergy, leaving the Christian masses in the shadows, as if they were somehow disreputable. This disparaging view of the role of the simple faithful has its roots in the heart of the Middle Ages. As early as 1296, in his famous decretal *Clericis laicos*, Pope Boniface VIII did not hesitate to assert: "That laymen have been very hostile to the clergy antiquity relates; and it is very clearly proved by the experiences of the present time."[2] Although it was framed in a particular context—the conflict between the pope and Philip the Fair, king of France—this polemical formula nevertheless seems, in the mind of the pontiff, to express a fundamental truth which consistently underlay the historical development of the Church: the hostility between the two constituent elements of the Christian people, the clergy and the laity, with the clergy considering the laity to be their rivals or even adversaries. In fact, although medieval anticlericalism was a phenomenon of major importance, we know that the concrete reality was infinitely more complex, and that, until the time of the Reformation, only rarely did the violence of their arguments and conflicts of interest cause the antagonists to lose sight of the necessary complementarity of their respective roles. Nonetheless, the cultural superiority of the clergy and their dominant role in determining ideology and interpreting events allowed them to portray the history of the Church as a formidable combat between the champions of Good, identified as the case may be with the bishops, the papacy, or members of religious orders, and the forces of Evil, that is to say, the laypeople whose rapacity and impiety were continually deplored by the Church. What is most surprising is that this Manichean rhetoric has influenced Catholic historiography up to our times: the volume of the famous *Histoire de l'Église*, edited by Fliche and Martin, entitled *L'Eglise au pouvoir des laïcs (888–1057)*, which was published in 1943, is a telling example.[3] The authors, Emile Amann and Auguste Dumas, presented the decadence of religious life which in their eyes characterized the West in that epoch as the result of the faithful's dominion over ecclesiastical institutions. But eventually redemption came from the reaction of the best of the monks—the Cluniacs—and of the papacy, who sought to wrench the spiritual (identified with the clerical world) from the grasp of the temporal, the domain proper to the laity.

The progress of historical studies over the last thirty years allows us to judge how arbitrary this interpretation was and how much it undervalued both the efforts at reform set in motion by the emperors, in the German Holy Roman Empire and in Rome itself, and the role of popular religious movements like the Pataria of Milan, recently rehabilitated by Italian historians, as well as the role played by the hermits in diffusing the ideal of the "apostolic life" among the masses.[4] Beyond any particular errors or blind spots for which we might reproach this "neo-Guelf" historiography, our major complaint is its inability to comprehend the evolutions that modified the physiognomy of the medieval Church except in terms of reformist impulses emanating from the top and the resistance they met with from below: in the face of good prelates and saintly monks, the wicked laity, out of ignorance or self-interest, seemed intent on creating obstacles to the triumph of justice and truth.

It would be naïve and scientifically unpersuasive to replace this simplistic and willfully reductionist vision of Church history with an interpretation of the medieval past based on an idyllic or mythical conception of "popular religion," or on the contrast between a corrupt hierarchy, insensitive to the religious aspirations of the time, and the faithful populace, attracted spontaneously to evangelical values. The "noble masses" existed no more in the Middle Ages than they do today, and popular devotion, in the areas in which it did not conform to the mandates of the clergy, was not always positive in content. One of the studies in this volume (chapter 12) demonstrates, for example, that medieval anti-semitism was much more virulent among the masses than among the members of the clergy, who themselves held various opinions on the subject. Our purpose, therefore, is not to replace one form of Manichaeism with another, but rather to extend the effort, now several decades old, of some medieval historians—including Etienne Delaruelle, Raoul Manselli and Gilles Gérard Meersseman—to reintegrate the unjustly neglected history of the laity into the history of the Church.[5] Their efforts were much in keeping with the ecclesiology of Vatican II, one of whose most significant innovations was the definition of the Church as the people of God marching toward the Kingdom of God, in which all of the baptized are called to play an active role inspired by the Holy Spirit. In this theological perspective, it seemed essential to emphasize the fundamental role of lay religious movements in the life and history of the Church, movements as varied as the Crusades, the confraternities, and the Beguines and Beghards. This issue has lost none of its vitality, as the studies in part I of this collection attest; but we must also recognize that this rediscovery of the common people as actors in history—and not merely objects of the pastoral solicitude of the clergy—gives rise to new questions about the relationships between religious life, social structures, and "folk culture," both urban and rural. These are the concerns which inspire the studies in part II.

Moreover, it is desirable to approach the study of the relationship between the clergy and the laity free of preconceived notions. During the Middle Ages, this relationship was characterized by ambivalence. On the one hand, many of the faithful gave voice to an anticlericalism, often violent, which was at the origin of most heretical movements. It is no surprise that a work essentially consecrated to orthodoxy contains no mention of them, but we should be careful not to forget their existence, and the success which their denunciations of clerical vices and deficiencies found among the laity. On the other hand, we note at the same time the laity's desire to appropriate the spiritual riches of the clergy, particularly those of the monks and religious, in order to ensure their salvation, which remained the fundamental goal of religious life. This impulse explains the importance in the Middle Ages of all forms of association between clergy and laity, whether they be prayer unions or ties of solidarity that allowed laypeople to benefit from the merits and suffrage of the clerics. This general aspiration could lead in particular cases either to an exact imitation of clerical forms of piety—pious laypeople reciting canonical hours, for example—or, on the contrary, to the quest for a direct relationship with the divine, by means of an imitation of Christ pushed to the point of total conformity. This is what we see in the flagellants of the fourteenth and fifteenth century, who adopted and diffused an ascetic practice which until then had been reserved for the religious alone. Whether they considered the clergy to be models, foils, or useless intermediaries, the medieval laity were fascinated by them and could conceive of their own spiritual destiny only in relation to them. If we wish to present a true image of the religious history of Western Europe, therefore, it is not enough to simply graft some "popular" elements to a trunk that remains chronologically and institutionally clerical. We need to investigate the precise nature of this fundamental relationship, the forms it assumed in various places and countries, and its evolution between the twelfth and fifteenth centuries.

Another essential question which guided the writing and compilation of these studies is the underlying meaning of the emergence of the laity, which was one of the major novelties of the era in the religious domain. Beyond any particular sets of circumstances that might be offered in explanation, the growth of the laity's role in the Church seems to me to be related above all to the rehabilitation of the active life in Christian spirituality. Whether it be holy wars or works of charity, the practice of poverty or the exercise of justice, all forms of concrete action in the world aimed at bringing it into conformity with the evangelical ideal grew in importance in the twelfth and thirteenth centuries, in the context of an incarnational Christianity which exalted God's humanity. At the same time, wider social categories were called to participate actively in religious life. In the feudal era, only sovereigns—emperors and kings—were involved, along with a small number of great lords and noble women, who were recognized as benefactors of the clergy and of churches. By the end of the twelfth century, the movement in Italy included the milieux of artisans and even merchants who had remained faithful to the Catholic faith, on whom the hierarchy was to rely in combatting the spread of heresy. This same course was later followed in other parts of Christendom, where bourgeois milieux provided the nucleus of the recruits for the Beguines; and it is not entirely surprising to see a simple peasant girl like Joan of Arc, considered a prophet in her day, at the head of a movement of national liberation that was political in its objectives but religious in its inspiration. As the evolution of the typology of sanctity at the end of the Middle Ages demonstrates, the fourteenth and fifteenth centuries constituted the golden age of the laity, which is all the more remarkable for its striking contrast with the epochs that immediately preceded and followed.

This perspective must also take into account the new prominence of women, who emerged from the shadows to suddenly assume roles of primary importance in the religious domain. The mention of a few names—Bridget of Sweden, Catherine of Siena, and Joan of Arc are the most famous—will suffice to suggest the importance of their actions and influence in this time of troubles and doubts. Already noticeable in the thirteenth century, the emergence of women, especially laywomen, in church life became more pronounced with the Great Schism and the crisis of the conciliar period. Here again we are in the presence of a phenomenon that was both important and ambivalent, which I have tried to study in its various aspects in parts III and IV. Although women were at center stage between approximately 1370 and 1450, this does not mean that all aspects of the female condition improved. None of the obstacles set up by canon law and the weight of tradition was removed. But at a time when ecclesiastical authorities were losing their prestige by tearing each other to pieces in petty quarrels, women, excluded by definition from power in the Church, were able to turn the situation to their advantage by taking on the role of privileged depositories of sacred utterances: revelations, visions, and prophecies were the main forms of their action in the world and the source of their influence. In contrast to the bookish knowledge of the clergy, women affirmed the primacy of spiritual experience and the possibility of contact between people and God in mystical relationships. To be sure, the success of these visionaries was partial and short-lived; their prestige was too closely tied to extraordinary situations and spiritual gifts for them to be able to change mentalities in any lasting way. But this "Indian summer" of feminine religiosity at the end of the Middle Ages is well worth pondering and evaluating.

In concluding this introduction, it remains for me to set forth my reasons for compiling this volume, which contains various articles previously published in journals or conference proceedings, along with some unpublished studies. I know that I am taking liberties with the tradition according to which scholars do not publish collections of scattered works until the autumn of their days, when they are certain that the ideas have aged well. I have decided to break this unwritten rule, which in any case is increasingly less honored nowadays, because the conditions of university research have changed significantly in the past few decades: periods of tranquility, favorable to the creation of works on a grand scale, have become more rare, and, what is more, it has become usual for specialists to meet frequently in national and international conferences, whose proceedings, often published after long delays, are not easy to come by, especially when they are published in foreign countries. Given these conditions, the coherence of the subject matter becomes the main criterion for judging whether an enterprise of this kind is worthwhile. The reader will decide whether this group of studies actually constitutes a homogeneous ensemble. More prosaically, it seems to me that this publication is justified by the simple fact that it makes available to a new and larger public research which otherwise would only have found a limited audience.

PART I

THE EMERGENCE OF THE LAITY
WITHIN THE CHURCH

(11th to 13th Centuries)

ONE

THE
IDEA
OF GOD

IN COMMON PARLANCE, the medieval world is frequently designated by the name of "Christendom." This is well founded, because, between the sixth and sixteenth centuries, the only religion
known and practiced by the inhabitants of France, with the exception of a tiny minority of Jews, was Christianity, or, more precisely,
Catholicism. Although it is on the whole valid, in that all French
people received baptism, and unbelief was an extremely rare phenomenon, this equation between the Middle Ages and Christianity
runs the risk of smoothing over a reality infinitely more complex
than was long believed. Historians cannot be satisfied with this
oversimplification. Indeed, their experience teaches them that the
exceptional religious continuity long ascribed to this millennium
of our history is in large part illusory. How can we overlook the
distance separating the faith of a recently converted barbarian in
Merovingian times from that of a fourteenth-century Beguine? For
this reason, we must abandon at the outset all synthetic or static
approaches to the religious reality of the period and treat the
problem from an evolutionary perspective.

This procedure is particularly advantageous for the earliest period, for the transition from paganism to Christianity took place
gradually between the second and ninth centuries, and in the span
of the early Middle Ages there were significant disparities among
the various regions which now constitute the country of France:
the south, Provence and Aquitaine, an area which was profoundly

marked by Roman influence and converted to Christianity at an early date, was at quite a different stage of Christianization than the France north of the Loire, both more rural and more directly affected by the impact of the great Germanic invasions. In the sixth century, when Clovis and his successors united the majority of ancient Gaul under Frankish rule, the canvas of religious life was particularly full of contrasts: on one hand, there was the old Gallo-Roman senatorial aristocracy from which the bishops were recruited, heir to the Mediterranean traditions and spokesman for the new Christian culture; on the other hand, a mass of conquering warriors who received baptism in emulation of their chiefs, who had been clever enough to understand that they could win the support of their new subjects only by adopting their religion. Thanks to this perspicacity, France was the only barbarian kingdom which did not experience the kind of religious conflicts that everywhere else set the native Roman Catholic populations against the invaders, followers of a heterodox sort of Christianity, Arianism, which held that Christ's nature was not fully divine. Between the two groups, which were still clearly distinct in the beginning of the sixth century, an osmosis progressively took place, facilitated by the rapid decline of classical culture and the gradual loosening of the ties that connected Gaul with the Mediterranean area.

The new Frankish aristocracy, which was born of this fusion, settled down to the protracted task of Christianizing the rural populace—the *pagani*—a Latin term from which, significantly, the French word "païen" [and the English word "pagan"] were derived. To grasp properly the reality of this process, which we call conversion or evangelization, it is necessary to take account of the religious mentality of the people of those times and their conception of the divine. At the end of Antiquity and the beginning of the early Middle Ages, Gallic or Germanic paganism did not consist of a corpus of clearly outlined doctrines. The old Celtic religion, which had survived from prehistoric times, had already been profoundly shaken by Romanization. The spread of Latin, the growth of the cult of the emperor, and finally the penetration of mystery religions of Oriental origin had laid the groundwork for the advent of Christianity, especially in urban settings. And, though cults of springs and worship of pre-Roman agrarian divinities survived in the countryside, they should be considered expressions of a "folk culture" that was certainly still alive but fated to be marginalized because of its "rusticity" in a world where the cities long continued to play a dominant role. The same was true of the beliefs of the Germans, who frequently had already been influenced by Christianity before they settled in the Roman world; in their eyes, the Christian religion was an integral part of this civilization, which they felt to be superior, and into which they longed to be integrated. For them, as for Clovis, it was a question of efficacy: if the God of the Christians procured for them victory over their adversaries, why not recognize his superiority and join his cult?

But even more than God's power, the people of that epoch were conscious of the power of his servants, the saints. Indeed, they played a deciding role in the conversion of Gaul to Christianity, through both their works while alive and the attraction exerted by their relics after their death. The most typical case in this regard is that of St. Martin in the second half of the fourth century, who combatted paganism in the region between Tours and Poitiers, destroying rural sanctuaries without encountering significant resistance. But his lasting fame was due above all to his powers as a miracle worker and protector. Numerous miracles were witnessed at his tomb, and the sick, the crippled and, most significantly, the possessed flocked to the basilica of Tours, which soon became a very popular pilgrimage center. Clovis credited him with the victory over the Visigoths at Vouillé in 507. From then on, the Merovingian sovereigns placed themselves under his protection, and the saint's mantel (the *capa*) became the military emblem that led their armies into battle. Other cults arose for martyrs like St. Mauritius and the saints of the Theban Legion venerated by the Burgundians, in whose honor King Sigismund founded the abbey of St. Mauritius in Valais, or St. Saturninus in Toulouse. But the number of martyrs in Gaul was not large, and in most regions, the catalysts of the new devotion were bishops like St. Desiderius in Cahors, St. Germanus in Auxerre, St. Leodegar in Autun, and St. Ouen in Rouen.

It is appropriate to linger over the spread of cult of the saints, which had such an important role in the Christianization of Frankish Gaul and which was to remain one of the characteristic traits of medieval piety. Interested neither in the complexity of relationships within the Trinity—a subject which fascinated the Christian

Orient at the time—nor in the mystery of the Incarnation, which they often misunderstood or considered a kind of disgrace, the masses in the West thought of God as a beneficent power, capable of triumphing over the various forms of evil that held sway in this world and in society: natural catastrophes, epidemics, and illness of all kinds, but also the violence of the powerful, political anarchy, and social pressure exerted by groups over individuals. However, this God was too impersonal and too distant to be approached. For that reason, the religious mentality of the time attached great importance to the intermediaries who surrounded the celestial Powers: first of all, the angels, whose cult experienced exceptional development throughout the early Middle Ages, and the most celebrated of whom was St. Michael; but also the saints, whose remains, it was believed, conserved some part of their *virtus*, that is to say the supernatural dynamism that had imbued them in their lifetimes. From the beginning, the Church had admitted cults of martyrs, but as of the fifth century, these cults, now extended to confessors who had not shed their blood for their faith, took on fundamental importance in Christian life. In a society in which the notion of the state had almost disappeared, every community, and soon every person, sought to establish a direct relationship with a personal protector.

This evolution, which could already be felt in the relations between men, was gradually extended to the religious domain. The bishop who during his lifetime had often made possible the survival of his city and had defended it against the arbitrary exercise of royal power quite naturally became its patron after his death. The influence of these saints spread from the city to the surrounding countryside through church dedications, which displaced the pagan divinities. Gregory of Tours recounts the story of how the bishop of Javols, in Auvergne, put an end to the worship offered by the mountain dwellers to a volcanic lake and built a chapel on its shores dedicated to St. Hilary, the former bishop of Poitiers. Although the annual procession was not abolished, its objective and the framework in which it took place were modified: from now on the diocesan Church took charge. However, to consider the Christian saints to be no more than successors to the pagan gods would be to underestimate the dimensions of the religious transformation that was taking place. The destruction of the sacred woods and the desacralization of the springs and lakes not only affirmed the power of the supporters of the new faith: these gestures illustrated their will to anthropomorphize the cosmos by substituting for the veneration of the forces of nature a new relationship between the divine and the human, mediated by historical personages—the "friends of God" whose intercession could be obtained through prayer and faith.

The massive adhesion to the cult of saints had profound repercussions on the very nature of the religious comportment of the faithful. Almost everywhere in the Frankish kingdom people took up the search for relics, fragments of bone which sometimes took them to distant spots—to Italy or the Orient—when none were available locally. Those who were able kept the relics on their persons as amulets or acquired objects that had been in contact with a reliquary: dust, oil from the lamps burning in the sanctuary, cloths placed in the tomb. The remains of certain prestigious saints held particular fascination for pilgrims, like those of St. Julian in Brioude, St. Martial in Limoges, St. Denis in Paris, and St. Remigius in Reims. But the sanctuaries where famous relics were kept did not attract only the living, for they also furthered the evolution of funerary custom: the Roman or Germanic necropolises, located far from habitations and often of considerable size, were replaced between the fifth and the seventh centuries by cemeteries, where the dead were brought together and sometimes even piled up in the limited area surrounding a *martyrium* or a basilica containing relics. The fashion of interment *ad sanctos* [near the saints] helped to make the churches themselves burial-places and served to reintegrate the deceased into inhabited space. In medieval Christianity, the dead were never to be distant from the living, and all would await together the day of the final resurrection.

Even the topography of the cities was modified by the anarchical proliferation of the sanctuaries, resulting from the discovery and translation of relics. At that time there were 40 churches in Metz, 29 in Paris, and 22 in Reims, each serving a very small number of inhabitants. If we add the churches located in the old necropolises outside of the cities, we end up with a veritable nebula of places of worship in which the devotion of the faithful was dispersed. But this is just one of the many ways in which the communitary dimension that had characterized early Christianity was dissolving. The progress of religious individualism was even more marked in the area of sacramental life. Penance in particular underwent significant changes: during the first centuries, it was conferred in public during a liturgical ceremony and could not be repeated. Those who had received it had to behave as if they were henceforth dead to the world, abstaining especially from all sexual relations as well as from bearing arms. In the Merovingian era, these requirements seemed too extreme, and very few of the faithful did penance before they were at the point of death.

The obstacles were removed thanks to the Irish and Scottish monks who, beginning in the late sixth century, arrived in large numbers on the Continent, not only in what is presently Brittany, where the monastery bishoprics established by St. Samson and St. Malo were to be of profound importance, but in all of Frankish Gaul, where St. Columbanus and his disciples introduced a model of ascetic Christianity that held great fascination for the laity. These monk-missionaries, who were responsible for the evangelization of a large part of northern France, from Picardy to the Vosges, spread the practice of private penitence, in other words, the use of re-peatable confession, already known to the Celts and Anglo-Saxons. So that the penitent could expiate the sins he had confessed to the priest, the monks emphasized works of penance, which little handbooks known as "penitentials" carefully calibrated: for each fault there was stipulated a precisely corresponding penance. The penalties (essentially consisting of fasts, expiatory pilgrimages, and flagellations) may seem extremely burdensome and harsh to us; but we must not forget that justice in those days was based on the idea that all crimes required concrete compensation, often quite costly, in the form of reparations that varied according to the social positions of the guilty person and his victim.

The new forms of penitence met with considerable success. The faithful who lived sinful lives and prayed little had been burdened throughout their lives with a generalized sense of guilt. For this rea-son, they welcomed the possibility of obtaining absolution when-ever they wished. The spreading practice of confession resulted in an evolution in religious feeling, and by this means Christianity was able to extend its influence to the domain of morality, where it had hardly made itself felt before that time. A new kind of relationship was established between man and God, who was considered the guarantor of moral law. Moreover, the new penitential discipline brought about the valorization of the works which the faithful could perform to atone for their faults.

Indeed, as early as the eighth century, the draconian canonical sanctions prescribed by the penitentials, especially the long and drastic fasts, began to be replaced, through a process of commutation, by prayers and alms. Although the latter were considered equivalent obligations, they were easier to carry out. It was then that the custom of redeeming all or a part of one's penance by donating a sum of money to churches or to the poor began to gain popularity. This further development, combatted at first by the ecclesiastical hierarchy but to no avail, was to lead to the practice of indulgences in the eleventh and twelfth centuries. In any case, the practice of donating money was at the origin of the spread of works of beneficence or charity, which is one of the characteristics of medieval religiosity.

The final stage in the Christianization of France was the establishment of a network of parishes between the eighth and twelfth centuries. This was the culmination of a process through which all churches were afforded the rights which had once been reserved for the cathedral or the mother church of the village. Henceforth, in every town or district, the parish church had its own baptistry, where baptisms were performed year-round. Divine offices were celebrated there, as in the monasteries, and the parish priest was supposed to preach there. This presupposed the existence of a resident, stable clergy, supported in their daily needs by the local community. In a world where the decayed cities had lost their importance, the religious life of the faithful was centered around rural parishes. They gathered there to hold assemblies or sought refuge there in times of need, because these sacred places guaranteed the right of asylum. Church bells, whose use became widespread in that era, marked the rhythm of time as a function of religious offices, and the fence around the church enclosed the remains of the dead.

The Carolingian sovereigns, anointed with holy oil, showed themselves to be more conscious of their religious duties than their predecessors and supported the bishops' efforts to enforce obedience to the commandments of the Church. Because of their pressure, the obligation of all of the faithful to attend Sunday mass was better observed. It was accompanied by a ban on engaging in manual labor on that day, with the exception of the preparation of food. The parishioners were compelled to pay tithes, originally intended for the maintenance of the parish priest. In this way, the essential elements of what sociologists call religious conformism took shape. Indeed, the sacraments soon came to delimit all social life: baptism, for example, no longer merely signified entrance into the Church, but also admission into society, into that Christianity which was defined from then on as a community of faith.

Through a parallel evolution, the religion became clericalized, and the sacred was made the exclusive domain of the priest. Although laypeople attended mass every Sunday, they behaved more as spectators than as participants. Moreover, prayers were pronounced in Latin, now clearly differentiated from the vernacular, and the celebrant turned his back to the people; he recited the canon, in which the people were no longer invited to participate, in a low voice. "Common bread was replaced by unleavened bread, as if the Mass had become estranged from everyday life" (E. Delaruelle). At the lateral altars in the side aisles, private masses multiplied—votive offerings for the most part, celebrated for the sake of the defunct, whose posthumous destinies were the object of ever growing apprehension for their families. The priests, obligatory intermediaries between the faithful and God, were not distinguished by their particularly high level of culture: most only had a meager notion of Latin and fragmentary knowledge of the Bible. But in the eyes of their flocks, they represented a superior order with which they could commmunicate through a series of rituals, gestures, and efficacious formulas. For this reason, the liturgy evolved in the direction of increasing ritualism. In the dedication of churches, as well as in the consecration of bishops, a whole series of new signs furthered the sacralization of space and individuals. The gesture of making the sign of the cross, considered to be a talisman, became common, and benedictions were increasingly given. The religious habit itself was considered to be endowed with sacramental effectiveness: at this time, the lords of this world began to adopt the custom of "dying in the cowl" to guarantee their eternal salvation.

The second wave of invasions, flooding the West in the ninth and tenth centuries, did not spare France, and in many regions shook the ecclesiastical structures that the Carolingian sovereigns had just restored. The Normans in northern France, and the Saracens—Moslems from Spain in the south—pillaged and destroyed many abbeys. In some areas, like present-day Normandy, the majority of episcopal sees remained vacant for several decades. The decline of the monarchy and the growing impotence of the sovereigns deprived the Church of the support of the secular arm and entailed the renunciation of the reforms begun in Charlemagne's time to improve the level of the clergy, especially in the cultural domain.

New feudal structures took shape between the end of the ninth and the beginning of the eleventh centuries, and ecclesiastical dignities participated in this general evolution. The warrior aristocracy that held the real reins of power considered bishoprics and abbeys its own property and appropriated them. The same was true for the parish churches, whose property and revenues were enfeoffed, divided, or sold. The secular clergy became more dependent than ever on the lords, and the Church ran the risk of dissolving into the ambient society.

Nevertheless, even in the depths of these "dark ages," there were some signs of a renewal of religious vitality. It was amazing enough that Christianity survived the collapse of the institutional structures on which it was based, an accomplishment that testifies to the depth of its roots. The pagan invaders rapidly adopted the religion of their subjects, and the dukes of Normandy in particular were to demonstrate themselves to be strong supporters of the monastic restoration, as the splendor of the abbeys of Caen, Jumièges and Fécamp attests even today.

Indeed, it was monasticism that provided the major stimuli. Cluny, founded in Burgundy in 910, led the reaction against the movement toward secularization, whose baneful effects were making themselves felt in most French Benedictine monasteries. To shield themselves against the intrusions of princes and episcopal authority, which had often fallen into unworthy hands, the abbots of Cluny decided to attach themselves directly to the Roman Church, or more precisely to the figure of St. Peter, under whose protection they placed the new abbey. Given the low prestige of the papacy at that time, theirs was fundamentally a symbolic gesture, intended to guarantee the liberty of their religious life and to affirm the autonomy of the spiritual sphere. After the Church had spent centuries in submission to the temporal powers, and in the face of the danger that Christianity would end up being diluted by an ever more invasive religious anthropomorphism, reformed monasticism was prepared to incarnate the most profound aspirations of the people of that time. As uncultivated and coarse as they may have been, they were nonetheless convinced that God actually intervened incessantly in the history of peoples and individuals, and that He was the supreme judge. Everyone therefore had to fear Him, revere Him, and implore Him to turn away the effects of His anger and the actions of the forces of Evil. In the feudal world, whose structures were taking form in that epoch, prayer was at least as much a social function as an individual act. The result was the paradox of those lords who, while they secured bishoprics and sold prelacies to the highest bidders, helped monks build monasteries where people would pray for them and their defunct relatives. Convinced that they were sinners and that their condition as laypeople prevented them from avoiding sin even if they had wished to, people of the feudal era delegated the task of salvation to an elite of specialists in spiritual matters, who discharged this obligation for the benefit of society as a whole—except for those people who decided to swell their ranks to guarantee their own salvation.

Given this mental context, it is easier to understand the extraordinary success of Cluny, which in the space of two centuries founded and reformed several hundred monasteries and priories, and received enormous donations from the seigniorial aristocracy, thus enabling them to reconstruct the basilica of the abbey three times between 950 and 1130, making it one of the great centers of Romanesque art. The monks of Cluny did not conceive of themselves as ascetics or pioneers. They were men of praise to God, of perpetual prayer, and of eucharistic sacrifice, who snatched from the Devil the souls of the living and the dead. An anticipation of heaven here on earth, the monastery celebrated God in His glory and sought to provide an idea of His grandeur through the splendor of its singing and its decoration.

Not all of their contemporaries shared this conception of the exaltation of the spiritual, and it is striking to realize that the monastic reform took place at the same time as what is known by the general term of the heresies of the year 1000. In fact, this term covers various movements and uncoordinated flashpoints—but all were expressions of a common malaise. In Vertus, in Champagne, a peasant by the name of Leutard destroyed the cross in his village church and urged the villagers to stop paying their tithes; in Orléans, certain canons, some of whom were part of the entourage of King Robert, were accused of belonging to a Manichaean sect and were accordingly burned at the stake; and in Arras, in 1025, some illiterate laymen were unmasked who denied that the sacraments of the Church had any value and rejected marriage in particular. Behind these accusations and in the heretics' professions of faith, it is possible to discern a set of themes common to all of these dissident movements. Shocked by the corruption of the Church and the reification of the sacred which characterized the religious life of their day, the heretics objected to the widespread magical interpretations of the sacraments and vehemently rejected all forms of the incarnation of the spiritual, from the cross to the eucharist. On this point, the heretics of the year 1000 were obviously as distant as possible from the monastic reformers. But the two shared the conviction that in order to survive, Christianity had to tear itself free from the ascendancy of the world and the material, and that humanity could only be saved by the efforts of fervent communities living on the fringe of the secular Church and bringing together those who wished to worship God in spirit and in truth.

The weakness of royal power—which did not end with the change of dynasties in 987, and indeed was to last until the beginning of the twelfth century—as well as the renewed outbreak of violence caused by the installation of new feudal structures, soon led the monks, especially the Cluniacs, to abandon their isolation and actively intervene in profane society. Only a spiritual authority was capable of restoring the minimum of order necessary for the survival of the Church itself, as well as for that of the poor and the humble. This was the reason for the assemblies and institutions of peace organized by bishops and abbots between 987 and about 1050, first in Aquitaine and Languedoc, then in the whole of France. In order to arrive at the desired pacification, the Church used the arms it had at hand. It threatened pillaging barons with the pains of hell; it inflicted spiritual sanctions on rebels, including excommunication and interdiction, which excluded laypeople from all participation in the sacraments and the liturgical activities of the churches; it had the lords swear oaths of peace on saints' relics and on the Gospels. But above all, it brought together the peasant and urban masses in manifestations of reconciliation during which those present raised their hands toward the heavens and cried "Peace, Peace!" God, with whom all participants believed they had concluded a solemn pact, thus became the guarantor of a social order that was more just, in which unarmed people—women, children, pilgrims, poor peasants—were granted the right to safety, and where war was to be gradually limited to the warrior class and restricted to certain days. Around the year 1000, then, the dream of a messianic era took shape, in which, according to the words of bishop Fulbert of Chartres, inspired by the prophet Isaiah, "the lance will be turned into a scythe, and the sword into a ploughshare" ["they shall beat their swords into plowshares, and their spears into pruning hooks" (Isaiah 2:4)].

To be sure, the concrete results did not live up to these expectations, but the peace movements nevertheless marked a decisive step in the religious history of France: the masses, passive up to that date, now emerged on the scene. Their feelings and beliefs were revealed in the course of the eleventh century, which also happened to be the great era of Romanesque art. The popular Christianity of that time had a marked eschatological tone: it was intent, that is to say, on the imminent return of Christ. But far from causing pessimism or despair, the perspective of the arrival of a new age gave rise to and stimulated initiatives. In preparation for the coming of the Kingdom, people were willing to deprive themselves, individually or collectively, of their worldly goods. Fasts became longer and more frequent; freed from their attachments, the faithful did not hesitate to set out for prestigious sanctuaries like Sainte-Foy of Conques and especially Santiago de Compostela, which at that time was beginning to attract an exceptional number of pilgrims; or else they became followers of men of God, poor and illiterate hermits and errant preachers whose ascetic exploits and fiery sermons stirred the enthusiasm of the faithful. It is in this climate that we must situate the extraordinary response to the appeal launched by Pope Urban II when, presiding at an assembly of peace in Clermont in 1095, he urged the Christians of the West to go on a crusade for the first time. Immediately repeated by popular preachers like Peter the Hermit and Robert of Abrissel, the papal exhortation was answered not only by the warriors, the seignorial aristocracy for whom it was intended, but also by the simple people, the poor and even women and children, who were the first to leave for Jerusalem.

This idea was truly new and apparently paradoxical, for Christianity had long classified the voluntary shedding of blood as defilement, and the peace movements promoted by the Church were based on its explicit wish to reduce and limit violence. At the same time, however, the clerics were trying to endow the new seignorial class—the knights—with ethical ideals. To this end, they attempted to sacralize the relationships of vasselage, which had originally been purely profane, by valorizing oaths, fidelity to one's plighted troth, and, later, dubbing, the rite of admittance to knighthood.

But the decisive turning point occurred in the second half of the eleventh century when, responding to the appeal of Cluny and Pope Alexander II, some knights spontaneously offered their services to the Holy See to go to war against the Moslems in Spain. The Church promised to those who lost their lives in the combat an indulgence, in other words remission of the punishment owed for the expiation of their sins, thereby giving their actions a religious character. From this time on, military service ending in supreme sacrifice would win exceptional merit for the knight who carried it out in a spirit of faith, merit comparable to that earned by martyrs. In this way, as the *Chanson de Roland* demonstrates, chivalry became the Christian form of the military life. The struggle against the infidels made the combatant a soldier of Christ whose task was to avenge the honor of his Lord, who has been deprived of his land by the pagans. The idea of transmitting the Christian faith to those who were not familiar with it was foreign to the mentality of the times: God can only be on the side of his people (this is the ultimate meaning of the expression "*Gesta Dei per Francos*," so dear to the chroniclers of the Crusades), while Islam was considered to be the incarnation of infernal powers with whom one could not compromise. The combat of the Crusades thus became part of the tradition of monastic spiritual combat, since it too sought to drive back the limits of Evil. The experience of the First Crusade, which ended with the capture of Jerusalem in 1099, gave rise to a living synthesis of all of these elements: exalting the valiant knights who hoped to conquer a place in heaven through their suffering, it also glorified the poor, stirring in them the hope for revenge in this Holy Land, the goal of everyone's messianic expectations.

This was, however, a fragile synthesis, which was soon to be challenged by the upheavals experienced by the West, and particularly France, in the course of the twelfth century. Progress in agriculture, demographic growth, the renewal of commercial exchanges, and urban life constituted the most visible signs of a splendid expansion, whose consequences were also felt in both the cultural and religious realms. An original literature in the vernacular blossomed in the *chansons de geste* and courtly poetry, while clerics enriched the meager heritage of books on which they had lived since the Carolingian renaissance. As the eschatological longings became attenuated, the image of God as judge and avenger of the Apocalypse slipped into the background, without totally vanishing from people's minds. The secular Church, led by the papacy, undertook reform and the construction here on earth of a Christian society which it would guide and encourage. There were stirrings of great intellectual ferment; and at the same time that St. Anselm, abbot of Bec, ushered in a renaissance of philosophical thought, a multiplicity of heretical movements appeared, a sign of new religious vitality.

Among the fundamental questions being debated in this century of great progress, one of the most important concerned the place of the Creation and man in God's plan. In a country which was emerging from underdevelopment in every domain, and where the levels of life and culture were improving rapidly, it was becoming difficult to dismiss the world as nothing but a vale of tears. The idea of *contemptus mundi*, the contempt for the world, preached by monastic spirituality, which considered profane reality of little value, continued to attract spirits like St. Bernard, who found both the new urban schools and the communal movement disturbing and worthy of condemnation, but it no longer held much appeal for many of his contemporaries. The rediscovery of whole sections of ancient philosophy, beginning with Plato and some treatises by Aristotle, led the clerics of the school of Chartres and soon the Victorines of Paris to emphasize the autonomy of the natural order and to stress the legitimacy of the procedures by which the human mind strove to learn about it.

In the works of these first Christian intellectuals of the Middle Ages, God is presented as the creator from whom everything originated but who has in some way moved away from his work, entrusting it to the laws which he had established to guide its operation. This process of the desacralization of nature, which on the conceptual level marked the end of the magical nature of the world, was accompanied by the exaltation of man's role. He was no longer defined as a substitute creature, with whom God replaced the fallen angels after their revolt. In fact, the opposite was true: he was the real center of the universe, which had been created for him. He had been endowed with the ability to know the reality of things through the exercise of reason, a process that was not at all sacrilegious since it consisted simply of the search for God's will and his plan for salvation, which extends to the material world. From Anselm to Alain de Lille, an entire current of thought, which started out with a small number of adherents but ended up with a majority, affirmed that reason and faith, far from being in opposition, were complementary. God himself became the object of knowledge; and theology—born in the Parisian schools in those years through Abelard's efforts— broke away from monastic exegesis to become an autonomous discipline with Peter Lombard, who in his *Book of Sentences* demonstrated the rationality of dogma without appealing to the authority of either Scripture or tradition.

This valorization of man and his intellectual faculties was accompanied by the rediscovery of Christ's humanity and its eminent place in the history of salvation. The Crusaders were the first to experience it, as they came in direct contact with the places where Jesus had lived and suffered. This new awareness did not take long to find echoes in popular devotion: from the East came a flood of relics, both authentic and counterfeit, which had some connection with Jesus or his mother, ranging from the innumerable pieces of the true cross to the crown of thorns for which St. Louis had the Sainte-Chapelle built in 1245. The Marian cult experienced tremendous growth, which is attested to by the dedication of most of the new Gothic cathedrals to Our Lady. These are merely the superficial signs of the very profound conviction that the Incarnation represented neither an illusion nor a disgrace, but instead the intervention of God in nature and human history.

Moreover, the best minds of the day tried to reach across the centuries and renew their ties with the experiences of the first Christian community, that of the apostles, and to promote in their Church the ideal of the apostolic life, based on the practice of charity and poverty. This ideal influenced the reinvigorated monasticism of Cîteaux and Grandmont as well as the various congregations of canons regular, like that of Prémontré, created around 1121 by St. Norbert. In this new ambience, which allowed greater scope for human freedom and man's capacity to act on the world, entering a monastery no longer constituted the only means of arriving at Christian perfection. Among the laity themselves, the conviction began to take hold that it was possible to ensure one's salvation in any human condition, and that neither marriage nor involvement in worldly affairs constituted an obstacle to salvation. Thus, to use the apt expression of father Chenu, a "new equilibrium between nature and grace" took shape.[1]

One of the fundamental characteristics of twelfth-century French civilization was the place it afforded to love, and as a consequence, women. After centuries of male dominance and misogyny, the problems of happiness and the relationship between the sexes came to the foreground, as witnessed by the success of courtly literature, which celebrated the "joy of love" rather than martial exploits. To be sure, these poems, particularly the ones composed in the south of France, very often sang of adulterous relationships and not of marriage, which the Church at that time was at pains to valorize and stabilize. The same is true of the Celtic romances, with their *"matière de Bretagne"* [Breton subject matter] which had such a profound influence on Western sensibilities. A prime example is the legend of Tristan and Isolde, which glorifies passionate love and awards amorous relationships the highest rank.

The omnipresence of love could not fail to have repercussions in the religious domain, because it called into question not just morality but the very meaning of life: if a man and a woman could reach beatitude through carnal emotions and sensual pleasure, what became of God's role? Spurred by this challenge, the clergy responded to this fundamental question by defining God himself as the power of love and by presenting the relationship of the human soul with its creator as the prototype of the perfect amorous relationship. In his *De diligendo Deo* [Treatise on the Love of God] and in his commentaries on the Song of Songs, St. Bernard speaks of Christ as a friend, whose terrestrial existence he relives with intense participation, moved to pity at his humble birth and shedding tears over his painful Passion. He insists above all on the importance of desire in the quest for God. Like that offered to the chosen Lady in courtly poetry, the love given to the divine Spouse can be only perfect, disinterested, and pure. The lover must banish all fear and offer himself without contamination and with no hope of recompense. The soul that reaches this grade of purity is transported outside of itself and raised to a state of ecstasy. United with Christ, it feels itself becoming celestial, engulfed in God's very being. Stripped of any will of its own, it is restored to the state of innocence and harmony of the earthly paradise.

More systematic than the abbot of Clairvaux, Richard of Saint-Victor elaborated a veritable mystical theology, which allotted a major place to psychology. Love, in his view, was not—as in Tristan—a force of destiny that crushes man and sweeps him to his death but, instead, was based on free will and liberty, which were concomitant with the royal dignity of the soul. His spirituality stressed the trinitarian relationship: more than a mere dialogue between distinct Persons, it is that perfect charity which makes them delight in what each one gives and receives. God has placed in the human soul a piercing desire, a sort of yearning for the love which transcends these differences without abolishing them. Through contemplation, the soul can enter into the intimate life of the divine Persons and merge with God in an *excessus mentis*, a state of transport, which is more an illumination of all of its faculties than a true ecstasy.

From our distant vantage point, the importance of this religious transformation of the twelfth century, which threw Christianity open to knowledge and to love, appears truly considerable. But we must not lose sight of the fact that access to interior life and con-templation was reserved to a very small number of persons. The masses thus remained largely unaware of these advances, whose repercussions were to make themselves felt most strongly in the following century. However, a new spiritual sensibility developed in the laity, making them more sensitive to the contradictions between the way of life of God's representatives—the clerics and monks—and the injunctions of the Gospels. This uneasiness was further nourished by the very success of the Gregorian reform, whose consequences included a notable influx of wealth of every kind into the hands of the religious, thanks to the restoration of tithes and churches. The newfound wealth and the moral turpitude of a good part of the clergy, who claimed, moreover, increased authority over the faithful, were major themes for popular preachers like Pierre of Bruys, the monk Henri, or the Breton Eon de l'Étoile. These preachers, who presented themselves as messiahs, often found success with rural audiences, whom they advised to refuse to receive the sacraments from the hands of priests and to reject all of the material aspects of Christian devotion.

This exacerbated spiritualism, accompanied by virulent anticlericalism, was combatted by the hierarchy: in Aquitaine, St. Bernard had to take a personal hand in checking the progress of the subversion. After a brief pause, the movement gained new vigor with the implantation of Catharism in the West. The French Cathars, known as the Albigensians, constituted a veritable Church in the South beginning in 1167. They presented themselves as the emissaries of evangelical truth, which they accused the Catholic clergy of having obscured, and they claimed to have returned to the perfection of the primitive Church through the practice of poverty, asceticism, and itinerant preaching. In their view, the world was the theater of a permanent struggle between two opposing principles: Good, which was associated with God, and Evil, incarnated by Satan. Men's souls were particles of spirit ensnared in matter from which they should try to extricate themselves, following the example of Christ, who was not the son of God but rather the greatest of the angels or the best of men, and whose incarnation and sufferings had been only illusory. If Christ had redeemed mankind, it was not by his Passion on the cross but through his teachings. The Old Testament, the work of the forces of Evil, was worthless; only the Gospels were divine. Beyond its apparent simplicity, which corresponded well to the spontaneously dualist vision of the masses, Catharism was attractive because of the extreme sobriety of its liturgy: it was reduced to the *consolamentum* alone, the rite of laying on of hands, performed by the *perfecti*, which afforded believers the certainty of being reborn in the next world to a life of the spirit, after having led a very free existence in this world.

Other movements of religious dissidence arose in France during the second half of the twelfth century. The most significant among them was the Waldensians, a group of laymen founded by a merchant from Lyon named Valdes, who after hearing the call of the Gospels in 1176, decided to practice poverty and preach the Good News. Living in simplicity and penitence, the Waldensians had the Gospels translated into the vernacular. It did not take long for *v* them to come into conflict with the clergy, who would not permit uneducated laymen to have direct access to the sacred texts and to dedicate themselves to preaching. Condemned as heretics in 1184 by Pope Lucius III, the Waldensians were forced into hiding, but their numbers continued to grow in such regions as the Dauphiné, Provence, and Languedoc. Although they were often compared to the Cathars and persecuted on those grounds, the Waldensians were no more than superficially similar to them. Indeed, theirs was an evangelical movement which in the beginning was opposed to Catholicism only in the area of discipline, and did not question its fundamental dogmas.

For the first time in its history, at the end of the twelfth century the medieval Church found itself confronted with a massive outbreak of heresies which in some regions such as Languedoc had prevailed over orthodoxy. When warnings and persuasion proved useless, the Church appealed to the secular arm and promulgated severe penalties, going as far as incarceration for life or death on the stake for those who refused to abjure. This reaction seemed perfectly legitimate to the clerics of this time, since heresy endangered both the unity of the faith, which was considered to be the supreme good, and the social order desired by God, which it was sacrilegious to disturb. For this reason, thirteenth-century theologians, while reaffirming the liberty of the act of faith and condemning violence toward the Jews, had no scruples about justifying the killing of apostates. To render the repression more efficient, the papacy then instituted the Inquisition, a tribunal entrusted for the most part to Dominican monks, who were instructed to seek out and prosecute heresy. Before long it extended its activities to magic, sorcery and all forms of religious and moral deviance.

But the Church did not limit its activities to simple repression. Now that the success of the heresies had made it aware of the beliefs and aspirations of the masses, it set out to bridge the religious gap that had opened between the masses and the clerical elite that had taken charge of the reform movements. In this respect, the thirteenth century marked a period of stasis, especially in France. Innovations came from other places, from Italy in particular with St. Francis and St. Clare. But the essential contribution of this epoch consisted in the popularization of earlier achievements. This was the import of the actions taken by both the secular clergy, spurred on by the bishops, and the mendicant orders, led by the Franciscans and the Dominicans. The impact of the mendicants was considerable, especially in the cities. Their way of life, which emphasized poverty, and their rule, which consisted of living in conformity with the Gospels, won them the sympathy of the humble folk, to whom they began to address themselves in a style which was less dogmatic and more picturesque than that of school-bred clerics.

For these new kinds of religious did not remain closed up in their convents and their churches. Their principal objective was the apostolate: through confession and preaching, they brought to people's awareness a religious ideal founded on penitence, the practice of virtues, and devotion to Christ and Mary. No figure incarnated their religious ideal better than St. Louis, who was profoundly influenced by them and tried to put into practice in his private life and in his actions as sovereign the principles taught to him by the Franciscans and the Dominicans. As a good and pious layman, he relied on the Church and the clergy to define the doctrines which he was ready to defend with the sword against any adversaries, whether heretics or pagans. His personal devotion was centered on the Passion and the sufferings of Christ. Twice it led him to leave for the Crusades, where he finally met his death in 1270. But above all, this valiant and impetuous knight conceived of religion as service. Although he was very devout, he knew well that "an honest man is worth more than a Beguin," and sought perfection not in religious practices but in the performance of his duties of state. For this reason, he was attentive to the needs of the poor and the sick, for whom he had hospitals and hospices built, in keeping with the spirituality of the times, which considered the outcasts of fortune to be the representatives of Christ. As king, he tried to establish the reign of justice, sending investigators into the provinces to gather the complaints of his subjects and trying to remedy the abuses and injustices to which the humble were victim. He protected the peasants by outlawing private wars and limiting seigniorial high-handedness in judicial matters. With him, the king's peace, which substituted legal procedures for the practice of trial by combat, followed the path of the peace of God.

The effort to invest secular reality with religious spirit, which in St. Louis found its highest expression, was shared by many of his contemporaries. Almost everywhere the trade corporations took on the character of confraternities, whose statutes called for collective exercises of piety and organized prayers for the dead. They also stressed assistance to needy members and to the poor, for whom periodic distributions of food or money were provided. In the same period, there appeared communities of Beguines, lay women who divided their lives between work and prayer; some, like St. Douceline in Aix-en-Provence (†1274), reached the highest pinnacles of mysticism.

This century of equilibrium and majesty—that of the "Beau Dieu" [Beautiful God] of the cathedral of Amiens and the smiling Virgin of Reims—was followed by a more troubled era. It was an age of crises, of the Hundred Years' War and, most significantly, of the Black Death, which beginning in 1348 mowed down millions of people in a few decades, both in the cities and in the countryside. These events, which made the fourteenth and fifteenth centuries a particularly tormented time, wrought changes in spiritual outlook. The questions of death and the Last Judgment became leading preoccupations of Christians, obsessed by the tragedy of their condition.

In this period, confraternities devoted to the souls in Purgatory multiplied. Purgatory, defined by thirteenth-century theologians as an intermediate place between heaven and hell where the dead were required to finish expiating their sins, offered new perspectives of redemption, because the intercession of parents and friends, through prayer and good works, could shorten their trials. People of that era feared nothing more than sudden death, which allowed them no time to receive the sacraments of the Church or to make a will, or with no one to attend to their remains. The interiorization of religion through the practice of confession had insinuated anxiety into their consciences, and individual judgment became more important to them than the Last Judgment. When Pope John XXII declared in 1331 that before the resurrection of the body, the souls of the just enjoyed neither eternal life nor the beatific vision of God, this imprudent statement, running counter to the opinion of most theologians and the sentiments of the faithful, aroused such a general outcry of indignation that the pontiff had to retract it on his deathbed. For every person was preoccupied above all with his own salvation and was convinced that life in the next world must be the direct and immediate reward for the existence led on this earth.

The omnipresence of death, felt especially keenly after 1348, also had an influence on people's conception of Christ. The preceding epoch had exalted his glorious humanity. The last centuries of the Middle Ages were more attuned to the agonies of his Passion. New themes appeared in religious art: the man of sorrows, the descent from the cross and the entombment, and, finally, the *pietà*, in which the Virgin Mary presents the lifeless body of her son to the disconsolate onlookers. Not satisfied with evoking the physical and moral suffering of Christ, the Christians of that time tried to relive them. Such was the aim of the religious dramas known as "mystery plays," the most famous of which, Arnoul Gréban's *Le Vrai Mystère de la Passion* [The True Mystery of the Passion] was devoted precisely to representing the drama of Calvary. Some Christians went even further, trying to avert God's wrath by identifying with the holy Victim. This was true of the flagellants, whose excesses were condemned by the French monarchy and the Avignon papacy, but whose processions reappeared spontaneously with each grave calamity.

Alongside these spasmodic manifestations of a Christianity awash in pathos, the era of Jean Gerson and Joan of Arc also experienced the personalization of faith. Many of the well-to-do laypeople of the fourteenth century owned books of hours, which were French translations of the Gospels. Piety flourished around the edges of the liturgy: in the churches, the host was permanently displayed in order to satisfy the faithful's desire to contemplate it at greater length than was allowed by the brief moment of its elevation in the mass. Devotion to the holy sacrament, which was born in northeast France and what is now Belgium early in the thirteenth century, gradually spread. It became common for Corpus Christi processions to gather the urban or village community every year to celebrate the real presence of Christ in the sacrament of the altar. But the crisis of ecclesiastical institutions during the Great Schism and the conciliar period led many Christians to wonder about the means of attaining salvation and the necessity of recourse to priestly authority. Fervent groups of "friends of God" sprang up almost everywhere: having lost all faith in institutions which they deemed incapable of self-reform, they attempted to enrich their own interior lives by meditating on the Holy Scriptures and reading devotional works. The calamities of the age inspired the proliferation of private revelations. Some women did not hesitate to speak in God's name, denouncing the clergy's inability to restore the visible unity of the Church and transmitting prophetic warnings to their contemporaries.

This splintering of the great Christian community into a host of small groups weakened the idea of Christendom. Hardly anyone was interested in the Crusades; there was no talk of building cathedrals, but only of multiplying the chapels within them and decorating them lavishly in an assertion of group identity. With the growth of flamboyant piety, the quest for God, which had been the foundation of all medieval religiosity, degenerated into bookkeeping for the Beyond. The average Christian of the fifteenth century had masses celebrated by the hundreds or thousands; he counted the days of indulgences he had earned and the beads of his rosary; he took pleasure in the symbolism of numbers which he used to enumerate vices and virtues, sorrows and joys.

Nevertheless, a minority of the population, rejecting this mechanization of religious feeling, stressed the presence of God in the hearts of believers, and the fact that sanctification takes place less through works than by the conformity of man's will to that of Christ in the practice of the Gospel. This is the lesson of the *Devotio moderna*, which advocated an ascetic, intimate conception of Christian life, based on inwardness, examination of conscience, and reading. Its fullest expression was the *Imitatio Christi*, a group of brief spiritual treatises in which the soul engages in a dialogue with Christ, conceived as a friend and the object of tender attention. Thus, several decades before the Reformation, a break was taking place with the religion of works, which formerly had allowed medieval man to satisfy his "immense appetite for the divine," but now, at the time of the spread of printing and the voyages of discovery, no longer corresponded to the cultural expectations and needs of the emerging classes.

TWO

THE
MIDDLE AGES
OF "THE PEOPLE"

WHEN MEDIEVALISTS REFLECT on the notion of "the people" in their own discipline, they are confronted with a dual image, or rather with two antithetical images. On the one hand, specialists in economic and social history evoke an immense crowd of starving serfs, totally dependent on their masters and toiling without respite to win their sustenance: in short, a mass of exploited helots, too preoccupied by material necessities to care about any other order of reality. On the other hand, some authors, generally more interested in cultural and religious phenomena, present what Michelet has called an "enormous and delicate" Middle Ages, capable of enthusiasm and creativity. To be sure, no one would claim today that medieval common people built the cathedrals or composed the *chansons de geste*, if only because works of art and writing long remained the monopoly of clerics. But these historians properly emphasize the massive and spontaneous participation of elements external to the clergy and the nobility in the great movements which fashioned medieval Christianity: assemblies of peace, the first Crusades, the development of Romanesque art, flagellant processions, or heretical gatherings. All of this presupposes that the people of that age, even the most humble among them, had a basic understanding of doctrines and forms of expression which were not always simple, along with the ability to live up to quite exacting ideals—which flatly contradicts the image of the socioeconomic school. Were they beasts of burden or demigods? While admitting the difficulty of reconciling the two images, let us seek the source of these contradictions by examining representations of the common people in the works of both their contemporaries and the historians who have studied them.

As historical subjects, the common people emerge from obscurity only around the year 1000 or, more precisely, between the end of the tenth and the middle of the eleventh century. This does not imply that in the preceding epoch there was no differentiation between dominant groups and subaltern classes, who were sometimes at odds with one another. But we lack the sources to define these social entities precisely, and even when evidence exists, for example in certain hagiographic documents from the early Middle Ages, it is difficult to interpret, for there is no way of determining whether it reflects an exceptional situation or an enduring reality. Moreover, we can affirm without fear of oversimplification that between the end of Antiquity and the beginning of the second millennium, ethnic factors were often more significant than social distinctions. A person was Frankish or Lombard before being a farmer or a lord; in a world where all except for a tiny minority led a precarious existence and everyone suffered from endless waves of invasions, the consciousness of belonging to a specific population and the requirements of common defense against the enemies of the group took precedence. The climate began to change only in the final thirty years of the tenth century, when the situation in the West was stabilized. Ethnic cohesion was to remain strong for a long time in border areas, where "nations" in the medieval sense of the term were in open and permanent conflict with outside enemies: the Saracens in Spain, the Slavs and Hungarians in the Germanic countries. But everywhere else, the dominant ethnic groups fused with the populations who were their subjects, and social struggles reappeared in the forefront, as the situation in Normandy at the end of the tenth century exemplified.[1]

Almost everywhere, from Catalonia to the Rhineland and from England to Latium, a new economic and social structure—manorialism—was put into place between 950 and 1100, while internal relationships within the ruling class were organized along feudal-vassal lines. This marked the birth of feudalism, if by that term we mean both a mode of production and a system of human organization and control. The new regime seems to have been much more rigid and burdensome for the lower classes than the earlier domainial system. In many regions, landowners now tried to concentrate the people dependent on them for purposes of control. This phenomenon of *incastellamento*, thoroughly studied in all of its aspects for central Italy by Pierre Toubert, led to more or less forced displacements and regroupments of the population.[2] It was accompanied by coercive measures which aimed to draw the greatest possible profit from the productive forces, by extracting both work and monetary revenue from them. Between the minority, who held the power of arbitrary command within their lordships, and their dependents, whose varied juridical statuses tended to be reduced to a common mediocrity, a deep gap opened: on one side were the people, the rural masses subjected to forced labor and monetary exactions of all kinds; on the other side were the lords, who were also warriors, and soon were to be the only ones permitted to do battle on horseback, the knights.[3]

This rigid structure was not put into place without difficulties or violence. In his *Roman de Rou*, Wace, a twelfth-century author, handed down the memory of the famous Norman peasant revolt of 997, savagely crushed by Duke Richard II and his barons, who had the hands of the ringleaders cut off to set an example.[4] Because of the military superiority of the lords, popular revolts in the form of armed insurrections were relatively rare, and in any case were doomed to failure. But the peasants' struggle against the "wicked customs"—that is, the new practices introduced by their masters without their consent—took more cunning forms, as Robert Fossier has shown for Picardy in the eleventh and thirteenth centuries.[5] Historians would have no knowledge of these expedients if judicial documents did not conserve their muted echo, which allows historians at least to imagine how this multiform resistance to seigniorial rule may have looked: deliberate inertia on the part of the peasants, sabotaged forced labor, gathering of wood from forbidden forests, individual attempts on the lives of the lord's agents, sometimes even the rape of his daughter at a turn in the road, or the burning of his haystacks. When all this proved to be useless, the peasant could still decamp, in other words abandon his property to move elsewhere, especially to areas being cleared or reclaimed, in the hope of finding conditions of life that were less harsh, and, above all, greater freedom. This explains, at least partially, the extraordinary mobility of the rural populace in the feudal epoch. Far from being attached to the soil, the rural masses seem to have been prey to a fever for change; and recent research has confirmed the aptness of the metaphor used by Marc Bloch, who compared this mobility to the Brownian movement of cells within an organism.[6]

It was precisely at this time, marked as it was by profound transformations, that a model of social organization first appeared in the Occident which allotted the people a large role, while keeping them strictly subordinated to the dominant classes. This was the so-called functional tripartition—or model of the three orders—presented and expounded between 1027 and 1030 by Bishop Adalbert of Laon in his *Carmen ad Rotbertum regem*.[7] This text, which served as the starting point for Georges Duby's work *The Three Orders: Feudal Society Imagined*, set forth the precept that the terrestrial world is comprised of three orders (*ordines*): the clergy (*oratores*), whose function is prayer; the warriors or nobles (*bellatores*), who fight to maintain order and justice; and finally, the workers (*laboratores*), in other words everyone, particularly the peasants, who provides for human subsistence. Over these groups or categories sits the king, whose role is to guarantee the harmonious operation of the system.[8] Commentators on this document have not failed to emphasize the complementary of the three functions, in line with what Georges Dumézil ascertained for other civilizations and other eras: each order fulfills an essential function in society and no one of them can function without the other two.[9] In theory, then, the working people are assigned the same importance as the clergy and the warriors. But Adalbert's vision is set within a hierarchical framework. If we make too much of the solidarity of the orders, we risk losing sight of the fact that the *laboratores* were at the bottom of the social ladder and that the bishop of Laon accorded them no respect. In his view, workers were nothing more than slaves, human beasts of burden. Their work was unvarying: the peasant who endlessly followed his plow, prod in hand, was excluded from history and change; moreover, he was ugly and ignorant. Everything tended to classify him among the beasts, not only because his profession brought him into close contact with animals, but also because he was not part of the world of speech. It was therefore fitting for this mute being to be doomed, like a sort of Caliban, to performing physical tasks and satisfying alimentary needs. The clergy, in contrast, had to be chaste and abstemious; remaining aloof from all contact with the earth and flesh, they dedicated themselves to the goal of instilling in people's minds the Christian doctrine of purity and grace. In opposition to the food the serfs provided, they offered the sacred nourishment which led to salvation: the eucharist. The priest, called to perform supernatural tasks, had to be free from the contamination of servile occupations. As for the warriors, they were distinguished from the common people because they were free and they defended society militarily. Moreover, they did not work with their hands, and beauty, an attribute of nobility, was their birthright.[10]

In his recent study, Georges Duby has demonstrated the importance and longevity of this taxonomy, which partitioned French society throughout the Middle Ages and the Ancien Régime, until the Third Estate, descendents of the medieval *laboratores*, put an end to the society of the orders in 1789.[11] Nevertheless, we need to situate Adalbert's schema of the three functions in its proper perspective: his was a normative text, not a description of social reality. The author himself affirmed that human society would not know peace until the rules he set out were respected, and he called on the king to take appropriate action. Among those who obstructed the proper functioning of the social order as he conceived it were the monks of Cluny and certain bishops who did not hesitate to seek the support of the peasants in reestablishing peace. For Adalbert this was an unnatural alliance, for, from his markedly "Carolingian" perspective, authority in temporal matters belonged exclusively to the king; the clergy's role should be limited to praying for the success of his enterprises. In fact, faced with weakening royal power, part of the clergy had chosen another route at this time: collaboration with the common people to restore a minimum of order to a society threatened with disintegration resulting from feudal violence. This was the epoch of the peace assemblies and movements which spread from Languedoc and southwest France to the borders of the Empire between 980 and 1040. On several occasions, a spectacle could be seen which Adalbert and the supporters of his ideology considered absolutely scandalous:

clerics brought peasants and city dwellers together in military operations aimed at reestablishing peace. In Le Puy in 990, the *pauperes* helped the bishop subdue recalcitrant nobles; in Angoulême in 1020, Corbie in 1021, and Beauvais in 1023 popular militias, composed of simple faithful under the command of knights, took up arms in the name of the Church. In 1038, at the urging of Aimon, archbishop of Bourges, a veritable peasant army was formed, and the villagers, led by their curate, marched forth to assail rebel castles.[12] But this movement, interesting as it may have been in many ways, was short-lived; the peasants' ardor in taking it upon themselves to mete out justice soon aroused fear in certain elements of the clergy. The lay aristocracy rallied and chose to join the peace movement in order to assume its leadership and turn it to their profit. As Robert Fossier has shown, the collective oaths that the knights finally swore secured the foundations of ecclesiastical property and consecrated the newly recovered solidarity of the ruling classes in the temporal sphere.[13] After 1050, the prospects which antifeudal combat had opened to the people were closed off one by one. Brought to a halt in the countryside, the process continued nonetheless in some regions, in urban settings, where it led some decades later to the communal movement.

In general—and this is the point—the common people in the eleventh century emerged from their passivity and began to play an active role in history. In the religious domain, this phenomenon has been brought to light by the work of the Italian historian Cinzio Violante and, for France, by that of Étienne Delaruelle.[14] Both have recognized that during the crisis which shook ecclesiastical institutions at the end of the tenth century and the beginning of the eleventh, laypeople in some areas took the place of the crumbling hierarchy and seized the initiative in clerical reform or supported it where the clergy itself had already undertaken it. These popular movements, the best example of which was the Pataria of Milan, were not anticlerical, at least not at the outset. On the contrary, they opposed any secular taint in the clergy— from clerical marriage or institutionalized concubinage to trading in ecclesiastical dignities as if they were personal patrimonies— and sought to restore in the clergy that purity which befitted the servants of God, a necessary condition if the eucharistic sacrifice they offered was to be the source of salvation and grace for the faithful. As Étienne Delaruelle wrote,

> perhaps more than in any other epoch, for the eleventh century we can legitimately speak of the "Christian people." At this time, indeed, the elite failed in its educational mission [. . .] the Christian masses remained alone, with no guides or leaders.[15]

This situation did not last very long: in the 1070s, the papacy assumed leadership of the reform movement. On occasion, as in Milan, it relied on laypeople in its struggle against prelates who were unworthy or too attached to the imperial Church system. But when the papacy, beginning with the pontificate of Gregory VII, took matters in hand, it was for the sole benefit of the clergy. In order to combat more effectively the imperial power which was opposed to the liberty of the Church, Gregory and his successors strove to exalt the superiority of the clergy ("It is they who are kings") over the laity. This polemical statement was aimed primarily at the sovereigns; but the lay condition on the whole ended by being devalued, and the distance grew within the Church between the sacerdotal elite, called upon to live in chastity like monks, and the population of the faithful, kept far from perfection by their condition itself, which entailed marriage and work, and of whom nothing more was asked than that they pay their tithes, give charity, and obey their curates.[16] Although most laypeople fell into line, some resisted. Affirming ever more exacting moral and religious standards that sometimes verged on spiritualism, they became estranged from the Church and ended by breaking completely with the institution and forming heretical groups, even before the influence of dualistic doctrines, and especially Catharism, could offer them a corpus of coherent doctrines in the second half of the twelfth century. Thus the common people, who in the eleventh century had demonstrated their creative dynamism, in the course of the following century found themselves doubly brought into line. In the social arena, the close collaboration between the clerical and lay aristocracies—despite attention-getting conflicts like the Investiture Controversy—kept the townspeople and, even more, the peasants firmly subordinated.[17] The same was true in the religious domain, where the ecclesiastical hierarchy turned to its own advantage the evangelical aspirations that had arisen among the faithful. With the Crusades, in which the *populus christianus* came together at the summons of the papacy in apparent unanimity, without class distinctions, and with the assumption of the leadership of reform by the monks and canons regular, the specifically popular movements were forced back into the shadows or out to the dissident fringe.

The consequences of this transformation were felt even in religious circles. At the end of the twelfth and throughout the thirteenth centuries, in some sectors of the urban bourgeoisie, and often among its most dynamic elements, there was a kind of return to the common people—in the new sense of the term—which took the form of the glorification of the poor and of poverty. Many newly rich merchants renounced their fortunes to share in the existence of the most underprivileged or fled from urban civilization and its refinements to return as hermits to the harsh life of the wilderness.[18] St. Francis of Assisi, the most famous among them, contributed through his own experiences and his sanctity, quickly acknowledged by the Church, to the perceived identification between economic and social poverty and evangelical values. He voluntarily renounced all of his wealth and gave to his first followers, and then to the order which grew up around him, the name of *minores*, a term which not only had moral connotations, but also referred explicitly to the conflicts in the Italian communes which set the world of the small artisans and impoverished workers against the *maiores* who lorded it over them.[19] But with its rapid clericalization, the Franciscan order soon lost sight of its original anchoring in the social realities of the day; already in St. Bonaventure's generation, the label *minores* was simply interpreted as an invitation to humility in the most general sense. The same was true for poverty, which tended to become either a slogan progressively emptied of all concrete meaning or a controversial religious program. Polemics raged on this question between the Spirituals and the majority of the order at the end of the thirteenth and the beginning of the fourteenth centuries. But this was an internal debate among clerics, which did not concern lay society except for a few devout groups. Rather, it can be argued, paradoxically, that the increasingly sibylline character of these quarrels and the violent turn they took often ended by exasperating public opinion, which was in any case increasingly hostile to poverty and the poor. Indeed, the economic crises of the fourteenth century, the ravages caused by the wars and epidemics which afflicted many countries, and the ensuing problems contributed to making indigence a social plague.[20] Popular revolts—the *jacqueries*, the Ciompi rebellion, the English insurrection of 1381—made the laboring classes seem dangerous, a permanent menace to the social order.[21] The most feared and hated of the poor were the uprooted drifters, who often tended to constitute a sort of society of deviants, a hotbed of banditry and insecurity; a sudden influx of them could cause famine in the cities. To protect themselves against the swelling numbers of marginals and vagabonds in the late Middle Ages, almost everywhere the public authorities issued edicts which, for example, forbade giving alms to beggars able to work, and reserved the benefits of charitable works to those needy who were native to the region. At that time, "the needy" referred to certain categories of the poor: invalids, pilgrims, women in labor, and the maimed and crippled. To be sure, there were many other kinds of poor people, especially in the big cities—in particular unskilled workers with families, whose miserable salaries barely allowed them to scrape by. These strata of the population attracted neither the attention nor the sympathy of the well-to-do. Even if the latter had been more generous, they probably would have seen no reason to take an interest in the difficulties of these "working poor." The religious conception of poverty, on which charitable works were based, had created a sort of screen which blocked any accurate perception of the realities of destitution. The only people considered to be poor, and thus deserving of assistance, were certain categories whose situations matched those in biblical texts quoted by the clergy in their sermons. Ill-paid laborers had no place there.[22] For this reason, these outcasts filled the ranks of the troops who fought in the popular revolts that shook most of western Europe between the last third of the fourteenth century and the famous Peasant War of 1524-1525. These uprisings, which were all brutally quelled, explain the harsh measures taken almost everywhere, from the end of the fifteenth century, to confine the poor and reduce the influence in urban life of trade groups, especially of petty artisans.

It therefore does not seem excessive to conclude, in the final analysis, that the reality of the popular condition in the Middle Ages has almost always been hidden from view by the ruling classes and remains in large part unknown. One reason for this is that numerical data, precise statistics on the income and social composition of the populace, are totally lacking until the mid-fourteenth century, and sometimes into the fifteenth century. Even tax rolls, where they survive, are not very useful, because people who had no possessions were exempt from taxes and therefore do not appear on these lists. But the essential obstacle was ideological and cultural. Throughout the entire period under consideration, clerics held a monopoly on writing; they applied to their society interpretive grids which sometimes emphasized the necessary solidarity and complementarity of the orders, as in the schema of the three functions, and at other times applied religious or moral concepts to a real situation of which they furnished a deformed picture, as we have seen in the case of late-medieval poverty. Far from diminishing, the mistrust with which the elite and the ruling classes viewed the masses only grew with the passage of time. It can be gauged by the efforts of the Church, and later the States, to eradicate, by force if necessary, the hidden remnants of a specifically popular culture or discourse.[23] Nevertheless, paradoxically, it was in the fourteenth and fifteenth centuries, when the repression of the Inquisition was at its height, that the national monarchies and great cities began for the first time to consult their own subjects. To reinforce their hold on the masses, the authorities organized a generalized collection of opinion by means of inquests and proceedings. To be sure, the right to speak was granted to the mutes only to enable them to voice their assent to the decisions taken by those who know and decide, or to express their approval of the dogma and beliefs under discussion. The *vox populi*, the voice of the people, was less than ever identified with the *vox Dei*, the voice of God. Nevertheless, it was symptomatic that the opinions and beliefs of the common people were sought at all. This was an implicit admission that the survival of institutions could not be guaranteed by coercion alone, but to a certain extent required general consent. In this way, the part was no longer identified with the whole, and the elite recognized the existence and otherness of the popular classes, if only to engage them in battle. In the place of medieval conceptions whose aim was to bring human society into conformity with the divine nature, at the same time one and trine, at the dawn of modern times there emerged a dualist vision, founded on a keener awareness of concrete realities.

THREE

THE LAITY
IN THE
FEUDAL CHURCH

FROM THE TIME OF CONSTANTINE, if not before, a distinction was drawn within the *Ecclesia* between a minority of clerics, summoned by God and ordained as ministers in the service of the cult, and the mass of the baptized, the population (*laios* in Greek) of the faithful, known as the laity. All, however, were members of the Church, the mystical body of Christ. This theological schema has remained valid for Catholicism, yet it does not adequately account for reality as Christians actually experienced it, for, depending on the era, the emphasis has been either on the distinction between the two categories of the baptized or, instead, on their solidarity within the ecclesiastical body. In this regard the Middle Ages is a particularly important period, because it was marked by considerable shifts of emphasis in this fundamental relationship between the clergy and the laity.

Between the end of Antiquity and the Carolingian era, a process of Christianization took place in the West, by the end of which, around 800, all of the population (except for a small Jewish minority) had received baptism. But the Christian faith had as yet only superficially penetrated this society, which continued to be marked by its barbarian origins and Germanic culture. Beginning around the eighth century, an enlightened minority of prelates, abbots, and great lay dignitaries, of whom the Carolingian sovereigns were foremost, tried to create a Christian society, first of all by

exalting the function of the king—and, after 800, the emperor—
who was considered by virtue of his anointment to be the visible
image and the earthly representative of Christ. The Church, the
population of the baptized and the faithful, was assimilated to a
Christian society governed by a sovereign, who was advised and
inspired by clerics. As the monk Walafrid Strabo wrote in 841,
"through the union of the two orders [the clergy and the laity]
and their mutual love, a single house of God is built, a single
body of Christ is realized." In this perspective, the Church and
the State remained distinct, though they were assigned the same
objective: to lead the people of God to salvation. The emperor,
a modern-day Joshua or David, was the leader of this new Israel.
He issued "capitularies" to reform the clergy and did not hesitate
to intervene in liturgical questions or theological arguments. The
clergy, from the pope down, prayed for the success of his political
and military endeavors. This was a system quite similar to that of
the Byzantine Empire throughout its history, and to that which
endured in Russia until 1917.

In the West, however, this balanced system of "condominium,"
or joint leadership of Christianity shared by the clerical and lay
elites under the guidance of the emperor, did not last for long:
only in the Germanic world did it survive until the twelfth century. Everywhere else, beginning in the second half of the ninth
century the episcopate and the papacy sought to regain their
liberty and autonomy. The dominance of a lay chief, which was
admissible as long as he was the sole, powerful emperor, became
intolerable to the clergy once they were faced with powerless
kings and, soon, with short-sighted local potentates. The dissolu-
tion of the great political entities, which resulted from the dis-
membering of the Carolingian Empire, and the reconstruction of
power on the basis of seigniories and castles plunged the tenth-
century Church into an entirely new situation: the lay lords actually considered themselves to be the proprietors of the churches
and abbeys which they themselves or their ancestors had built
on their lands. Not satisfied with appropriating their revenues,
the lords laid claim to the ecclesiastical dignities and did not
hesitate to name parish priests, and even bishops and abbots,
who would suit with their patrimonial interests and their political
strategies. By means of investiture—a feudal ceremony of purely

lay character—men without the slightest aptitude for religious life were assigned high offices in the Church. The papacy itself did not escape this evolution: it emerged from the control of the Roman nobility to fall under that of the Germanic sovereigns, more benevolent but still self-interested. Thus the entire Church, from bottom to top, ran the risk of dissolving into the feudal society which surrounded it.

But in the tenth and especially in the eleventh century, movements sprang up almost everywhere in the West in reaction to this situation. This was true particularly of reforming monasticism, which, first in Cluny then in a growing number of monasteries, aimed to liberate the world of the cloisters from the confusion of roles and states of life that was considered to be at the origin of all of the disorders. Even if their efforts were supported in some cases by laypeople like Emperor Henry III and Countess Mathilda in Italy, in their own writings the monks tended to emphasize the superiority of the spiritual over the temporal to justify their demand for freedom from the secular authorities. In order to bring about the regeneration of the Church, the reformers were thus led to accentuate the distinction between clergy and laity and to relegate the latter to a subordinate position, while extolling the eminent dignity of the priesthood. And, since at this time monks increasingly tended to be priests, and sometimes even became bishops or legates of the Holy See, monasticism, which once had been a sort of common ground for the clergy and the laity, gravitated definitively toward the clerical side. Thus, as early as 999 Abbo of Fleury, abbot of Saint-Benoît-sur-Loire, applied the parable of the talents to the three "orders" of the Church (monks, clergy, and laity), establishing among them a hierarchical ranking:

> Among the Christians of both sexes, we know that there exist three orders and three degrees, so to speak. Although none of the three is exempt from sin, the first is good, the second better, the third excellent [. . .] The first is that of the laity, the second that of the clergy, the third that of the monks [. . .] As for the conjugal state (which characterizes the laity), it is permitted only so that man, at the age when the temptations due to the fragility of the flesh are the strongest, does not fall into an even worse situation.[1]

As the last sentence makes clear, monastic authors of this bent defined Christian perfection as a function of distance from material life. Reforming monasticism proceeded from the postulate that the flesh is evil and that marriage is no more than a concession to human weakness. If the monks were at the top of the hierarchy, it was primarily because they were virgins. Even if this vision of things was not the only one that existed, it was the one which prevailed among the clergy; the laypeople themselves came to be convinced of their own inferiority in the religious sphere and ended by adopting the idea that salvation could only be attained by those who lived in cloisters and wore monastic habits, even if the habits were only donned at death's door.

Even more fraught with consequences was the struggle which the Roman Church carried on in the second half of the eleventh century to recover its autonomy and put an end to trafficking in ecclesiastical dignities. To guard against the risk that parish patrimonies would be dispersed if left in the hands of the families of priests who passed their function from father to son, the reformers took up arms against "Nicolitanism," or all forms of clerical marriage, and simony, or the peddling of spiritual powers. To attain these high objectives the Gregorian reformers—named for Pope Gregory VII, the most illustrious figure in the movement— undertook to subject temporal matters, or the world of the laity, to spiritual authority, which was identified as that of the clergy. This is the program set out, for example, by a monk from Lorraine, Humbert of Silva Candida, named cardinal in 1049, who in 1057 wrote the famous treatise *Adversus simoniacos* [Against Simony]:

> Just as secular matters are forbidden to the clergy, ecclesi-
> astical matters are forbidden to the laity [. . .] The clergy is
> the first order in the Church, like the eyes in one's head.
> The Lord was speaking of them when he said "He who
> touches you touches the apple of my eye" (Zechariah 2:8).
> The power of the laity is like the chest and the arm whose
> might is accustomed to obeying the Church and defending
> her. As for the masses, likened to the inferior members and
> the extremities of the body, although they are subject to the
> ecclesiastical and secular powers, they are at the same time
> indispensable to them.[2]

This is a prophetic text if ever there was one, and a good illustration of the ambiguities inherent in the Gregorian reform. On the one hand, the Church fought for its autonomy and won it progressively by affirming its independence from the emperors and kings whose power it desacralized. But on the other hand, it accentuated the tendency of the clergy to consider the Church as their own and to identify with it. The laity, relegated to their temporal tasks, in this view represented nothing but the simple object of the pastoral ministry of the clergy. The conception of a people of God guided by its pastors was supplanted by the exaltation of the roles of the clerical hierarchy and its supreme leader, the pope.

Moreover, the clergy's claims to exercise hegemony over the laity found support in their cultural superiority. At a time when Latin was the only language of culture in the West, and when the rare individuals capable of writing had extraordinary power and prestige in society, the clerics, who had a monopoly over learning and abstract thought, were the cocks of the walk. In particular, they alone had access to the sacred texts, for the Bible had been little translated into the vernacular. Many churchmen were proud of this fact and felt only scorn for the "unlettered" laypeople, that is, cultural outsiders unable to attain true wisdom, which was reserved for those who lived in cloisters or attended the schools that sprang up around cathedrals in the twelfth century.

However, it would be incorrect and unfair to emphasize only the negative consequences of the Gregorian reform for the situation of the laity in the Church. The laity was not insensible to the struggles for clerical reform, and in certain regions like Lombardy, the simple faithful—called "Patarines" by their adversaries—took the initiative in fighting abuses and bringing corrupt priests back to the straight and narrow. Almost everywhere in the Occident, around the years 1090-1100, popular religious movements sprang up, sometimes led by hermits or monks, but in which the laity played a decisive role. Some remained within the bounds of orthodoxy: among these were the Crusaders who left for the Orient to liberate Christ's tomb, in answer first to the call of Urban II after 1095, then to that of St. Bernard in 1147; this is also true of the lay brothers and sisters who associated themselves with new monastic and canonical orders, particularly the Cistercians, in order to share in the monastic merits and benefit from their prayers in exchange for work. Others went further and slid toward heresy. Indeed, the reform movement of the eleventh century had emphasized the invalidity of any sacraments administered by morally unworthy clerics. This radical position was soon abandoned by the papacy, but many laypeople remained faithful to it and sought to make their own obedience to the clergy dependent on the quality of the evangelical testimony offered by the ministers of the cult. Some of them went so far as to affirm that Christians who lived their lives in conformity with the Word of God were entitled to announce the Good News, and claimed for themselves the right to preach. The result throughout the twelfth century was a series of increasingly violent conflicts, as the growing wealth of the clergy—an indisputable fact at this time, when the lords were beginning to pay tithes to the Church—helped to nourish the virulent anticlericalism of the faithful. All of these themes came together with the Waldensians in 1170, and even more emphatically with the Cathars, whose exacerbated spiritualism led them to reject all of the institutions and visible realities of Christianity.

Thus, in the course of the eleventh and twelfth centuries, the masses emerged from their passivity and aspired to play an active role in the religious domain. But this demand, which provoked increased intractableness on the part of the clergy, ended by weakening the Church, whose very existence was soon threatened. Once again in the history of the Church, salvation was to come not from institutional reform but from a surge of Christian sensibility, expressed through new spiritual experiences and a flowering of sanctity.

FOUR

The Crusades:
The Masses Appear
on the Scene

IS THERE ANY REASON to speak of the Crusades again? The time may seem ill chosen to recall events which run the risk of reawakening alarming feelings of nostalgia. Indeed, not long ago Franco in Spain launched with notorious results his "crusade against Bolshevism"; immediately denounced by Georges Bernanos, this imposture was to experience a sinister prolongation in France during the Vichy period and the Nazi occupation. Moreover, the almost unanimously negative judgment of contemporary historians of the Crusades makes reopening the dossier even less pressing: these great expeditions, which followed upon each other at irregular intervals but without interruption, only succeeded in widening the already significant gap between Christians and Moslems. It is no coincidence that two of the three "divisions" of the Palestinian Liberation Organization took the names of battles from the era of Saladin and Rukn ad-Din Baibars. And some of the discussions in Beirut or Damascus about the future of Lebanon demonstrate an unfortunate tendency to overlook the distinction between Christian minorities long present in that country and the Franks of the thirteenth century. Far more than the Spanish *Reconquista*, the Crusades caused profound trauma in the Moslem world, which is apparent to this day in its attitude toward Christians.

The outlook is no more positive when it comes to Judeo-Christian relations. As Bernhard Blumenkranz demonstrated long ago, although the Jews did not enjoy especially favorable status, they did live for the most part in harmony with the Christians until the end of the eleventh century.[1] There is no doubt that with the Crusades their situation deteriorated rapidly and profoundly. The exaltation of the cross and the constant references to the Passion of the Savior kept the accusations of deicide in the limelight; and despite the opposition of the ecclesiastical hierarchy and a religious leader of the status of St. Bernard, the mass departures of Christians for Jerusalem in 1095 and 1146 were accompanied by pogroms and violent persecution, which only grew more widespread as the Jews were treated like veritable scapegoats.

Even among the Christians the Crusades sowed discord and hatred. The first Crusade was, to be sure, the result of an appeal for Western help launched by the Byzantine Empire after the defeat at Manzikert (1071), which opened the doors of Anatolia and Armenia to the Turks. Gregory VII saw in a rescue expedition organized by the papacy the opportunity to put an end to the schism which had separated Rome from Constantinople since 1054. Events did not allow him to carry out his plans, which were adopted by Urban II. At Clermont in 1095, Urban moved his audience by recounting the sufferings of Christians in the East. But what could have been a great manifestation of ecumenical spirit turned instead into discord, followed by open conflict. Relations between Roman and Byzantine Christians were strained from the outset, and occasions for complaints and rancor did not take long to accumulate. The breaking point was reached in 1204, when the Fourth Crusade, which had set out to liberate Jerusalem, was diverted to Constantinople by the Venetians and resulted in the conquest and plundering of the capital of the Byzantine Empire. Here again the emotional shock must have been deep and lasting. It is from this moment, not from 1054, that we can date the profound hatred of the common people and clergy of the Orthodox Church for Western Christendom, and all of the reconciliation agreements negotiated in later years between the popes and the emperors or patriarchs of Constantinople could not erase this memory and end this rancor. Perhaps the only people to welcome the arrival of the Crusaders were the Christian minorities in the Middle East—especially those persecuted by Byzantium for their doctrinal differences—whose good relations were attested by the large number of marriages between Frankish men and Armenian women, to cite only a single example.

Useless and even noxious in religious terms, the Crusades were no more profitable by secular standards. It is significant that the Frankish crusader kingdoms—which nevertheless lasted for almost two centuries—gave birth to no literary or artistic works of lasting value, unless the chronicle of Fulcher of Chartres or the system of fortifications at the Krak des Chevaliers can be considered such. Unlike what happened in Spain or Sicily, where, to be sure, relations between Christians and Moslems were also full of tension, the graft which could have merged or connected the contributions of the two civilizations did not take in Syria and Palestine. The most we can say is that a certain osmosis in their ways of life took place, with the uncouth Frankish conquerors quickly coming under the influence of the Orient, which newcomers condemned as perverse and enervating. But this was not enough to make the Holy Land the crucible of a new civilization, nor even a filter through which the cultural riches of Islamic civilization could reach the West.

In the sphere of economics, finally, where it was long believed that the Crusades were of decisive importance, the balance sheet is quite meager. Without going as far as Jacques Le Goff, who claims that the only thing the Crusades brought to the West was the apricot[2]—which in any case came to Italy through Sicily—we must nevertheless discount the importance of the Syrian and Palestinian ports in the exchanges between the West and the Moslem world. Indeed, as early as the tenth century, the merchants of Amalfi were engaged in close commercial relations with Alexandria; and the Pisans, like the Venetians, were to maintain economic ties with Egypt. The opening of counting houses by Italian merchants in Tyre or Acre doubtlessly made it possible for this trade to increase; but after 1291 trade was not interrupted for long, and goods from India, Persia and even China continued to reach the West, just as pilgrimages to the Holy Land—which were already frequent before the Crusades—quickly picked up again under the sponsorship of the Franciscans, to whom the Moslem authorities entrusted certain Christian holy places in 1331.

Nevertheless, despite this clearly negative assessment, people have always been fascinated by the Crusades, and the number of studies which specialists continue to devote to this theme testifies to their enduring interest for modern-day historians and for the public at large. Is this because of the exotic nature of the subject—there is always need for an Orient which represents an "elsewhere"—or, even more simply, because we feel a necessity to accept our past in its totality, with its moments of glory but also with all of its flaws and faults? None of these explanations should be excluded, but, as we vaguely sense, none hits the mark precisely. The real reason should be stated very clearly: it is only from a strictly Western perspective that the Crusades can be positively evaluated, as they relate to the origins of our civilization and our religious culture. Indeed, they mark a decisive stage in that evolution: this was the moment when the masses, emerging from their age-old passivity, came onto the scene of history in response to the summons of the Church. It marked the birth of Western Christianity. For the first time, the European populations, who used Latin as their language of culture and who recognized the religious primacy of the bishop of Rome, became aware of their own unity over and above ethnic particularities and joined together in a common enterprise: the deliverance of Jerusalem, the only city which could have inspired such a large-scale gathering because it was the symbol of both the presence of God among men and his eventual coming at the end of time.

This Western Christianity, which made its presence felt at the end of the eleventh century, was still crude. Like all adolescents, it asserted its own existence by matching itself against others and attacking them brutally: Moslems, Jews, and Byzantines in turn paid the price of this growing dynamism, which at first saw nothing in other civilizations but obstacles and enemies. The just war and the holy war were to offer to these masses, unenlightened but animated by ardent religious zeal, a simple ideological justification that was well adapted to their fundamentally Manichean mentality, which opposed good and evil, faithful and infidels, loyal men and traitors, with no concern for fine distinctions. Out of this vigorous human mass, the Church attempted to make a people, the people of God. Even before the year 1000, Cluny had shown the way with the peace movements. After 1050, the papacy took up the challenge and, mobilizing feudal society against the Germanic emperor and the sovereigns, with Gregory VII (1073-1085) set out to build a Christian society here on earth which would acknowledge Peter's successor as its supreme leader. The Crusades thus participated in the mainstream of church reform. Beginning in the eleventh century, the Church had been engaged in keen struggle with the forces of Evil: against pillaging lords and anarchic violence, it tried to impose the peace of God; then it fought against simoniacal priests and clerical concubinage in what is called the Gregorian reform. Its efforts to establish the reign of Christ in human society found their logical conclusion with the Cluniac Pope Urban II in the great expedition to aid the Christians of the Near East, in the hope of reestablishing Christian unity by liberating Jerusalem. The fact that these dreams of universal peace and reconciliation centering on the holy city generally came to naught does not diminish the boldness and originality of the plan. The best proof of the power of this dynamic myth is its very longevity: even after the debacle of Hattin, the Moslem recapture of Jerusalem, and the successive defeats suffered by the Christians, the call of the Crusades continued, at least until the end of the thirteenth century, to stir a profound response full of emotional and religious reverberations, and militias of the simple faithful took the place of sovereigns and lords in going "over there to avenge the honor of God," as the expression of the day went.

In associating the mystical elements of pilgrimage with devotion to the Cross, the Crusades illustrate the birth of a new religious sensibility within Western Christianity: what is known as "penitential spirituality." Detaching themselves from routine, ritual practices, laypeople gave themselves wholeheartedly to the prospects of salvation offered by the Church, which presented the Crusades as a period of grace, an opportunity to erase the consequences of sin by means of the plenary indulgence reserved for pilgrims to Jerusalem. This was the beginning of a religion of the Incarnation, based on the imitation of the Redeemer and, soon, of the bloody victim of Calvary. A single certainty took root in people's minds: the only path to salvation lay in the imitation of Christ, in following his footsteps. At first interpreted quite literally, this drive to conform to his pattern led to the quest for mortification and ascetic exploits. But while monks had the leisure to undertake daily deprivations or to flagellate themselves in their cells, laypeople entangled in marriage and worldly life could only purify themselves through pilgrimages, preferably the longest and most arduous: journeying overseas and, if necessary, engaging in armed battle against those deemed to be enemies of God. The fundamentally penitential and religious character of the Crusades prevents them from being considered mere manifestations of Western imperialism. If the point of the enterprise had been colonization, why did almost all Crusaders hurry home at the end of their wanderings and ordeals, leaving in the Holy Land only a small number of "Franks" who were constantly forced to appeal to the West in order to hold their ground?

In conclusion, with the Crusades, Western Christianity for the first time in its history called into question the absolute primacy of contemplation over action. The conception of the Crusade as *gesta Dei* (the intervention of God in history through man) offered warriors a means of sharing directly in the benefits of salvation, without having to give up their status and the values it entailed, as St. Bernard was to make clear. To our twentieth-century eyes, killing infidels may seem to be a strange way to live a Christian life. But from the perspective of the history of Western spirituality, the Crusades interest us less in their historical unfolding than as evidence of the appearance of a new religious mentality. Behind the knights, who found a place in the Church thanks to the Crusades, we can discern the outlines of the masses of the poor and unarmed, who were the ones who believed the longest in this undertaking. Refusing to let themselves be confined to a purely passive or instrumental role, they were to make this hope their own and would try to construct in this world a peaceable, egalitarian, and fraternal society. To be sure, beginning with the thirteenth century, the royal assumption of control over the Crusades and their deflection to suit the temporal interests of the papacy gave rise to many failures and much disillusionment. But in the hearts of many medieval Christians there remained the memory, which soon became mythical, of a population which forgot its political divisions and transcended its social cleavages, the forefront of a humanity reconciled with itself in the service of God. The masses spontaneously discovered and preserved the true spirit of the biblical message, in which the sufferings of the poor prepared the way for the triumphs of Jerusalem, and the Messiah, bearer of an emblem of salvation—the cross—would be the sign of the gathering of the nations.

FIVE

A Twelfth-Century Novelty: The Lay Saints of Urban Italy

THE PURPOSE OF THIS STUDY is to highlight, on the basis of a number of case studies large enough to constitute a representative sample, the appearance in the twelfth century of a new phenomenon in the religious history of the West: the fact that simple laypersons were able to become officially recognized saints and enjoy the honors of a cult.[1] At an epoch when the prevailing opinion was that Christian perfection could only be attained by fleeing the world, and the leading figures in ecclesiastical life were monks and founders of religious orders like St. Bernard and St. Norbert, it may seem strange that the public took an interest in figures who were exceptional neither for their ascetic exploits nor for their devotion to prayer and contemplation. Nevertheless, this was the case in some Mediterranean countries, where the evolution of religious mentalities took place earlier than elsewhere because of the importance of urbanization beginning in the early 1100s, and because of the peculiarities of their political and social structures. And it is surely no coincidence that northern and central Italy, the cradle of the communal regime, was the privileged setting where most of the people whom we will discuss lived.

When we speak of lay sanctity as a phenomenon unique to these areas, it goes without saying that we set aside the very particular cases of sainted kings, about whom important studies have been published in recent years.[2] In fact, by virtue of the coronation ceremony, the sovereign assumed a religious rank comparable to that of the bishops by whom he was anointed. In the eyes of the clergy and the common people, the king was an exceptional being, a mediator between the spheres of the sacred and the profane.[3] Thus we cannot in all fairness consider sainted kings, who were relatively numerous at that time, to be typical representatives of the laity. In fact, as French jurists were to specify in the thirteenth century, the king was not a "pure layman," and the historian is justified in treating the holders of royal power as a special case simply because of the halo of sanctity which surrounded their function.[4]

This does not mean, to be sure, that the notion of lay sanctity was totally unknown in the West before the twelfth-century figures to be discussed below. Indeed, as early as the tenth century, the monk Odon of Cluny had tried to provide a model for the rising feudal aristocracy in his *Vie de S. Géraud d'Aurillac*. But despite the interest of this text, which historians have commented on extensively in recent years,[5] we must recognize that it was not influential, and that the only saints outside of the ecclesiastical world, in the eleventh and twelfth centuries, were almost all selected—except for a few hermits—from among the holders of power, such as Emperor Henry II, Empresses Mathilda, Adelaide and Cunegund, and Queen Margaret of Scotland, which brings us back to the model of royal sanctity.[6] The absence of sainted laypersons is nonetheless astonishing in an epoch when St. Bernard, in his *De laude novae militiae*, praised the knights who had consecrated their lives and their arms to the service of the Holy Land as members of the new Knights Templar. But the time for a modern notion of sanctity had not yet arrived in most of the West. As Michel Parisse demonstrated in 1980, the Christianization of knighthood, which the Church achieved in the twelfth century, was based among other things on hagiographic models, but these models were borrowed from an earlier period, that of Christian Antiquity.[7] The iconographic representations found in Romanesque churches and the statues on the portals of Gothic cathedrals provide a good illustration of the cult rendered by the Church to warrior saints; but it was St. George, St. Mauritius, and St. Theodore, not the crusaders of the twelfth century, who bore witness to this rehabilitation of the warrior. In hagiography as well, the obstacle caused by the preponderance of clerical and monastic ideals proved to be equally insurmountable, and yearnings for a chivalric sanctity incarnated in "modern" heroes could only be satisfied through epics and popular devotion ("Saint" Roland's horn was venerated as a relic in Blaye) or through courtly romance (Perceval and Galahad in the Grail cycle).[8] And when the Roman Church became open to the idea of the modernization of the saintly ranks, the figures who took precedence were those of bishops like St. Thomas Becket, canonized in 1173, or of monks. It was not until 1199 that a simple layman, St. Omobono of Cremona (†1197) was granted the glory of the altars. In any case, his canonization was an isolated instance, since until the fifteenth century all of the newly promoted lay saints were kings or princesses.[9]

This did not prevent local cults from developing in Mediterranean countries, which rendered sometimes intense and long-lasting devotions to figures like St. Domingo de la Calzada, a pious layman who distinguished himself among his contemporaries by preparing the pilgrimage road to Santiago de Compostela with his own hands, or St. Bénezet (†1184), who began the construction of the Avignon bridge and who is credited with the founding of the confraternity of the "Frères Pontifes."[10] But the only region of Western Christendom where lay sanctity as defined above could take root and blossom was communal Italy. For this reason, we will deal exclusively with saints of this geographic area, with the goal of bringing to light their unique characteristics.

I. The Lay Saints and Their Social Milieux

Before proceeding further, it is necessary to survey the common features of the figures we have included under the generic term of lay saints. We must state at the outset that the list we have drawn up does not pretend to be exhaustive. The fortunes of our research and the availability of documentation have led us to highlight nine figures. More extensive investigation of the *Acta Sanctorum* and Italian archives would probably have enabled us to add some names to the list. But it is unlikely that they would have significantly modified the general profile that emerges from these individual portraits.

The first of these figures chronologically speaking (based on the dates of their death, which in the case of saints is also considered their *dies natalis*, the day of their birth to eternal life) was Gualfardo of Verona, who is supposed to have died near that city in 1127.[11] According to his *Vita*, which was probably written toward the end of the twelfth century, he was an artisan and tradesman who plied the trade of harnessmaker; he came from Augsburg to Verona in 1096. His name itself seems to lend probability to the hypothesis that he was on a pilgrimage, since it is the Italianized version of the German word "Wallfahrer," which means pilgrim. Interrupting his trip, he settled in an impenetrable forest on the banks of the river Adige, not far from the city. One day he was found there by hunters and brought to Verona, where he set up shop near the abbey of San Salvatore. But at the time of a large flood, Gualfardo left the city and built a cell near the Church of Santa Trinità, in the nearby countryside. The Veronese sought him out there to ask him to work miracles, which he accomplished in great number until his death.

The case of Allucio of Campigliano (†1134) is rather different. Born in Valdinievole, in western Tuscany (near Pescia), he is known to us through a *Vita* which was found in 1344 on the occasion of the translation of his relics, but which, according to the report drawn up on that occasion, dates from the twelfth or thirteenth century.[12] Allucio was the son of a rural landowner who was probably fairly well off. After spending his youth as shepherd of the family flock, he devoted himself to works of charity and devotion, building two churches, a bridge across the Arno, and three hospices for pilgrims and travelers, one of which was on his lands at Campigliano, near Uzzano. He also distinguished himself in his generosity toward the poor, whom he showered with alms, and in his actions on behalf of peace, which led him to play the role of mediator in the conflicts which were already setting the leading cities of the area against one another.

Teobaldo of Alba (†1150), in Lombardy, is probably the best documented figure of this group. Indeed, in addition to his *Vita*, which was composed in the mid-thirteenth century, we are fortunate in having an important collection of miracles attributed to him and a second medieval biography, intended to be used for preaching. This beautiful hagiographic dossier is conserved in its entirety in a fourteenth-century manuscript, still to be found today in the Archivio Capitolare of Alba; it was published in an excellent edition in 1929, after having been overlooked by the Bollandists.[13] According to these documents, Teobaldo was born in Vicoforte, near Asti, in 1100. Orphaned at the age of twelve, he went to Alba as a cobbler. After he spent ten years as an apprentice, his master offered to give Teobaldo his daughter in marriage and hand on his workshop to him. But the young worker refused and left on a pilgrimage to Santiago de Compostela. Upon his return, he chose the profession of porter out of humility and distinguished himself through his works of charity on behalf of the poor. After his death in 1150, his tomb became a very popular pilgrimage destination, since in the thirteenth and fourteenth centuries records were kept of miracles brought about through his intercession on behalf of visitors from Franche-Comté, where his cult seems to have been extensive at this time.[14]

Ranieri of Pisa (born around 1115 or 1117, died 1160), the patron saint of his native city, is known to us through the very long *Vita* that Canon Benincasa devoted to him in 1161 and through the fresco cycle by Antonio Veneziano that illustrates it at the Campo Santo.[15] He was the son of a rich Pisan merchant and shipowner. After a very worldly adolescence, he was converted by the saintly hermit Alberto, a Corsican nobleman who had withdrawn to the monastery of San Vito in Pisa and had become famous for his actions on behalf of the poor. Ranieri then travelled to the Holy Land to see the places where Jesus had walked, and lived there for several years as a hermit, graced with many visions and revelations. He returned to Pisa in 1153 and spent seven years in penitence, unmasking demons and performing countless miracles.

Although he was the only saint in this group to be canonized by the papacy, St. Omobono of Cremona (†1197) is not the best known.[16] His hagiographic documents, which consist of three thirteenth-century *Vitae*—one of them by Bishop Sicardo of Cremona (†1215)—remain unpublished for the most part, and the texts which figure there are not always very explicit about his life and his activities.[17] Judging by the data in *Quia pietas*, the bull of canonization promulgated by Innocent III in January 1199, Omobono was a pious layman who distinguished himself through his charitable works on behalf of the poor and through his great piety, as his death, which occurred during mass at his parish church, demonstrates. In the eyes of the pontiff, Omobono incarnated the penitential ideal, which was presented as a privileged way for laypeople to attain salvation.[18] But other sources emphasize his participation in the battle against heresy and the exemplary fashion in which he practiced his profession of draper-tailor.[19]

In 1212, shortly after his death, Raimondo Palmerio (†1200) was the subject of a *Vita* composed by a canon from Piacenza, Master Rufino.[20] Raimondo is depicted as a shoemaker who made a pilgrimage to the Holy Land in his youth; because of this journey, he was given the surname of "Palmerio" (palmer or pilgrim) upon his return. He then married, had children, and returned to his workshop. But he stood as a model of comportment for his fellow workers and constantly edified them with moral and religious teachings. After the death of his wife, he made a pilgrimage first to Santiago de Compostela and then to Rome. While he was dreaming of another voyage to the Holy Land, Christ appeared to him and asked him to return instead to Piacenza to care for the poor whom nobody was tending. Obeying this behest, he devoted himself, with the support of the bishop and the canons of the Church of the Twelve Apostles, to succoring all of the dispossessed of the city, from pilgrims and abandoned children to prostitutes and invalids, and he founded various institutions on their behalf, in particular a hospice. He also intervened in the internal conflicts of the city to promote the cause of peace; his vain attempt to prevent armed conflict between Piacenza and Cremona resulted in his imprisonment in Cremona. After his release, he turned his efforts to aiding prisoners and earned the hostility of the young aristocrats by working to have tournaments outlawed. He died in 1200 in the midst of the poor, who revered him like a father. Between 1209 and 1247, many miracles attributed to his intercession were recorded in various locations in Lombardy.[21]

Unlike the preceding saints, Obizio (†1204) is known not through a *Vita*, but through miracles collected by the Bollandists, and especially through a rather long passage devoted to him in the *Chronicon* of Giacomo Malvizzi (*Malvecius*), a chronicle of the history of Brescia beginning in 1412. Giacomo claimed that the substance of the passage came from manuscripts then conserved at the abbey of Santa Giulia.[22] To this day, there is a sixteenth-century fresco cycle in the Church of San Salvatore which illustrates the story of the Blessed Obizio. According to this dual textual and iconographical tradition, Obizio, who was born in Niardo, a town near Breno, was a knight and the lord of Valcamonica. Fighting in the service of Brescia, he was seriously wounded on the bridge over the Oglio in a battle against the Cremonese and left for dead. During the following hours he experienced a horrifying vision of Hell. Saved by a friend who had found his body, he recovered from his wounds and converted to a better life. From then on, he led the existence of a penitent, sharing his possessions with the poor and putting himself at their service. In addition, he constructed a bridge over the Oglio at his own expense. After separating from his wife, who also dedicated herself to good works, he retired to Brescia, where he became a lay brother in the monastery of Santa Giulia. He died there in odor of sanctity in 1204.

Gerardo Tintori (†1207) also was not the subject of a medieval *Vita*, but we possess a good deal of information about him from two sources: the passage devoted to him by Bonincontro Morigia, in his fifteenth-century *Chronicon Modoetiense*, and the diocesan canonization proceedings organized on his behalf in 1582 by Carlo Bascapè, the bishop of Novara, on the orders of St. Carlo Borromeo, the archbishop of Milan. On this occasion many medieval documents which illustrate Gerardo Tintori's reputation for sanctity were gathered and published.[23] Here again we have a saint of charity who distinguished himself in his actions on behalf of invalids and lepers, for whom he founded and directed a hospital at Monza. Both during his life and after his death, numerous miracles were attributed to him, and his memory lived on in the charitable institution he established, called the Hospital of San Gerardo.[24]

The last of our lay saints, Gualtero of Lodi (†1223 or 1224), closely resembled Gerardo Tintori. Born in Lodi, a town in Lombardy, Gualtero chose upon reaching adulthood to place himself in the service of the poor and worked for several years in the hospice that Raimondo Palmerio had founded for them at Piacenza.[25] Then, with the support of the ecclesiastical authorities and the commune of Lodi, he established a shelter for pilgrims and travellers not far from his native city in a place which previously had been dangerous to pass, remaining the shelter's director until his death. He also founded three other hospices of the same type in the region. His *Vita*, which contains no miracles, even though the author claims that several occurred through his intervention, was written shortly after his death by Canon BonGiovanni of Lodi, who, according to the editor of this recently published text, had joined the community of men, women, and hermits that had gathered around Gualtero.

As is evident from this list, all of the Italian lay saints of the twelfth and early thirteenth century belonged to the masculine sex. This should come as no surprise, since, as we know, it was unthinkable for an uncloistered woman to accede to sanctity at this time, except for a small number of empresses and queens, as the example of the Blessed Ubaldesca of Pisa (†1207) demonstrates *a contrario*. After becoming a nun at the Hospital of San Giovanni of Pisa at the age of fifteen, Blessed Ubaldesca received her abbess' permission to go out to beg and distribute the alms to the poor.[26] It was only a generation later, with St. Elisabeth of Thuringia (†1231) and the Blessed Umiliana dei Cerchi (†1246), that married women who had remained in the world as widows were first recognized as saints.[27]

It is also striking that the group of nine figures we are considering can be divided, unequally, between two geographic zones: western Tuscany (Allucio, a native of Valdinievole, and Ranieri of Pisa) and, overwhelmingly, Lombardy, from Alba in the west to Verona in the east, with the greatest concentration around Milan (Monza, Lodi, Cremona). In fact, these areas were unusual for their early urbanization, their precocious economic development, and their political evolution in the direction of communal government. Of these lay saints, only one had rural origins: Allucio of Campigliano, who happened to be one of the earliest. But there was nothing specifically rural about his activities, since they consisted of constructing hospices and a bridge to facilitate the movement of pilgrims and travellers. All of the others were city-dwellers, whether of old stock, like Ranieri of Pisa—scion of a good family of wealthy merchants who had made their fortune in maritime trade—Omobono of Cremona, Gerardo Tintori, Raimondo Palmerio and Gualtero of Lodi, or more recent immigrants, like Teobaldo, who had come from Vicoforte d'Asti to Alba to find work, and Obizio, lord of Niardo, in the Valcamonica, who moved to Brescia, where he became the object of a cult after his death.

As for their social origins, these saints were of rather modest extraction, especially compared to contemporary saints born north of the Alps. There was only one nobleman among them, Obizio— and even he was from the lower ranks of the knighthood.[28] As far as we can tell (for the hagiographical texts are not very specific on this subject), three of them belonged to the upper and middle levels of the "*popolo*," the bourgeoisie who grew rich through commerce and landed property: Ranieri of Pisa, who was wealthy enough to charter the ship which brought him to the Holy Land,[29] Gerardo Tintori, who established a hospital in Monza with his patrimony,[30] and Gualtero of Lodi, who sold his parents' house after their death and distributed the proceeds to the poor.[31] The last four were probably artisans, two of whom were masters— Gualfardo of Verona[32] and Omobono of Cremona[33]—and two were journeymen: Teobaldo of Alba, a cobbler who became a porter,[34] and Raimondo Palmerio, a shoemaker.[35] It is worth noting that all four were members of the leather and textile trades, from which a large number of heretics were recruited, as demonstrated by the research of Eugenio Dupré Theseider on the registers of the Inquisition in Bologna at the end of the thirteenth century.[36] Whatever the case may be, it would be incorrect to say that these saints had poor origins, even if they later became poor. The hagiographers who wrote their *Vitae* emphasize the fact that they owned their own property and lived in modest but real luxury before their conversions. Rather than being "popular" saints, in the sense of "coming from the common people," they were actually saints of the "*popolo*," that is to say, born in the middle classes, which were alert to the economic and social realities of the day.[37] No more typical text exists in this regard than the beginning of the *Vita* of Raimondo Palmerio of Piacenza, whose author tells us: "parentes habuit ne illustres nec viles admodum, sed cives privatos eosque, si rem spectes domesticam, nec pauperes nec opulentos."[38]

This social milieu constitutes an excellent reflection of the urban society of the Italian communes in the mid-twelfth century, which Otto of Freising described in such scornful terms: "they do not disdain to give the girdle of knighthood or the grades of distinction to young men of inferior station and even some workers of the vile mechanical arts, whom other peoples bar like the pest from the more respected and honorable pursuits."[39] In the case of sanctity as well, the same distinctive process of betterment was to be found, according to which membership in the elite came about not through birth or bloodlines, but rather through strenuous and productive activity in the service of the city.

II. The Components of Lay Sanctity: Asceticism, Pilgrimage, and Charitable Activity

All of the figures mentioned above were laymen, that is, they did not have clerical or monastic status. But this negative definition obviously does not provide a comprehensive account of their spirituality. In fact, their spirituality had three main components, present in varying degrees in the lives of each one.

The first was asceticism, especially prominent in the first of our lay saints, Gualfardo of Verona (†1127), who chose to live as a hermit for twenty years in an impenetrable forest on the banks of the Adige, and who, when he was found and brought back to the city by hunters, left once again as soon as he could. But his love of solitude did not reach the point of unsociability, since he gave a warm welcome to city dwellers who came to ask him to work miracles, and who brought him food at the same time.[40] The hermit's existence was also a feature of the *Vita* of Ranieri of Pisa: converted by the ascetic Alberto, "who wore a cloak of animal hair, like a goat," he went to the Holy Land and did penance for seven years at the Holy Sepulchre in Jerusalem, then at Mt. Tabor, Hebron, and Bethlehem. Since his austerity had become excessive, God, according to his biographer, intervened to ask him to eat normally. On his return to Pisa, he led the life of a wandering preacher, spending his time preaching in ragged clothing.[41]

The role of pilgrimage was even more important in the existence of these figures, whether they went on pilgrimages themselves— like Teobaldo of Alba, Obizio, and Raimondo Palmerio—or worked for the benefit of pilgrims by building bridges and hospices for travellers, as almost all of the others did. There is no doubt that going on a pilgrimage, whether to Compostela or to Jerusalem, conferred on the pilgrim the kind of religious prestige which could, under favorable circumstances, be the starting point for a reputation for sanctity.[42] But the most interesting case in this connection was certainly that of Raimondo Palmerio, the shoemaker from Piacenza. Having visited the Holy Land with his mother at the age of fifteen, he went to Santiago after his wife's death and continued via Sainte-Baume, Saintes-Maries-de-la-Mer, the tombs of St. Bernard (at Menthon?) and of St. Augustine in Pavia, finally reaching Rome. He intended to leave for Jerusalem, but Jesus appeared to him to advise against continuing his wanderings and ordered him to return to Piacenza to devote his attentions to the poor.[43] This turning point in his existence undoubtedly illustrates the growing importance of works of mercy in the religious ideal presented to the laity in the late twelfth century.[44]

Indeed, what all of these saints, despite their diversity, had in common were charitable activities for the benefit of the dispossessed; this was at the very heart of their sanctity. All, with the possible exception of Gualfardo, were patrons of the roads and bridges, devoting their efforts to improving communications and coming to the aid of travelers.[45] Some, especially among those in the late twelfth century, went further and tried to relieve all kinds of suffering, including that of the lepers whose wounds Gerardo Tintori bandaged in his hospital in Monza. His zeal on behalf of the impoverished won him the name of "Father of the poor," as it did for St. Omobono, who transformed his house into a hospice.[46] But the most interesting case, perhaps because it is the best documented, is that of Raimondo Palmerio, who seems to have had a keen sense of the social realities of poverty and marginality. Not satisfied with fighting against prostitution and protecting the poor against unjust magistrates and magnates, he did not hesitate to organize a demonstration of beggars and poor people in Piacenza, who marched through the streets shouting "Help me, help me, cruel harsh Christians, for I am dying of hunger while you live in abundance." He also took care of abandoned children. After his death, the commune took charge of his institutions, grouped under the name of *Hospitale sancti Raymundi*, the Hospital of St. Raimondo.[47]

Love for the poor and humility were thus the common denominators of the lay sanctity that arose in twelfth-century communal Italy. The saints in question interpreted the monastic precept of the *sequela Christi* in a concrete and practical manner, as an appeal to fight against the insecurity which made all travel dangerous and, especially after 1160, against the traumas of urbanization: famine, begging, prostitution, child abandonment, and so on. All of these initiatives were based on the conviction that the poor are the image of Christ and represent a privileged means of access to God.[48] At the same time, the traditional practice of alms-giving was taking on new forms: in the view of these saints, it was no longer enough for those with possessions to donate their superfluous goods; they were called on to share their necessities, so as not only to practice charity but also to establish justice in social relations.[49] For it would reduce the stature of these figures if we were to consider them as no more than apostles of poor relief. The most outspoken among them, Raimondo Palmerio, for example, did not hesitate to make scathing denunciations of the defects of the communal form of government, with its unequal justice and its incessant conflicts involving both factions within the same city and among neighboring cities. The poor were always the appointed victims of the discord, while the rich used it to embellish their own reputations.[50] Given these circumstances, it is not surprising that Raimondo Palmerio was imprisoned for his efforts to promote peace, or that St. Omobono was beaten black and blue by his enemies.[51]

In fact, pilgrimages and combat on behalf of the impoverished found a logical point of contact in the keen sense of the connection between the humanity of Christ and his divinity, between the incarnation of God and the Christian obligation to fight for the dignity of man in order to restore it when it was violated. In this new religious context, the active life, far from being inferior to the contemplative one, as it had hitherto been considered, assumed irreplaceable importance and value, because it held out the possibility of reunion with Christ through his suffering offspring. It would be incorrect, however, to seek in these statements a reflection of thirteenth-century spirituality, marked by the influence of St. Francis. To be sure, echoes of this later spirituality cannot be ruled out in the case of the last *Vitae* to be written. But it is in a text that clearly antedates St. Francis—the *Vita* of Ranieri of Pisa, composed in 1162—that we find the explicit affirmation that Ranieri, through the practice of *imitatio Christi* and particularly in his charity toward the poor with whom he had shared his meals, had come to resemble the Son of God.[52]

Beyond the charitable dimension—in the strongest sense of the term "charity"—that is apparent in most of the records concerning these saints, are there explicit signs in their biographies of a specifically lay spirituality which would give them the same prospects of salvation as monks or clerics?[53] Our response to this question cannot be categorical, because the corpus of hagiography which we are working from is not homogeneous and its contents reflect the fact that it is made up of texts composed over a period of two centuries. In fact, the text with the most extensive indication of lay spirituality happens to be one of the oldest: the *Vita* of Ranieri of Pisa, composed by the Canon Benincasa in 1161-1162. It is a unique work, very much engaged in the battles of its day. The author claims for his hero, and in fact for all of the baptized, a royal priesthood in Christ, and makes several mentions of conflicts between him and certain elements of the clergy, both in Jerusalem and in Pisa. In his opinion, Ranieri, though a layman, attained priestly rank both through his self-inflicted mortifications after his conversion and through divine election, for God had chosen him to be his prophet and had granted him numerous visions and revelations.[54] There is a very clear echo here of the tensions between clergy and laity which made their presence felt throughout the West in the middle of the twelfth century, tensions centering on the question of whether the power which priests exercised depended on the propriety of their manner of life. For his part, Ranieri prayed "that priests would become the light of the people" and stated that "even if they were wicked, they still had the power *ex officio* to bind and to loose," but reported that God had told him in a vision that He "had delivered the priests into the hands of Satan."[55] His biography is therefore the expression of a reformist current which rejected the radical attack on the priesthood by the heretical sects of the day, while at the same time harshly criticizing the deficiencies of the Catholic clergy.[56] The *Vita* also asserted, through the person of St. Ranieri, that the laity should have the right to preach.[57] Indeed, his biographer showed him evangelizing the common people with appeals to conversion and penitence. Benincasa justified these public orations by associating them with the royal priesthood of the baptized and with the prophetic charisma of his hero. But he remained within the bounds of orthodoxy, emphasizing that Ranieri did no more than exhort the faithful and urge them to go confess their sins to priests.[58]

Dating from the thirteenth century, the other biographies provide a more standard image of the situation of the laity within the Church, stressing their respect for clerical prerogatives. Thus Raimondo Palmerio is shown acting in every instance with the blessing of the bishop of Piacenza, whether he was leaving on pilgrimage or working on behalf of the poor of the city—though this did not prevent him from reproaching the prelate for his failure to condemn the factional battles in the city.[59] The same *Vita*, composed as we have seen in 1212, contains a very suggestive passage on the problem of lay preaching, which some decades earlier had brought the ecclesiastical hierarchy into conflict with certain evangelical movements, particularly the Waldensians. This passage states that after his return from the Holy Land, Raimondo addressed exhortations to his fellow workers and gave them doctrinal and moral instruction. Since this "preaching" was quite successful, he was asked to continue it in the public square, but he refused on the grounds that this activity belonged to priests and educated men. He did not, however, cease his spiritual discussions, and always urged his interlocutors to speak further with a monk or a priest.[60] The whole episode indicates the kind of compromises forced on the Church in this area at the time of Innocent III. But it is important to note that the distinction between forms of religious discourse permitted or forbidden to laypeople was based not on the opposition between the *aperta* (moral teachings) and the *profunda* (exposition of the fundamental doctrines of faith), but rather on the difference between private exhortation, which is allowed to all, and public preaching, which is reserved for the clergy alone.[61] In general, this *Vita* and those of St. Omobono, which were more or less contemporary—the first was composed by bishop Sicard before 1215—depict *laici religiosi* actively engaged in works of mercy, involved in city life, particularly in the struggles against heretics, and respectful of clerical prerogatives. At any rate, this is the picture which emerges from the bull *Quia pietas*, with which Innocent III announced the canonization of the Cremonese merchant in 1199.[62]

On the other hand, there are two other fundamental problems specific to the laity which do not seem to have been resolved, except perhaps in the kinds of personal experience of which we obviously have no record (at least in hagiographic documents): work and marriage.

To be sure, in their various ways all of these saints were active, hard-working people. Several spent their lives in the world of artisans and manual laborers.[63] But in the eyes of the hagiographers, the place of work in their religious experience was secondary and marginal. In fact, their professional activities were presented purely as a means of providing for their subsistence and procuring alms for the poor, or even—in the case of Teobaldo of Alba—as an ascetic exercise: after starting out as a shoemaker, he chose voluntarily to become a porter, because that was a rougher and more humble profession.[64] It would therefore be pointless to seek in our texts some kind of ethic or spirituality of work. But the fact that the exercise of very humble, often manual, trades did not constitute an obstacle to sanctity is in itself a remarkable development. As long as the profits were used for the benefit of the poor, even the profession of merchant did not seem to be incompatible with the search for Christian perfection, as the late thirteenth century *Vita* of St. Omobono emphasizes.[65] But it is worth noting that, in many of these *Vitae*, when the religious experience of the saint becomes richer and more intense, his earthly work is no longer mentioned, either because he actually abandoned it or because the weight of hagiographic conventions led the biographer to remain silent about these temporal activities in order to display more prominently his hero's progress in spiritual life.[66]

The same discussion is more or less valid for the subject of marriage, *mutatis mutandis*. Of the nine lay saints under consideration, only three were married: Obizio, the knight who was converted as an adult and then separated from his wife and children, leaving a dowry, and, more significantly, Omobono of Cremona and Raimondo Palmerio of Piacenza. We learn in the *Vita* of Omobono that he was married and a father. But this aspect of his life was only mentioned for negative reasons: his wife was presented as a cantankerous woman, constantly criticizing and scolding him for his excessive generosity toward the poor, and thus making it necessary for him to conceal his charitable activities on several occasions. Petty and uncomprehending toward her husband, she was portrayed only as an obstacle to his sanctification.[67]

In fact, the only text in which the questions of marriage and its compatibility with the pursuit of Christian perfection are discussed in any detail is the *Vita* of Raimondo Palmerio of Piacenza, where the problems posed by the entrance of one member of a couple—the husband, in this case—into penitential life are analyzed in depth. According to his biographer, Raimondo let his family arrange a marriage for him upon his return from a pilgrimage to the Holy Land; this did not keep him from being a good husband to his wife, "whom he instructed like a daughter, loved like a sister, and venerated like a mother."[68] Indeed, five children were born from this union. All died in the same year, however, probably because of an epidemic, and Raimondo suggested to his wife that they live in chastity from then on. But she energetically refused, declaring: "If I wished to be a nun, I would follow this advice. But since you have married me, it seems right to me to behave like a married woman, not like a widow or a nun." The saint yielded to these arguments, "in consideration of the weakness of his wife," and they had a final son, Gerardo, whom he dedicated to the clergy without his wife's knowledge; the son was to become a canon in the Church of the Twelve Apostles in Piacenza. Finally, the wife fell gravely ill, thus becoming "providentially" unfit for conjugal life, and died. Raimondo was free to go on another pilgrimage, leaving his son with his wife's parents, and to set his course decisively toward sanctity.[69]

We have analyzed this very interesting example in some detail because it allows us to see that in the thirteenth century, even in the best of cases, marriage—or married life, to be precise—remained an obstacle for lay saints on the road to perfection, a handicap that was not to be overcome until the following generation.[70] But here again, as in the case of commerce, we need to be aware of the evolution then in progress. Around 1130, Teobaldo fled from Alba when his employer offered him his daughter in marriage, and he remained unmarried during his entire life.[71] Several decades later, Raimondo Palmerio and Omobono were venerated as saints, even though they had been married for a good part of their lives. To be sure, marriage was not presented as a state that in and of itself was conducive to sanctification. But at least it was no longer considered an insurmountable obstacle on the path to Christian perfection. The extremely close ties between sanctity and virginity that had existed until this time were losing their force as the Church came to recognize the existence of an *ordo conjugatorum*, an order of married people, and the possibility of achieving salvation within it—even though the clergy retained serious doubts about the "weakness" of the female sex, as the fact that all of these saintly figures were men clearly illustrates.[72]

Thus, in terms of lay spirituality, the Italian saints of the twelfth and early thirteenth centuries lived in a period of transition. If, in the eyes of their clerical biographers, their modest social origins and their "ignoble" professions did not prevent them from achieving a certain level of perfection, it was because their involvement in serving the poor and social peace, as well as their fidelity to the Church, qualified them to be servants of God and models for emulation. Marriage, on the other hand, was seen essentially in terms of sexual life; it continued to be considered permissible, certainly, but nevertheless not conducive to the development of a vocation for sanctity.

III. Between Church and City

In this final section, it remains for us to consider the birth of the cults of these lay saints, the milieux which promoted them, and the success which devotion to these intercessors enjoyed in the Middle Ages. As we have already stated in our survey of the relevant documentation, most of these figures are known through hagiographic texts—*Vitae* and collections of miracles—which were the work of educated clerics, persons thoroughly familiar with Latin. For some, however, like Gerardo Tintori of Monza and Obizio of Brescia, the only literary source is a passage in a chronicle written in the fourteenth or fifteenth century, which mentions in passing the life and deeds of a purely local figure who was not lucky enough to find an ecclesiastical biographer. The question thus arises of why some of these saints were quickly forgotten, whereas others attained a certain fame.

Among the clerics who were sufficiently interested in these laymen to write their biographies and promote their cults, monastic milieux seem to have played an important role only in the cases of Obizio of Brescia and Ranieri of Pisa, whose *Vita* emphasizes his very close association with the abbey of San Vito during his life.[73] But it is significant that when Ranieri died, his body was borne triumphantly to the cathedral and buried there. Indeed, the relations between the lay saints and the secular clergy were particularly close.[74] If Master Rufino, the biographer of Raimondo Palmerio, was surely a canon regular, the author of Ranieri's *Vita*, Benincasa, was a canon of the cathedral of Pisa, and Gualtero of Lodi's *Vita* was written by BonGiovanni, who belonged to the cathedral chapter of Lodi.[75] The role of the bishop and the cathedral chapter was equally important for St. Omobono, whose earliest *Vita* was written by Bishop Sicardo himself,[76] and for Teobaldo of Alba. While the author of the latter's *Vita* remains anonymous, the text emphasizes the collaboration between Teobaldo and the canons of San Lorenzo; and it was the Archpriest Giacomo who recorded his miracles between 1285 and 1331. Moreover, at his death the cathedral bells began to ring of their own accord, and his body was buried by the bishop, probably to avoid arousing jealousy, half-way between the cathedral and his parish church, San Silvestro.[77] Even in cases where no *Vita* has survived, there are traces of close collaboration between the lay saints and the secular clergy, as we see in Monza, where Gerardo Tintori was always careful to seek the approval of the archpriest and canons of San Giovanni Battista for his generous initiatives on behalf of the poor and the sick.[78]

The secular clergy also played an important role in the survival of the cults of these servants of God. Not only did they keep careful records of their miracles, as we see for example in the case of Raimondo Palmerio between 1208 and 1247, but they also organized various translations of relics, which lent renewed energy to the devotions.[79] For instance, the *Vita* of Allucio of Campigliano was rediscovered in the course of a translation in 1344, which gave the clergy of Pescia an opportunity to organize a diocesan proceeding whose transcript has survived.[80] The same is true for Teobaldo of Alba, whose relics were "invented" in March 1429 by the bishop of that city, Alerino dei Rembaudi.[81] Paradoxically, the cult of St. Omobono went through a similar process: although he had been canonized by Innocent III, even in Cremona his cult was of little importance until 1356, when his remains were transferred to the cathedral and Bishop Ugolino established a large confraternity of devout patricians, the *Consortium sancti Homoboni*, thereby giving decisive impetus to the cult of the patron saint of the city.[82] All of these problems of cult dynamics are quite complex, and on this point the case of each saint should be given detailed and careful study. But despite the differences that may have existed between them, there is no doubt that the promotion of lay saints was essentially the work of the secular clergy and that it was limited to the local city or diocese, thus explaining the extremely localized character of these cults. This can be contrasted with the universalism of the mendicant orders, beginning with the late thirteenth century, who could take advantage of their centralized structures and their network of convents and tertiaries covering all of Christendom to recommend a small number of figures on whom the faithful were to concentrate their devotion.[83]

Another factor which helps to explain the relative obscurity of most of these lay saints is the civic dimension that their cults soon assumed.[84] When the commune where the body was located took charge of the devotion, it provided a solid anchoring for the cult, which in some cases ensured its survival to this day. But at the same time, this limited its diffusion, because a given saint could seem so closely associated with the city that venerated him that it became extremely difficult to introduce his cult elsewhere— assuming that anyone tried. For instance, Teobaldo's *Vita* does not fail to point out that God had accomplished great deeds in Alba in his honor: the offerings of the pilgrims who flocked to his tomb funded the construction of the bell tower of the cathedral of San Lorenzo and, at its side, a sort of covered portico where the municipal meetings took place. Moreover, these offerings made it possible to build on the sites of two preexisting buildings a church dedicated to him and a hospice for the poor which also bore his name.[85] It is not surprising, therefore, that in the communal statutes of the fourteenth century he was given the title of *custos civitatis*, guardian of the city. Similarly, St. Ranieri, who once announced the future greatness of Pisa to his fellow citizens, soon assumed the same role for his city as St. Mark had for Venice at the time: patron saint and talisman, as was demonstrated by the fact that merchants leaving for the Byzantine East never failed to carry with them water that had been in contact with his tomb, which would shield them against shipwreck.[86] In varying degrees, the same was true for all of the others, particularly for founders of hospitals like Gerardo Tintori in Monza, Allucio in Uzzano, and Raimondo Palmerio in Piacenza, whose popularity was linked to the vicissitudes of the institutions they had founded. When these institutions ceased to exist, or were absorbed by a hospital order or an "Ospedale Maggiore," the saints associated with them sometimes sank into oblivion, as was the case for some in the fifteenth century.[87]

The only members of the group to escape this unpropitious fate were Teobaldo (or Thibaud), whose cult spread as far as the Franche-Comté and whose tomb continued, at least until the end of the Middle Ages, to attract numerous pilgrims because of the miracles that occurred there,[88] and, more significantly, St. Omobono. In the case of St. Omobono, one might think that his fame was due to the fact that he was the only one of the group to be canonized. For reasons which I will present in a future work, I do not believe that this factor played a decisive role, for even though Innocent III canonized him in 1199, there was little mention of Omobono throughout the thirteenth century, even in Cremona. If his cult spread to most of the large cities in the Po Valley in the fourteenth century, and then to the rest of Europe (with the exception of France, it seems) in the fifteenth and sixteenth centuries, it was the profession he was engaged in during his life that enabled him to become the patron saint of confraternities of tailors and clothing merchants everywhere.[89] But he represents in some way the exception that confirms the rule; and we may truthfully say that, because of their failure to win the support of the papacy or the religious orders, most of these lay saints sank into undeserved obscurity, except at the local level.

In concluding this lengthy but still incomplete study, it is worth emphasizing (to the extent that it has been forgotten) how precocious and important the cults of lay saints actually were in the Mediterranean world at a time when the rest of Christianity was oblivious to this notion and chose as its new intercessors only sovereigns, bishops and monks.[90] Even when less elitist forms of sanctity were developing, as was the case in the thirteenth century in what is now Belgium, with Marie of Oignies and the female Beguine saints extolled by Jacques de Vitry and Thomas de Cantimpré, the content of these religious experiences, turned as they were toward ascetic exploits and the pursuit of mystical states, was quite different.[91] With these female figures, we are far from the saints of the Italian communes, who distinguished themselves in the eyes of their contemporaries through their keen sense of the need for charity in a civilization marked by uncontrolled urbanization and growing mobility, as well as through their efforts to furnish the active life with a spiritual dimension. Differences in the social and mental structures of the two parts of Europe can probably explain the limited success of a hagiographic model that represented the quintessence of the religious aspirations of the Lombard and Tuscan *"popolo."*

But it is less easy to understand why this model, so vital in the twelfth century and the first half of the thirteenth, rapidly lost its appeal in Italy itself, as is demonstrated by the ever smaller number of saints associated with this movement after the 1270s. In fact, this decline was connected with the success of the mendicant orders and the diffusion of their spirituality. To be sure, our saints had much in common with St. Francis, and it would not be an exaggeration to describe their movement as "pre-Franciscan," if this term has some meaning for historians. Like St. Francis, they were all associated with penitential spirituality, and the most characteristic aspects of his sanctity are sprinkled throughout their biographies: imitating Christ to the point of absolute conformity, valuing humility and poverty, tending to the disinherited and the marginalized not only with generous almsgiving but with fraternal assistance, desiring to help others work out their own salvation through exhortation and evangelical example, and so on. But at the same time, their insistence on remaining *laici religiosi*, lay religious, set them apart from St. Francis, or rather from the image cultivated by his spiritual sons. This desire was rooted not in some kind of laicism or need for autonomy—their frequently close collaboration with the secular clergy contradicts this argument— but in a very practical ideal of charity and a heightened sense of the importance of social and "civic" values. Now, the growth of the mendicant orders was accompanied, especially in Italy, by the growth of an increasingly contemplative form of mysticism, which was difficult to reconcile with this rather down-to-earth, or at any rate very concrete, conception of sanctity; and it was surely no coincidence that, through their confraternities of penitents and later of tertiaries, the Franciscans and Dominicans had an especially strong influence on women, as the great names of Italian lay sanctity after 1250 testify, from Rose of Viterbo to Margaret of Cortona and Angela of Foligno, culminating with Catherine of Siena.[92]

If the preceding reflections are correct, we must reject the statement, too often repeated, that the mendicant orders were responsible for promoting the laity: rather, their actions served to bring on the "monasticization of the laity" ("Mönchisierung des Laientums"), to use A. von Harnack's apt expression.[93] Because of the success of their enterprise, the criteria of sanctity were to become more and more extraordinary, in the etymological sense of the term—visions, revelations, exchanges of hearts, anorexic crises, and other mystical and paramystical phenomena—and in reaction to this, the doctrinal and intellectual dimensions of Christian perfection were newly emphasized. In the end, this evolution led inevitably to the disappearance of the modest and useful movement of lay sanctity, a victim of the dual processes of clericalization and spiritualization of religious life which characterized the final centuries of the Western Middle Ages.

SIX

Two Laypersons in Search of Perfection: Elzéar of Sabran and Delphine of Puimichel

ST. ELZÉAR (†1323) and his wife, the blessed Delphine (†1360) are usually considered Provençal saints. Their family origins and the social milieu in which they grew up lend support to this claim: Elzéar, who was born in 1286 and lost his mother in 1293, came from the powerful family of the Sabran, which was native to the region of Bagnols-sur-Cèze near Nîmes, and entered the service of the counts of Provence in the thirteenth century. Delphine, born in 1284, was the daughter of Guillaume de Signe, lord of Puimichel, and Delphine of Barras. She lost her parents in 1291 and was raised by nuns, under the guardianship of her uncles. For his part, young Elzéar was entrusted to his uncle Guillaume of Sabran, abbot of Saint-Victor of Marseille, and so he too grew up in monastic surroundings. In 1299, the two young people, aged thirteen and fifteen respectively, were joined together in marriage. Theirs was a union imposed for patrimonial and political reasons by Charles II of Anjou, king of Naples and count of Provence.[1] Delphine, who wished to maintain celibacy, began by refusing this marriage, which ran counter to her aspirations. Then, yielding to the wishes of her family and her sovereign, she conceived of the entirely original plan of conserving her virginity throughout her married life and managed to obtain her young husband's consent to the project.[2]

Their purely Provençal existence ended in 1310, when Elzéar succeeded his father, Ermengaud, who died that year, as count of Ariano. Ermengaud had lived in Italy since 1292 in the entourage of Charles II, who in 1301 had appointed him chief justiciar of the kingdom of Sicily. Elzéar inherited the title of count and was named chief justiciar of Abruzzo Citra upon his arrival in Naples. Through his biography, we know that he fought in Rome in 1312 against the troops of Emperor Henry VII and the Ghibellines. After the defeat of the imperial armies, he had to reconquer the county of Ariano, which had taken advantage of the disorders to rise up against the Angevins. By 1313 he had stamped out the rebellion and entered into conflict with Filippo of Taranto, who advocated violent repression. In 1314, with calm restored, Delphine came to join him in Naples. A period spent in Provence in 1316 provided them with the opportunity to make a vow of chastity in the presence of Gersende Alphant, their trusted adviser. But in 1317 they were back at the court of Naples, where King Robert, who had succeeded his father in 1309, entrusted to their care Duke Charles, the heir to the throne, who had just married Catherine of Austria. Delphine struck up a friendship with Queen Sancha, Robert's wife, and became her confidante, while Elzéar's influence in the ruling circles of the kingdom of Naples continued to grow. In 1319, he presided over the Royal Council in the king's absence; and in 1323, he was given a delicate diplomatic mission at the court of King Charles the Fair of France: negotiating the marriage of the recently widowed Duke Charles of Calabria with Marie, daughter of Charles of Valois and Mahaut of Châtillon. Accompanied by Delphine as far as Provence, Elzéar died alone in Paris on September 27, 1323. A short time later his body was returned to Provence and entombed in the Franciscan church of Apt.

As this brief biography makes clear, Elzéar's residence in Italy was rather limited—1310–1323, interrupted by repeated visits to Provence—and we can understand why the devotion which soon surrounded his memory and his tomb had no roots in the kingdom of Naples. Nevertheless, his biographer claimed that he distinguished himself there in two ways. First of all he comported himself as a perfect gentleman in military and judicial matters—after his participation in the battles between Angevins and Ghibellines in the streets of Rome, Christ had appeared to him, chastizing and scourging him for taking too much pleasure in war. But more important, he was able to restore order in the county of Ariano without useless bloodshed, and refused to take revenge on his defeated enemies. Although he displayed firmness toward wrong-doers, he always acted with mercy and gentleness: he personally admonished those sentenced to death, exhorting them to repent of their sins. Moreover, he urged his associates to mete out prompt and fair-handed justice to all and often remitted between one-third and one-half of the monetary fines imposed by his functionaries. This interesting depiction of a good administrator remains, however, somewhat abstract and atemporal. The author of Elzéar's *Vita* was clearly better informed about his role at the court of Naples: the picturesque description of this milieu and the portrait of the perfect Christian courtier are certainly the reasons for the success Elzéar's biography enjoyed in the seventeenth century.[3] Indeed, from 1317 to 1323, while holding high offices in the service of the Angevin sovereigns, he managed to live in the world without being taken in by its seductions. Not only did he have a positive effect on Charles of Calabria, the heir to the throne, whose mentor he was, but he disdainfully refused the presents offered to encourage him to use his considerable influence to advance private interests. In addition, while concealing his good deeds, he instituted a sizable "purse" to receive the complaints and petitions of poor people, thereby acquiring the reputation of being a defender of the humble, who came to him with their needs.[4]

Like his wife Delphine, Elzéar, who had been under the influence of the Franciscans from his earliest years, seems to have been marked by the crises which set one faction of the Franciscans against Pope John XXII between 1317 and 1323. It must be remembered that it was in Marseilles in 1318 that the first Spirituals, advocates of absolute poverty, were burned at the stake because of their conviction that Christ and his apostles had lived devoid of all possessions.[5] However, to the best of our knowledge, the count of Sabran does not seem to have been influenced by the Italian Franciscans, but rather by the more moderate beliefs of the Provençal theologian François of Meyronnes, his spiritual director who was present at his deathbed.[6] This may be the sense of Elzéar's somewhat sibylline statement to Delphine, reported in the *Vita*:

> If brother Jean Joli, my confessor, if Madame Gersende who has nourished me unceasingly on faith and devotion, if brother François of Meyronnes, this master and doctor who is so profound and learned in theology, came to me and said: 'Elzéar, let us recognize that you and I have been improperly instructed in our faith, and that the pope and the Church wish to change the faith'—because at this hour we are all in a fog of uncertainty and delusion—I tell you that this would not make me deviate on one single point from the faith that the Holy Spirit has taught me and God has breathed into my soul, even if I had to die ten times.[7]

And the Latin *Vita* adds:

> Neither the Antichrist nor his disciples could dissuade me from this position, nor from any article of the faith now upheld by our Holy Mother Church.[8]

Serenity seems to have been one of the characteristics of St. Elzéar. It stands in clear contrast to the extreme sensitivity, and even anxiousness, of his wife, who to be sure lived through one of the most difficult periods in the history of the Church.

Indeed, if only because of her exceptional longevity, Delphine, far more than Elzéar, was present at the center of the tempests that were then shaking all of Christianity, and particularly the Franciscan order. From the time of her childhood in Provence, she had been under the influence of the Franciscans; one of them, Brother Philippe Alquier de Riez, had vigorously urged her to refuse the marriage that her family and the king wanted to impose on her.[9] She was again in contact with Franciscans when she resided in Naples, from 1314 to 1323, from 1326 to 1328 or 1330, from 1332 to 1339, and finally from 1340 to 1343, for a total of at least twenty-two years.[10] The court of Naples, especially after 1323, was the refuge of Franciscans persecuted by Pope John XXII, and of the Beguines, devout laypeople, numerous in Provence, Languedoc and Catalonia, whose way of life was inspired by the precepts of the Spirituals, particularly Peter John Olivi.[11] King Robert himself was quite attracted to the ideal of poverty; his wife, Queen Sancha, was even more strongly drawn to it, and to chastity, to such an extent that, in 1317, the Neapolitan sovereign had to appeal to the pope to convince his wife to satisfy her conjugal debt.[12] In this intense and even exalted religious climate, Delphine decided after Elzéar's death to give away her landed patrimony and seigniorial rights, which were truly immense since her husband had left her all of his possessions in a will drawn up in Toulon in 1317.[13] Because the king was initially opposed to the liquidation of her domains and castles, in 1327 she arranged for 3000 lire of gold left to her by her husband, and another 1000 florins in 1328, to be delivered to her nephew Guillaume of Sabran, who was charged with distributing it to the poor of the region. At the insistence of the queen, Robert finally yielded, and Delphine gave away all of her possessions between 1329 and 1332, in order to live a life of absolute poverty.[14] In 1333, free of her patrimonial burden, she made a vow of poverty in the hands of Brother Isnardo Risi at Casasana (or Quisisana), the summer residence of the Neapolitan court. Delphine then proposed to her ladies-in-waiting and her half-sister, Alayette, a cloistered nun, that they form a community where all would live on equal footing, since she was not able to "go out wandering in the world" as she would have liked. To those who did not wish to follow her, Delphine offered financial support for the rest of their lives.

It is worth asking what inspired Delphine, who up to that time had distinguished herself primarily through her passionate attachment to virginity and chastity, to become a proponent of absolute poverty. More than to a specific person, whose name is lost to us in any case, we must ascribe it to her entire milieu. In addition to Queen Sancha, whom we have already mentioned, there was also her brother, Philip of Majorca: the former regent of the kingdom of Majorca, he had become a Franciscan and taken refuge in Naples, where in 1329 he delivered a vehement sermon against the theses of Pope John XXII on the question of poverty.[15] Delphine, who undoubtedly knew him and associated with him, seems to have shared his opinions on the matter, which joined uncompromising strictness with the desire to remain loyal to the Church and the Avignon papacy. This was also the position of brother Andrea da Galiano, Queen Sancha's confessor, a moderate Spiritual who preached poverty and came to the aid of "brothers of the poor life," or *fraticelli*, who had fled to the Abruzzi to escape the Inquisition.[16] After the rift between John XXII and Michael of Cesena, the new minister general of the Franciscans designated by the pope, Guiral Ot, persecuted Andrea and brought various charges against him; he was saved only by the intervention of the queen and of Neapolitan lords and prelates who vouched for his orthodoxy. In 1332 a furious John XXII complained to King Robert that his wife was interfering with the proper functioning of the Inquisition and protecting Beguines and *fraticelli*.[17] Two other members of that wing of the Franciscan order were in contact with Delphine at this time. The first was Guillaume Espitalier, who in 1331 was accused by Neapolitan Franciscans of being "Michaelist"—that is, a supporter of Michael of Cesena, the dissident minister general—and in 1332 was denounced by Adhémar de Mosset, a Catalan noble suspected of Beguinist sympathies, for having criticized John XXII; he was, however, never condemned.[18] This friar must have been close to Elzéar, since he was mentioned in Elzéar's will in 1317, and we know that he was Delphine's confessor in Naples between 1333 and 1335.[19] The second was none other than Philippe Alquier, with whom Delphine had been in contact during her youth in Provence. From Avignon, where he had resided at that time, he went to Assisi, residing in the Carceri for several years, before going to Naples at the request of the sovereigns. As Sancha's confessor, he had been charged by her with the guidance of the monastery of Santa Maria Maddalena, which the queen had founded to shelter repentant prostitutes, and at the same time was the spiritual director of the convent of Santa Chiara. His fervent devotion to the Passion—he bore self-inflicted stigmata on his feet and hands—his prophecies, and the miracles that were soon attributed to him led the common people of Naples to consider him a saint. When he died in 1369 at the age of nearly 100, his body was carried across the city by a delirious crowd, and an active devotion sprang up at his tomb.[20]

But the monk who seems to have had the greatest ascendance over Delphine was Angelo Clareno, with whose life and influence we are now better acquainted, thanks to the work of Lydia von Auw.[21] Delphine probably entered into contact with him through

Philip of Majorca, the brother of Queen Sancha, who corresponded regularly with him, and in whom the leader of the Italian Spirituals had great confidence. After his flight from Avignon, where John XXII had imprisoned him and then forced him to adopt the Benedictine habit, Angelo Clareno took refuge in the Abruzzi, on the lands of the abbey of Subiaco, and remained in epistolary contact with all those in Italy who did not agree with the decisions of the pope in Avignon regarding the order and rule of St. Francis.[22] Delphine was mentioned in this correspondence on at least two occasions. In letter 43, addressed to Philip of Majorca, Angelo wrote:

> Do not be surprised if I do not write to our venerable Mother and Lady, Dame D[elphine] and to the brothers whom I love in Christ with all my heart.[23]

In letter 29, there is a more detailed mention:

> They [those who adhere to absolute poverty] are, in the eyes of God, foreign to the ownership of all possessions and truly behave as foreigners and sojourners on this earth. For they possess nothing and do not want to possess anything, except for Jesus Christ, and eternal life is their lot, their holy and eternal possession. If the King and Madame the Queen, your sister, are of this opinion, it would bear fruit and be advantageous for you to remain among them and under their authority. If they waver and their hearts are divided, then you will be sowing in the sand, and God will not allow you to remain with them for long. I think that Madame D[elphine] will understand this also and will recognize that what regards the senses does not regard the spirit.[24]

The last, rather mysterious sentence, must refer to discussions which took place in the pious circles that gravitated around Philip of Majorca, to which great lay lords like Robert of Mileto seem to have belonged as well. This statement would not suffice to demonstrate a connection between Angelo Clareno's message and Delphine's spirituality if this connection had not also been attested by the strict parallelism of their conceptions about certain themes, such as poverty. Thus, in Angelo's words, he who is truly poor no longer has a body, nor a soul, nor reason, nor spirit, nor will, but lives for God and no longer for himself and is dead to the world.[25]

This statement echoes and extends Iacopone of Todi's definition, which states that "poverty is having nothing, wanting nothing."[26] To Delphine as well, poverty meant not only the refusal to possess wealth, but also the intimate renunciation of a soul which abandons everything to God and no longer has desires or wishes of its own.[27] And her flight from the world—beginning with her vow of poverty in 1333—was surely inspired by the old Spiritual, who in his letters called his Neapolitan friends and disciples "those whom Lord Jesus drew from the world by his grace to sanctify them through truth."[28] A few years later, the countess of Ariano would not hesitate to go begging like a pauper through the streets of Naples, earning for herself the insulting epithet of *bizoca* (beguine) from onlookers.[29]

Delphine's last years in Italy were saddened by the loss of her best friends and spiritual masters. Angelo Clareno, who, hounded by the Inquisition, had to flee to Basilicata in 1334, died in 1337, probably without meeting with Delphine again. Philip of Majorca followed him to the grave sometime between 1340 and 1342, and King Robert in 1343. Delphine decided at that time to return definitively to Provence. It is not likely that she felt threatened in Naples after the death of her royal protector, for Queen Sancha, who survived her husband by two years, maintained her affection for her. But the times had changed, and there was no reason for her to linger at the court of Naples: the "third party" which had tried to form around Philip of Majorca and find a middle ground between the authoritarianism of John XXII and the excesses of certain *fraticelli* did not survive the death of its leaders. Guiral Ot, loyal to Avignon, brought the Neapolitan Franciscans under his control; and the Inquisitors indiscriminately persecuted whoever had taken the liberty to discuss or criticize the decisions of the sovereign pontiff, as we can witness in a series of clamorous trials in central and southern Italy at the end of the pontificate of John XXII and during that of Benedict XII. For their part, the new leaders of the Spirituals, like Bernard of Azona, whom Delphine must have known well because he succeeded Philip of Majorca as leader of the group of Franciscan dissidents, the Vital refugees from France (who arrived in Naples in 1342), and Barthélemy of Provence, advocated breaking completely with the Roman Curia and going underground.[30] Even if she understood their reasons, Delphine could neither join them nor approve of them: her master Angelo Clareno had taught her that it was necessary to remain faithful to the authentic Franciscan message, but without being tempted to break with the hierarchical Church. It is even possible—but this is pure hypothesis on our part—that she was inspired to return to a more moderate position by the spectacle of the excesses of some Franciscans, who went so far as to deny the validity of sacraments conferred by clergy who had remained faithful to John XXII and his successors. In any case, Delphine could not have been seriously suspected of heresy, since during her canonization proceedings Cardinal Philippe Cabassole testified that when he met her in Naples in 1341, she converted him to a better life in a conversation during which she read the most secret thoughts of his heart and assured him of her virginity. At the time of this encounter, this prelate—a friend of Petrarch and bishop of Cavaillon since 1334— held an important position in the curia of Avignon, to which he was later to return, after acting as chancellor of the Kingdom of Sicily.[31]

But Delphine's return to Provence did not signal the end of her relations with Italy. During her canonization proceedings of 1363, her doctor and confessor, the Canon Durand André of Apt, illustrated her orthodoxy by recounting an incident whose exact date is, unfortunately, unknown, but which must have taken place sometime between 1350 and 1360, since it was during this period that the witness was on familiar terms with the saintly countess. Delphine told the canon one day that she had just been visited by a Franciscan, "a friar of great learning who feigned great piety," who had come to Apt "*de partibus Neapolitanis,*" from the area of Naples, and tried to convince her that the will was the fourth person of the Trinity. Delphine, angered, set out to persuade him of his error, and when he persisted, she sent for the inquisitor who resided at L'Isle-sur-la-Sorgue. But the suspicious visitor took flight and did not reappear.[32] This information, though interesting, is too condensed and imprecise to be absolutely conclusive. Nevertheless, it is revealing in its suggestion that Delphine had maintained contact with the *fraticelli* of Southern Italy and that they considered her to be an important figure, and someone likely to agree with their ideas—even if in this case we cannot pin down the precise doctrinal context of this trinitarian debate, in which, oddly enough, we see a Franciscan adopt the idea of a quadruple divine nature. This was the very concept for which Joachim of Fiore had reproached Peter Lombard, who, by insisting so emphatically on the unity of the three persons, had made of them a hypostatic entity, according to the Calabrian prophet.

Delphine's response—her denunciation of the heretic to the local inquisitor—tallied with the spiritual orientation that typified the end of her life. But this does not mean that she had repudiated her previous beliefs. To the very end her spirituality remained marked by the encounters that stood out as landmarks in her life, in both Provence and Italy: Philippe Alquier and Arnold of Villanova,[33] but also Ubertino of Casale, who (probably during his residence in Avignon between 1310 and 1314) had taught her to pray better and to recover the "spiritual consolations" she had been deprived of for a time,[34] and especially Angelo Clareno, who had persevered to the end in his indefectible fidelity to the Gospels and the Church. Transcending our modern political boundaries, the parallel lives of Elzéar and Delphine bear witness to the existence—from Catalonia, through Languedoc and Provence, to Sicily—of a world of devout laymen and laywomen, one of whose most original expressions around 1300 was the religious ideal of the Spirituals and Beguines, which had so profoundly marked both husband and wife.

PART II

RELIGION IN PRECEPT
AND IN PRACTICE

Lay Belief
around 1200:
Religious Mentalities
of the Feudal World

WE ARE ACCUSTOMED to thinking of the Middle Ages as a time when the Christian faith was intense and universally shared, and this is especially true of the eleventh and twelfth centuries, which were marked by the Crusades, the flourishing of monastic orders, and the construction of the great Gothic cathedrals. In quantitative terms, this estimation is substantially correct: except for a minority of Jews, all of the inhabitants of western Christendom at the time of Innocent III had received the sacrament of baptism and professed the Catholic faith. But we need to go beyond this objective statement and investigate the contents of this faith. The question is a particularly acute one for those who did not belong to the clerical world—in other words, the immense majority of the faithful who, because of their "lack of culture," could not have direct access to the texts that transmitted the Christian revelation.

More than on theological notions, the faith of the laypeople of the era rested on a certain number of convictions and certitudes that permeated the general outlook. In the first place, everyone believed in the afterlife and the existence of another world where the dead were rewarded or punished according to their behavior on earth. The Church therefore had no trouble convincing the faithful that their posthumous destiny was at stake in this world.

But if clerics emphasized the survival and immortality of the soul after the death of the body, laypeople for their part did not set up rigid barriers between the world of the defunct and that of the living. In their view, the spirits of the deceased faithful did not head immediately for the unknowable place—heaven or hell—to which their actions should lead them. For a certain period of time, they were thought to linger in a state of "amortality": these undead sometimes returned to the places they had frequented during their lives to solicit prayers or to settle accounts for unkept promises, especially during the weeks and months immediately following their deaths. This is the source of the widespread belief in ghosts who haunted their past homes during the night and had no qualms about bothering their relatives and friends. In connection with the evolution of penitential practices and also, probably, to put an end to the ritual ceremonies organized by the faithful to drive the dead back into their own universe—like the dances in cemeteries condemned by synodal legislation—beginning in the second half of the twelfth century, the Church affirmed ever more resolutely the existence of a place where distressed souls were received: purgatory. Over the following centuries, preachers gradually diffused among the laity a belief in this transitory stay, thereby freeing them of the haunting presence of the dead while allowing them to assuage their consciences by celebrating masses to shorten the time that their dead spent in expiation.

It would be wrong, however, to think that the fear of death was the foundation of the religious beliefs of the era. Death was too banal and too omnipresent in daily life to be considered more than a fact of nature. Still, it was necessary to die well and to make one's passing on an occasion for salvation. At the beginning of the thirteenth century, people feared the end of life less than they dreaded the possibility of dying without the comfort of the sacraments, intestate or excommunicate. In fact, beginning at this time the Church provided specific criteria for the "good death," emphasizing the requirement that the dying make confession to their parish priests and receive extreme unction. In addition, it obliged anyone with possessions to bequeath a portion of them to the poor and the clergy. In exchange, the defunct would obtain their prayers and "suffrages," which would enable them to face their individual judgment in the best possible circumstances. For if it is useless to wonder whether all people believed in God at that time—the available sources, clerical in origin, are not at all explicit on this subject— we can at least be sure that they were all convinced of the existence of hell, the Devil's kingdom. The fear of eternal damnation led even the most callous of people— plundering knights or greedy usurers—on the point of death to return illegitimately acquired goods and make impressive donations to the Church. The more serious the offenses against God and the violations of ecclesiastical laws, the greater the bequests: the amount of compensation had to match the gravity of the faults committed in this world. Of course, not all laypeople had committed crimes for which they reproached themselves, but everyone had guilty consciences for the simple reason that they had led worldly and carnal lives, honoring temporal values during their lifetimes instead of scorning them. For this reason, it often happened that the faithful would retire to monasteries as they advanced in years or take the veil as the end of their lives approached. By dying in a Cluniac or Cistercian habit, they affiliated themselves with a religious community in the hope of benefitting from the merits that the servants of God had accumulated through prayer and ascetic exercises. Others, without going to that extreme, made gifts to abbeys or collegiate churches and established ties of confraternity with them, thereby obtaining the privilege of having their names added to the obituary list of the community and the assurance that prayers would be said to keep their souls and those of their deceased relatives out of the clutches of the Devil. Clerics and laypeople shared the conviction that this world was the battleground for continual warfare between the forces of Good, identified with God, and those of Evil, incarnated by Satan. This cosmic struggle had its counterpart in the hearts of men, where the virtues fought with the vices.

Twelfth-century artists delighted in representing this "psychomachia," in which human forces acting alone were unable to obtain victory or even offer resistance, or in depicting the processions of equal numbers of wise and foolish virgins. Indeed, in the eyes of the people of that time, Evil had as much reality as Good, and the Devil made frequent appearances to tempt them, mock them, or beat them black and blue. But God was no abstraction either: his presence was apparent in events, and natural catastrophes or abnormal phenomena were immediately interpreted as signs of divine anger or heavenly warnings which were dangerous to ignore. In individual lives, just as in the history of groups, everything was a sign, a premonition or a symbol. But it was still necessary for people to have the wisdom to recognize them and grasp their importance before it was too late. The belief in immanent justice was widespread: did God not see all actions and judge even the most hidden thoughts? Thus the failures of the Third and Fourth Crusades in 1192 and 1204 found a ready explanation in the conduct of the Christians and the temporal ambitions of the participating sovereigns. And no one doubted that, if God permitted Saladin's Moslems to take Jerusalem after the battle of Hattin in 1187, it was because of the sins of the Christians, "*exigentibus peccatis nostris,*" in the words of Pope Gregory VIII, echoing an expression used by St. Bernard after the failure of the Second Crusade.

But God did not limit himself to permitting the forces of Evil to chastise sinners. He also intervened beneficently in history by performing miracles, whose reality no one in that epoch doubted. Indeed, miracles played a central function in people's lives: they reestablished in the human body and in society that divine order which had been perturbed by sin. As he cured the maladies that stymied doctors, freed prisoners miraculously, or broke the rope that hung a condemned person from the gallows, God manifested his power and presence by overturning the logical order of things. His interventions brought a ray of hope to a world in which the individual was defenseless in the face of nature, of whose laws he was ignorant, and in the face of an oppressive system in which the unarmed were subject to the whims of the powerful. It was rare, however, that God, who by definition was invisible and whose infinite grandeur surpassed understanding, was directly implored. In general it was preferable to have recourse to closer and more accessible intermediaries: the saints, whose cults, then at the height of their development, played a major role in Christian religious life. In the twelfth century, people were more interested in their miracles and relics than in their glorious deeds, which, recorded for the most part in Latin, were inaccessible to the masses. Indeed, the precious remains of the saints constituted palpable realities, and the beneficent influence that radiated from them attested to the presence of the supernatural here on earth. The most solemn oaths were sworn on relics, and they were frequently carried in processions to put an end to calamities or ensure the fecundity of the earth before the new harvest. But some bodies of saints were more renowned than others, and the places where they were enshrined exercised a powerful attraction over the crowds. This was the case of Rome, for example, where the remains of St. Peter and St. Paul were venerated, and of Conques, where the statue of St. Foy, covered with gold and precious stones like an idol, received the pilgrims who had come to beseech her, and, most strikingly, of Compostela in Galicia, where a body presumed to be that of the apostle James was conserved. This sanctuary enjoyed extraordinary prestige after 1100 and attracted believers who came from all directions, following various routes that merged beyond the Pyrenees to form the *camino francès*. Those who, at the price of long effort and harsh trials, managed to reach this sacred place, hoped to find solace for their ills and the promise of salvation. For the Church considered pilgrimages meritorious actions which had an important place in the penitential process, in some cases acting as substitutes for the punishments needed to expiate sins. And even if after 1150 the most progressive theologians and moralists emphasized the idea that a confessed sin was already pardoned as soon as the priest granted absolution, the faithful—more realistic or more matter-of-fact—remained viscerally persuaded that their souls were not totally free of the blemishes of sin until they had carried out a sufficient number of acts or works of reparation, which meant inflicting on their bodies enough suffering and privation to compensate the offense caused to God.

This is the mental context in which we must situate the fascination aroused in all levels of society by the idea of the crusade. For the "passage" in the direction of the Holy Land and Jerusalem was no more, all things considered, than an armed pilgrimage to the tomb of Christ and the places where he had lived. For their active participation, laypeople earned a plenary indulgence, in other words complete remission from the penance required for their sins. Was this certainty of eternal salvation, occasionally accompanied by certain temporal gains, not worth the efforts and risks that all expeditions to remote lands entailed? Without hesitation, the men of the twelfth century responded to this question in the affirmative.

Thus a certain number of characteristics of the popular belief of the year 1200 have come into view. It was a faith in which doubt and uncertainty were nonexistent. It felt nothing but scorn for infidels—with Moslems and Jews considered enemies by definition—as well as for the schismatic Greeks, which explains the ease with which the knights of the Fourth Crusade allowed themselves to be diverted to Constantinople instead of reaching the objective the pope had assigned them, the Holy Land. Scarcely interiorized at all, piety was expressed principally through exterior signs and practices. The extreme sensitivity of the people of that time and their changeability, caused perhaps by physiological factors, were manifested in abrupt shifts in their moral and religious behavior: a lord who had lived for years in debauchery, engaging in the worst kinds of violence, could make a spectacular conversion and switch overnight to the most rigorous asceticism. Such reversals, which were common in those days, testify to the success of eremitism, at least to a certain extent. Indeed, many men, having led an entirely worldly existence, retired to the depths of caves or forests to expiate their past sins with penitence. Even when they avoided the fascination of these extremes, laypeople were drawn to concrete enactments, and their efforts to be virtuous were displayed in tangible signs. Those in positions of power were called on to uphold justice, which, in the perspective of the times, meant respecting custom and giving each person his due. But it was charity above all that lay at the center of the religious life of the faithful: the pious layperson distinguished himself through his generosity and his sense of hospitality. He welcomed and lodged the poor, pilgrims, and vagabonds, gave alms to the indigent and, if he had the means, founded at his own expense or with his kin a hospice or a leper hospital on a road frequented by travellers.

If we wonder what led the most generous of the faithful to undertake such projects, we are led to explore their most intimate religious convictions and the amount of knowledge that they possessed about the Word of God. In the absence of catechisms, and given the generally mediocre level of the secular clergy, they surely could only have had partial and indirect access to it. Since most of them—especially women and peasants—did not know how to read, the transmission of the fundamental elements of the Christian message certainly could not have taken place through personal contact with the text of the Scriptures. But their ignorance of the Bible, a book which curates themselves only rarely possessed, did not exclude the existence of other modes of assimilating religious culture. The first initiation into Christianity took place in the family circle, under the influence of the mother, from whom the child learned the Our Father, the Ave Maria (at least the first part) and sometimes the Credo. In noble or urban settings, a cleric introduced the child to the reading of the psalter. Those adults who were especially devout recited the hours at set times of the day like monks or canons, because there was nothing distinctive about the piety of laypeople: in the best of cases—those of princes or kings—it remained an imitation of the piety of priests and religious. Lay piety tried to follow that model as faithfully as possible, for deeply rooted in people's minds was the conviction that the faithful living in the world were less likely to achieve salvation than those who, because they had renounced their worldly goods and given up the pleasures of the flesh in order to lead a life of penitence agreeable to God, enjoyed a reputation—whether deservedly or not—for greater spirituality.

At the heart of the religious activities of the people of this era was the search for a relationship with the divine. This relationship was established by means of signs and rituals which thereby took on fundamental importance; and the prestige of the clergy—however virulent the criticisms leveled at them—came from their special knowledge of the formulas and gestures that allowed people to enter into communication with the hereafter. Laypeople did not clearly perceive the distinction, established by the theologians in the course of the twelfth century, between the sacraments and the sacramentals. Baptism, to be sure, was universally practiced, and penitence certainly had an influence on behavior. But confirmation does not seem to have played a large role at that time, and even communion continued to be a rare event. It was not until the Fourth Lateran Council, in 1215, that the faithful were officially obliged to confess and receive the eucharist at least once a year, at Easter. But in the eyes of the majority, rituals such as benedictions or exorcisms, and ceremonies such as the dubbing of knights or royal coronations had as much importance as marriage or penitence. The Church itself was in part responsible for this confusion, to the extent that it had striven to sacralize certain privileged moments of existence, particularly the rites of passage from one age category to another, or certain social functions such as knighthood or royalty. At the threshold of the thirteenth century, the hierarchy was becoming more sensitive to and troubled by the ambiguity of these undifferentiated sacralities, in which the Christian reference points were sometimes no more than superficial. This, for instance, is what lay behind the condemnation of ordeals—that is, recourse to the "judgment of God" (trial by combat, or by fire and water) to distinguish truth from falsehood and the guilty from the innocent. The Fourth Lateran Council forbade trial by combat and enjoined ecclesiastical courts to take into account only rational evidence. Innocent III's institution of canonization proceedings must be seen in the same perspective: they tended to reduce the role of the *vox populi* in evaluating the sanctity of servants of God by subjecting their lives and miracles to the scrutiny of the ecclesiastical hierarchy and compelling the promoters of a new cult to provide evidence of the degree of perfection attained by their hero.

If the Church had some trouble regaining control of and purifying the domain of the sacred, it had far less difficulty making obligatory such ascetic practices as fasting and abstinence, for they met with general approval. These concrete requirements were all the more popular in that they suited the realism of the faithful, who were skeptical about the goodness of human nature and more inclined to believe in the virtue of works than in the operation of grace. This kind of heroic Christian life obviously meshed with the feudal mentality: was God not the Lord to whom one prayed with joined hands, in the typical posture of a vassal giving homage to a more powerful lord? The Crusades themselves—which had initially been dominated by eschatological concerns—acquired new meaning because of this. The Crusades of the twelfth and early thirteenth centuries were primarily motivated by the desire to "avenge the honor of God," which the Saracens had offended. Pope Innocent III adopted this feudal model when, in a call to succor the Holy Land, he compared God to a sovereign driven from his kingdom and Christians to vassals bound by their sworn homage to do everything possible to restore his honor and his rights. Here is still more evidence, if any were needed, that the history of religious beliefs takes on its full meaning only if it is seen in the larger context of the history of mentalities.

EIGHT

THE PASTORAL TRANSFORMATION OF THE THIRTEENTH CENTURY

CHRISTIANITY IS BY ITS NATURE a missionary religion, and the Church was instituted by Christ to disseminate the faith; for this reason, it may seem that its catechetical and pastoral functions must always have been indispensable. If this were true, the historian's task would be simply to study the various forms that the transmission of the revealed truth assumed at different times, with any changes being merely a matter of the modalities in which this kerygmatic announcement was made. But the reality of the matter is quite different; and it would not be an exaggeration to maintain that the continuity which we tend to ascribe to the Church in this area is to some extent illusory. Even a superficial knowledge of the history of Christianity reveals that from the beginning, periods of intensive missionary effort have alternated with epochs during which the major preoccupations of the Church lay elsewhere, whether they concerned the establishment of harmonious relationships with secular society or the anxious expectation of the new age. This alternation was present in the very heart of the centuries we usually call the Middle Ages. Roughly speaking, we can distinguish three successive periods between the eighth and the fifteenth centuries. The first, which more or less coincided with the Carolingian and post-Carolingian periods (the eighth and early ninth centuries), saw the completion of the Christianization of Europe, in the statistical sense of the term. By the end of a process that had begun with the fall of the Roman Empire, all Western peoples—the last being the Hungarians and the Scandinavians—had received baptism whether they liked it or not. The prevailing pastoral letter of the day was the *Compelle intrare*. For the Carolingians, propagating Christianity meant extending their own power, since in their view the emperor was not only a temporal ruler but also the leader of the whole *populus christianus*, which it was his responsibility to lead toward salvation with the aid and collaboration of the clergy. For this reason, they did not hesitate to use violence to uproot what was left of the Germanic religion and to impose Christianity on the Saxons, for example, who were not at all disposed to receive it peaceably. As Pierre Riché demonstrated in a recent work of synthesis, this first Christianization, a "political problem as much as a religious one," was accompanied by the Church's effort to organize the rural populace in areas where ecclesiastical structures had long been in place.[1] The civil and religious authorities were struggling to restore the dignity of religious practice by requiring the clergy to respect strict and uniform norms in the liturgical domain and by insisting that the faithful fulfill their Sunday duties more conscientiously. This era seems to mark the establishment of conformism in Western religious practices, even if that conformism was far from being as generalized and restrictive as people commonly believe.

It is difficult to evaluate the exact impact of this pastoral campaign of the Central Middle Ages. Because tenth-century texts that mention it are very rare and we have so little information about the realities of parish life between 950 and 1050 for most regions, historians have tended to call it a failure. Nevertheless, it would be surprising if the movement ran aground simply because of the arrival of new waves of invaders—the Normans in northwest Europe and the Saracens in the Mediterranean—and the disruption of Carolingian political structures. Moreover, it would be difficult to explain the rash of more or less heterodox religious movements which sprang up all over the West in the early eleventh century without acknowledging that biblical or evangelical themes must have permeated the mental climate to some extent. But we must admit that the concrete modalities of this phenomenon remain unknown to us for the most part.

From Salvation by the Righteous to the Christian Reconquest of the World

During the next period (c. 1050–c. 1200), which was characterized by the establishment of the feudal system, the spiritual climate was no longer the same. Except in peripheral regions— like Scandinavia and the Slavic countries—where the missionary effort continued along the same lines as in preceding centuries, pastoral preoccupations waned. This was the golden age of monasticism, whose prestige and influence far outclassed those of the secular clergy. It is paradoxical that, in a world that was generally Christian, the religious aspirations of the elites could only be satisfied within the walls of a cloister, in the midst of fervent communities devoted to the *vita angelica*, the angelic life, in a sort of anticipation here and now of the heavenly Jerusalem.[2] But the monks had no illusions about the degree of Christianization of the society in whose midst they lived. Far from idealizing it, they even tended to deprecate its realities and values, sometimes in a systematic fashion. For this reason, they could only conceive of salvation through "contempt for the world," which manifested itself concretely in *fuga mundi*, flight from the world. Only groups of righteous, by devoting themselves to asceticism and prayer, could hope to mitigate the divine wrath on Judgment Day; that is why many laypeople aspired to die wearing monks' habits or establish ties of confraternity with the great abbeys. This does not mean that the monks had no interest in the religious destiny of the Christian people. In certain regions, they even multiplied their efforts to acquire churches. But as a rule, they seem to have been more concerned with parishes than parishioners, and the care of souls was never at the center of their attention. More precisely, the care of souls was limited in general to an effort to Christianize chivalric institutions and aristocratic mores, particularly in the areas of conjugal morality and family life. In effect, in feudal society as in previous eras, the clergy was convinced that if the ruling classes of society led a life that conformed to the injunctions of the Church, the faithful would follow in their wake.

Nevertheless, this was the period during which some elements in both the secular and regular clergy developed an awareness which led in the long term to a renewal of the pastoral spirit. In the milieux where the so-called "Gregorian" reform germinated, people realized that, despite its dazzling appearance, the Church was in danger of splintering because of the spread of the feudal system; it ran the risk of being absorbed into a society which it served more than the society served it. Beginning with Gregory VII, the resistance of the reformers was translated into a vast program for the Christian reconquest of the world. In their view, the fundamental elements in this program were the liberation of the Church from the temporal powers aspiring to dominate it and the rejection of all forms of clerical worldliness, particularly in sexual matters. This explains the measures taken by the popes and synods against simony and clerical concubinage at the end of the eleventh and throughout the twelfth centuries. The first problem has long attracted the attention of historians, who are fascinated by the vicissitudes of the investiture controversy and the struggle between the papacy and the empire. But these conflicts, which occupied center stage until the middle of the twelfth century, in fact concerned the ruling classes alone. At stake was the leadership of western Christendom. The masses, with few exceptions, played no part here; they remained mere spectators on the sidelines of this prolonged contest. At the summit of the ecclesiastical hierarchy, the political and military struggle against the emperors absorbed all energies for a long time: the reform of the secular clergy in particular remained no more than a pious wish, and the canonical movement, founded on the ideal of the apostolic life, resulted for the most part only in the creation of new religious orders such as the Premonstratensians.

It was not until the final third of the twelfth century, with the primacy of the Roman church now assured, that it could tackle the second point in its reform program, whose aim was to bring about the triumph of the religion not only *in capite*, at the head, but also *in membris*, among its members. But conditions were quite different from those of the eleventh century, and it was no longer enough for people to be organized by Christian leaders and forced to pay tithes to the clergy. In every area, the masses were beginning to emerge from their passivity, as shown by the affirmation of the communal movement, the aspiration of the rural world for charters of liberties, and, most significantly, the success of the first great popular heresies. Thus, at the very moment when the Crusades were projecting the expansionist dynamism of medieval Christianity toward the exterior, a new campaign was emerging: the campaign of interior reconquest, whose first exponent and inspiration was St. Bernard. This combat soon became more important than the first, and required more energy. The progress of Catharism and other heterodox religious movements forced the clergy and the papacy to react promptly, before the entire edifice was undermined. The result was a vast effort, begun at the Third Lateran Council and reaching its apogee with the Fourth Lateran Council, to make the religious beliefs and practices of the faithful conform to the requirements of the Church.

Pastoral Zeal and Cultural Resistance

In what manner did this pastoral turning point of the thirteenth century, whose importance has properly been emphasized by recent historians of medieval Christianity, from Gabriel Le Bras to Etienne Delaruelle, manifest itself? First of all, through the Church's exaltation of apostolic action over contemplation. In the thirteenth and fourteenth centuries, the papacy no longer chose to canonize monks, but rather bishops, clergy, and laity who had distinguished themselves by their desire to win souls for God. This orientation towards one's fellows and toward the world, with the aim of converting them in order to bring about their salvation, was designated in contemporary texts by the expressions *zelus animarum* or *zelus spiritualis*. Thus, St. Dominic, after making plans to bring the faith of Christ to the Kumans and the Saracens—like his contemporary St. Francis—finally chose to devote all of his efforts to the struggle against heresy in Languedoc and the county of Toulouse. One witness at his canonization proceedings, held in Bologna in 1233, declared that he "seemed to have more zeal than anyone else for the salvation of the human race;" a second added that "his charity and his compassion were extended not only to the faithful, but also to the infidels, the pagans, and even the damned in hell."[3] Among the sainted bishops of the thirteenth century, the pastoral dimension was equally dominant: in canonization proceedings of the day the accent was placed on the exemplarity of their diocesan visitations and on their efforts to make the clergy more worthy of their mission. Contemporary synodal statutes sound the same note, and allow us to follow in detail the measures taken to raise the religious level of the clerics and the faithful.

However, it would furnish a misleading image of this new dynamic to reduce it to a mere intensification of the pastoral effort and to the implementation of a program of reorganization of ecclesiastical structures. Rather, it was a radical transformation of the catechesis, based on the valorization of the word as an instrument of mediation and seduction.[4] This may seem banal, because primitive Christianity had already experienced a brilliant efflorescence of preaching. But in the course of the Middle Ages, the religion that was lived and practiced by the masses had been reduced to a complex of ritual signs and gestures. The liturgical language, even in the "Roman" regions, had become unintelligible to the faithful. Bishops had other preoccupations than to speak to them about God and the Christian life; even when they made the effort to preach, they were not always understood by their flocks, who asked their bishops above all to protect them from famine in times of want and to perform exorcisms or miracles. As for the monks and the canons regular, they rarely addressed themselves to the people, for that was not their vocation. It was the historic role of the mendicant orders to resume, after long lapse, the diffusion of the evangelical word. As a contemporary noted, St. Dominic, founder of the Preaching Friars, "devoted himself to preaching with such fervor that he exhorted and constrained his friars to announce the Word of God day and night, in churches and in homes, in the fields and on the road, everywhere, in short, and never to speak of anything but God;" while another emphasized the remarkable impact of his speech: "When the saint preached, he found words so disconcerting that quite often he was moved to tears himself and made his audience cry, such that never did we hear a man whose words so effectively moved people to compunction and to tears."[5]

Except for a few minor nuances, we find the same admiring comments about the first Franciscans, who were equally tireless preachers: the *Poverello*, St. Francis himself, harangued his audience "as is done in public assemblies," and St. Anthony of Padua's sermons drew large crowds.[6]

But saints were by definition exceptional beings, and the success of a few "stars," no matter how great, was not enough to solve the problems the Church faced in carrying out its mission. In practice, these difficulties were exacerbated by the fact that the parish clergy was not capable of diffusing and explaining beliefs which could no longer be imposed on everyone by the sheer exercise of authority. Contrary to the papacy's hopes, the growth of the universities in the thirteenth century did not appreciably modify the situation, because the total number of secular clerics who attended them was low, and those who did attend generally found positions of responsibility on the staffs of prelates and princes. The merit of St. Yves (†1303), the only parish priest to be canonized in the Middle Ages, was precisely that he voluntarily went to live among the Breton peasants and devoted his efforts to the care of souls, whereas his social origins and university education would have allowed him to lead the privileged existence of an ecclesiastical judge in the bishop's palace at Tréguier. At the inquest on his sanctity in 1331, his parishioners emphasized that, unlike his predecessors, he frequently preached in the church and even in the fields, and that, under his influence, "the people of the land became twice as good as they had been before." It is certain that he emphasized the relationship between religion and behavior, because the same source indicates that through his sermons and his example he chased immorality and sin from the village of Louannec, where he was curate.

But this was an exceptional case, and the incapacity of the parish clergy to correctly announce the Good Word remained a dominant theme of synodal statutes and pastoral visits until the end of the Middle Ages. For a long time, this failure was attributed to a series of "abuses" that the normative texts of the era complacently listed: the dubious morality of the parish clergy, the plurality of benefices, absenteeism, and so on. All of these certainly existed, but their role was not necessarily decisive, nor would it have been sufficient to explain the limited efficacy of the pastoral effort, especially in rural milieux. In fact, a thirteenth-century Alsatian chronicler noted that the peasants of the region did not complain about the fact that their pastors were living in concubinage, because that made them less fearful for the virtue of their daughters.[7] The true problem lay elsewhere: in the incompatibility, at least in part, of clerical and lay culture. Even when they had only a thin veneer of Latin and theological culture, the priests were convinced of their superiority over the faithful, who, although *illiterati* — that is, ignorant of Latin—were not necessarily untutored. The twelfth and thirteenth centuries were marked, as we know, by the rise of courtly literature among the aristocracy and of more "bourgeois" literary genres, like farces and fabliaux, in the towns. Among the peasants, who constituted the majority of the population, vast areas of "folkloric" culture survived, about which we still know little but whose importance has been signaled by recent studies.[8] Certain religious, particularly Cistercians and mendicants, understood this early on and tried to "domesticate" their audiences by making use of themes or stories borrowed from profane texts in their sermons. This is the reason for the vogue of the *exemplum*, the study of which, begun several years ago, has opened new perspectives. However, the fact that preachers had frequent recourse to them does not mean that they were ennobled in the telling. For those who used them, they were simply a technique of ideological popularization, a technique based, in the final analysis, on a pejorative conception of profane culture. Thus the use of *exempla* has seemed to some scholars to be no more than a preacher's stratagem.[9] Moreover, as Michel Zink has demonstrated in his study of medieval preaching in the vernacular, even when the clergy preached in the local idiom, the messages that they were communicating still had some oppressive features.[10] Indeed, in contrast to the situation today, their audiences had no means of checking the sources of their instruction or verifying its accuracy. Until the sixteenth century, with the exception of a few high-placed laypeople, only members of the clergy had access to the Holy Scriptures and sacred books. For this reason, their discourse, larded with references to biblical, literary or fictive authorities, tended to inspire assent much less often than emotional reactions, ranging as the case may be from delirious enthusiasm to vehement protestation.

Mass Languages and Specialized Languages

The catechetical effort undertaken by the Church *ad intra* met with another difficulty. In a society as diversified and as rapidly evolving as that of the West during the late twelfth and early thirteenth centuries, the languages of mass communication—using this term to designate the liturgy, hagiography and religious art— no longer sufficed to ensure that the Gospel suffused people's outlook. The clerics involved in the evangelization of the urban populace were the first to realize that the *populus christianus* was no longer unitary, just as society was no longer trinary. The old distinction between *bellatores, oratores,* and *laboratores*— those who fought, prayed, and worked—no longer corresponded to reality. In order to reach all of the various social groups and settings, it was necessary to speak to their specific areas of interest. To this end, the Church inaugurated the pastoral of the *status vitae,* the stations of life—or, more precisely, extended to the world of workers the same effort of adaptation that it had been extending toward the knightly class for more than a century. The warrior saints, exalted by the preaching and hagiography of the twelfth century, were joined by artisan and merchant saints who appeared in the Italy of the communes. Innocent III ratified this evolution in 1199 when he raised to the glory of the altars St. Omobono, a Cremonese draper who had died two years before, after distinguishing himself by his zeal in charitable activities and in the struggle against the heretics. A few decades later, Federico Visconti, the archbishop of Pisa, did not hesitate to propose St. Francis as a model for a confraternity of merchants. "How it must please the merchants," he exclaimed in a sermon in 1261, "to know that their brother [St. Francis] was a merchant and that he was sanctified in our times!"

Manuals of confessors and sermons *ad status,* which multiplied in the thirteenth century, likewise tended to emphasize people's professions and stations.[11] But the efforts of the clergy and especially the mendicants to christianize professional ethics signalled more a shift in their strategy than a change in their attitudes toward secular realities and work. Fundamentally, the ecclesiastical culture continued to exalt rural values, and even a great Dominican preacher like Humbert of Romans would still, in 1260, point up the contrast between the peasants, who because of their condition were barred from the worlds of violence and money and redeemed their sins through labor, and the merchants and townspeople, who risked corruption since they lived from the exchange of goods and wealth, not from the products of nature.[12]

Orthodoxy and Orthopraxy

This observation brings us back to the fundamental problem of the catechesis of this era: its objectives. The goal of the mendicants and secular clergy who devoted themselves to the care of souls was not so much the struggle against unbelief—which was very unusual at that time and limited to a few resolute souls— as the eradication of erroneous beliefs. In short, the goal was to inspire correct belief and correct behavior. Some of the faithful had been influenced by heterodox movements, especially the numerous varieties of Cathar dualism; others remained attached to practices that the clergy trained in schools and universities readily termed magical or diabolical. Preachers tried to find a middle ground between heresy and superstition for their audience by transmitting a few essential notions of doctrine and especially by recommending pious or devotional practices. Among the latter, the Church favored the practice of the sacraments and, above all, of confession. The importance of the canon *Omnis utriusque sexus*, decreed by the Fourth Lateran Council (1215), which requires all of the faithful to make confession and take communion at least once a year, is well known. In fact, most of the sermons that have survived from this era exhort the laity to make confession often and well. Moreover, many of them were delivered during Lent, which was the yearly high point for both preaching and penance. To convince their listeners of the benefit they would reap for avowing their errors, some clerics did not hesitate to state that confession would not merely guarantee the salvation of their souls in the next world, but would also protect the faithful against fire, shipwrecks, and other catastrophes in this one. At the same time, they brandished terrible threats against those who refused to make confession; and we know how medieval iconography exploited the themes of the death of unrepentant sinners, misers, and lechers as they were portrayed in art ranging from cathedral statuary to fifteenth century woodcuts illustrating treatises on the *ars moriendi*, the art of dying. The results of this insistent orchestration were noteworthy: in the fourteenth century, it was a rare layperson who did not make confession at least once a year. The most devout went as far as confessing themselves several times a day, so obsessed were they with the fear of dying in a state of mortal sin. To be sure, frequent communion was not the norm; it remained the preserve of an extremely limited spiritual elite. In any case, as time went on the catechesis put more and more emphasis on the problem of the afterlife. Beginning in the twelfth century, some clerics had asserted the existence of a place where the corporal sufferings that the faithful deserved for their sins would be administered after their death. We are well aware of the speed with which this theme of purgatory, which was destined to have a great future in Christian piety, grew in importance, both in sermons and in stories of journeys to the hereafter.

———— ⚬⚊⚬ ————

Any attempt to measure the effectiveness of the medieval catechesis would obviously be beyond our scope here. In such an evaluation, it would be just as misleading to rely on the laments collected in the normative texts as on the manifestations of remarkable spiritual vitality shown by some fervent groups of "friends of God." Nevertheless, without falling into pure subjectivity, we can assert that in the final centuries of the Middle Ages a devout elite took shape in the confraternities and third orders, an elite which did not recruit its members solely from the ranks of the high aristocracy. These laypeople, among whom women were a majority, demonstrated themselves capable of conducting a dialogue on equal terms with the clergy, and sometimes even of dominating them spiritually, as St. Bridget of Sweden and St. Catherine of Siena dominated their entourage. However, they were but a small minority; the majority, except for a few ephemeral manifestations of enthusiasm, seem to have remained relatively indifferent to the religious program that the clergy was trying to draft for them, a program that was essentially an imitation of clerical practices and spirituality. In fact, everything seems to have been done as if the ultimate goal of catechesis was the clericalization of the laity, not its advancement. This disparity was the consequence of a cultural situation whose peculiar nature we have already stressed. The pastors, increasingly influenced by the culture of the university, now claimed to be the sole repositories of true Christianity, and tended to think of the minds of their flocks as soft wax on which they needed only to leave their own impression. It was at this time that the Church was demarcating ever more strictly the bounds of the believable, and when ignorance was beginning to be identified with error. The growth of preaching with the aim of convincing and stirring up the audience coincided with the spread of the Inquisition and witchcraft trials. Wishing to impose a religious model that required adhesion to a particular cultural and social system, medieval clerics ended by marginalizing a large portion of the faithful and provoking the exasperation of others who were no less Christian than they, as the Reformation would show, but who aspired to be Christian in their own fashion.

NINE

"ORDO FRATERNITATIS": CONFRATERNITIES AND LAY PIETY IN THE MIDDLE AGES

MY PERSONAL ACQUAINTANCE with Father Meersseman is limited to meeting him, I believe, a total of two times at professional conferences. It is not as a result of personal friendship, therefore, that I am speaking this evening. I accepted Monsignor Maccarrone's invitation to participate in the tribute to Father Meersseman in celebration of the publication of the volumes entitled *Ordo fraternitatis: Confraternite e pietà dei laici nel medioevo* because of my admiration for his work and everything I owe him.[1] Forgive me if I speak personally for a moment. For me, Father Meersseman's name will always be associated with the great impression that reading a number of his articles on Dominican confraternities produced in me. My friend Charles de La Roncière called these studies, which were published in the *Archivum fratrum praedicatorum* in the 1950s, to my attention when I had just begun to specialize in medieval religious history. They were a revelation to me; and I can say that Father Meersseman, along with Canon Etienne Delaruelle, whose work I discovered in those same years, was one of the scholars who truly opened new perspectives to the medievalists of my generation. In effect, Delaruelle and Meersseman brought about the same kind of "Copernican revolution" for historical studies that Father Congar, for example, accomplished for theology in those same years: that is to say, the rediscovery of the Church as the people of God, and not only as a hierarchically structured institution. This insight was to lead to a new understanding of the place and role of the laity in the Church and of its history, and I believe that it was no coincidence that the *Dossier de l'ordre de la Pénitence au XIIIe siècle*—which in my opinion is Father Meersseman's masterpiece—was published soon after the *Jalons pour une théologie du laïcat*.[2] What I found most striking at the time in the works of Father Meersseman was the novelty of the material. He brought to view a hitherto unknown world, the world of lay penitents and confraternities of devotion about which almost no worthwhile studies had existed. Thus, he brought to the surface a whole unsuspected part of our history, just as a few years earlier the work of Charles Dereine, Jean Becquet, and Cosimo Damiano Fonseca had rescued from oblivion another area of medieval religious life, the history of the canons regular.[3] Because so much work has since been published on the history of the penitents, the importance of the subject now seems self-evident. But we must not fail to credit Father Meersseman for opening the way.

One of Father Meersseman's characteristics is his intellectual probity as a historian. Although a Dominican friar, he did not hesitate to affirm that neither St. Francis nor St. Dominic invented the order of penitence and that, several decades before their time, laymen and women had practiced the penitential ideal and way of life. He even demonstrated that it was not until a relatively late date that the Franciscan and Dominican tertiaries were constituted in the form whose tradition has come down to us today: that is, sometime after 1289, when Nicholas IV promulgated the bull *Super montem*, in which he placed or attempted to place the Italian penitents under the direction of the mendicant friars. But the papal admonitions did not have an immediate effect, and the movement long maintained its fundamentally lay character. At the time, it took considerable insight and, above all, great courage to counter the received wisdom as energetically as Father Meersseman did. Defending his positions earned him the vilification of a certain number of his mendicant brothers, who would not forgive him for debunking centuries-old myths. But Father Meersseman is not a man who fears polemics, and his evidence was so solid that his arguments on the whole carried the day, even if later research by historians of the Franciscan order has added nuances to some of his conclusions, establishing indisputably, for example, that in the thirteenth century there were some penitents who belonged to an *Ordo penitentium beati Francisci*, the Order of the Penitents of St. Francis, whose exact characteristics still remain obscure.

We must therefore rejoice at the initiative of the directors of the *"Italia sacra"* series in publishing a collection of Father Meersseman's studies on lay involvement in religious life. This enterprise is worthwhile for three reasons: first, because it brings together studies scattered in journals and collective volumes which are sometimes difficult to find; secondly, because it allows us to measure the breadth and coherence of Father Meersseman's work, which is hard to grasp from reading the same articles in a piecemeal fashion; finally, and not least important, because this project has provided the author with an opportunity to take another look at his own work, correcting a few substantive errors and adding new elements. It is fitting to point out the humility of Father Meersseman, who in the evening of his life has placed at the disposal of scholars all of the materials he has painstakingly gathered. At first glance, what is perhaps most apparent in these three volumes is Father Meersseman's admirable editing of texts. When we think of his work, we tend to remember only its conclusions; but the wonders he has worked in his preliminary research, manuscript studies, and critical editions are equally impressive. We are also grateful to him for organizing the various aspects of his research in a clear and up-to-date synthesis, while leaving open certain perspectives and indicating in his final chapter the paths that he did not have the time or the opportunity to follow and the directions which he hopes future researchers will choose. He has given us a lesson in methodology—as Father Meersseman often said, with good reason, we should beware of premature syntheses—and also one of great modesty.

————— ◁▦▷ —————

I do not intend to provide a summary or even an analysis of these three large volumes, which together contain 1400 pages. I would simply like to explore several issues that emerge from the work of

Father Meersseman, particularly in the first part, which includes a large number of unpublished studies that have been revised for this publication. Most of them deal with the origin and formation of devotional confraternities. The author has concentrated on the prehistory of these groups, which extended from the Carolingian period to the twelfth century, and the sections he devotes to this subject represent the freshest portion of the collection. The impulse which from early in the Middle Ages stirred the faithful to meet in confraternities whose primary purpose was devotional had many causes. Father Meersseman has correctly situated this process in the context of the vast movement of association which characterized this period and whose varied terminology was so incisively studied by the late Father Michaud-Quantin.[4] But Michaud-Quantin himself emphasized the difficulty of distinguishing, for these early periods prior to the thirteenth century, true confraternities from rural or urban guilds—like those whose excesses in feasting and drinking were denounced by Hincmar of Rheims in the ninth century—and from professional corporations, which arose as early as the eleventh century in the Low Countries and northern France. These corporations often doubled as mutual aid societies and sometimes put themselves under the protection of a patron saint: for this reason they could easily be confused with the confraternities of devotion. Meersseman also points out the relationships which could exist in some cases between the confraternities, peace movements, and communes, at least initially. Of particular interest in this connection is his study of the military confraternities—for example, the confraternity of the Virgin of Puy, which was established in 1182 through the initiative of a lowly carpenter, Durandus *de Orto*, and known as the Confraternity of the Capuciati because of the distinctive white hoods its members wore.[5] This movement was born out of the peasants' desire to see a modicum of order restored to the countryside of Auvergne. When this objective was reached, the group began to attack the injustices of the feudal system; it was then condemned by the hierarchy and classified as more or less heretical, at the same time that the French bishops were repudiating the Waldensians. The historian is thus confronted with a swarm of communitarian initiatives in the professional, political, and even military sectors, among which, given the available documentation, it is difficult to identify with certainty the ones which were specifically confraternities of devotion.

In this new section, Father Meersseman demonstrates the connection between the founding of lay confraternities and clerical, or, more precisely, priestly confraternities: he cites, for example, the Carolingian *Kalendae*, some of which survived until the twelfth century, or associations which can without exaggeration be called clerical unions, like the *Romana Fraternitas*, which constituted pressure groups that enabled the lower clergy to intervene actively in episcopal elections. Whether the lay people formed their groups as a reaction to these associations, whether they tried to imitate them, or whether they infiltrated them, thereby gradually transforming them into mixed confraternities—as was often the case in Northern Europe but much more rarely in Italy— there was almost always some connection between lay and clerical confraternities, which the new research of Father Meersseman allows us to grasp in all of its complexity. His investigation is not limited, however, to reflection on the various forms that the relationship between clergy and laity assumed in different times and places. In the eleventh and twelfth centuries there occurred an event of singular importance for the religious life of the faithful: the approval of penance as a way of life and as an ideal suitable to the aspirations of the faithful. The work of Cyrille Vogel has traced the process through which, between the fourth century and the twelfth century, the ancient form of penance, public and irrepeatable, was transformed into the essentially private and repeatable penance characteristic of medieval and modern Christianity.[6] By the end of this evolution, which was not accomplished without difficulties and attempts to reverse course, particularly in the Carolingian period, penance was no longer a mere penalty; it had become a choice open to those who aspired to perfection while not desiring or being able to enter monastic life. Father Meersseman has made repeated references to this question, particularly in a paper on the laity which he presented in 1965.[7] How did this happen? How did the notion of penance as punishment come to be transformed into the idea of penance as a positive value, and even as a way of life to be pursued by the laity? This phenomenon was, I believe, related to the prestige of monasticism. In the eleventh and twelfth centuries, monasteries were the great

centers of penitential spirituality. All who were drawn to this ideal
turned to them, either to become monks themselves or to serve
the monks while remaining among the laity, according to legal
formulas which varied over the course of the centuries. As early
as the Carolingian period, servants and followers gravitated to the
monasteries. But if the serfs often preferred to be attached to an
abbey instead of to a lay lord, what attracted them was less the
fascination of the penitential life than the superior organization of
the monasteries and the hope of being treated less roughly: it is
good, the saying went, to live under an abbot's crosier. Nevertheless, we can suppose that the example and encouragement of the
monks exercised a certain spiritual influence on the members of
their circle. Father Meersseman points to the example of the ninth-
century confraternity of Fulda, which brought together lay people
from very different social milieux in a prayer union centered on
the abbey. During the eleventh and twelfth centuries, the foundation of many large abbeys and the multiplication of rural priories
put monks in more extensive contact with the people, which
helped to increase their influence. The impact of the apostolic
ideal must also be considered: its enormous success in the West
in the twelfth century helps to explain the communitarian dimension which the penitential movement often assumed. From the
conjunction of these two themes—the penitential ideal, inspired
by monasticism, and the apostolic ideal, spread by canons regular
and popular preachers—a lay movement was born, whose major
stages have been traced by Father Meersseman. In the first phase,
the faithful embarked on penitence while still following in the
monks' footsteps. This period was marked by an increase in the
numbers of lay brothers and *conversi*, who were associated with
a monastery and were a part of the community, but in the end
proved to be no more than second-class monks, separated from
the "choir" monks by their lack of education. In the second phase
the penitential ideal was identified instead with the practice of
eremitism. This way of life was obviously not limited to the laity,
since many hermits were priests or monks. But whether lay or
clerical, the eremitic movement, which experienced tremendous
growth in the West between the late eleventh and early thirteenth
centuries, was nevertheless inspired by the penitential ideal and
valued it, while distinguishing it from the institutional forms of

monasticism. By the end of this evolution, in the second half of the twelfth century, movements of specifically lay character were springing up. The idea that ordinary believers could lead fervent religious lives while retaining their lay status did not meet with true popular acceptance until sometime between 1160 and 1180. This period was marked by the simultaneous appearance of Waldensian brotherhoods, industrious groups of *Umiliati*, and rural communities of penitents, to whom Father Meersseman has devoted one of his most elegant studies. After 1210–1220, the movement expanded under the influence of the mendicant orders, particularly that of the Franciscans, whose penitential origins have been amply demonstrated. Although they were in no way the inventors of the *Ordo poenitentiae*, they lent it wider distribution than it otherwise would have found.

As different from one another as these groups may have been, they all shared the same preoccupations, as their statutes, so accurately published by Father Meersseman, attest. Their common goal was to bring together pious laymen and laywomen who desired to ensure their salvation while remaining "*in domibus propriis*," that is to say, in the world and in the midst of other people. This meant adopting a certain number of exterior signs, beginning with distinctive clothing, to indicate one's membership, for, at least in the beginning, there was no profession in the juridical or canonical sense of the term, but simply a *professio in signis*: all it took to be recognized as a penitent was to wear a certain habit, for the exterior would bear witness to the interior. Poverty, asceticism, and periodical continence, all prescribed by the famous *Memoriale propositi fratrum de penitentia* of 1221, were the virtues required of the brethren. After much hesitation, the clergy finally yielded in the face of so much enthusiasm; and in the mid-thirteenth century, the canonists were forced to recognize the existence of a hybrid being which did not fit properly in any of their categories: the *laicus religiosus*, a person both lay and religious. Henry of Susa, Cardinal Hostiensis, wrote around 1255 in the *Summa aurea*: "In a broad sense, we use the term 'religious' for people who live in a holy and religious manner in their own homes, not because they are subject to a precise rule but because their life is simpler and more rigorous than that of other laypeople, who live in a purely worldly manner."[8]

As Father Meersseman says in his conclusion, this study should be extended to the end of the Middle Ages in order to analyze the evolution of the penitential ideal in the third orders, as these lay movements gradually lost their autonomy.

I would now like to call attention to another point which seems to be of particular importance in the work of Father Meersseman. In discussing the confraternities dedicated to the Virgin, he provides a concise definition of the attitude of these laypeople, who sought a form of religious life that would be independent of and yet close to that of the clergy: "They want to become clerics while remaining lay." This formula epitomizes all of the ambiguity of the movement. Indeed, the confraternities of penitents and flagellants were clearly animated by the desire to appropriate the spiritual resources of monasticism. Laypeople aspired to escape from their subordinate position in religious life. To this end, they did not hesitate to borrow religious practices and devotions, which they slanted in new directions. The most telling example of this was flagellation—a monastic practice which some laypeople in the thirteenth century appropriated in order to win the rewards associated with it. The same could be said of the cult of the Virgin, the quest for indulgences associated with the cults of St. Dominic or St. Peter Martyr, and so on. All this makes it seem as if laypeople in the Middle Ages were incapable of conceiving of their own spiritual destiny without imitating the ideals and way of life of the religious orders. But although they were fascinated by the clergy, the laity maintained a certain distance. This was particularly clear in the area of discipline. The penitential confraternities sought to remain autonomous. In northern Italy in the thirteenth century, the penitents even tried to form their own order, institutionally structured along the lines of the mendicant orders, with chapters general, provincial and general ministers, etc. Above all, they clung to the freedom to meet when and where they wished, to recruit their own members, and to choose the monks or priests they wished to have as their chaplains. In all of these movements, whatever their form, there was a clear desire for autonomy which occasionally reached the point of secularism or even anticlericalism, as paradoxical as this may seem at first glance. As proof, we need only consider the difficulties the papacy encountered in enforcing the bull *Supra montem*. Father Meersseman notes perceptively that, when the master general of the Dominican Order imposed the *Regola dei fratelli e delle sorelle della penitenza di S. Domenico* on the confraternities affiliated with the Dominicans, thereby making the admission of members subject to the authorization of the Dominicans, the male members withdrew. And is it not the case that the only noteworthy members of these pious congregations in the fourteenth century were women, *mantellate*, like St. Catherine of Siena and Maria of Venice?

In the domain of spirituality as well, there were perceptible differences between the clergy and laity. The lay confraternities attached particular importance to works of mercy and mutual aid. This emphasis on charitable activities led to an erosion in the religious role of some groups whose original objective had been devotional, such as the confraternities of the Virgin. This was the source of a more or less latent conflict with the mendicants, who, as time went on, tended to give increasing attention to the strictly spiritual, or even mystical, aspects of religious life. This situation is clearly reflected in hagiography. Numerous lives of penitent saints, such as Lucchese of Poggibonsi, Pietro Pettinaio, and Facio of Cremona, have come down to us from the thirteenth century. But there is nothing of the kind for the fourteenth century, because the Franciscan and Dominican hagiographers were only interested in contemplative and mystical holy women like Vanna of Orvieto, Clare of Montefalco, Catherine of Siena, and others. In short, we can say that the penitents—whatever form their confraternities assumed—constituted a lay elite, whose importance varied from region to region, which wished to participate in the religious privileges of the clergy while remaining apart from them institutionally and even spiritually. These contradictions were resolved with greater or lesser success in various periods, which explains the alternating phases of decline and rebirth in the existence of these groups. But in the final analysis, behind the complex vicissitudes of their history, there always lay an implicit rejection of the schema of the states of perfection propounded by the clergy, who in distinguishing between the *doctores*, the *continentes*, and the *coniugati*—the learned, the chaste, and the married—consistently placed the latter on the lowest rung of the ladder, judging the condition of layperson and especially of married layperson to be least perfect of all.

In conclusion, I would like to mention some paths for research to which Father Meersseman has pointed in passing but has not been able to follow. They concern the meaning of penitential behavior and the mental and cultural reasons which may have impelled some, and perhaps even a large number, of the simple faithful to make this religious ideal their own. A recent study listed twenty-five confraternities that were identified in the city of Perugia, while Charles de La Roncière found twenty-seven in the rural Valdelsa in the fourteenth century.[9] Their membership certainly constituted an elite with respect to the masses, but it was a representative and numerically significant elite. It would be interesting to determine why the lay people of that time flocked with such enthusiasm to these pious associations. (An anthropological approach may be helpful: Ida Magli, in her book *Uomini della penitenza*, has attempted this, with interesting but uneven results.[10]) This question cannot help but come to mind upon rereading the works of Father Meersseman, for it is one of cardinal importance. The evangelical passage of Matthew 4:17—"Repent, for the kingdom of Heaven is at hand"—is obviously at the origin of the choice of penitential behavior. The summons to conversion, and thus to the renunciation of sin, is intimately bound up with the prospect of the imminent coming of the Kingdom. This implicit connection of cause and effect was quite clearly perceived in the Middle Ages, when doing penance did not merely mean punishing oneself or seeking forgiveness for one's sins. It also meant adopting the only attitude that is suitable before God: acknowledging in all humility that one is a sinner and repenting in order to restore a relationship that sin had disrupted. From the medieval perspective, insofar as man was defined as pure nothingness before the divine majesty, God was virtually obligated to reveal Himself. But this result could only be obtained through an effort of purification effected by the triple rejection of power, sex, and money. This idea of sanctification through penance, through the triple renunciation, pleased the laity because it corresponded to one of the most typical tendencies of popular piety: seeing everything as either black or white, in Manichean terms. In the thirteenth century, the penitential ideal shifted toward asceticism modelled on the Victim of Calvary. For a lay person of the time, flagellation meant actualizing and reliving in one's own body the Passion of the Son of God, in order to arrive with him at the glory of the Resurrection. This was all quite orthodox. But the risk of deviating from ecclesiastical norms was not imaginary, for the faithful tended to believe that the simple fact of inflicting harsh penance on themselves and engaging in meritorious practices would eventually allow them to establish a direct relationship with the supernatural and thereby dispense with clerical mediation. Thus, in the case of the flagellants in the fourteenth century, it is noteworthy that although priests were not excluded from their ranks, those who were admitted were treated on the same footing as the lay members who had founded the group and had every intention of remaining its directors. This, moreover, explains why the processions of 1348–1349 provoked the hostility of most clerics and finally the condemnation of Clement VI. Toward the end of the Middle Ages, a rift opened between the Church, which tended increasingly to identify the function of the priest with that of master and to attach sacred meaning to the word, which, through preaching and catechism, became the principal means of access to the divine mysteries, and the laity who still clung to a penitential religion based on the quest for identification with the suffering Jesus.

TEN

MEDIEVAL PENITENTS

THE PENITENTIAL MOVEMENT, which began at the end of the twelfth century in the West, expressed the aspiration of many laymen and laywomen to lead a religious life without submitting themselves to the rigid structure of monastic or canonical orders. It represented an ulterior evolution of the institution of *conversi*, lay brothers or sisters who actively contributed to the community life of Cistercians or canons regular and worked for their own sanctification. But the penitents went further, claiming that it was possible to lead authentically religious lives while carrying on their trades, unaffiliated with any community of regular or secular clergy. Remaining in the world without living in a worldly manner was the goal of individuals and groups in the Middle Ages who adhered to the penitential ideal and strove to make their lives conform to it.

The first experiments of this type took place in 1170–1180. In the Low Countries—taken in the large sense of the term as the group of regions stretching from the territory of Liège to Brabant and Flanders—women called Beguines appeared, living either alone or in communities under the direction of one of their number, without pronouncing vows. Their way of life joined manual labor and care for the sick with fervent prayer. In the early thirteenth century, the outstanding figure in the movement was Marie of Oignies (†1213), who epitomized the spiritual richness of the penitential movement. Thanks to her biographer, Jacques de Vitry, who wrote her *Vita* as early as 1215, we are well informed about her.[1] Born in Nivelles (in present-day Belgium) in 1178 and married at the age of fourteen, she and her husband soon retired to a small leper hospital where for fifteen years they dedicated themselves to helping the sick. Widowed, she gave away all of her possessions and withdrew to the priory of Oignies-sur-Sambre as a Beguine, where she devoted herself to her love of poverty, begging from door to door to help the destitute. Her charitable activities found their natural extension in her devotion to the humanity of Christ and in her genuine mysticism. Although certain elements of the clergy disapproved of these women at first, they eventually managed to win ecclesiastical recognition of the appropriateness of their way of life, though they were still urged to gather into stable communities.

In the same period, in Lombardy, and especially in Milan, groups of laymen were formed who called themselves *Umiliati*. According to a contemporary chronicler, they were "citizens who, although living at home with their families, had chosen for themselves a certain form of religious life: they abstained from lying and lawsuits and pledged to do battle for the Catholic faith."[2] The movement arose and found popularity among artisans who wished to lead an evangelical life while continuing to practice their professions. These laymen thus asserted the sanctifying nature of all human and social conditions, while at the same time expressing their refusal to be confined to the domain of the temporal, which the clergy brusquely characterized as a purely material and transitory universe. This audacity led initially to their condemnation as heretics in 1184 by Pope Lucius III. But at the beginning of the thirteenth century, Innocent III reversed this sentence and approved the movement of the *Umiliati*, after endowing it with a juridical structure. From then on, it was composed of three orders: two orders of clerics and laymen leading a monastic form of communal life under the same roof, and a third made up of laymen who remained in the world, living not according to a rule but in conformity with a program of life, or *propositum*. This document, dating from 1201, is of great importance: it represents the first official recognition by the hierarchical Church of the validity of the penitential movement in one of its institutional manifestations. A few years earlier, the same pope had already removed any suspicion that might have still been attached to this innovative spiritual movement by canonizing

St. Omobono of Cremona (†1197), a merchant who had distinguished himself for his piety, his devotion to the poor and his ardor in the struggle against heresy.[3] With this gesture, the pope had given his own endorsement to the religious aspirations of the penitents, and most importantly to their fundamental claim that they could win salvation while remaining faithful to the requirements and values of their lay station: work, family life, and aid to the indigent.

The movement of the Penitents strictly speaking, the *Ordo poenitentiae*, developed in this spirit. A detailed description of its program can be found in a text, probably written around 1215 but approved by the papacy in 1221, known as the *Memoriale propositi*, which defined the status and the obligations of its members.[4] The Penitents had to wear a robe made out of poor and undyed fabric. Indeed, at the start there was no ceremony or ritual to mark entry into the penitential life: to be considered a member, one needed only to wear this characteristic habit. The Penitents were required to fast more often and at greater length than other faithful, and had to recite the seven canonical hours daily (for which uneducated people could substitute a certain number of Our Fathers and Hail Marys). In addition, they were expected to make confession and take communion three times a year. Taking the Gospels literally, the Penitents refused to shed blood, and hence to bear arms, nor would they take solemn oaths (James 5:12: "Let your yes be yes")—demurrals which soon brought them into conflict with the public authorities, especially in the Italian communes. In 1221, the papacy took the Penitents under its protection and asked the bishops to support them, but it took some time to arrive at a compromise: in practice, the Penitents were exempt from military service, but the cities assigned them a variety of tasks, from distributing poor relief and comforting the condemned to managing the municipal treasury, thus constituting a sort of "civil service" before its time.

Women were also admitted to these confraternities. Those who were married had to obtain the consent of their husbands; the couple could continue to practice conjugal relations except for certain periods of the liturgical year. That is why the Penitents were sometimes called "the continent," a term which should not be taken in an absolute sense. Meetings were held monthly for the most part; they took place in a church, where a priest or monk would address them on a sacred subject. But these lay confraternities were independent of the clergy and obeyed only their own ministers, whom they freely elected.

The status of penitent enjoyed wide diffusion after 1220, under the influence of the mendicant orders. St. Francis and his companions had themselves begun as a brotherhood of penitents, which, after Innocent III granted his approval, gave rise to the order of the Franciscans and the order of the Poor Clares, headed by St. Clare. The Franciscans and the Dominicans, anxious to extend to all the faithful the call to penitence issued by their founders, promoted the establishment of lay communities of this type, which followed their lead without—at least at first—maintaining any special institutional ties with them. Only at the end of the thirteenth century did the third orders earn juridical recognition; their constitution resulted from the desire of the hierarchy to win control over and rein in a typical lay religious movement. In the past, these groups had been quite diverse: some were strictly devotional; others preferred to emphasize the important problems then being faced by the Church, such as the struggle against heresy and the political and military defense of the orthodox faith; others, lastly, dedicated themselves to works of charity, generally placing themselves under the protection of the Holy Spirit or the Virgin of Mercy. But behind these different orientations there was a single spirituality, which is worthy of closer examination.

For the Christians of this time, in fact, penitence did not mean simply repenting of one's sins and carrying out the sacrament of penance, which the Fourth Lateran Council of 1215 had made obligatory for all of the faithful at least once a year. What it meant was taking literally the word of Christ: "Repent, for the kingdom of Heaven is at hand" (Matthew 4:17). Indeed, it was not simply a question of preparing for this kingdom, but of actually entering it during earthly life, a step which was manifested by a radical change in one's conduct and by the renunciation of sin. Penitence was a condition, virtually a way of life. It meant assuming a humble and repentant attitude, the only one suitable for a sinner before God who wished to be joined to Him through love. This was why he had to seek nakedness and poverty, rather than authority, knowledge, or the dignity of the priesthood. Moreover, we must keep in mind that in the Middle Ages the coming of the Kingdom of God was generally considered to be imminent. We know that a certain number of Franciscans adopted for their own purposes the speculations of Joachim of Flore on the beginning, now at hand, of a "new world age" which was to be the last: the age of the Spirit and the eternal Gospel. But even if they had never heard of the prophecies of this Calabrian abbot, the ordinary faithful were inclined to share with many clerics the conviction that they were living "in these, the last of times." The popes themselves did not hesitate to present their chief adversary, Emperor Frederick II, as the true Antichrist, whose appearance in the world was a premonitory omen of the coming end of time. Thus the penitential movement often took on a marked eschatological tone, especially in Italy. This was the case in 1260, when a penitent from Perugia, Rainieri Fasani, read to the townspeople a letter from the Virgin instructing him to flagellate himself publicly and to spread this practice to others so that the city would convert as Nineveh once did. Distressed by the prospect of imminent chastisement, the populace responded overwhelmingly to the appeal of this lay preacher. They followed the example of Rainieri—who was, after all, simply popularizing and performing in public a ritual of private penitence long practiced in the monasteries—and took to beating themselves until the blood ran, in order to avert God's anger by assimilating themselves with Christ through sharing his sufferings. The movement of the flagellants thus embodied an essential component of the spirituality of the penitents: ascetic conformity with the person of the Son of God, which was based on a belief in the redemptive value of physical suffering. In this conviction we recognize the influence of monastic asceticism, which the laity had adapted for its own purposes, retaining only its most rigorous aspects.

But if we consider only its most flamboyant features, we will misunderstand the true nature of this movement. At the same time as they flagellated themselves, the penitents of Perugia also performed the gestures of conversion: reconciliation with their enemies, restitution of ill-gotten gains, especially the fruits of "usury," confession, and so on. There is nothing particularly macabre in the accounts of this episode in various Italian chronicles. When the *battuti* or *disciplinati*—as the flagellants were called in Italian—

went in procession, they composed hymns in honor of God and the Virgin Mary which they sang while going from city to city.

Once the fateful date of 1260 had passed, the movement, which had spread like a shock wave from central Italy through the Germanic countries to eastern Europe, did not die out. Brought into the Church's sphere of influence and provided with a defined structure, it gave rise to confraternities of flagellants which flourished in the Mediterranean countries and the Germanic world, particularly during those massive collective perturbations which shook the West in the late Middle Ages: the Black Death of 1348–1349; the last years of the fourteenth century, marked by the great processions of the *Bianchi* in 1399; and the Great Schism and the conciliar crisis, not to mention more local "popular movements" like the pilgrimage in 1335 which brought throngs of penitents from all corners of Italy to Rome, led by the Dominican Venturino of Bergamo. The statutes of these confraternities, often translated into the vernacular in the fourteenth century, provide us with an idea of their membership and activities. Women were excluded from them for obvious reasons. The meetings generally took place every Friday, every other Sunday, and on principal religious holidays, particularly during Holy Week. Upon entering the oratory of the confraternity, everyone knelt on a marble platform and begged forgiveness for his transgressions against the statutes, which were noted in a special register. Then they read in unison a votive office like those which were found in manuscript books of hours for devout laypeople; the office consisted of the seven penitential psalms, the fifteen gradual psalms with the litany of the saints, the office of the Virgin, and the office for the dead, usually reduced to the first nocturn. On Sundays and feast days, a mass was celebrated, during which offerings were collected and the kiss of peace was exchanged. At the Friday night meetings members flagellated themselves with scourges: after donning special robes, they went barefoot to embrace the crucifix in their chapel, then whipped each other, each one receiving on his bare back as many blows as he deemed necessary to expiate his sins. All faces were covered with hoods to conserve anonymity. During this ceremony, a choir made up of the members with the best voices sang vernacular hymns—called *laude* in Italian—exalting the bloody sacrifice of Christ and its redemptive powers. From the fourteenth century on, as a rule, the flagellants no longer put on public display, except to lead the ritual procession that paraded through the city on Good Friday. But on occasions when mass terror or anguish erupted, such as during the great epidemic of the plague known as the Black Death, they put aside their reserve and poured into the streets. For example, in 1349 almost 200 flagellants followed their banners from town to town in Alsace, singing this hymn of supplication:

> Christ went to Jerusalem.
> He carried a cross in his hand.
> May the Lord help us!
> We must become penitents
> To be more pleasing to God,
> On high, in his Father's kingdom.
> That is why we all give prayer,
> We pray to Christ most holy
> Who governs the whole world.

When they entered churches, they knelt and sang:

> Jesus was given gall to drink.
> We must all throw ourselves to the ground,
> Arms outstretched like crosses.

Once they were prostrate on the ground, their leader cried:

> Now raise your hands toward heaven
> So that God may turn this deadly epidemic from us.
> Reach your arms toward heaven
> So that God may have pity upon us.

The growth of religious lyric poetry in the vernacular, which was characteristic of the late Middle Ages, was undoubtedly linked in large measure to the penitential movement. The earliest confraternity of *laudesi*—the *laude* being a kind of religious ballad with a refrain—was founded in Siena in 1267 by the Dominican Ambrogio Sansedoni. The movement later spread to numerous confraternities, which adopted the names of the churches in which they gathered to sing. Each confraternity had its own *laudario*, a book of vernacular songs; the oldest surviving one comes from the Fraternity of Santa Maria della laude in Cortona, which was associated with the Franciscans. But the fundamental themes were always the same: praise of the Virgin Mary, "the Lady of Paradise," the celebration of her joys and her sorrows, the commemoration of the patron saints and, above all, the Passion of Christ, which was, of course, the central point of the repertoire.

In addition to the confraternities of penitents or flagellants (composed mainly of married men, although unmarried men were also admitted), other forms of solitary penitent life continued to attract adherents in the thirteenth and fourteenth centuries. They ranged from reclusion in a cell adjoining a monastery or the city walls to more flexible kinds of urban eremitism, which combined a life of retirement lived within the family home with charitable activities on the outside. The numerous *cellane* or *incarcerate* mentioned in Italian communal statutes were typical of these solitary penitents, but the phenomenon could be found in most of the countries which then made up western Christendom. This category included holy women such as Delphine of Puimichel (†1360), who spent the last part of her life in Provence as a "recluse" in the towns of Cabrières and Apt and was the object of canonization proceedings in 1363, and Jeanne-Marie of Maillé (†1414), who belonged to the Franciscan movement and worked many miracles in Tours and the Loire Valley. But the person who best exemplified the spiritual richness of the penitential ideal was surely Margaret of Cortona (†1297), who, after a very troubled youth, finally placed herself under the direction of the Franciscans in the convent of this small Tuscan city. Having converted to a better life, she was allowed to wear the habit of a penitent in 1275; from then on she consecrated herself to prayer and charitable works. She inflicted extremely rigorous mortifications on herself to expiate her past faults: she fasted, flagellated herself, slept on the bare ground with a stone for a pillow. Soon she began to be blessed with visions, revelations, and ecstasies, mostly concerning the Passion of Christ, the central theme of her meditation. Her director of conscience, the Franciscan Giunta Bevignate, recorded her confidences and thus was able to write her biography immediately after her death.[5] In this text, which constitutes a veritable program of Christian life for lay women, the hagiographer presents Margaret as a modern-day

Mary Magdalen and emphasizes the merits she acquired through penitence which had allowed her to become "the mirror and mother of sinners."

The number of penitents, both isolated or in communities, remained large until the end of the Middle Ages. But beginning with the early fourteenth century, the papacy tried to channel this kind of religious life, which was popular with both laymen and laywomen, in the direction of greater regularity. The confraternities of penitents were absorbed by third orders, which recruited their own members primarily among women, and which themselves often evolved toward claustral forms of life, ending up as semi-monastic congregations. In this way the originality of this typically medieval movement was progressively lost—though the movement was to be reborn in new forms in the sixteenth and seventeenth centuries.

ELEVEN

LITURGY AND FOLK CULTURE IN THE *GOLDEN LEGEND*

WE ARE SO USED TO THINKING of the *Golden Legend* as a collection of saints' lives that we sometimes forget that Jacobus de Voragine constructed this well-known work in the double register of the spiritual and the temporal, and that it closely associated the great festivals and important moments of the liturgical year with the commemoration of the servants of God. Among the ceremonies in the temporal cycle that Jacobus describes in his work, the Greater and Lesser Litanies have an important position; they are placed immediately after the feast day of Saint John Before the Latin Gate (May 6).[1] His account merits our attention, even if it is not noteworthy for its originality, because for its main points Jacobus de Voragine closely followed the *Rationale divinorum officiorum* of the liturgist Jean Beleth, written between 1165 and 1180.[2] By examining these two texts—the original source and the edifying interpretation provided around 1260-1265 by the future archbishop of Genoa in his *Golden Legend*—we can try to elucidate the attitude of medieval clerics toward a group of ceremonies celebrated each year at the beginning of springtime with the principal aim of ensuring the protection of the crops.

In the passage concerning these festivals, Jacobus de Voragine informs us that there are two kinds of litanies in the Catholic liturgy: the one, known as the Greater Litany, takes place on April 25, the feast day of St. Mark; the other, known as the Lesser Litany or Rogations, takes place on the three days preceding the

Ascension. The first of these was supposedly instituted by Pope Gregory the Great in 590, during an epidemic of the plague in Rome. It was originally called the Septiform Procession, because on that occasion the Roman people walked in a procession of seven rows, according to their respective ranks; but since this organization no longer corresponded to social realities, the Romans adopted the tradition of reciting the litanies seven times before laying down the banners which had been paraded through the city. Finally, it was called the "Black Crosses," because the men and women paraded in black robes as a sign of penitence, and the altars and crosses were draped that day with black cloth.[3]

The creation of the Lesser Litany was attributed by our hagiographer, following the traditional account, to St. Mamertus, bishop of Vienne between 458 and 470. It was supposedly instituted as a result of earthquakes which ravaged the city of Vienne in the fifth century: a fire destroyed the royal palace, and the city was invaded by wolves that devoured a number of its inhabitants. To put an end to these calamities, the prelate called for a three day fast, which had the desired effect. Observance of this festival spread under the name of the Rogations, because during it the help of all of the saints is sought. According to Jacobus de Voragine, its purpose was to keep away the scourge of war—which often breaks out in the spring—to protect the tender shoots, and to mortify the flesh, which is subject to dissoluteness at this time of year. Moreover, it prepared the faithful to receive the Holy Spirit. As the processions made their way, church bells were rung at full peal, and the cross was paraded as a banner to put to flight the demons, who were preparing storms in the heavens. In some churches, especially in Gaul, dragons stuffed with straw were carried around; their tails were full and stiff on the first two days, but flaccid on the third.[4] The passage ends with a list of the various reasons for which people should call on the saints and an account of the eastern origins (Constantinople, to be precise) of the formulary of litanies which, according to Jacobus, was approved by the council of Chalcedon in 451.

Up to this point, we have limited our discussion to a summary and analysis of the rather extensive passages which Jacobus de

Voragine devoted to the two litanies. Now we must compare this information with what we know from other sources about the origin and the evolution of these ceremonies from late antiquity to the medieval era. Jean Beleth and, following him, Jacobus de Voragine dated the origins of the Greater Litany at the year 590, the inception of the pontificate of Gregory the Great; Jacobus provided abundant detail on this point in his account of the illustrious pontiff.[5] After a severe flood of the Tiber, a swarm of serpents and a dragon died on the banks of the river, poisoning the air of Rome and causing an epidemic of the plague which claimed numerous victims among the inhabitants of the city. Pope Pelagius organized an expiatory procession, but he himself died during it. Gregory was elected Pope, and, despite all of his efforts to decline the office, finally had to accept it. Shortly after assuming his duties, he led a new procession. At the end of the ceremony, he beheld the archangel Michael atop the Mausoleum of Hadrian— from then on known as the Castel Sant'Angelo—a vision which was taken as confirmation that God had decided to put an end to the epidemic. Gregory ordered therefore that a litany be celebrated everywhere once a year to commemorate the event. In the future, this procession was to take place annually at Eastertime "according to custom" and end at the church of Santa Maria Maggiore, after parading through the city the church's image of the Virgin, which was "not made by the hand of man." The obvious contradictions in Jacobus de Voragine's account—for example, there is no reason why a new procession should proceed "according to custom"— testify to some degree of confusion in his information, a confusion that is increased still further by his mention of the Constantinop- olitan origin of the Litanies, a statement found at the end of his account of these festivals.[6] As a matter of fact, it seems that an April 25th procession already existed before Gregory the Great's time, as a sermon by St. Leo (pope in 440-461) attests.[7] This text describes how the Roman people gathered at St. Peter's to thank God for ending a plague. The path of this litany later became fixed by tradition: the procession left from the church of San Lorenzo in Lucina, touched San Valentino on the Via Flaminia, crossed the Tiber at the Milvian Bridge, and ended at the Vatican basilica. It took place during the Easter season and so cannot be identified with the litany instituted by Gregory the Great, which was celebrated in the month of August and finished at the church of Santa Maria Maggiore. On the other hand, its dates correspond to those of the Litany of St. Mark, whose origins are recounted by Jacobus de Voragine in the chapter he devotes to the Evangelist in the *Golden Legend*:

> At one time there came a dearth over all the land of Apulia, and no rain fell to water the earth and make it fruitful. And it was learned that this calamity had befallen because the people did not celebrate the feast of Saint Mark. They made haste therefore to offer prayers to the saint, and promised that they would honor his feast-day with all solemnity; and immediately Saint Mark dispelled the drought, and brought to them pure air and the rain for which they longed.[8]

To be sure, this does not prove that the Greater Litany originated in Apulia, but the fact that it undoubtedly took place in Rome on April 25—the feast day of St. Mark—leads many historians to think that it replaced the *Robigalia* of the Roman religion, a festival which called on the gods to protect the young shoots and the future harvest. Whatever the validity of this hypothesis, it seems certain that Jacobus de Voragine, following the liturgists from whom he drew his inspiration, confused the various litanies or processions connected with Roman seasonal rituals. And since by tradition the litany of April 25 was called the Greater Litany, it would have somehow seemed logical to claim that a major personage like Gregory the Great had instituted it, even if that attribution entailed some contradictions.

The *Ordines romani*, recently edited and studied by Monsignor Andrieu, attest to the existence of the Greater Litany throughout the early Middle Ages. Considerable space was devoted to it in the *Ordo romanus L*, written around 950 at the abbey of Saint Alban in Mainz, and here its origin was already attributed to Gregory the Great.[9] "It has the name of *Litania septena* [litany by sevens]," wrote the author of the *Ordo*, "because each group departed from a different Roman church" to gather there.[10] Thus, as early as the tenth century the liturgists dated the institution of the Greater Litany from the plague of 590. But the division of the Roman people into seven categories—which Jacobus de Voragine also mentioned—was no longer understood by this time; as we have seen, the German commentator provided his own interpretation for it.[11] The *Ordo romanus L* provides a detailed list of the scourges that this procession aimed to eradicate: in essence, the supplications addressed to the saints by the clergy and the faithful attempted to make the specters of war and inclemency recede "so as to preserve the harvests."[12] It was a penitential ceremony: on that day, Christians were not supposed to ride on horseback or wear expensive clothing, but instead donned hair-shirts and covered themselves with ashes. This is all corroborated by what Jacobus de Voragine, following Jean Beleth, had to say about the expression "Black Crosses."[13]

Unfortunately, with the exception of these texts, we have very little information about the celebration of the Greater Litany in the medieval West. Since Jacobus de Voragine dwelled at length on the observance and symbolic significance of the Rogations, the fact that he provided no precise details about the Greater Litany, after having treated its origins in detail, might suggest that it no longer was of much importance in his day. On the other hand, we know from other sources that the festival of the Invention of the Holy Cross (May 3) enjoyed great popularity from the eleventh century on. Could this be a case of osmosis or confusion between the two festivals, whose dates were rather close to one another? There is nothing improbable about this, since both were celebrated at a crucial period for the crops, which were still delicate and could be threatened by late frosts. (The famous "ice saints' days" were from May 11th to May 13th.* The first of these was the feast day of none other than St. Mamertus, who was credited with the creation of the Rogations!) In any case, in nineteenth-century French folklore, according to Arnold Van Gennep, masses were celebrated in many regions on May 3rd "to ward off storms and preserve the fruits of the earth."[14] Priests blessed cruciform breads, which were then conserved as a protection against storms, and consecrated crosses, called "croisettes," were planted in the ploughed fields. It thus seems that, despite a minor change of dates (from April 25th to May 3rd) which occurred at an unknown time and may not have taken effect everywhere, the rites of the Greater Litany have survived in rural areas to our century.

The history of the Rogations is both clearer and more complex.[15] Established around 470 by St. Mamertus, bishop of Vienne, they probably owed their name of Lesser Litany to the fact that a Greater Litany already existed in the Roman liturgy and not (as Jacobus de Voragine would have it) to the difference in dignity between a simple bishop and a pope. Having rapidly been extended to the entire Burgundian kingdom by King Gontran, they were adopted and generalized in all of Frankish Gaul by the council of Orléans in 511, as the *Homilia de rogationibus* of St. Avitus, bishop of Vienne from 494 to 518, attests.[16] In the middle of the tenth century, the *Ordo romanus L* devoted a long passage to the Rogations: the author mentioned the custom of making processions for the three days preceding Ascension "for various calamities," among which he listed the incursions of wild beasts, epidemics, and inclement weather.[17] On this occasion, he related, the faithful were supposed to practice fasting and abstinence, walk barefoot singing "*Kyrie eleison*," and implore the saints' help in obtaining peace and preserving the fruits of the earth. The prayer in the Romano-Germanic ritual catches nicely the tone of the ceremony:

> Surgite, sancti, de mansionibus vestris, loca sanctificate, plebem custodite et nos homines peccatores in pace custodite, Alleluia.[18]

According to Jacobus de Voragine—who here again followed Jean Beleth very closely, but simplified the liturgical discourse and amplified the symbolic interpretation of his source—the primary purpose of the Rogations was to implore the saints' aid and protection against the calamities of the season.[19] Jacobus provided a lengthy description of the processions and the roles that the cross and bells played in them: by carrying the cross and ringing the bells, the faithful cleansed the atmosphere of the evil influence of the Devil, who, as everyone knew, was responsible for storms. Singing was also a part of this process of reestablishing harmony in the heavens: "[We sing the hymn] *Sancte deus, sancte fortis, sancte et immortalis miserere nobis . . .* since it has the power of inspiring a special fear in the demons."[20] All of this is perfectly congruent with what ethnologists and historians have to say about the apotropaic function of noise in folk culture, especially its usefulness in averting storms and other threats to the prosperity of the group: in many rural communities, until fairly recently, certain men were employed by each village for the specific purpose of sounding the bells at the approach of black clouds, which carry hail.[21] Thus hagiography easily merged with popular beliefs, furnishing them with a spiritual meaning. Jacobus de Voragine inscribed the procession in an ascensional symbolism: placed under the sign of the cross, the token of resurrection, it was a mystical representation of the procession of saints escorting Christ in his ascent to Heaven amidst the acclaim of the angels.[22] Without wishing to accord excessive importance to this exegesis, we nevertheless cannot help but be struck by the fact that Jacobus de Voragine did not make the least allusion to processions in sacred places or fields, of the kind that are explicitly mentioned in the *Ordo romanus L*. While the latter text named "to sanctify places" as one of the objectives of the Rogations, Jacobus only retained their celestial or vertical dimension, emphasizing their effectiveness in purifying the atmosphere. Now, everything we know about these ceremonies, from both the liturgical rituals and the work of folklorists, confirms that the desire to sacralize space and stimulate the fertility of the earth and the animals had a major role in the festival.[23] After a short, early-morning Mass in the church, the procession would get under way: a first circuit, usually rather brief, led the faithful to the various churches and chapels of the region. Next, there was a more extended itinerary along the boundaries of the territory; the choirboys would shake rattles and ring bells, and consecrated crosses would be planted in the ploughed fields. At the limit of the cultivated lands, wax crosses would be placed on the boundary stones. Finally, in certain regions, the priest would bless the houses, beehives, and stables. But this entire aspect of the Rogations goes unmentioned by Jacobus of Voragine. It is difficult to determine whether this attitude was conscious and deliberate, or if it was simply due to his ignorance of rural matters; but the question is at least worth posing.

The other aspect of the Rogations that Jacobus de Voragine emphasized (following Jean Beleth) was the presence in the processions "in certain churches, and especially in the churches of Gaul," of a dragon with a huge tail "filled with straw [or some other similar material]."[24] The question of processional monsters, especially dragons, has already attracted the attention of many folklorists and historians: Louis Dumont, in his pioneering study on the Tarasque, Arnold Van Gennep, and more recently Jacques Le Goff have shown that as of the thirteenth century, dragons figured in annual processions in certain cities of France and Provence from Douai to Marseilles, including Rouen, Paris, Metz, Poitiers, Provins, Troyes and Tarascon.[25] In all of these cities, they were associated with local saints (Martha in Tarascon, Clement in Metz, Marcel in Paris) who were said to have defeated the monsters and were iconographically represented as tamers who domesticated them. According to Dumont's interpretation, which was adapted and amplified by Le Goff, the dragon was a protector (or a mascot) for the urban community. By accentuating the domestication of the wild and ferocious beast by the holy patron of the city, the legend and the processional ritual illustrated "the victory of the civilizing hero, and, through him, that of the urban community, over the quagmires and the swamps" that filled the original sites of settlements before man's intervention.[26] In the mocking parade of the defeated monster, the city commemorated its own foundation in a region now purged of all traces of rurality and wild beasts. It celebrated the arrival of the urban economic order and affirmed its immunity from the maleficent forces which were arrayed outside the city walls.

Is this really what the accounts of Jean Beleth and Jacobus de Voragine were about? The answer seems clear, even if these churchmen obviously emphasized the moral and religious significance of the allegory of the dragon rather than any reference to the mythic origins of the city. In the view of these authors, the monster was above all the classic incarnation of evil and sin.[27] Jacobus reported that the tail of the processional dragon was long and swollen on the first two days (because it was stuffed with straw or tow) but empty and drooping the third day.[28] His source, Jean Beleth, added that on the first two days the dragon marched in front of the cross and on the third day behind it.[29] In both cases, the ritual was interpreted as symbolic of the three steps in the history of salvation, *ante legem, sub lege, sub gratia,* before the Law, under the Law, and in the age of Grace: the Devil ruled the world during the first two ages, but "on the third day . . . he was driven from his kingdom by the Passion of Christ."[30] For Jacobus, the future archbishop of Genoa, everything was made to pertain to the Christian era; and his typically clerical interpretation of the monsters in the procession precluded any other reading, particularly the obvious one which would establish a relationship between the attention paid to the tail of the monster, the organ in which its potency was concentrated, and fertility rites.

If Jacobus de Voragine's account agrees with what other sources have to say about the place of dragons in urban processions, it is nevertheless surprising that his description of the Rogations makes no mention of the rural world. On the contrary, he emphasizes the urban origin of the festival: it was supposedly established at Vienne after a series of calamities struck the city, of which the worst was an invasion of wild beasts who devoured old people, women, and children in the city streets; the other places mentioned in his account of the Litanies are Rome, Constantinople and Chalcedon.[31] These processions are presented as manifestations of unanimity which, whether the dragon was present or not, brought together the various groups that made up the city population, marching according to their established hierarchical order. In contrast, the rural Rogations, as we understand them from the modern period, had a markedly different appearance. They seem to have been more fervent and less festive, because the stakes were extremely high: in the three days of processions, usually dedicated to the three principal crops of the region, the very survival of the populace was in question. There were no monsters here, because unlike the city-dwellers, the peasants could not allow themselves to mock the animals they feared and needed.[32]

It would seem, therefore, that the medieval liturgists and hagiographers, ending with Jacobus de Voragine, knew or wished to know only about the urban side of the Rogations. Can this mean that in the twelfth and thirteenth centuries this festival was primarily celebrated in the cities, and only later spread to the countryside? Let us merely note that the synodal statutes of Paris make no mention of them, whereas they do note the procession of St. Mark, that is to say the Greater Litany of April 25.[33] The paucity of information at our disposal on this subject does not allow us to come to any conclusions, and a large-scale, systematic inquiry for all of Christendom would have to be conducted for the problem to be resolved. But we can also venture another interpretation: in the rural Rogations, beginning with their earliest documented manifestations, the rites turn fundamentally on the sanctification of space and on an appeal to God for the fertility of the earth; this seems to be corroborated by the various interdictions in the *Ordo romanus L* and the Parisian synodal statutes strictly forbidding female dancing during the processions.[34] If this hypothesis is correct, Jacobus de Voragine would have preferred to remain silent about ambiguous practices that verged on the folklorization of religious ritual and emphasize instead urban customs that lent themselves more readily to an edifying interpretation in terms of the opposition between the forces of Good and Evil (symbolized by the dragon), God and the Devil. Eliminating anything that smacked of "chthonic" religion in the Rogation processions, the hagiographer mentioned only the classical symbolism of the dragon and the "uranic" combat for the mastery of the heavens between the demons, perpetrators of atmospheric perturbations, and the faithful, sustained by the saints and by the Christian armaments *par excellence*: crosses, bells, and hymns.

In the final analysis, should we consider the author of the *Golden Legend* an adversary of "popular religion," seeking to suppress it by hiding its most obvious manifestations? The reality of the matter seems more complex: Jacobus de Voragine did give a nod in the direction of folk culture—both urban and rural—when he emphasized the community's need for collective penitential practices, without which fertility would not be possible. Such is the anthropological basis of the liturgical procession, a veritable collective exorcism which alone can rescue the earth from the grasp of the forces of Evil, and particularly from atmospheric catastrophes. And the same need is expressed—*mutatis mutandis*—in the raucous ritual of the charivari, when the group turns against one of its members who has transgressed the norms governing selection of marriage partners.[35] On the other hand, our hagiographer, by eliminating all references to the rural world and fertility from his description of the Rogations, and by interpreting the rites in a spiritualist sense, modified their meaning significantly. This mixture of acceptance and rejection of the most popular liturgical manifestations was entirely consistent with Jacobus de Voragine's general attitude toward supernatural phenomena and his conception of the relationship between the human and the divine.[36] Far from denying their existence, in all of his works he tried to enclose them within the framework of ecclesiastical ritual and to place them in the context of Christianity as he understood it, that is to say, as a religion which sanctifies time and not space.

Anti-Semitism and Popular Canonization: The Cult of St. Werner

THE SUBJECT OF THIS STUDY falls into a well-known category of medieval sanctity: those saints—almost always children or youths—who were canonized because they died in tragic circumstances and were venerated as martyrs, victims of the Jews. Cults of this type were quite frequent in the latter centuries of the Middle Ages. The first appeared in France and England in the twelfth century with William of Norwich (†1144), as well as Richard of Pontoise (†1179), who was buried and venerated at the cemetery of the Innocents in Paris. The phenomenon grew in the thirteenth century, as shown, for example, by the cult of the child-martyr Hugh of Lincoln (†1255) in England, and reached the Germanic countries, where it enjoyed a wide diffusion in the fourteenth and fifteenth centuries. These devotions were very popular and, early on, inspired various vernacular writings, but their evolution is difficult to pin down because the Church generally did not ratify them, at least during the Middle Ages. As a result, the sources available for studying their origins and spread are rather sparse and fragmentary: some allusions to them can be found in chronicles, versified laments, and accounts of pilgrimages; in some cases there is an abundant iconography, but specifically hagiographic documentation is sporadic and often late in date, especially if the cult was not recognized or approved by the Roman Church through formal canonization proceedings.

Among these saints, there is one exceptionally well documented case: that of St. Werner of Bacharach or Oberwesel, two towns on the banks of the Rhine in the diocese of Trier. For St. Werner, who died in 1287, we have a canonization proceeding, or more precisely a preliminary investigation whose aim was to obtain permission from the pope to open such proceedings, which was concluded in 1428–1429 by local authorities in order to provide a juridical foundation for very widespread and flourishing devotion to the saint. Two manuscripts from this inquest are extant: one at the municipal library of Trier, which contains interesting illuminations, and the other at the Vatican Library, in the Palatine collection. The Bollandists have published lengthy extracts in the *Acta Sanctorum*.[1] Using these documents and certain thirteenth- and fourteenth-century chronicles, we will attempt to clarify the vicissitudes of this cult, whose history spotlights the complexity of the relationship between popular and clerical religion in medieval and modern times.

To begin with, here are the facts: some of the chronicles from the Rhine Valley and southern Germany mention that a certain Christian ("quemdam christianum") by the name of Werner, whom the *Annals of Colmar* call "der guote Werher," the good Werner, died in 1287. According to their accounts, he was murdered by the Jews of Oberwesel in the Rhenish Palatinate and buried in Bacharach, a large neighboring village. Miracles immediately began to take place at his tomb, and to avenge his death the local populace engaged in a massacre of Jews in the entire region. The *Chronicon Colmariense* adds that the leaders of the Jewish community complained to the Emperor Rudolf about the violence being inflicted on them. He recognized the justice of their complaints and imposed heavy fines on the inhabitants of Oberwesel and Boppard, where the pogroms had taken place. In addition, the source states that on his orders, the archbishop of Mainz pronounced a public sermon on this theme, declaring that

> the good Werner, who was commonly said to have been killed
> by the Jews and who was revered almost like a god by certain
> Christians of simple spirit, should be burned in the flames

and the ashes of his body should be scattered and reduced to nothing.

It was certainly not new or unusual for the faithful and the hierarchy to have different opinions about the Jews. As early as 1146, St. Bernard had to use all of his religious prestige to oppose the wave of popular anti-Semitism that had accompanied the preaching of the Second Crusade by a fanatic hermit; Bernard's intervention had been requested by the bishops of the Rhineland, when the events proved beyond their control. In 1247, Innocent IV addressed a bull to the archbishops and bishops of Germany, defending the Jews against the accusations of ritual murder used to justify the persecution and violence unleashed against them there. He condemned the accusations as false, emphasizing that, contrary to popular opinion, there was nothing in the laws of the Jews that enjoined them to "take communion by sharing the heart of a child." Emperor Frederick II reacted in the same way in 1236 to a pogrom in Fulda which followed the accidental death of a miller's five children who perished when the mill went up in flames.

However, in Werner's case, the ecclesiastical hierarchy soon changed its attitude. In 1288, work was begun to enlarge the chapel consecrated to St. Cunibert on a hill overlooking Bacharach, where the body of the "martyr" had been laid to rest; the next year, twelve prelates of the Roman curia granted indulgences in support of the construction project. Rapid progress must have been made on the work, since in 1293 the new altar of the chapel was solemnly consecrated by the auxiliary bishop of Cologne, in the name of the archbishops of Cologne and Trier. For this occasion indulgences of forty days were granted to the pilgrims who came to venerate the reliquary of St. Werner, which was placed in the newly completed apsidal chapel. Further indulgences for the chapel of St. Cunibert were granted in 1320 by the archbishop of Mainz and quickly confirmed by the archbishop of Trier, Baldwin of Luxemburg (1307–1354). One might wonder what brought about this sudden reversal. The answer seems clear: it was caused by popular enthusiasm and the success of the pilgrimage of St. Werner, not just in the Rhineland but even in Hungary and the Slavic countries. His tragic death must also have had strong resonance in the Western regions of Christendom, since as early as the end of the thirteenth century or the first decades of the fourteenth, a lament was composed in Flemish—*Van sente Waerneer*—which described at length and in detail the murder of this innocent victim of the Jews. But another element certainly played a decisive role in the fortunes of the cult: the support given it from the start by the count palatine of the Rhine, Ludwig II the Severe, in whose lands the little town of Bacharach was located (Oberwesel and its neighbor Boppard were incorporated into the temporal domain of the archbishops of Trier in 1307). As early as 1288, Ludwig created a little collegiate church (*domus sancti Wernheri*) in the locality of Winzbach, on the spot where Werner's body had been found after his death. This princely foundation was placed in the care of a few Williamite monks and remained under the jurisdiction of the curate of Bacharach. The support of the local dynasty, which stands in contrast to the hostility of the Emperor Rudolf of Hapsburg, did not diminish in the following years, since the canonization inquest was organized in 1428 at the request of another elector palatine, Ludwig III the Bearded.

Nevertheless, in the course of the fourteenth century the public cult of St. Werner seems to have been hobbled by the hierarchy. The reconstruction of the chapel broke off in about 1307 and did not resume for a long time. Witnesses at the inquest in 1428 saw a connection between the interruption of this building project and an act of brigandage perpetrated by the troops of the archbishop of Trier, the same Baldwin of Luxemburg who had conceded indulgences to the sanctuary in 1320 and 1324. This episode is odd and poorly documented. But we know that this prelate, anxious to increase his territorial domain, protected the Jews: in 1338 he harshly quelled pogroms that had begun shortly before in Boppard and Oberwesel. Since a large part of the chapel's treasure consisted of items plundered from the Jews of the region, it is quite possible that he confiscated it for his own profit. But a century later it was said that he never tasted the fruits of this robbery, because the waters of the Rhine mysteriously swallowed up the boat that was carrying the treasure.

If this conflict blocked the construction project, which did not resume until after 1420, it did nothing to impede the success of the cult and its exterior manifestations. The composition of the German version of the legend of St. Werner (*Gott Vatter in der Ewigkeit*), which the specialists place between 1360 and 1370, attests to this success. Sometime before 1400 it was followed by a Latin legend called *Passio antiqua sancti Werneri* and by an office in nine lessons known as the *Historia prima*. We know from witnesses at the 1428 proceedings that the text of the German *vita* was hung in the chapel for the instruction of pilgrims. The depositions also tell us about the cult: near the chapel there was a spring that Werner, while alive, had supposedly brought forth to soothe the thirst of some shepherds; its water kept its flavor even after sitting for a long time. A cult statue of the saint was placed in the hospital of the Holy Spirit at Oberwesel, the supposed site of Werner's torture. Many visitors came to touch the stake to which he had been bound by the Jews, which became so worn that it had to be moved to a less accessible place. Miracles continued to take place in the sanctuary, in particular for the benefit of newborns, whose mothers brought them to the tomb of the "holy child," and prisoners, whose miraculously broken chains festooned the walls of the chapel along with many other votive offerings. In his testimony at the inquest of 1428, a priest did not hesitate to contrast Werner's thaumaturgic dynamism with the paucity of miracles wrought by the traditional saints of the region, the eleven thousand virgins of Cologne and the martyrs of Trier. But the local clergy shied from rendering to St. Werner the honors of a public liturgical cult and were especially reluctant to celebrate the office that had been composed in his honor. This office was nevertheless known to all: poor schoolchildren sang it in the streets as they begged for bread from door to door. Werner became a popular first name, and his iconography seems to have been abundant: there is even mention made of a polyptych in which Werner was depicted at St. Martin's side. But the lack of official recognition on the part of the Holy See surely acted as a restraint on local priests, who were aware of the rules governing canonization and the cult of saints which had been instituted by the papacy in the thirteenth century. Torn between their devotion to St. Werner and their knowledge of his uncertain canonical status, they hoped to revive the cult from its position of marginality. On several occasions in the late fourteenth and early fifteenth centuries, earthquakes caused the chapel floor to crumble and the cover of the reliquary to gape open, letting a sweet smell escape. This was interpreted as a request for a cult voiced by a saint who lacked the consecration of official papal recognition.

An auspicious occasion presented itself after 1420: during the wars against the Hussites, a papal legate, Cardinal Branda Castiglione, came to the Rhineland to preach the crusade. At the insistence of Ludwig III, the elector palatine and duke of Bavaria, the cardinal went to Bacharach to see the sanctuary of St. Werner, a visit which was interpreted by some chroniclers as an actual canonization. This was not the case, however; and the official procedure was not begun until 1426, during the visit to Bacharach of another papal legate, Cardinal Giordano Orsini, bishop of Albano, sent by Martin V to spur on the zeal of the German princes against the Bohemian heretics. This prelate—whose retinue included the young Nicholas of Cusa—came to Bacharach with two other bishops and bestowed new indulgences on the chapel of Saints Werner and Cunibert. He conducted a brief inquest on recent miracles, opened the reliquary, and performed the elevation and translation of the martyr's relics, which were laid in the main altar of the new chapel, consecrated on the same occasion. That same year, the bishop of Besançon, Thibaut de Rougemont, made a pilgrimage to Bacharach and granted still more indulgences. The construction work, which had been discontinued more than a century before, resumed, and by 1428 the building was almost completed, as the indulgences granted by a third papal legate, Henry of York, known as the cardinal of England, attest. At the request of Ludwig III, Cardinal Orsini ordered that canonical proceedings be opened; the resulting local inquest took place between 2 September 1428 and 25 March 1429 and recorded the depositions of 211 witnesses—a sign of how deeply rooted this cult and this devotion were in the Middle Rhine region.

Despite the official recognition of the cult of St. Werner by three cardinals, it was not yet free of controversy. There are several possible reasons for this. First of all, Pope Martin V, who was well known for his interventions on behalf of the Jews, did not follow up on the informational proceedings of 1428–1429 and did not pronounce on the sanctity of the martyr of Bacharach. Perhaps Rome also shared the uneasiness of some German clerics about

this popular cult, an uneasiness that is documented by a short treatise called *De Sancto Wernhero in Bacheraco* [On St. Werner of
Bacharach] and most certainly written by the Dominican inquisitor
Heinrich Kalteisen in 1428. In this unpublished text, preserved in a
manuscript in Kolblenz, the author vigorously challenges Werner's
right to be called a martyr, arguing that a young Christian who
agreed to go work for the Jews on Maundy Thursday could not
have been an admirable individual and that, considering his age,
he must surely have had some mortal sin on his conscience that he
had no time to confess before his death, which would render his
sanctity very doubtful. A few years later, toward the middle of the
fifteenth century, another cleric, reading or copying the legend of
St. Werner in the legend collection of the abbey of Bodeken in the
diocese of Paderborn, added a very critical comment in the margin
which left little doubt about his feelings toward the populace's
devotion for the presumed martyr. This devotion seems to have
cooled somewhat in the course of the fifteenth century, because
the chapel of St. Werner was still unfinished in the mid-sixteenth
century, when the majority of the population of the Palatinate
joined the Protestant Reformation.

The convoluted history of the cult of St. Werner does not stop
there; but, before following its later vicissitudes, we need to give
closer scrutiny to the medieval documents concerning him and
study the stages through which his legend evolved, which have
some significant variations. In reality the earliest evidence, although clearly marked by anti-Semitism, remains rather vague. The
chronicles say simply that a Christian—whose age is not mentioned
in the first texts—known locally by the name of "good Werner,"
was killed by Jews at Oberwesel on Good Friday of 1287. One
of the sources, the *Continuation of the Annals of Niederaltaich*,
introduces the idea of a ritual murder, explaining that the killing
of Werner resulted from the Jews' need for blood to be used for
medicinal purposes ("*quo mederi dicuntur*"). It was not until the
Gesta Treverorum, dating from the early fourteenth century, that
a more elaborate version appeared, presenting Werner as a young
beggar ("*puer mendicus*") assassinated by his Jewish employers in
a cellar where he was transporting soil. The idea of ritual murder
was adopted and developed at length in the Flemish poem dating
from approximately the same time:

And when they had stripped off his clothes,
The dirty Jews, the stinking dogs,
They inflicted many wounds on him
With daggers and with knives
And then, still in the same place, caused
All of the blood to flow from his body
And collected this blood in a vessel.
They did this
Because with this blood, I know,
They wished to celebrate their sacrament;
For it was their custom, and this is no lie,
To obtain a Christian child every year
Young, healthy, and rosy,
This child they put to death
In order to have his blood. . . [2]

Finally, the German legend (c. 1370) and, above all, the Latin passion add the accusation of the profanation of the host. The story now had assumed its definitive form, and was embroidered with a wealth of details to recreate the thread of the events. Werner was born in Womrath in the Hunzrück region; having lost his father while still young, he left home to work in the Oberwesel area. He was hired by a Jew there, who, along with some other Jews, attacked him on the night of Maundy Thursday just after he had received communion. They hung him from a post to make him vomit the host. When this did not work, they proceeded to torture him in the most atrocious manner and slit all his veins to bleed him. While they were torturing him to death, a Christian maidservant saw them and informed the judge. He arrived on the scene quickly but, bribed by the Jews, took no action. Worried, the Jews tried to dispose of the body by taking it to Mainz, but the boat on which they had placed it travelled only one mile up the Rhine that whole night. So they had to bring the corpse ashore and got rid of it by tossing it into a hollow full of underbrush, near Bacharach. Drawn by a light, a peasant discovered the mutilated body of the young man, who was brought in procession to Bacharach and laid in state at the city hall. The news attracted large crowds, and the first miracles took place three days later. The servant came from Oberwesel to describe what she had seen and reveal the identity of the victim. The inhabitants of the two towns immediately fell upon the Jews and took vengeance, massacring everyone they could lay their hands on.

This late and complex story was obviously designed to conceal, by providing an apparently rational explanation, the contradictions and obscurities of the earlier tradition. In addition to the escalation of the anti-Semitic polemics and the accusation of the profanation of the host, which made it necessary for the authors of these legends to move the attack on Werner back from Good Friday to Maundy Thursday, the story contains a new element: for the first time, it is mentioned that a tool for pruning vines (*putatorium. . . laboris sui instrumentum*) was buried with the fourteen-year-old youth. This is not surprising, considering that at that time Oberwesel was in the middle of a wine-producing area, and that Bacharach was a transshipment center for the wines of the Moselle, the Franche-Comté, and Burgundy, which merchants exchanged there for those of the Rhineland. Moreover, we know that this mid-Rhine region contained large Jewish settlements and that hostility between the vinedressers and the Jews was intense and lasting, because the Jews lent or advanced at high rates of interest the sums the vinedressers needed to "make ends meet" or to tide them over until the harvest could be sold. Given this context, it is not surprising that Werner ended up, rightly or wrongly, portrayed as a worker in the vineyards. This aspect of his sanctity was to be amplified in later years; but even in the inquest of 1428, we can see how proud the inhabitants of these towns were to have as their patron saint a person "*de rustica stirpe natus*," born of peasant stock, and it is certain that this element played an important role in the growth of the cult.

Despite the efforts of their authors, fourteenth-century legends did not succeed in masking all the incoherences of a story that had obviously been composed to provide *a posteriori* justification for an already well-established cult. For example, the chronology of events poses a serious problem: in 1287 Easter fell on April 6, and Werner accordingly must have been attacked by the Jews on April 3 or 4; but the sources all agree that his feast day—that is, the anniversary of his death—was on April 19. Even though the legend makes much of his protracted agonies, the lack of verisimilitude is troubling. Moreover, from the beginning, the name of Werner was associated with two towns: Oberwesel, where he was supposedly martyred, and Bacharach, in whose vicinity his body was found. The episode about how his body was transported on the Rhine serves to explain the passage from one locality to the other. What really happened? Paradoxically, the sources from longest after the event—the records from the opening of the reliquary and the interrogatories of the witnesses in 1428-1429—are surely the ones that provide the most help in answering this question. Indeed, the remains of the saint exhibited all of the emblems of virginity: his face was surrounded by golden tresses and his head rested on a silk cushion filled with violets; he wore a silken robe and his body was wrapped in a bloody shroud fastened with a comb which, according to a witness, *"in istis partibus est verissimum virginitatis signum"* [in these regions is the most authentic sign of virginity]. To a Rhenish local historian, F. Pauly, this emphasis on the innocence and virginity of the victim is evidence that this was a sexual crime.[3] The body of a horribly disfigured and mutilated young man was indeed found in a hollow near Bacharach by a peasant in April of 1287. At his side there was a sort of hoe, which must have been the murder weapon. The body was brought back to the town, where it was displayed to the public. Upset by this sight, the population spontaneously declared the youth a saint, which is nothing surprising if we consider the large number of "holy innocents" in the Middle Ages—boys or girls, savagely murdered, whose tragic deaths were enough in themselves to excite veneration or give rise to a cult, despite the misgivings of the clergy. It was only later that a maidservant from Oberwesel, where the young beggar had plied his trade, identified him and blamed the Jews for his death. What is more, this whole episode may have been no more than an attempt to justify after the fact a massacre of Jews, such as the one which took place in Oberwesel and its environs in May of 1287. When Werner's body was placed in its first reliquary and carried to the chapel of St. Cunibert, the murder weapon, which lay next to him, came to be considered the tool of his trade, which of course was vine-dressing. The latent anti-Semitism of the Rhenish population did the rest, and St. Werner soon came to be venerated everywhere as martyred by the Jews. But the local memory of the original theme—virginity—did not, however, entirely disappear, as the inquest of 1428-1429 demonstrated.

However interesting it may be, the question of the origins of the cult should not claim all of our attention, because, for both laity and clergy in the Middle Ages, St. Werner was clearly a saint of anti-Semitism. This was not however, his last transformation. In 1548, just before the Reformation came to Bacharach, a canon of Besançon, Jean Chuppin, obtained the index finger of Werner's right hand, which he took back to the capital of the Franche-Comté. The relic was placed in a reliquary in the Church of the Magdalen, in the parish of the vinedressers of the Battant neighborhood. The parish established a confraternity dedicated to St. Vernier (the French form of Werner), which met with great success and survived until the French Revolution. The reasons for the canon's actions are worth investigating: was Werner/Vernier already known in the Franche-Comté in the fifteenth century? We have seen that the archbishop of Besançon, Thibaut de Rougemont, had come to Bacharach in 1426 and granted indulgences to visitors to the chapel where the martyr lay. Did he introduce the cult into his diocese? We do not know, and we must also confess that there is no trace of a medieval cult of St. Werner on French territory. In any case, the greatest growth of the devotion took place in the early modern centuries. A legend in French, written and published in Besançon, dates from the sixteenth century. Although it certainly portrays Werner as a martyr, it primarily shows him as the patron of the vinedressers. The cult soon spread to Burgundy; in the seventeenth century, on the banner of the confraternity of St. Vernier in Auxerre, the saint was depicted crucified head down with a spring of fresh water gushing miraculously from his head. In Auvergne, he was revered by the vinedressers under the name of St. Verny.[4] The memory of his martyrdom and the context of anti-Semitism characteristic of the Rhineland soon evaporated completely. The cult, enthusiastically adopted by the vinedressers of eastern and central France, where St. Vernier often displaced St. Vincent, became a part of folk culture. Cult statues and processional banners represented Vernier as a young vinedresser in work clothes, whose attributes were a pruning knife and a vine-stock heavy with grapes. This development eventually came to alarm the ecclesiastical authorities, and the bishops of Clermont protested against these "misshapen or unseemly" images or statues and against some aspects of the festivals or processions in his honor, which could be occasions for disturbing excesses.[5] In his treatise on the canonization of saints, Benedict XIV displayed some misgivings in his discussions of the cult of the martyr whom he curiously calls "*Vincentius Wernerius.*"[6] The process was finally completed in the nineteenth century: with the Revolution and the phylloxera crisis, many of the confraternities of St. Vernier disappeared. The Church made no great effort to keep them alive: after all, in 1848 it had seen the statue of St. Vernier, dressed in a phrygian bonnet, paraded around the city of Issoire to celebrate the news of the revolution in Paris. But St. Werner's ecclesiastical career ended only very recently, for it was not until 1963 that his name was removed from the liturgical calendar of the diocese of Trier, where his feast day had been a holy day of obligation since 1742. Despite this, his memory survives to this day; and in the Franche-Comté, particularly in Arbois and Ornans, confraternities placed under his sponsorship continue to exist and even appear to have enjoyed something of a revival.

It would be hard to exaggerate the exceptional interest of the case of St. Werner. This case allows us to track over a long period of time the complex and shifting relationships between a popular cult and the ecclesiastical authorities. When the pressure from the faithful and the princes was too strong, as was the case in the Middle Ages, the hierarchy was inclined to be flexible, approving the devotion without officially recognizing it, while attempting to eliminate its nastier aspects. Thus the victim of the Jews came to be portrayed as an innocent vinedresser, whose figure the clergy of the early modern period used to try to Christianize that profession and the work it did. But this graft took too well, and the model rapidly became "secularized" to the degree that the saint became totally identified with his followers and the religious dimension of the patronage evaporated. Above all, the story of St. Werner serves to illustrate the extreme plasticity of saints' cults and their capacity to adapt to their surroundings, at the price of profound modifications. The very longevity of this cult testifies to the strength of an acculturation process which was able to keep the memory of this young beggar alive in the collective consciousness. Of Werner himself, we must resign ourselves to knowing only that one day in 1287, he may have been an innocent victim of the forces of Evil.

THIRTEEN

PATRONAGE OF SAINTS AND CIVIC RELIGION IN THE ITALY OF THE COMMUNES

LATE-MEDIEVAL EXAMPLES of the fundamental role of communal authorities in organizing cults of saints in northern and central Italy are quite abundant, although they have not yet been studied systematically. The documentation, which is found mainly in communal statutes and the *Libri di riformanze* [Books of decrees], allows us to measure the extent to which municipal officials were engaged in a domain which at a first glance would seem to lie entirely within the purview of the Church and the clergy. As we shall see, civic authorities were most often involved in the process of promoting devotion to recently deceased figures, but their activities were not limited to these cases.

When it wished to honor a saint, a commune began by making him an annual offering of wax: on the anniversary of his death, a messenger brought the candle given by the city to the church where the body or relics reposed.* The value of the offering—and therefore its weight—varied according to the importance that the officials ascribed to the saint and, actually, to the particular group which was honoring him. For example, in 1350 the commune of Orvieto sent a candle weighing fifty pounds on August 15, the feast of the Assumption, to the cathedral of Orvieto, which was dedicated to the Virgin, and another, smaller one on May 21, the feast day of a local saint, the Blessed Pietro Parenzo (†1199), who was buried there. For their part, the Dominicans received a twenty-pound candle on the feast day of St. Dominic and another of the same size in commemoration of the Blessed Vanna or Giovanna (†1306), a pious woman of Orvieto who during her life had gravitated to the preaching friars. This was repeated by the Franciscans on the feast days of St. Francis and the Blessed Ambrogio of Massa, and by the Augustinians on the feast day of the Blessed Clement of Osimo. Ambrogio and Clement were monks who died in odor of sanctity in Orvieto or its environs—the first in 1240, and second in 1291—and whose remains were preserved in the local monasteries of their respective orders.[1] These donations were made with very specific conditions: the candles presented to the churches by the municipality had to remain on the altars of the saints for the whole year until they were replaced. In Orvieto, a statute enacted by the Council in 1314 declared that the commune's candles should serve exclusively to illuminate the body of Christ, and that they should remain lit until the end of the Elevation. If a candle donated by the city was not kept until the end of the year, it would not be replaced. Moreover, a notary public was supposed to visit the church every three months to make sure that the candle was still in its place.[2]

A commune demonstrated deeper involvement when it stipulated that designated authorities—generally the *podestà*, the elders, and a delegation from the council—would march in procession on the feast days of their patron saints to bring the city's offerings to the churches and monasteries. The confraternities and guilds were sometimes required to participate in the procession, which thus took on the character of an official city holiday. For example, in 1315 the town council of Poggibonsi, in Tuscany, decided that the merchants, the artisans, and all of the officials of the commune would carry candles in the procession of the feast day of the Blessed Lucchese, a local Franciscan tertiary who was venerated at the Franciscan church from the time of his death in 1260.[3] Beginning in 1321, the commune determined annually the number of candles to be carried and donated on this occasion to the Franciscan monastery: depending on the year, it varied between 200 and 500. An equal number of individuals, chosen from among the wealthiest men in the city, were required to buy the candles and participate in the procession.[4] This convenient procedure allowed poor communes to avoid large outlays and to adapt the expense of honoring their patron saints to the current economic situation. Surely it is no coincidence that the number of candles for which the citizens were responsible went from 500 in 1348 to 350 in 1350.[5] Moreover, the annual vote on how the ceremony was to be celebrated gave the Council an opportunity to introduce useful changes. For example, in 1361, when the commune decided to finance the construction of a chapel in the Franciscan church of Poggibonsi dedicated to the Blessed Lucchese, the Council decreed that that year all of the usual offerings should be "converted" to funds for the project.[6]

Communal activity on behalf of the cults of saints was a phenomenon that went far beyond the case of new intercessors who merited local promotion. In many cities at this time, public authorities took up commemoration of the feast days of earlier saints in order to celebrate the anniversary of events that had benefited the entire community. For example, after the battle of Montaperti in 1260, Siena gave thanks to St. George for having granted their victory by making his commemoration a public holiday. The Council decreed that henceforth no work would be done on that day, and that a church in Siena would be consecrated to that saint at public expense.[7] This was not an isolated occurrence: in fourteenth-century Treviso, the feast day of St. Francis was a public holiday because October 3rd was the day that the exiles were able to return to their city after the flight of the tyrant Alberico da Romano; St. Bartholomew's Day [August 25] was a holiday also, because on that day the same Alberico was captured and burned by his enemies.[8] From that time on, these feast days were holidays for all, and the bishop and clerics joined the civil authorities in processions to the churches dedicated to these saints.[9] Even the Assumption became a civic holiday, because, as an addition made to the communal statutes in 1314 states, "at the call of the church bells of the church of Santa Maria Maggiore in Treviso, which began to sound early in the morning, the men of the city rose up and, with the help of the blessed Virgin Mary, reestablished communal rule, order, and peace."[10]

On the other hand, for quite logical reasons, some saints' days were considered to be black days for the community. In Faenza, for example, the feast day of St. Anthony and St. Brice of Tours was celebrated in mourning to commemorate the treason of Tebaldello Zambrasi, who at dawn on November 13, 1280, had opened the gate of the city to the *geremei*, the Guelfs of Bologna, bringing on the death or exile of many Ghibellines.[11] The same feast day was celebrated with joy in Imola, after the passage of a decree in 1282 which recalled how "on that feast day, the city of Faenza was occupied by the party of the holy Church." Every year on that date, the *podestà* brought gifts of candles and silver to the cathedral of San Cassiano.[12]

What was involved in these festivities which were organized or financed by the commune to honor the saints? For lack of precise descriptions, we must settle for the sparse data provided in communal statutes or certain papal documents. The feast day, first of all, was the anniversary of the death of the saint—unless, as sometimes occurred, the commune modified the date by its own authority. For example, in Poggibonsi, the feast day of the Blessed Lucchese, usually celebrated on April 28, was transferred as of 1340 to the first Sunday in May by a decision of the town council.[13] On the eve of the appointed day, there was a torchlight procession led by municipal authorities, in which the various guilds were required to participate. The procession made its way to the church where the saint's body lay; there the torches, whether paid for by the commune or by individuals, had to be left or a fine would be exacted.[14] The next day, after a procession culminating in a religious service, the constituted authorities placed the wax offering from the city on the saint's altar. A trumpeter hired by the city announced the beginning of the celebration.[15] The afternoon was devoted to manifestations of public joy: sweets were distributed to the children, and, in Tuscany at least, the commune organized a "running of the *palio*" in the city streets.[16] Sometimes a market was held on the day of the festivities; in the case of San Gimignano, a five-day long fair accompanied the feast day of the Blessed Bartolo (†1300).[17] For one case, that of Bevagna in the region of Umbria, where the memory of the Dominican Giacomo Bianconi (†1301) was venerated, we have somewhat more detailed information about the way the feast day itself was celebrated. A festive triduum took place in his honor every year on the first three days of the month of May (whereas the anniversary of his death was August 22). It was preceded by a vigil on April 30, during which the magistrates, guilds, confraternities, religious orders, and canons of the main church of Bevagna made a candlelight procession to the Dominican monastery. They then paraded the reliquary of the saint around the city and returned it to the church, singing the *Te Deum*. Next, an office was celebrated in the church (whether it was a mass is not specified) during which the reliquary was opened—the relics would remain exposed to the devotion of the faithful for three days—and a Dominican pronounced an encomium to the saint. On the final day, the crucifix which, according to the legend, ran with blood that bathed the Blessed Giacomo as he prayed before it, was presented to the adoration of the faithful. After a panegyric of this miracle, the popular festivities began.[18]

In general, despite the absence of precise information on this point, it seems that the liturgical aspect of these ceremonies was quite minor. The fact that we are dealing with uncanonized saints should not be overlooked: according to canon law, they could not be honored with a public cult. This explains the rather unusual nature of these commemorations, in which the civic and popular element was fundamental. Contemporaries were aware of this, especially outsiders who observed with astonishment that exceptional honors were being rendered to figures on whose sanctity the Roman Church had pronounced no judgment. In the case of two beatified Italians affiliated with the Dominican order—Vanna of Orvieto and Margherita of Città di Castello—the German Dominican Johannes Meier, in his *Liber de viris illustribus ordinis Praedicatorum*, written in about 1466, emphasized the fact that "although they have not been canonized, their compatriots honor their memories in their native cities *festive et solemniter suo modo* [with celebrations and ceremonies as they see fit].[19]

The words *suo modo* express the Dominican friar's uneasiness about the ceremonies that the festive city offered on its own initiative to commemorate the anniversary of its heroines and protectresses.[20] This same discomfort, but better defined this time, is apparent in the bull *Regimini universalis*, in which in 1515 Pope Leo X granted official recognition—pending her canonization, which did not come about until 1728—to the cult of Margaret of Cortona, who had been venerated in her native city since her death in 1297. Speaking of the commemoration held in her honor every year on February 11, the pope noted that on that day

> a solemn and public festival, with the ceremonies that the communes usually organize for these occasions, is celebrated in Cortona. To celebrate this great feast day, not only do the people of Cortona flock there, but the inhabitants of neighboring cities, villages and towns also come in large numbers. However, since no mention is made of Margaret herself in the masses and offices which are celebrated that day, for she is neither canonized nor listed in the catalog of saints, many of those who go there are filled with astonishment.[21]

Leo X granted permission for a special office to fill this liturgical void, which had lasted for more than two centuries but which, despite what he said, does not seem to have greatly preoccupied the clergy and the faithful of Cortona and its region.

Nevertheless, it would be wrong to conclude that the communes where the bodies of these saints lay were not interested in obtaining official recognition of their cults from the Roman Church. On the contrary, many documents demonstrate that in the thirteenth and early fourteenth centuries the Italian cities spared no efforts in attempting to secure their canonization. For example, in 1260 Perugia sent ambassadors to the Curia to request the canonization of Bevignate, a local penitent who had died in odor of sanctity several decades earlier.[22] Treviso had the same goal in mind in 1317, in the early days of the devotion for the Blessed Rigo, (or Enrico of Bolzano).[23] In 1318, the commune of Cortona sent two priests to Avignon to try to interest some cardinals in the cause of St. Margaret (†1297).[24] But all of these efforts to induce the Holy See to ratify the new local cults failed, some because of insufficient evidence of the genuine sanctity of the candidates for pontifical approbation, others—this happened more often— because the cities in question lacked financial resources and influential friends in the Curia.[25] Indeed, after the mid-thirteenth century, canonizations became rarer and more difficult to obtain. The procedure had become more complex, and local collectivities quickly realized they lacked the resources for this subtle game whose rules were unfamiliar to them.[26] Even when they ventured into it, they soon discovered that they were not equal to it and that their objective was beyond their grasp.

What could be done under these circumstances? The papacy paid no attention to the great majority of local saints, but the popular pressure in their favor kept on intensifying.[27] The Italian communes did not hesitate: they proceeded on their own initiative and with the support of the local clergy, both secular and regular, to *de facto* canonizations, rendering the honors of a civic cult to those whom they considered to be authentic servants of God. The first sign that they had taken charge of the process was the inclusion of the saint's day among the holidays on which no work was done. The communal statutes of each Italian city contained a rubric *De feriis*, which sometimes varied considerably from one city to the next and which evolved in the course of time, moreover, as it was enriched by successive additions. In these texts, the notion of *feria* [holiday] originally had a precise juridical meaning. A distinction needs to be drawn between holidays *in criminalibus*, which were quite rare (generally, these were major holidays like Christmas, Good Friday and Easter), and holidays *in civilibus*, that is to say, when the ordinary tribunals did not hold session. The latter were far more numerous: they corresponded to the feast days of a number of saints, headed by the Virgin and St. John the Baptist, who were venerated in all of Christendom, to which were added those of the particular intercessors designated by each city in the course of its existence.[28] On these occasions the shops had to remain closed or risk being fined; crimes committed then were punished twice as severely as usual. In addition, penalties were set for those who blasphemed the names of the saints, and measures were sometimes taken to prevent prostitutes on the day of the ceremony from stationing themselves around the church where the relics lay.[29]

The final step in the formation of a civic cult was proclaiming the new saint the official patron of the city. The speed with which this happened varied from city to city. In Treviso, the Blessed Rigo appears in the official records alongside St. Liberale, the traditional patron of the commune, in 1316, scarcely one year after his death.[30] The new intercessor generally had to be content with a place beside the older official protector of the city. Sometimes, however, he took over entirely, as we see in the case of Poggibonsi, where the Blessed Lucchese, at first invoked along with and in the same capacity as St. Lawrence, supplanted him definitively as of 1320 in his function as "defender and protector of the said commune."[31] This promotion was usually marked by the construction of a church or chapel placed under the protection of the new patron and entirely financed by the commune, whose property it remained. This was the case in Perugia at the end of the thirteenth century, where the municipal authorities arranged for a church dedicated to St. Bevignate to be built. To avoid difficulties with the ecclesiastical hierarchy, a chapel under the patronage of St. Jerome was added, thus allowing John XXII to approve the founding of a "church commonly called St. Bevignate, with a chapel to St. Jerome."[32] In Cortona, in as early as 1297 the commune began construction of a new church adjoining that of San Basilio, where the body of St. Margaret lay in a magnificent stone tomb. The two edifices together took the name of *ecclesia sancti Basilii et sanctae Margaritae de Cortona*, the church of St. Basil and St. Margaret of Cortona. When it was completed, the municipality entrusted it first to the secular clergy, and then in 1392 to the Franciscan order.[33] If a city was more modest or less wealthy, it settled for building a chapel to honor its new patron in the cathedral or the local monastery of the religious order to which he had belonged in his lifetime; of course, the city retained the right of patronage over the chapel.[34]

Thus in fourteenth-century Italy, cults of saints came under the jurisdiction of public authorities, just like the policing of the markets or the streets. What if a religious community desired the translation of the remains of one of its members from a monastery in the town? It had to obtain the assent of the municipal authorities as well as that of the bishop.[35] What if the bishop wanted to authenticate the relics? He was always accompanied by the *podestà* and representatives of the public authorities.[36] Nothing that concerned the servants of God escaped the attention of the commune, so strong was their conviction that by their intercession the prosperity of the city was guaranteed and concord maintained among the citizens. And if by chance the clergy were remiss or failed to perform their duty toward the patron saints of the city, civil authorities took their place in rendering to the protectors their rightful honors. The communes considered themselves principally in charge of and responsible for the cults honoring their heavenly patrons. For example, when in 1378 the council of Poggibonsi pondered how the feast day of the Blessed Lucchese could be celebrated, since the city was under an interdict and the Franciscans had had to leave town, it decided that the ceremony would take place nevertheless, and took measures to endow it with its usual solemnity.[37]

––––––⟨⟩––––––

Now that we have described and analyzed the importance of civic cults of saints in the communes of fourteenth-century Italy, we must do our best to account for this singular phenomenon. We can accomplish this by proceeding backwards, retracing the steps that lead back to the inception of these devotions. Sometimes they were rooted in popular enthusiasm: when a "man of God" (or a saintly woman) died, his fellow citizens who had known him during his life would proclaim him saint, and a "popular outpouring of emotion" like that in Treviso following the Blessed Rigo's death in 1315 would force the commune, as it were, to take charge of the newborn cult.[38] However, this was not the most frequent case. Most commonly, devotions arose and developed within the boundaries of limited groups which gradually endeavored to convince the urban collectivity to adopt the cult in question. For example, the recognition of the cult of the Blessed Andrea Gallerani (†1251) by the commune of Siena in 1347 probably testified to the increased power held by the hospital and the confraternity of the Misericordia which he had founded, and which alone had venerated this pious layman for almost a century. It could also have been a sign of the growing influence of the Gallerani family within the Sienese ruling class, as a phrase in the petition addressed to the Council by the promoters of his cult might lead us to think.[39] A similar case dates from that very year, 1347, in Orvieto, where the Council passed a decree instituting the feast day of the Blessed Pietro Parenzo (†1199) and placing the city under his protection.[40] Pietro was no unknown figure in that city: as *podestà* of Orvieto at the end of the twelfth century, he had distinguished himself by his ferocity in the struggle against the heretics, a category he seems to have enlarged to include all of his political adversaries, whether Cathar or not—and who eventually assassinated him.[41] When asked to raise Pietro Parenzo to the altar, Innocent III refused to pronounce on his sanctity, but the clergy and the Guelfs in Orvieto organized a local cult nonetheless. In the thirteenth century his feast day was regularly celebrated in the cathedral where his remains were buried, and a *vita* composed around 1250 was added to the lectionary. But the commune did not officially recognize this cult until a century later, when the Guelf party triumphed definitively in the city.[42]

Among the groups who brought pressure to bear on the civil authorities, religious communities were not the least active: they intervened both directly and through the confraternities that grew up around them. But they still needed an important event to spotlight the worth and above all the powers of their hero. The small town of Amandola, in the Marches, has exemplary documentation on this subject. Its *Libri di riformanze* allow us to follow over more than a half-century the vicissitudes of the cult of a monk in the local monastery of the Hermits of St. Augustine, the Blessed Anthony. This figure, renowned for his ascetic ardor and the sanctity of his life, must have been highly esteemed by the townspeople because the day after he died in 1450, the commune decided to bring a candle worth 50 soldi to the church of the Augustinians each year on the anniversary of his death.[43] The contribution from the commune remained at this modest level until 1477, when a member of the council put the following resolution to a vote:

> Since the almighty and all powerful God in his mercy has saved our land, that is Amandola and its territories, from the plague which contaminated various regions, and since we believe that this happened thanks to the prayers of the blessed Anthony, who prays and intercedes for us with God and his heavenly court, do you agree that a gift should be made to the chapel of the blessed Anthony in the church of the Augustinians of this town, so that the blessed Anthony himself will pray to the divine majesty and the heavenly court to deign to protect our city and its *contado* in the future from epidemics, plague, and the illness of cankers, and he will deliver us in his clemency and his mercy?[44]

The thirteen counselors present voted unanimously in favor of the resolution.

One might wonder what reasons lay behind this promotion of the Blessed Anthony, who twenty-seven years after his death replaced the traditional patron saint of the town, St. Donatus, and henceforth enjoyed an annual offering of candles worth ten pounds, instead of the 50 soldi of the period before 1477.* The Hermits of St. Augustine probably influenced the decision of the public authorities: in a period of crisis, the order succeeded in winning recognition of the merits of a monk who, although he certainly was well known, had remained in the lower ranks of the local pantheon until then. But other factors could have played a role in this decision, whose exact motivation escapes us.

Such reclassifications of civic cults generally took place in a harmonious atmosphere, because the decision of the municipal authorities accomodated popular sentiment and the aspirations of some element of the ecclesiastical institution. But in cases where differences of opinion happened to arise, they disclosed even more clearly the roles of the various groups in the life of the cults. In Spoleto, for example, at the end of the fourteenth century, a polemic flared over who should be given credit for the victory of the city troops in 1391 over Tommaso da Chiavano and Gaspare Pazzi of Arezzo, who had attacked them with a thousand men. After the combat, the local leader of the Guelf party claimed that he had witnessed an apparition of St. Peter Martyr, the famous Dominican inquisitor, and that his supernatural intervention had played a decisive role in the victory of the Spoletan forces, a victory which moreover had taken place on his feast day. The Council of Spoleto immediately passed a decree stating that henceforth the feast day of St. Peter Martyr would be celebrated by the commune every year, and that all of the city's clergy and civil authorities would make a procession to the church of the Dominicans to present an offering of 30 pounds of wax, at the city's expense. This clause must have seemed exorbitant to the secular clergy: in 1397, when Spoleto had returned to the jurisdiction of the Holy See, they had the decree revoked by the rector of the duchy. In the new text that the rector published, the victory of 1391, on the strength of certain "prophetic persons," was reascribed to the Virgin Mary, patron of the cathedral of Spoleto. As a result, from then on the solemn ceremony of thanksgiving was to take place in the cathedral, where civil and religious authorities would go to offer candles of three pounds each. But to avoid open conflict with the Dominicans and the Guelfs, it was stipulated that the procession would then go to San Salvatore, the church of the Dominicans, bringing two candles of three pounds each. The remaining twelve pounds were to be distributed as alms to the religious who participated in the procession.[45] This kind of incident is significant insofar as it demonstrates how the balance of power among the groups and their respective dynamism condition the life of the cults. Thus many conflicts over patronage reflect internal tensions among the clergy, in particular the conflict between regular and secular clergy or the rivalry between the mendicant orders. For when the commune assumed responsibility for a cult, the associations which constituted the basic building blocks of urban society received what they had sought: the legitimation and public recognition of their own role in public life. It was rare, however, that these rivalries led to violent conflicts. More often, a compromise would be reached that satisfied all parties, as was the case in Spoleto in 1397, or else a new cult would find a place next to the older ones without overshadowing them.

If the reasons which led various groups and collectivities to promote the cults of their own privileged intercessors to the highest level—that of the city—are obvious, we still may wonder what advantages the communes could derive from multiplying the number of their patrons in this way, especially in cases where they already had prestigious patron saints. What did a city like Siena (which already was the city of the Virgin, as the inscriptions on its coins indicated) have to gain from placing itself under the protection of obscure or at least secondary figures like the Blessed Ambrogio Sansedoni, Pietro Pettinaio (or Pettignano), or Agostino Novello, as it did in 1328?[46] To answer this question, we need only cite the words of the guardian of the Franciscans of Siena, when he addressed the council that year to urge the passage of a statute that would mandate the regular celebration of the feast day of the Franciscan tertiary Pietro Pettinaio (†1289): "The more advocates—good advocates—our city has in the court of the One who is its defender, that is, God himself, the greater its chance of remaining entirely secure."[47]

In saying this, the monk clearly knew that he was sounding a sensitive note. The quest for the greatest possible number of intercessors was indeed one of the characteristic traits of religious piety in the later centuries of the Middle Ages. It even influenced the "cultic policy" of the Italian communes which, as they extended their influence over the surrounding *contado*, secured any relics found there and transferred them to the city. This was true of Perugia, which deprived the town of Antoniola of the body of St. Ercolano in 1278 and built a beautiful church dedicated to this sainted bishop within its own walls between 1295 and 1300.[48] Similarly, in 1440 Astorgio II Manfredi, lord of Faenza, had one of St. Savino's arms, which belonged to the rural church of San Savino in Fusignano, brought to the cathedral, where a silver tabernacle was built to receive it.[49] This aspect of the subjugation of the countryside to the city has been little investigated, but it is worth studying because it would bring to light an important step of the process which led to the formation of city-states in the fourteenth and fifteenth centuries.

The search for new protectors was not haphazard. What the communes particularly desired were saints who could be theirs exclusively. St. Ercolano was a bishop of Perugia who was decapitated by the Goths in 547, and the city therefore considered that it had a legitimate title to his body. For similar reasons (though they operated in the opposite direction), Bologna stopped counting St. Ambrose among its protectors and promoted its former bishop, St. Petronio, to the position of sole patron saint, because the name of Ambrose was too closely connected with Milan, the city with which he had come to be identified.[50] In the fourteenth century, every urban agglomeration, no matter how small, aspired to possess its own saint. This is apparent in the case of Siena, where in 1329 the Dominican prior reproached in these terms the members of the council of the commune, who had decided for financial reasons to suspend the participation of the municipal authorities in the feast days of new saints: "There is no Tuscan city which does not have a saint of its very own and which does not venerate him with a ceremonial feast day."[51] The argument was clever and bore fruit. Moreover, the prior found opportune words to evoke the merits of the Blessed Ambrogio Sansedoni (†1287): "your noble fellow-citizen whom you knew, to whom you listened, whom you loved in entire purity of heart and with great respect, one whom your own hands touched."[52]

For his part the guardian of the Franciscans used similar arguments, emphasizing the fact that "the blessed Pietro [Pettignano] was a native of this city and because of this natural love he feels particular benevolence toward your city and his fellow citizens."[53]

Similar examples could easily be multiplied, but I will cite only the case of Bevignate, in Perugia. Nothing specific was known about this figure, whom the papacy had repeatedly refused to canonize in the thirteenth century, but that did not prevent the commune from celebrating his feast day from 1342 on. A century later, in 1453, the Council sought to justify this public cult in the following terms: "St. Bevignate, whose church is in an outlying part of town, near the Porta Sole, was born and lived in our *contado*, and, his legend tells us that it was in our city that he met a commendable and pious death."[54] We could hardly find it stated more explicitly that the cult of "Saint" Bevignate was ultimately based on the fact that he was a native of the region of Perugia and that he had left his remains to his townspeople! In this way, new patron saints—beatified locals who had died a few decades before, or traditional saints whose relics had been brought to the city—took their place next to the old ones. The strict signification of the notion of "patron" thereby yielded to vaguer concepts like "special protector" or "defender of the commune," titles which the new intercessors shared with the traditional ones. What had come to matter most for contemporaries was that both old and new saints be considered the city's property.

─────── ⊂⊙⊐ ───────

Various explanations might be offered for the development of this civic religion, which we have attempted to delineate in one very interesting, but certainly not unique, manifestation, the cult of the saints. Some have claimed to see in it the signs of a decline of Christian universalism: the proliferation of new intercessors, often chosen from among the "minor" uncanonized saints; the strictly local patriotism which in every city predominated in their selection—all this seemed to testify to a Christianity splintered by the pressure of emerging particularism. From Salimbeni to Salutati, many clerics and cultivated people lamented the perverse spirit which drove the faithful to turn away from the great traditional saints of the Church and embrace these obscure personages.[55] But were not these moralizing clerics—not to mention the modern historians who have placed so much trust in their diatribes—perhaps committing an error of valuation? It is true that in becoming more popular, the cult of the saints was vulgarized as well, and it came to fulfill certain functions that were not specifically religious, in the sense this term has today. In the countryside, the devotions became folklorized, and their eventual forms have attracted the attention of ethnologists and, more recently, historians.[56] This phenomenon has its parallel in urban settings: in late-medieval Italian communes, cults of saints were so thoroughly integrated into social life that they became a fundamental element of it. In this privileged form of civic religion, laypeople found a way to safeguard their autonomy from the encroachments of the clergy. But perhaps it was precisely these inextricable overlappings of the sacred and the profane, the political and the religious, that enabled the cult of the saints to hold its ground and flourish in new ways for many centuries in Italy. In the North, in contrast, where this cult was essentially managed by clerics, wherever the Reformation prevailed, it had no trouble expunging with the stroke of a pen a set of beliefs and practices which the urban bourgeoisie of the sixteenth century considered to be nothing more than superstitions nourished by the Church to maintain its hold on the masses and exert its influence on the life of the city.[57] In what only seems to be a paradox, the civic religion of the late Middle Ages, by establishing a close relationship between religious life, popular piety, and civic institutions, ensured the survival of devotions which were not imposed from above but instead emanated from the basic constituent elements of urban society. Beginning in the seventeenth century, the papacy's attempt to regularize the canonical position of these intercessors, most of whom had no official status, led to a large number of beatifications and canonizations *ex cultu immemorabili*, of which the majority of these local Italian saints were beneficiaries.[58] It was the least the Church could do for them, for they had rendered her more service than she could imagine!

A final comment will help to fix the exact meaning of this study and the implications of its conclusions. As the reader has surely noticed, the appearance of new intercessors and the doubling of the number of civic patrons, with new saints reigning next to the old, were phenomena witnessed most often in cities with small or middle-sized populations. The largest Italian cities, with rare exceptions like Siena, generally remained faithful to their traditional patron saints or, in any case, to traditional saints with whom they tended to identify in their mental representations and sometimes even in their iconography: in the fourteenth century, Milan remained the city of St. Ambrose and Venice was identified more than ever with St. Mark, and even his lion.[59] In contrast, communes that achieved their liberty late or with difficulty, like Cortona or Poggibonsi, demonstrated a marked preference for modernizing or renewing the city's calendar of saints. But it is by no means certain that the growth of civic cults of saints which we have noted in the fourteenth century is a sign of the vitality of communal government. Instead, various indications could lead us to think that this proliferation of urban devotions was a symptom of the crisis, or even the decadence, of these institutions: cities tended to exult all the more in their own particularism in this sphere as their real power and their ability to resist lay or clerical pressure groups grew weaker.[60] Like noble families that jealously treasured their emblems and coats of arms in periods when their political decline was well underway, Italian communes of moderate size in the fourteenth century seemed to vaunt the particularity of their own cults of saints just at the time when their spheres of influence and their margins of autonomy had begun to shrink. If this assertion is justified, the growth of civic religion at the end of the Middle Ages, rather than being evidence of the splintering of Christianity, would testify to the profound crisis of communal government, condemned to unavoidable change.

PART III

WOMEN'S CHOICE: HUMAN MARRIAGE OR SPIRITUAL NUPTIALS

FOURTEEN

FEMALE SANCTITY IN THE FRANCISCAN MOVEMENT

AT THE RISK OF OFFENDING my readers, I will begin this essay with a few statistics—not in order to conform to the current fashion for quantification, which is not a great help in a domain as complex and as delicate as the history of spirituality, but to call attention to some especially striking evidence. Thus, if we consider the group of women who were the objects of canonization proceedings instituted by the papacy between 1198 and 1431, we find that five, that is to say fully half of them, were attached in some way to the Franciscan movement. In chronological order, these five were St. Elisabeth of Thuringia or Hungary (†1231), Rose of Viterbo (†1251), St. Clare of Assisi (†1253), St. Clare of Montefalco (†1308) and Delphine of Puimichel (or of Sabran, if we use the name of her husband), who died in 1360. This is a high percentage whose significance is obvious. Moreover, the conservation, at least in part, of the original transactions of these investigations, which provide the historian with material of the highest value, makes possible a thorough study of the religious experience of these women and of the impressions they produced on their contemporaries.[1] It is more difficult to measure the impact of the ideal of St. Francis at the level of local cults—those not officially recognized by the Roman church—because we are not able to compile a complete list of the women who had an aura of sanctity in the eyes of their contemporaries in the final centuries of the Middle Ages. But the surviving *vitae* and collections of miracles, as well as iconographic

171

evidence, allow us to be certain that a significant number of holy women were affiliated with the Franciscan movement, even if we exclude those who at a later date, and without foundation, were said to have been members of the third order. Without any claim to exhaustivity, we can cite the names of Filippa Mareri (†1236), Umiliana dei Cerchi (†1246), Douceline, the sister of Hugues of Digne (†1274), Margaret of Cortona (†1297), Angela of Foligno (†1309), and Micheline of Pesaro (†1356). All of these women were natives of Italy or Provence, but the Mediterranean region did not have a monopoly in this regard. For central Europe, we need only mention Agnes of Bohemia or of Prague (†c. 1280), and two queens of Poland, Salomea (†1268) and Kinga (†1292), who joined the order of Poor Clares as widows; and, elsewhere in Christendom, tertiaries or penitents like Elisabeth of Portugal (†1336), Jeanne-Marie of Maillé (†1414) in France, Elisabeth of Reute in Austria (†1420) and many others whom space does not permit us to list here.

This burst of Franciscan sanctity was part of the more general efflorescence of female sanctity characteristic of the end of the Middle Ages. It stands in sharp contrast to previous centuries, during which Heaven—or at least the official pantheon—remained relatively closed to women.[2] While fewer than ten percent of the new intercessors venerated in the West between 500 and 1200 were female, the proportion rose markedly after that date. Of all of the canonization proceedings instituted by the papacy between 1198 and 1431, more than 18 percent concerned women (though only 14.8 percent of those resulted in approved canonizations). The increase may seem meager in global terms, but if we eliminate the canonized bishops, all of whom were necessarily male, and the members of the traditional religious orders (Benedictines, canons regular), much higher percentages result: 21.4 percent of the saints belonging to mendicant orders were female, and of the lay saints, more than half (58.5 percent) were women! Thus if we consider the total number of candidates for canonization after 1200 that the Roman church acknowledged, or at least was willing to take into consideration, we can speak without exaggeration of a very clear tendency, especially marked among the new categories, toward a feminization of sanctity.[3] There is no doubt that the Franciscan ideal and the activities of the Franciscan friars—and those of the

Dominicans as well—played an important and even decisive role in this change of direction.

This was no easy task, because the image of woman transmitted by the clerical mentality hardly favored assigning the title of saint to a daughter of Eve. Monastic tradition, outdoing even the misogynist observations of St. Jerome, who was much read and discussed in the eleventh and twelfth centuries, had insisted on the close ties between woman and sin.[4] In the numerous treatises of the era devoted to the *contemptus mundi*, women were generally presented as creatures incapable of spiritual reflection and understanding: frivolous, fickle and inconstant, they aroused nothing in these authors but mistrust and castigation.[5] The acerbic criticism spared only a few rare women, mostly queens or great aristocrats, who by force of character had been able to overcome the faults common to their sex.[6] Women operated under a dual handicap that usually prevented them from attaining sainthood: their physical and moral weakness, about which their male contemporaries had no doubt, and their status in the Church, which condemned them to a passive role, except in the rare cases in which birth or marriage opened the way for actions which they could take to support clerical undertakings. Even when they aspired to a more intense religious life, they could only satisfy their desires by entering a monastery.[7]

In the second half of the twelfth century, this situation began to change, under the impact of a group of phenomena that cannot all be studied here, but whose consequences were soon felt in the religious realm. Under the influence of Marian spirituality, which was then at the height of its popularity, the role of women in the history of salvation came to be evaluated in a less negative fashion. "If our Lord wanted to be born of a woman, it was not only for the sake of men but also for the sake of women," wrote Pope Alexander III in 1173 in a letter addressed to the master of the Order of St. James, where he stated unequivocally that the wives and widows of knights who belonged to it could legitimately be considered members of a religious order with the same privileges as their husbands.[8] A few years later, St. Hugh of Avallon (†1200), a Carthusian monk who had become bishop of Lincoln, went even further, stressing that "to no man was it granted to be called the father of God, but to a woman alone was it accorded to be God's mother."[9]

We cannot rule out the possibility that the Church's new open-
ness was largely opportunistic, given that this was a time when
women were responding with particular warmth to heretical
movements, which offered in them a way of overcoming the handi-
caps that burdened their existence.[10] Thus we see how new forms
of religious life adapted to the needs of the laity were developed
between 1180 and 1230. In the Low Countries (in the broad
sense of the term) numerous groups of Beguines joined work and
prayer within the framework of communal, non-cloistered life.[11]
Similar congregations soon sprang up in the Rhineland.[12] Comparable associations existed in Italy as well, but there the pious
faithful seem to have preferred to pursue holiness *in domibus
propriis*, in their own homes, which accounts for the success of
the third order of the *Umiliati* and, especially, that of the Order of
Penance (or of Penitents) in its various forms.[13] Often, the widows
and unmarried girls who joined these groups remained in their
own homes, where they led an existence consecrated to prayer,
penitence, and works of mercy. In some cases they obtained the
authorization of the bishop or local clergy to shut themselves up
in cells or other places of reclusion, where they lived from the
work of their hands and from alms given by individuals or by the
community.[14] For their part, married women, like their husbands,
could belong to communities of penitents, or later to tertiaries,
who ordered their lives according to a *propositum*, which was
more an ideal standard than a rule in the strict sense, since it did
not entail taking permanent vows and transgressing its injunctions
was not considered to be a fault, juridically speaking.[15]

It is within this rapidly changing spiritual and institutional framework that we must situate the various forms of female sanctity.
The prominence that the Franciscan movement quickly assumed
amid this cultural ferment is not surprising, given the great impact
of their preaching on the laity from the start. Women seem to
have been particularly susceptible to the lure of the Franciscans,
if we can believe the many literary texts in which the friars are accused of systematically trying to win their favor in order to extend
their influence over lay society.[16] However, it would be wrong
to see nothing more in this movement than a simple reflection
of the masculine model, as defined by the Church through the
canonization of St. Francis of Assisi and St. Anthony of Padua. The

situation of women in thirteenth-century society prevented them from putting the rule of St. Francis into practice without modifying it in important ways. Besides, the *Poverello* initially had no more intention of founding a female religious order than had St. Norbert in the twelfth century or his own contemporary St. Dominic. The evangelical life of the Franciscans, defined by surrender to the will of Providence, apostleship by example and word, and mobility, could not have been thought suitable for the "weaker sex." Thus, when St. Francis received St. Clare and her first companions, all he could imagine doing was having them enter a monastery to lead a claustral life. This institutional setting was evidently not propitious for the realization of the ideal which he heralded and which had drawn the women to him.[17] But a careful examination of St. Clare's canonization proceedings, writings, and biography shows that, despite being hemmed in by constraints, she was able to bring to fruition an original spirituality that was quite different from that of the Benedictine nuns. It was distinguished, first of all, by its emphasis on humility and poverty. Her desire for abasement long led her to reject obstinately all hierarchical offices and titles; and we know that even when she was forced to accept the title of abbess, she willingly washed the feet of the sisters placed under her authority.[18] Above all, throughout her life she manifested a jealous and single-minded zeal for defending and winning papal recognition of the "privilege of poverty," which she correctly considered to be the cornerstone of her rule.[19]

In matters of piety and devotion, Clare's spiritual experience may seem relatively commonplace. As with most female saints of her era, meditation on the Passion of Christ and his suffering, along with contemplation of his humanity, played a central role.[20] She attempted to reach God by recalling the sorrowful mysteries, especially those of the Cross. She does not seem, however, to have experienced "mystic states" in the exact meaning of the term, even if some of the depositions at her canonization proceedings described phenomena related to rapture or ecstasy.[21] What distinguished St. Clare was rather her extreme asceticism and the severity of the penances she inflicted upon herself. Whereas for St. Francis and St. Dominic asceticism was simply a means of arriving at interior liberty, and thus excluded the pursuit of pain for its own sake or suffering taken to an extreme, in the female Franciscan (or Dominican) saints moderation was completely lacking and mortification seemed rather to be a fundamental feature of Christian perfection. Clare's abstinence, as evidenced by her taking only a little bread and water during two Lenten seasons and sleeping on a bed of vine-shoots, was admired by her companions.[22] This is not simply a hagiographical commonplace, for we know that St. Francis intervened to ask her to mitigate her fasts, a request to which she assented with sorrow, out of a spirit of obedience. In her opinion, in fact— and this connects her with the penitential movement that had developed in lay circles—asceticism was the best way to prepare oneself for the meeting with the heavenly Spouse. This same desire for ever greater conformity with Christ also informed her longing for martyrdom and her fierce attachment to safeguarding her virginity.[23] These attitudes were present as well in the male Franciscan saints of the period, but in a less pronounced form, and in their lives we do not find the atmosphere of exaltation which gave female sanctity its paroxystic quality. St. Clare and the women who in her footsteps sought holiness within the order of Poor Clares behaved as if they were striving, through their extremes of heroism, to transcend the narrow limits within which they spent their everyday lives.[24]

Most of the female saints who were associated with Franciscan spirituality in the final centuries of the Middle Ages were not nuns, however: it was clearly easier to remain faithful to the spirit of St. Francis by living in the world than by withdrawing to a cloister. Among the laywomen who achieved sanctity without renouncing their worldly status, it is possible, without being too arbitrary, to distinguish two principal movements, or rather two tendencies, because what separated them were differences of emphasis, not sharply contrasting features. The first group gave primacy to an evangelical spirituality centered on poverty and on love of one's neighbor, as manifested by the practice of works of mercy. The woman who best incarnated this ideal was undoubtedly St. Elisabeth of Thuringia, who can still be grouped with the Franciscan movement even if it is now certain that she never belonged to their third order. To her, the essential point was charity, which she conceived as an active commitment to the service of the poor, whose life and suffering she strove to share.[25] Having refused to enter a monastery after the death of her husband in 1227, she donned the robe of a penitent in order to be able to put herself totally at the service of the poor.[26] But this love for the underprivileged was inseparable from her search for humility. We know from her servants that she refused to let herself be called *domina* and that she insisted that they address her with the familiar form of the pronoun "you."[27] Her most heartfelt desire was that she be allowed to beg, but her spiritual director, the terrible inquisitor Conrad of Marburg, expressly forbade it, thereby provoking a bitter conflict between them.[28]

Elisabeth's sanctity was not defined by her charity alone, which went far beyond the ceremonial, and her compassion toward the poor, whom she considered to be figures of Christ. The picture would be incomplete if we did not prominently include her keen sense of justice and injustice. During her husband's life, this obsessive preoccupation led her to abstain from "impure" dishes, that it to say, all food produced by exactions levied on the humble people or the Church, consumption of which would have weighed on her conscience.[29] This refusal to compromise with evil, including its political and economic manifestations, led her eventually to engage in a veritable mysticism of impoverishment. After her husband's death, she renounced all of her worldly goods in order to give a little bit of joy and happiness to the ill and the leprous.[30]

The blessed Delphine of Puimichel took the same path of total poverty: in the middle of the fourteenth century, she still remained touchingly faithful to the original Franciscan ideals.[31] After the death of her husband, St. Elzéar of Sabran (†1323), who like her belonged to one of the leading families of the Provençal aristocracy, she gradually divested herself of all her possessions, to the horror of the local nobility. Despite the misgivings of King Robert, she then retired to an almshouse at Cabrières, then to Apt, where she lived as a recluse; from time to time she went out to beg in the streets, where she was sometimes scorned as a "crazy Beguine." Her experience of absolute poverty was entirely in conformity with the program of the Franciscan Spirituals, with whom she maintained very close relations.[32] But other themes, particularly her impassioned attachment to maintaining her virginity even in marriage, endowed Delphine's spirituality with genuine originality.[33]

However, this current, whose aim was to remain faithful to the fundamental ideas of the *Poverello*, was not the most representative of female sanctity within the Franciscan obedience. To be sure, all women who were inspired by the message of St. Francis devoted a large part of their lives to charity and the love of mankind. But very quickly, probably under the influence of the Franciscans themselves, the emphasis shifted from the exaltation of poverty to the pursuit of asceticism and, especially, of mystical experiences, which beginning in the last decades of the thirteenth century became one of the main criteria for the evaluation of sanctity. The historian's problem is to determine how and under what influences this change of emphasis came about. In some cases, this shift was visible in the biographies of these holy women, whose lives began with the most compassionate acts of charity and ended in lofty contemplation. Since it is not possible to study all of the cases in detail, I will limit myself here to a specific example, which is all the more significant in that it is very early: the case of the Blessed Umiliana dei Cerchi, whose life story was written as early as 1247 by the Franciscan Vito of Cortona.[34] Daughter of a rich Florentine merchant who had a beautiful house and a tower right in the center of the city, Umiliana was married at the age of sixteen to a man quite a bit older than her. From this union, which was manifestly not a happy one, two daughters were born. After six years of life together, Umiliana's husband died and she was left a widow. Her family pressed her to remarry, but she categorically refused, for she had "begun to scorn the pomp and ornaments of the world" and had thrown herself wholeheartedly into prayer and good works.[35]

Before going on, we should pause for a moment to consider the critical role of the theme of marriage—or rejection of marriage— in the lives of the female saints being discussed here. With rare exceptions, the most notable being St. Elisabeth, who felt deep (and reciprocated) affection for her husband, landgrave Louis of Thuringia, they seemed to have experienced conjugal life as a psychologically traumatic trial. In this they were not unlike many women of their day who, wishing to escape from the dismal conditions of a marriage contracted for economic reasons and in response to family pressures, could avail themselves of only two solutions: debauchery, which was abundantly illustrated by a whole literature of satire ranging from French *fabliaux* to Tuscan *novelle*, or continence, which, as the case may be, took the form either of the couple's *a priori* refusal of all sexual activity (as was the case for Delphine and Elzéar of Sabran), or the progressive renunciation of physical union on the part of the husband and wife. Far from representing an opportunity for personal growth, marriage was portrayed in the hagiographic texts of the thirteenth and fourteenth centuries as the consummate occasion for alienation.[36] Thus, in order to affirm their own existence and liberty, the female saints were led to reject the institution of matrimony in all of its forms, especially in its patrimonial aspects, which constituted its principal foundation in medieval society. For example, St. Elisabeth was forced to leave Wartburg after the death of her husband because her brother-in-law, Heinrich Raspe, allowed her only a single *sustentatio* at the common table, just one portion for herself and her children.[37] Similarly, their rejection of the matrimonial strategies mapped out by their families explains the violence of the conflicts provoked by female Franciscan saints when they decided to embrace religious life. In his life of St. Clare, Thomas of Celano vividly describes her parents' anger when she ran off to join St. Francis, and their efforts, which almost succeeded, to drag her sister Agnes away by force when she went to join Clare in the cloister.[38] Nearly identical scenes appear in the life of Filippa Mareri, the "baroness saint," who clashed with her brother Thomas when she left the family castle and whose monastery was actually assailed by the family when her mother Imperatrice also went there to retire from the world.[39] This psychological and social context helps to explain some of the extreme attitudes of the female saints who viewed their physical appearance with hatred and scorn. For some, this could lead to attempts at self-destruction through asceticism or deliberate self-mutilation: for example, every time her father, King Bela IV, tried to remove St. Margaret of Hungary (†1271) from her Dominican convent and marry her to a prince or a sovereign, she threatened to cut off her nose to make herself hideous.[40] Repulsed at being viewed as no more than bodies and pawns in marital strategies, women found that the religious life, which legitimized and sanctified virginity both inside and outside of the convent, provided the liberty and autonomy that civil society refused them.

Let us return to Umiliana dei Cerchi, whose refusal to remarry caused her many hardships. Her father used it as a reason to dispossess her of all of her goods, including even the portion of her inheritance which was rightfully hers, and her daughters were taken by her husband's family.[41] She was allotted only a small quantity of food, brought to her each day in the room, or rather the cell where she lived, in the tower of the familial palace. But this did not reduce her zeal for the poor, to whom she had devoted herself ever since the early months of her marriage. Now lacking resources of her own, she called on the wealthy ladies of patrician Florence and distributed the money she collected to the poor, particularly to the *pauperes verecundi* whom she visited in their homes.[42] According to her biographer, she tried in vain to join the Poor Clares of Monticelli. In the absence of any explanation, we can only note this fact and associate it with the rejection that another contemporary female saint, Rose of Viterbo, encountered when she sought to enter the ranks of the Poor Clares of her city.[43] Vito of Cortona considered her lack of success a providential event, since it allowed Umiliana to "shine for everyone in the house, that is, in the Church militant," and he did not hesitate to present her as the founder of a way of life as new as it was holy: the practice of penitence in the midst of the world.[44]

In fact, under the influence of her spiritual director, Brother Michele degli Alberti, Umiliana had taken the habit of a Franciscan penitent and had become a Beguine recluse. It is difficult to define Michele's role with precision on the basis of a hagiographic text, but some of the events and comments reported by Umiliana's biographer lead us to think that he influenced her piety in two ways. First of all, he seems to have turned her away from the "temptation of the desert" that was felt so strongly by women of the era. Let us recall that one of the very first Clarissan saints, Filippa Mareri, had created a community of female hermits in the mountainous region east of Rieti before she met St. Francis and adopted the rule and life of the Poor Clares.[45] In Umiliana's case, the theme of the solitary retreat to the desert was present on several levels. Her biographer indicated in passing that she was in contact with a Camaldolese hermit named Simon and that she herself would have liked to live in an inaccessible place in order to meditate freely on God.[46] Some of her friends seem to have shared that desire.[47] The actions of Brother Michele and the Franciscans of Santa Croce tended to channel and "socialize" these women's enthusiasm for asceticism, which they judged to be excessive and dangerous: that is why Umiliana had to constrain herself to remain in her tower in the middle of the city, and lead there in plain view the life of a recluse devoted to penitence and prayer.[48] This austere way of life, which Vito of Cortona affirmed to be in no way inferior to that of anchorites and monks, was thus enriched with a pastoral sense. Better than "savage" hermits could, Umiliana demonstrated that it was possible to live outside of the world while remaining in it, a lesson which constituted an authentic *exemplum*.[49]

But Umiliana's spirituality, as it appears in her *vita*, bore the mark of another orientation, which was certainly not foreign to the Franciscans in her entourage. Under their influence, the saint gradually renounced the works of mercy and charity to which she had devoted herself for many years, and dedicated herself ever more to contemplation and the pursuit of mystical graces. Indeed, her biographer inveighs in passing against a group of unnamed people, whom he designates with the vague term *carnales qui sunt in ecclesia*, whose principal fault is to have tried to involve Umiliana in worldly matters.[50] He is undoubtedly referring to clerics, perhaps secular clergy, who urged her to attend actively to the problems of the city and become involved in a militant way. Their promptings are presented in the form of a series of diabolical temptations which appeared to the saint in visions and urged her to leave her tower to go to people's aid. In a succession of visions she witnessed her own daughters dying, her sister-in-law Ravenna beset by grave difficulties, the prior of the Church of the Holy Apostles assassinated, and factional fighting raging in Florence.[51] But by dint of grievous effort, the saint managed to reject all worldly concerns and consecrate herself entirely to heavenly matters. Redoubling the severity of her asceticism (she wore a hair shirt and flagellated herself with a scourge), she meditated in her heart on Christ's suffering and was blessed with an apparition of the Baby Jesus. Her supernatural powers grew: not only could she read minds and uncover their most secret anguish, but at the end of her life she acquired the gift of healing, and her *vita* was soon followed by a collection of her miracles, put in writing by another Franciscan, Brother Ippolito of Florence.[52]

It is noteworthy, however, that unlike later female mystics and prophets, Umiliana seems not to have revealed much about the contents of her mystical experiences.[53]

This single but far from exceptional example outlines quite clearly the religious ideal which the Franciscans proposed to women and which would later be experienced and illustrated by a number of other sainted or beatified women. This spirituality corresponded to their desire to tear themselves away, like St. Francis and St. Clare, from the constraints of their social surroundings, from the crushing weight of their earthly families, and, finally, from marriage, to the extent that its principal function was to transmit or preserve patrimonies. But at the same time it channelled that current of contentiousness that so often took on extreme forms in women, by working to redirect their yearnings for the eremitical life. There was no need to flee the world to win salvation: it was better to live within it, not to sanctify oneself by turning profane realities (family and professional life, for example) to religious ends but to be a living example of absolute detachment and devotion to God in the midst of men, slaves to their passions. Persuaded of the superiority of contemplation over action, the religious who directed these women encouraged them to blaze a trail which was to become the highway to female sanctity at the end of the Middle Ages: the search for mystic union.

Their effort to spiritualize female religious life also made itself felt in another domain, which deserves mention as a conclusion to this chapter. In the thirteenth century, for obvious sociocultural reasons, female piety was principally expressed through the body. The body was viewed not only as a brother who must be made to suffer to expiate his failings and bring him into conformity with the Christ of the Passion; it also constituted a privileged means of communication for illiterate and powerless women. Decomposed, raised from the earth, ravished, liquified, irradiant, the body of the female saint constituted in itself a language for everyone to decode according to his ability. The most extreme case in the second half of the thirteenth century was that of St. Douceline, whose biography describes at length her raptures and mystical ecstasies, which gained her a large audience eager to see and touch the supernatural in its most concrete manifestations.[54] The Franciscans, like their Dominican contemporaries, tried also to transpose this spontaneous and, in their eyes, aberrant discourse to another register by enriching its symbolism—this is the meaning of the motif of the exchange of hearts, which appeared for the first time in St. Clare of Montefalco—and, more importantly, by endowing the female saints with speech, to make them the instruments of divine revelations. The mute saints of the thirteenth century, who were content to meditate in silence on the sorrowful mysteries, were replaced after 1350 by a wave of visionaries and prophets whose inspired words were to transmit to astonished clerics amplified echoes of their own messages.

FIFTEEN

Conjugal Chastity: A New Ideal in the Thirteenth Century

IN THE COURSE OF the thirteenth century—or more precisely, between 1199 and 1297—the papacy canonized as saints four lay men and women who had been married: St. Omobono (or *Homebonus*) of Cremona (†1197), St. Elisabeth of Hungary or Thuringia (†1234), St. Hedwig of Silesia (†1243) and St. Louis, king of France (†1270).[1] It is interesting to note that the bull *Quia pietas*, issued by Innocent III in January of 1199 did not even mention Omobono's family situation—he was a husband and father— and his later *vitae* speak of his wife only as an impediment to the fulfillment of her husband's vocation, because of her criticism of his excessive generosity toward the poor.[2] In the pontifical documents and hagiographic texts concerning St. Elisabeth, there are a few brief notes about her conjugal life with the landgrave Louis IV of Thuringia, to whom she bore three children and for whom she seems to have had deep affection, which he returned.[3] But this union was quite short-lived, lasting from 1221 to 1226; Louis's departure for the Crusades and subsequent death at Otranto in 1227 soon put an end to it. For this reason, the depositions of the four servants who lived intimately with her, like her later biographers, all emphasize other aspects of her saintliness, such as her love for the poor and the humiliations which she voluntarily endured during her widowhood. In the case of St. Louis, chronologically the last of our married lay saints, what obviously attracted most of the attention of contemporary clerics was the manner in which he conceived and exercised his royal functions, and Boniface VIII hardly mentioned his conjugal life in his important speech on the occasion of Louis's canonization.[4] In fact, it was only with St. Hedwig that this question came to the fore and was treated with special attention. Here was a woman in whose life the role of wife and mother was central, and it was necessary at all costs, if she were to be granted the glory of the altars and presented as a model, to resolve the suspicions that clerics harbored about sexuality, particularly that of women.[5] Although the text of the inquest ordered by Urban IV in 1262 and carried out in Silesia between November 1262 and March 1264 is lost, some documents that were directly inspired by it have survived: the bulls of canonization of 1267, the speech made at Viterbo by Pope Clement IV on the day of the ceremony, and, especially, the *Vita maior* in twelve chapters, composed around 1300 by an anonymous Silesian cleric, which cites many passages from the proceedings.[6] In the official documents of 1267, the theme of Hedwig's conjugal chastity is given a central place; what makes it even more noteworthy is that it is the first known case of its kind. In the bull of canonization, Clement IV began by describing the noble origins of the Duchess of Silesia, mentioning her blood kinship with many kings and emperors. He reminded his audience that her brothers and sisters included two bishops, a duke, a queen of France, a queen of Hungary, and an abbess. After this traditional panegyric to her *beata stirps*, the blessed roots from which she had sprung, the pope emphasized that she was able to turn her conjugal condition to the best account, not only by remaining perfectly faithful to her husband, but also by managing to avoid the traps of the *"libido."* In the pontiff's view, in fact, her feelings for her husband were not the result of an instinctive drive, but rather were always marked by judicious moderation, to such an extent that—long before the duke was lost to her love—they agreed to sleep in separate beds, in order to attend more assiduously to prayer and contemplation.[7]

The sermon pronounced by the pope in the Dominican church of Viterbo on the day of the liturgical ceremony of her canonization was even more explicit. After rapidly evoking her humility and her love of poverty, he stressed the fact that Hedwig had arrived at the perfection of chastity even within the state of marriage.[8] And to clarify the meaning of his praise—which was paradoxical in the case of a married woman—Clement IV elaborated on this theme at length, dividing the saint's married life into two equal parts of twenty-eight years each. During the first part the marriage was so spiritual in orientation that even in the conjugal bed "she was never excited by the fire of voluptuousness"; during the second part, on the other hand, the spouses lived separately.[9] If we follow the generally accepted chronology, which there is no need to question, the antithesis would seem a bit forced: married in 1185 at the age of twelve to Henry the Bearded, Hedwig actually spent 53 years, not 56 (twice 28) in the bonds of marriage, since her husband died in 1238. Moreover, if, as it seems, the couple took their vow of chastity in 1208, after the birth of their last child, the two distinguishable periods in their married life were not of equal length, but instead lasted 23 and 30 years respectively. Finally, we note that while the papal sermon commended Hedwig's husband, calling him *felix*, it emphasized nonetheless that Hedwig had played the decisive role in conceiving and putting into practice this unusual marital arrangement.[10]

As precise as the pontifical documents of 1267 are about her chaste marriage, the longest and most concrete discussion of the subject can be found in the *Vita maior* and its extension, the *Vita minor*, both of which were written around 1300 by a Silesian cleric.[11] The author, who drew his material from an earlier *vita* and from the records of the canonization proceedings, actually devotes the whole first part of his work to the sexual and familial life of his heroine. What he produced is unique in the hagiographical literature of the period: a very detailed text whose explicit aim is to present, through the example of Hedwig and her husband, the Christian ideal of marriage. We should note at the outset, for the fact is significant, that Hedwig had not desired this marriage but had entered into it to comply with her parents' wishes. Having married Henry the Bearded at the age of twelve, she bore her first child at the age of thirteen and thirteen weeks. Five others followed, making a total of three sons—Boleslas, Conrad and Henry (who succeeded his father and died at the hands of the Tartars in the battle of Legniça in 1241)—and three daughters, Agnes, Sophie and Gertrude. Thus the strictest Catholic doctrine was affirmed at the hagiographical level: the fundamental justification for marriage is the duty to procreate.[12] The primary difficulty for women was reconciling this imperative with the renunciation of the pleasure inherent in the sexual act. Hedwig's biographer explained how she set about to solve this problem and succeeded in "preserving in all things, in keeping with the teaching of the Apostle, an honorable marriage and an immaculate marriage bed," while observing to the letter the laws and rights of matrimony.[13] The hagiographer was obviously alluding here to the equal right of each spouse to the body of the other, and the obligation of each to pay the other the *debitum conjugale* [conjugal debt] whenever asked to do so.[14] To reconcile these requirements with her aspirations to chastity, St. Hedwig first of all limited the occasions on which the carnal union of the spouses was acceptable, a solution praised by her biographer. The *Vita maior* emphasizes the fact that as soon as she became pregnant with her first child, Hedwig did not allow further relations with her husband; and she repeated this practice with each pregnancy. Moreover, "she followed, with her husband's agreement, the law of the continent, as much of the time as she could."[15] This somewhat sibylline statement refers in fact to the observance of periodic continence that was customary in some movements or associations of devout laymen at the end of the twelfth century and became more common at the beginning of the thirteenth. Early examples were the *Umiliati* of Lombardy and the *Ordo poenitentiae* which developed in Italy in the years 1210–1220, whose members were often called the *continentes*.[16] The author of the *Vita maior* was undoubtedly referring to these rules, and particularly to that of the penitents, when he stated that this special kind of marital relationship was approved by the Church.[17] The validity of this connection is confirmed by the list of days and liturgical seasons during which Hedwig used to renounce all carnal contact: it matches, at least in its essential points, the list found in the *Memoriale propositi fratrum et sororum de poenitentia in domibus propriis existentium*, written in 1221–1228.[18] To be sure, the rule of abstinence on saints' days was in force for all Christians, as Gratian's *Decretum* shows; after listing the days of required fasting, it adds that "on these fast days it is proper to abstain from relations with one's own spouse."[19] But only a small elite seems to have obeyed these precepts. They were known from the early thirteenth century as "lay religious," people who sought to achieve a certain kind of Christian perfection without necessarily giving up life in the world, with its specific constraints.[20] By transforming the ecclesiastical interdicts into ascetic exercises, they put the spiritual ideal of conjugal chastity into practice. The Church soon recognized the validity of this ideal and encouraged its diffusion.[21]

In the thirteenth century, a list was drawn up that defined the major periods of the liturgical calendar during which continence was enjoined: besides Advent and Lent, it included all Fridays, the Ember Days, the vigils and feast days of the leading saints, especially those of the Virgin, and all Sundays—this last certainly being related to the reception of the Eucharist.[22] Thus, for Hedwig, as her biographer noted approvingly, the proper use of marital relations consisted in making as little use of them as possible, by restricting to an absolute minimum the time "left open" for copulation. For this reason, we are not surprised to learn that she sometimes abstained from relations with her husband for periods of as long as a month and even six or eight weeks.[23] It was a logical end to this process that, once a sufficient number of children had been brought into the world, sexual relations should be completely discontinued. This is what happened—undoubtedly in 1208—when the husband and wife pronounced solemn vows of chastity before a bishop. From that time on, Hedwig behaved like a widow, refusing to speak to her husband or approach him without being accompanied, and residing for ever-longer periods in the Cistercian monastery she had founded at Trzebnica.[24]

It may seem paradoxical that St. Hedwig's biographer should present this periodic restriction and then total renunciation of marital relations as if it were a new and original phenomenon, when canonists like Ivo of Chartres and Gratian had already discussed it long before the thirteenth century. Her *vita* seems in any case to exclude the possibility of any influence of the mendicant orders, which were to have an effect on the saint only later. An explanation for her adherence to this austere way of life can be found in her education and in the ideals that the nuns of Kitzingen had inculcated in her when she was young. But it is also undeniable that these ecclesiastical precepts were not usually followed. The author of the *Vita maior* emphasizes the fact that St. Hedwig actively tried to publicize this particular kind of conjugal relationship, first in the courtly circles of Wroclaw—where she instructed her daughter-in-law Anne about it—and then more generally all around her, by giving financial assistance to young girls of modest backgrounds, whom she urged either to lead chaste existences in convents, or to marry but conserve their "conjugal modesty."[25] The novelty of this idea therefore does not lie in the ascetic way of life it proposes, which was entirely traditional, but in the attitude of the Church, which turned the precept of periodic marital continence into an evangelical program that could lead married people to salvation and sanctity. Hedwig and her biographer—and Pope Clement IV, as well—did not question the hierarchy of the states of perfection, which, on the pattern of the Parable of the Pounds [Luke 19:11-27], granted virgins a return of 100 (to one), chaste widows 60, and good wives 30. But the life and behavior of the duchess of Silesia, an exemplary wife and mother, gave clerics of the second half of the thirteenth century an opportunity to map out for married women a path to perfection in which the suspicion of sin that stained all carnal relationships in the eyes of the theologians did not eclipse the notion of the spiritual progress of the spouses, which was judged to be more important. Marriage was not presented as an ideal—far from it. But it no longer constituted an inviolable impediment to sanctification, and the Church from then on would propose a Christian kind of marriage that was to enable a certain number of married men and women to accede to the glory of the altars in the final centuries of the Middle Ages.[26] Herein lies the significance of the canonization of St. Hedwig and the texts that exalted her sanctity between 1267 and 1300, from the perspective of the history—yet to be written, for the most part—of Christian marriage as it was actually experienced by laymen and laywomen in the Middle Ages.

SIXTEEN

THE VIRGINAL MARRIAGE OF ELZÉAR AND DELPHINE

AMONG THE ARTICLES on which witnesses were asked to testify at the canonization proceedings of Delphine of Puimichel, held at Apt and Avignon from May to October of 1363, the first was of particular importance, not simply because it appeared first on the list but because it was the one that prompted the greatest number of depositions. It was formulated in the following terms:

> It is true and generally recognized and it was held to be true and generally recognized that the aforesaid lady Delphine was a virgin and remained one throughout her life, and that she was a holy woman; and that precisely because of the life and sanctity of the lady Delphine, as well as because of her prayers and merits. . . , God has performed and continues to perform numerous and great wonders and miracles in this world in a visible, public, and manifest manner.[1]

This text was essential for the unfolding of the investigation, since it contains at one and the same time affirmations of Delphine's uncontaminated virginity, the saintliness of her life, and the performance of numerous miracles through her intercession both during her lifetime and after her death. When the pontifical commissioners who were conducting the local inquest asked the witnesses how long she had enjoyed this reputation for saintliness, many said it went far back in the past: for most it had begun forty years before, which would put it around the time of the death of her husband, Elzéar of Sabran (†1323); some, especially their intimates and elderly people, recounted even earlier memories or secrets heard directly from the mouth of one or the other member of the couple. But whatever their sources of information, everyone mentioned the event that had created the biggest stir in the region: the marriage of 1300 that had never been consummated, despite the fact that the couple lived together until Elzéar's death. The depositions unanimously emphasized that the rejection of the carnal aspects of marriage started out as Delphine's own idea. But the witnesses also stressed that, after some initial difficulties, the young Elzéar, who was fourteen at the time of their marriage, followed Delphine's plan with growing enthusiasm, and became a supporter not only of the couple's own virginity but also of the virginity of those around him.[2] A code of seigniorial governance—undoubtedly that of Ansouis—attributed to Elzéar illustrates his neophyte's zeal. It contains the following dispositions in particular:

> I order my officers to see to it that all live chastely on my lands, and to banish from them the carnal and the lewd. If any adulterer is discovered there, let him be publicly admonished the first and second times, and banished and punished the third time; for if nothing soiled should enter Paradise, nothing impure should be tolerated among Christians destined for eternal glory.[3]

The *Vie occitane d'Elzéar*, which drew its own inspiration from an earlier Latin *vita*, describes in great detail the life he led with Delphine at the castle of Puimichel between 1307 and 1310. Here again a sort of "rule book" that he drafted for his household demonstrates his zeal for purity and the cult of virginity which he now shared with his wife:

> First of all, he orders and establishes that married women may not regularly reside in his house: all must be virgins, widows, chaste. As for the men, whether they are nobles or servants, they must live chastely and honorably; otherwise, they will be excluded from his house and from his company.[4]

The climax of Elzéar's evolution came when in 1316, upon returning to Provence from Italy, the couple pronounced their vows of chastity in the presence of Alayette, Delphine's half-sister, and, most notably, of Gersende Alphant, who from the couple's youth had encouraged them to preserve their virginity.[5] From that moment on, their astonishing mode of behavior seems to have been common knowledge, at least among their intimates, and miraculous phenomena directly related to this virginal cohabitation began to be noted. For example, Alayette claimed that when she fell prey to the temptations of the flesh, she would go into the couple's bedroom and kneel before their bed, which thus became a sort of talisman, saying:

> Lord God, Jesus Christ, sower of chaste counsel, by the holy virginity and purity that this husband and wife preserve in this bed, deliver me from this temptation! Immediately, like a person who has taken off the clothes he was wearing, she was delivered from this temptation.[6]

After the death of Elzéar in 1323, Delphine spent many years at the court of Naples, where from 1326 to 1343 she was lady-in-waiting and confidante to Queen Sancha, wife of Robert of Anjou. Under the influence of certain Franciscans of Spiritual tendencies who were quite hostile to Pope John XXII, like Philip of Majorca, Philippe Alquier, and Angelo Clareno, she discovered a new dimension of religious and spiritual life: voluntary and absolute poverty, to which she vowed herself in 1333 at Quisisana, near Naples, before Brother Isnardo Risi.[7] From that time on, her main concern was to liquidate the extensive lands and lordships which Elzéar had left to her in the will he had made in 1317 in Toulon.[8] Acting directly or through her friends, she disposed of all of her possessions and distributed the proceeds of their sale to the poor. Her spiritual itinerary thus followed a trajectory that started with her passionate desire to preserve her virginity and ended in boundless charity and a very Franciscan desire to share the fate of the poorest of the poor, which led her to beg for alms in the alleys of Naples and, later, Apt.

The theme of chastity did not retreat to the background, however, and much of the testimony at her canonization proceedings indicated that it retained its fundamental importance in her eyes. One of her confessors, Brother Isnardo Risi, who had accompanied her after her definitive return to Provence in 1343, reported that "both in her confessions and elsewhere, she took pleasure in speaking about the conservation of virginity."[9] Moreover, she promoted continence so actively that it would be no exaggeration to call it proselytism. For example, a noblewoman of Apt testified that after the Black Death, in other words in 1349, she, now widowed, had been urged by Delphine to pronounce a vow of chastity; she did this in the hands of the bishop of Apt, along with seven other women who had also been "converted" by Delphine. She added that after a while she had been tempted to return to carnal and worldly life, but that Delphine had noticed this and led her back to the path of virtue.[10] Many depositions made in 1360 mentioned similar achievements: Delphine was credited with bringing a number of lax clerics back to the practice of chastity;[11] some claimed to have appealed to her both during her lifetime and after her death for strength to resist the temptations of the flesh;[12] finally, people spoke of the miraculous conversion of several prostitutes of Apt, who, after having come near her body, which was lying in state in the cathedral, could not continue to practice their shameful profession.[13] It is undeniable that, over the entire arc of her existence, the theme of chastity, particularly in the form of her virginal marriage, was at the origin and heart of the reputation for sanctity that Delphine, like Elzéar, had earned, even if each of them added their own individual merits to this common theme.

Although what sixteenth-century canonists were to call the heroic virtue of Elzéar and Delphine may have seemed obvious to the people of fourteenth-century Provence, the very unusual behavior of this couple, who were exceptional in every way, seems to have posed a problem for the ecclesiastical hierarchy, which had to pronounce on their sanctity. This could already be felt in the petition addressed to John XXII in 1327 by Raymond Bot, the bishop of Apt, requesting the canonization of Elzéar, a petition surely drafted by his friend and last confessor, the Franciscan François of Meyronnes. In this document, several possible models for their virginal marriage are proposed: Mary and Joseph, of course, but also St. John, the emblem of consecrated masculine virginity ("who renounced marriage when Christ called") and certain great figures from hagiography like St. Cecilia and St. Alexis. But the author was aware that none of these personages were in exactly the same situation as Elzéar and Delphine: Mary had certainly remained a virgin, but she had given birth to a son; St. John was only engaged to be married when, as tradition would have it, he left everything to follow Jesus. As for the saints mentioned above, they did not live with their spouses. For this reason, he concluded with some embarrassment that:

> this modern celibacy seems all the more astonishing. . . because he [Elzéar] shared a common bed with his wife for twenty-seven years while preserving his integrity, so that the sublime nature of this virtue seems more astonishing than imitable.[14]

This perplexity did not prevent Elzéar from eventually being canonized by his godchild Urban V in 1369; but, in the bull announcing this decision to the Christian world, what was emphasized was his generosity toward the poor, his intense mystic life and his indefectible attachment to the Church.[15] For its part, hagiographic tradition portrayed him above all as a great and pious lord, solicitous of justice and charity, and praised his exemplary conduct at the court of Naples; all this enabled his biographers up to the seventeenth century to present him as a model Christian courtier.[16] But the merits of Delphine, who was generally held to be responsible for her husband's chastity and who waged a two-pronged campaign for chastity and poverty throughout her life, have not been recognized by the Roman church; and, as a result, her cult has had only a very limited development. To be sure, some particular circumstances may help explain their different destinies: the problems of the schism that came to the fore after 1378 are enough to explain why her case, which was neither urgent nor topical, became bogged down. Nevertheless, the fact remains that Delphine's dossier "smelled heretical," and the failure of the canonization proceedings of 1360 can certainly not be ascribed to sheer chance.

Indeed, we should inquire into the reasons behind the passionate attachment to virginity that the "holy countess" already had when she was seven or eight years old, and investigate the precise meaning of this rejection of sexuality, which aroused first the astonishment and then the admiration of public opinion in Provence and the Comtat Venassin. Some of the testimony from the 1360 canonization proceedings and certain passages in the *Vie occitane de Delphine* clarify this delicate problem and demonstrate that her rejection of marriage was accompanied by a sense of repugnance at the prospect of maternity. For example, in responding to Elzéar, who early in their marriage insistently requested that she fulfill her marital obligations, she advanced the following arguments:

> Many people live in marriage who cannot have children. Even if they have them, the children live badly, die and have a bad end. For those people, it would have been preferable not to have had any children.[17]

One witness who had known her well, Guillaume Henri, reported that when he consulted her one day about his own plans for remarriage, she replied that she "would not have wanted to be the mother even of an apostle of Christ."[18] Other depositions corroborated the statement in the *Vita* that "whenever anyone came to speak to her of marriage, a great sadness filled her heart."[19] We may wonder why she held such a pessimistic conception of marriage. Perhaps its roots are to be found in her family background. Her father, Guillaume of Signe, does not seem to have been a paragon of virtue, since our documents speak of her two half-sisters, Alayette and Sibylle, the first of whom became a nun. They were surely illegitimate, since Delphine inherited everything in the estates of both parents when she was orphaned in 1291 at the age of seven. It is possible that at her tender age she reacted to the moral laxity of her prematurely deceased father by becoming exaggeratedly strict, but this can be no more than a hypothesis. It would be even more speculative to speak of possible Cathar influence. To be sure, as René Nelli has shown, chastity, defined as abstaining from sexual activity, was considered by Catharism in Languedoc to be the highest form of love, because an unconsummated marriage did not result in procreation.[20] But the direct influence of Catharism in Provence around 1300 is far from proven. More likely, it was a question of ideas in circulation among the aristocracy, perhaps through the agency of the troubadours, who wrote certain poems, widely diffused in the world of the *chateaux*, which could have contributed to creating a mental climate that was unfavorable to marriage.[21] Moreover, there was no need to look to the heretics for something that was readily available in orthodox doctrine. Delphine showed the way herself when, repelling her husband's advances on their wedding night, she justified her behavior by referring to hagiographical literature, in this case the *Vitae* of St. Cecilia and St. Valerian, as well as those of St. Alexis, St. Agnes, and St. Agatha.[22] These were precisely the texts that one of her relatives, Sibille of Puget, a nun who had looked after her during her childhood, had read to her to show her "in what way virgins were incomparably more pleasing to God than women bound by ties of marriage."[23] Now, these very old saints' lives—the Syriac *Alexis* goes back to the fifth century—transmitted traditions of rigorous self-control inspired by Montanism and by other movements of extreme asceticism that had flourished in early Christianity. Their influence can still be found in the *Golden Legend*, in particular in the *Vitae* of Sts. Nereus and Achilles, where the two heroes wage a war of eloquence to dissuade the young Domitilla, to whom they were preaching the Christian faith, from marrying:

> They exhorted her to virginity, recommending it as a virtue dear to God, sister to the angels, and innate in man. They told her that the wife was subject to the husband, that often she was exposed to blows and kicks, and often brought forth misshapen offspring: and that if it was hard for her now to bow to the kindly admonitions of her mother, still less could she bear humiliations from her husband . . . All the other virtues, once lost, may be recovered by penance. Virginity alone can never be regained. [24]

One can see at a glance that such texts, perfectly orthodox in appearance, contain all of the themes that were to reappear in Delphine's arguments: the enthusiastic praise for virginity, the rejection of marriage and procreation because of the risks of degradation they entail, the assimilation of physical integrity with moral perfection.

But there were certainly other influences besides that of hagiography that must have strengthened Delphine in her original choice. A witness tells us that she often cited this celebrated statement of St. Jerome: "Marriage fills the earth, virginity paradise. . . . Marriage ends with death; virginity finds its coronation after death."[25]

It was probably her first director of conscience, the Franciscan Philippe Alquier de Riez, who introduced these texts to her. Perhaps he also cited the example of one of the many women for whom Jerome acted as spiritual director, Melania the Younger: she had imposed chastity on her husband Valerius Pinian, who finally assented to it.[26]

But in the final analysis, the key to the behavior of Elzéar and Delphine is to be found by studying the atmosphere in which they were raised and which had guided them during their youth, before their departure for Italy. If Delphine was strongly incited to virginity by Sibille of Puget, Elzéar was no less inspired by two women who were often mentioned in his biographies and in the proceedings of 1360: Gersende Alphant and Mabille of Simiane. Gersende was the widow of a knight to whom she had borne a son; this child later became a Franciscan and gravitated to the young count's entourage. Gersende inculcated the love of chastity in the count himself until he was sent to the abbey of Saint-Victor of Marseilles, where his uncle Guillaume of Sabran saw to his education in the years preceding his marriage to Delphine. From then on, Gersende never stopped encouraging him to pronounce a vow of chastity, a vow that he finally made, as we have seen, in 1316. Mabille of Simiane, chatelaine of Castillon and Viens, had been widowed at the age of seventeen and, refusing to remarry, had led a pious and chaste life without entering a convent. Behind our two saints, then, a whole spiritual milieu begins to take shape, a milieu composed of members of the middle and high aristocracy of Provence, in which women, and especially young widows, seem to have played a particularly active role. A more detailed description of this milieu is provided by a document dating from 1299—the very year in which the marriage of Elzéar and Delphine was arranged by their families—which throws some light on the beliefs and behavior of members of these devout circles. The document in question is a decree of the council of Béziers, convoked and presided over by Gilles

Aycelin, archbishop of Narbonne, which vigorously denounced those members of an approved order, the Spiritual wing of the Franciscans, who "have been preaching that the end of the world is approaching and that the time of the Antichrist is almost upon us," and who make this a reason for suggesting "new ways of doing penance" to the faithful of both sexes and for recommending that these laypersons take vows of virginity and chastity which they themselves had taken but did not respect. The bishops of Languedoc then lashed out specifically against the Beguines, both male and female, who, meeting in secret to hear preached the word of God, tended to constitute a sect within the Church.[27] They were obviously referring to the groups of laypeople, particularly numerous in cities like Narbonne or Béziers, who had been influenced by the ideas and writings of Peter John Olivi: he had died the year before and was greatly revered in these circles.[28] Investigations conducted by the Inquisition at the time of John XXII would later clarify this spiritual connection still further, as the responses of a Beguine from Escueillens (in the Aude region) demonstrate. Put on trial in 1325 at Carcassonne, he declared that he had listened to one of Olivi's works, in which it was written that "marriage is a private brothel," and that he himself believed that "in having carnal intercourse with his own wife, a man commits a mortal sin."[29] Raoul Manselli, who quotes this statement, considers it to be a case—albeit a unique and exceptional one—of Cathar infiltration in Beguine circles. In my opinion, it would seem more correct to see in it the reflection, perhaps deformed but not totally inaccurate, of the celebrated Franciscan scholar's teachings on marriage.[30] Father Emmen's edition of a large part of Olivi's famous treatise *De perfectione evangelica*, which the Franciscan wrote in Narbonne in 1276, has made his beliefs better known to us.[31] In this treatise, Olivi develops the idea that marriage prevents the growth of divine love in man and impedes his progress in contemplation; moreover, it is an obstacle to the practice of poverty and humility, which are the cornerstones of evangelical life. In his view, marriage is not a true sacrament, and that is why he has no objections—quite the opposite, in fact—to people living in the world and pronouncing solemn vows of chastity. These ideas and others were condemned in 1282 by the chapter general of the Franciscans in Strasbourg. Olivi made a partial retraction in 1285 but continued to maintain that marriage was only a minor sacrament. After his death in 1298, polemics raged within the Franciscan order about his work, and the subject was raised during the violent controversy which pitted the Franciscan Spirituals against the Conventuals.[32] In 1311, the latter accused Olivi of having declared that "marriage was a hidden brothel" (*"matrimonium fore lupanar occultum"*). Ubertino of Casale defended him on this point as on others, and in fact his ideas on marriage were not condemned by the Council of Vienne, since some theologians, while not going as far as he did, nonetheless shared his inclination to consider marriage an imperfect sacrament.

Given the current state of our documentation, it is obviously impossible to prove that Elzéar and Delphine of Sabran knew Olivi or that they read his works. But we know that Olivi was not a solitary figure, and that some of his works were diffused in vernacular translation by Franciscans who were close to him and exercised a profound influence on the laity. This has been amply demonstrated by Raoul Manselli for the regions west of the Rhône. It is certain that tendrils of the Beguine movement extended into Provence, although it did not take firm root there; its followers in Provence seem to have belonged to a more noble and aristocratic milieu than those in Languedoc, where it met with success among the urban bourgeoisie and some artisans. Unfortunately, the sources for Provence, which are full of lacunae, do not permit us to go beyond these general impressions. But to my mind there is no doubt that the words of Elzéar and Delphine echoed with this Mediterranean spirituality, Franciscan in inspiration and "Spiritual" by inclination, which insistently emphasized the value of *castetat evangelical*, evangelical chastity, and advocated a new form of contempt for the world: not to flee from it, but instead to remain in it while rejecting its carnal and worldly aspects, thus bearing witness to a life lived according to the Holy Spirit. Marriage, especially in aristocratic circles, seemed to be a purely social and worldly phenomenon, whose primary goal was to ensure the preservation or extension of familial patrimonies and the continuity of lineages. Far from being a rejection of love, the denial of the physical aspect of married life seemed to represent love's culmination, as Elzéar made clear to Delphine at the court of Naples when he saw the Duke of Calabria openly rejoice at the death of his wife:

With many husbands and wives who love the world, it often happens that the carnal love which joins them collapses
entirely along with the flesh. But you and I are united by a
pure and spiritual love.[33]

The tone of this observation is very close to that of the diatribes
of the Spiritual Franciscan Mathieu of Bouzigues against corrupted
men and women "who are lustful and desirous of the vile pleasures
of this world, and lovers of the flesh," and reminiscent of his
affirmation that only a soul uncorrupted by sin *"ayssi que femna
verge"*—like a virgin—can hold out against the unicorn, symbol
of death.[34] But we can go further than a simple comparison: what
conditioned the attitude of Delphine and Elzéar toward marriage
was, in the final analysis, their profound conviction that the end
of time was near. Indeed, among the arguments that the young
bride offered her new husband on their marriage night was, first
of all, the "brevity of life"; the revelation that Elzéar received at
Sault some time later and that finally persuaded him to go along
with his wife's project consisted precisely in the fact that God had
made him share this conviction.[35] We know, moreover, that they
sustained one another in the face of the "evils and temptations
that will exist in the time of the Antichrist."[36] Their rejection of
[physical] marriage was actually an eschatological kind of behavior:
since the time of the supreme test was near, there were more
important things to be done than copulating or abandoning oneself
to transitory pleasures. And it is certainly no coincidence that their
ideas on this point seem very close to those of the famous Catalan
doctor Arnold of Villanova, to whom their families sent them for
consultation in Marseilles in 1304, when after many years of life
together they had not yet produced a child. Informed of the
couple's spiritual project by Gersende Alphant and one of their
Franciscan confessors, Brother Jean Joli, Arnold engaged them in
extended discussions; in the end he delivered a medical opinion
that met the expectations of their relatives while at the same time
allowing Elzéar and Delphine to persevere in their plan without being found out.[37] Let us not forget that Arnold of Villanova was not
only the most eminent physician of his day, but also a passionate
believer in apocalyptic thought and, late in his life, in the theses
of the Franciscan Spirituals. During a stay in Paris in 1300, he ran

afoul of the faculty of theology over his recent treatise *De adventu Antichristi*, which earned him a stay in prison.[38] Most importantly, he was the author of a commentary in Catalan on the pseudo-Joachimite treatise entitled *De semine scripturarum*. This work, which he—and Olivi as well—believed to have been the work of Joachim of Fiore himself, includes a passage in which the author defends the virginal marriage (or at least what had been considered since the twelfth century to be a virginal marriage) of Emperor Henry II and his wife St. Cunegund, and insists on the fact that the realization of a truly Christian life should not be deferred until the end of time.[39] It cannot be demonstrated with certainty that Delphine and Elzéar read this text or even knew of its existence, but it is noteworthy that they had dealings with its commentator and that their closest associates, both lay and clerical, were linked with him and fully shared his eschatological convictions.

We may wonder whether the spiritual dimension—in the double sense that the term had in the context of the times—of the virginal marriage of Elzéar and Delphine, along with their proselytism in favor of chastity, can fully account for the impression that their behavior made on large segments of Provençal public opinion in the first half of the fourteenth century. It seems unlikely, because to the east of the Rhône, Franciscans influenced by Olivi's ideas do not seem to have had the level of popular support that their confrères in Languedoc enjoyed. And when, during the pontificate of John XXII, violent persecution of the *fraticelli* and the Beguines spread in and around Marseilles, there is no evidence of any decline in the fascination excited by this unique couple's way of life. Thus we should also give due weight to the anthropological dimension of virginity, of which documents of the era give us a glimpse. For this married couple to remain virgin while living together was not only a novel ascetic exercise. It was also a feat of valor, an extraordinary achievement that must have deserved a reward. The clergy liked to say that continence meant depriving oneself of pleasure in order to store up for the next world a treasure of advantages equal or superior to the one renounced in this world. But, in the view of most people, such a heroic sacrifice necessarily had consequences here on earth, and they widely believed that those who managed to preserve their virginity in particularly difficult circumstances acquired thereby a sort of supernatural power.

For example, Inquisition records tell us that, to the heterodox Beguines of the fourteenth century, "a man and woman could not be considered virtuous if they were not capable of sleeping nude in the same bed together without performing the carnal act."[40] In this perspective, it is not surprising that the first article of Delphine's canonization proceedings associated her miraculous power with her virginity. Conversely, we know that in the following century rumors circulated that Joan of Arc had remained undefeated as long as she preserved her physical integrity, but that when she lost it—as she was reported to have done—she met with nothing but defeat and finished miserably on the stake.[41] In this context it becomes easier to understand those witnesses at Delphine's canonization proceedings who insisted rather morbidly that not only did Delphine herself incessantly affirm her virginity, but that it had been physically verified by matrons who swore to its reality.[42]

Obviously, Delphine's reputation for sanctity cannot be explained by this sole consideration: her gift for reading hearts, her love of poverty, and her actions to promote peace must also be taken into account. But for the public opinion of Provence in the 1360s, the "holy countess" nevertheless remained above all that extraordinary woman who managed to preserve her virginity in marriage, win her husband's assent to this unheard-of project, and propagate around her a way of life oriented toward the imminent coming of the Kingdom in which relationships between the sexes would preclude all stains and any form of domination.

SEVENTEEN

A HOLY WOMAN
DURING THE HUNDRED
YEARS' WAR:
JEANNE-MARIE OF
MAILLÉ

IN THE HISTORY OF the Franciscan movement in France, the century between the end of the pontificate of John XXII and the triumph of the Observance around 1430 is a shadowy one. This is particularly true for the west-central area, roughly coterminous with the Franciscan province of Touraine: created in 1239, it consisted of the regions of Berry, Anjou, and Brittany, in addition to Touraine itself.[1] With the exception of that of Brittany, now well known thanks to Hervé Martin's excellent synthesis, the history of the province remains particularly obscure: because of the Wars of Religion and the destruction of the Revolutionary era, the documentation is sparse and, in some instances, almost totally lacking.[2] This phenomenon is so striking that some historians have understood the silence of the sources to mean that Franciscan influence in these regions declined markedly during the Hundred Years' War.[3] For this reason, we are fortunate to be able to make use of indirect evidence, in this instance hagiographical: documentation furnished by the inquest that Father Martin of Boisgaultier, guardian of the Franciscan convent in Tours, organized in 1414 for the purpose of canonizing Jeanne-Marie of Maillé, for whom he had acted as confessor and spiritual director during the final part of her long life (1331–1414). These texts, published by the Bollandists in the *Acta Sanctorum*, actually contain precious information not only about the life and miracles of this woman, whose personality and visions were very interesting, but more generally on Franciscan influence in the Loire region during the fourteenth and early fifteenth centuries.[4]

Jeanne-Marie of Maillé was the daughter of Hardouin VI of Maillé, lord of Milly and Champchevrier (twenty kilometers northwest of Tours), and of Jeanne of Montbazon, who was a remote descendent of Robert of Dreux, son of Louis VI the Fat and therefore related to the French royal family.[5] The fourth of six children, Jeanne-Marie was born in the château of Roches-Saint-Quentin in 1331 and grew up in a family milieu that had long been steeped in Franciscan influence. Her grandfather, Hardouin V, a crusading companion of St. Louis in the Holy Land and of Philip III in Aragon, had been buried in 1285 in the Franciscan friary in Tours dressed in the habit of the order, as was his wife, Jeanne of Bauçay. Jeanne-Marie's own parents had a private chapel erected in the same church to receive their mortal remains. Finally, we know that her mother always arranged for a Franciscan to live in the family château, acting both as her confessor and her children's tutor. Jeanne-Marie's biographer tells us that this monk was "erudite and honorable" (*"litteratus et probus"*) and that he read and commented on the Holy Scriptures after their meals every day. It seems also that he had the young girl read saints' lives, since at the age of sixteen she was already able to cite *exempla et miracula* from them to her young husband.[6] By means of these few items, which are frustratingly brief, we glimpse a little known but probably important phenomenon: the role of the Franciscans as castle chaplains and tutors—or, in any case, religious instructors—of the children of the nobility.

We cannot retrace here all of the vicissitudes of Jeanne-Marie of Maillé's exceptionally long and complex life, but it is essential for our purposes to indicate its main stages. Having lost her father in 1340 and her mother soon thereafter, she was raised by her maternal grandfather, Barthélemy of Montbazon, who married her to the young Robert of Sillé-le-Guillaume in 1347 or 1348. Her biographer and witnesses at the 1414 proceedings assure us that she was reluctant to contract this union and that her husband allowed her to preserve her virginity during the marriage, which therefore was not consummated.[7] This statement, formulated in a clearly hagiographical context, could leave us perplexed, at the very least, if we did not find in it the specifically Franciscan theme of the rejection of carnal union within the sacrament of marriage and conjugal life, a theme that had already been illustrated by Delphine (†1360) and Elzéar of Sabran (†1323) several decades earlier. Obviously, it is impossible to demonstrate that the very unusual behavior of this saintly Provençal couple had a direct influence on Jeanne-Marie's milieu, but there is nothing to prevent a historian from seeing the mark of a common spiritual climate in her rejection of the carnal aspects of marriage.[8]

Jeanne-Marie and her husband suffered from the devastations of the Hundred Years' War. A brigand knight, Philippe of the Chèze, pillaged the château of Sillé and massacred forty-six men-at-arms. Robert, taken prisoner by the English captain Robert Knolles, was liberated only after a ransom of 3000 florins was paid, which forced him to sell part of his lands. Moreover, he died in 1362, and shortly after his death Jeanne-Marie was chased from the Sillé by her brother-in-law, William VII. She went to live with her family, who were soon vexed by her obstinate refusal to remarry. It was at this time that she supposedly had her first vision, an apparition of St. Yves Hélory (canonized in 1347), who told her: "If you are willing to abandon the world, you will taste here on earth the joys of heaven." His words were followed by an ecstasy (*raptus*) during which she believed she was transported to paradise.[9] Following this, she went to live in Tours to escape the family pressures. From 1363 on, she led a penitential life, dividing her time among prayer, assistance to the poor and the ill, and assiduous visiting of sanctuaries. It is worth noting that, at least in the early period, she did not seem to have been in contact with the local Franciscan community and had as her director of conscience a canon of Saint-Martin of Tours. She left Tours periodically to reside in Angers and at the hermitage of Notre-Dame of Planche-de-Vaux, near Ambillou, which was on her father's lands. Sometime between 1363 and 1372 she pronounced a vow of chastity before Simon Renou, the archbishop of Tours, and decided to embrace evangelical poverty. Despite the fierce objections of her relatives, she donated the château of Roches-Saint-Quentin to the Carthusians of Liget, and distributed her fortune to the poor and the Church. In 1386, after twenty-three years of penitential life, she affiliated herself with the Franciscans of Tours, moving into a cell next to their convent and taking Brother Martin of Boisgaultier, later to become her biographer, as her confessor and spiritual director.[10] The fact that this woman, whose spirituality and comportment were marked from the start by the message of St. Francis, took so long to join the Franciscans, cannot fail to surprise us. To find an explanation, we would undoubtedly need to know more about the history of the Franciscan convent of Tours, which perhaps went through a period of difficulty between 1362 and 1386 that made it less attractive to her. In the absence of any precise documentation on this subject, this can be no more than a hypothesis.

Whatever the case may be, after 1386 the specifically Franciscan aspects of Jeanne-Marie of Maillé's piety became more pronounced. In 1387, she had a vision of the Virgin and St. Francis, and, on another occasion, one of Brother Bonincontro (†1230), who had founded the friary of Châteauroux in the thirteenth century.[11] One day, her prayers stopped two Franciscan novices who had fled from the friary of Tours; stricken with remorse, they spontaneously returned to the community.[12] Finally, in 1396 she announced prophetically that a Franciscan would bring the Great Schism to an end; in the view of her contemporaries, this was fulfilled in 1409 when the Council of Pisa elected Alexander V pope.[13]

A miracle reported by witnesses at the 1414 inquest reinforces our impression that the recluse of Tours must have had a role in the spread of the reform movement within the Franciscan order.[14] The incident took place in 1410 or 1411: a Franciscan from the diocese of Luçon, François Bigois, arrived at Tours bearing letters addressed to the Franciscans of the dioceses of Poitiers and Luçon from Father Guillaume Tête d'Oye and Father Henri de la Baume, who bore the title of "confessor of sister Nicole, abbess of the Poor Clares of Besançon." This sister Nicole can only have been St. Colette of Corbie, commonly known as Nicolette or Colette. The monk spent a few days in Tours, residing not at the local monastery but at the home of a certain Franciscan tertiary (*de tertio ordine*

S. Francisci) named Guillaume, to whom the monk entrusted his letters. When he was ready to leave, his host pretended never to have received them, or even seen them. Desperate, Brother Bigois rushed to Jeanne-Marie of Maillé and explained the matter to her. A few hours later, the letters in question mysteriously reappeared, and the relieved friar went on his way and completed his mission. We will undoubtedly never know the precise contents of these letters, but it is likely that they dealt with the actions of St. Colette, to whom, during their colloquy in Nice in 1406, Pope Benedict XIII had entrusted the task of reforming the convents of the Poor Clares as well as the friaries of the Franciscans; she was trying to accomplish this without forming a separate congregation on the fringes of the Franciscan order, as the Observants then tended to do.[15]

Moreover, it is noteworthy that the Franciscan Observance first took root in France in the northern parts of the Poitou, the Vendée, and the Loire Valley, through the reform of existing houses and the foundation of new ones.[16] The monastery of Mirebeau, in the diocese of Poitiers, was the first to be affected by the movement, in 1390; it was followed by Bressuire and Chinon (founded in 1404), Sées (reformed in the same year), Cholet and Fontenay-le-Comte (founded in 1408), Saint-Jean-d'Angély and Loches (reformed in the same year), and Amboise (created in 1409). The convent of Laval, founded in 1396 by Count Guy XII and his wife Jeanne (whose first husband had been Bertrand du Guesclin) joined the Observance between 1404 and 1407. The two founders of Laval were intimate friends of Jeanne-Marie, and it was in their château in 1396 that she had prophesied the election of a Franciscan pope.[17] Thus, a number of converging indications lead us to believe that Jeanne-Marie of Maillé must have played an active role in the movement of renewal stirring among the Franciscans of western France, while at the same time it is likely that she remained attached to the "middle way" advocated by St. Colette. This problem was felt particularly acutely in the 1410s, since in 1409 Alexander V suppressed the privileges that the Observants had obtained from Benedict XIII. The Conventuals then hastened to disperse them, depriving them of the right to preach and imprisoning their leaders.[18] We know that in the provincial chapter of Touraine, in 1411, the Observants were denounced as heretics and *fraticelli* by their adversaries.[19] It is surely within this context of polemics and violence that we must place the episode of Jeanne-Marie's "miraculous" recovery of the letters transported by Brother Bigois, even if the precise modality of her intervention is not known.

Jeanne-Marie of Maillé died on March 28, 1414, at the age of eighty-two, dressed in the habit of St. Clare—a sure indication that she was not a Franciscan tertiary, whatever may later have been said on the matter—although it is certainly true that she belonged to the Franciscan movement broadly speaking.[20] The inquest that was held in Tours immediately following her death with the purpose of winning papal permission to open formal canonization proceedings is not only the source of much information about her life and miracles. It also allows us to distinguish the major aristocratic networks that were closely tied to the Franciscan order in the Loire Valley and beyond, in central and western France.

The first and most prominent network had at its center Jacques de la Marche, whose full title was Jacques de Bourbon, count of the Marche and "king of Hungary, Jerusalem, and Sicily."[21] As a matter of fact, the Tours inquest was jointly organized by Brother Martin of Boisgaultier and Jean of Pontlevoy, the procurator of Jacques de la Marche. The testimony gathered at the inquest was forwarded to Jacques de la Marche so that he could present the dossier to the pope and persuade him to open genuine canonization proceedings. Jacques de la Marche was certainly no nonentity. Born in 1370, he was the son of Jean I of Bourbon, count of the Marche and of Vendôme; in 1396, he participated in the crusade of Nicopolis and was taken prisoner by the Turks. After being ransomed, he became high chamberlain of France and waged war against the English beginning in 1397. In 1413, he was in charge of leading the Great Companies into Guyenne. The following year, the court of Naples chose him to be husband of Queen Joanna II, who had been widowed in 1406. At the time of the inquest of Tours, he had gone off to conquer his kingdom. The matter, as we know, turned out badly, and after a few months the ephemeral sovereign was imprisoned by order of his fickle wife, who did not release him until 1419.

Jacques de la Marche interests us here because of his very close ties, both before and after his return from Italy, with the reform movement within the Franciscan order, and particularly with St. Colette. His own daughter Isabeau entered the Poor Clares and joined Colette at the convent of Vevey; one of his granddaughters, Bonne of Armagnac, joined the same order and enjoyed a reputation for sanctity at the time of her death in 1462. After his Neapolitan misadventures and the political disappointments that followed his return to France, in 1434 he withdrew from the world and became a Franciscan tertiary, under the influence of Henri de la Baume. It was in this habit that he died in 1438, having resided in the friaries of Vevey, Dole and Besançon. Other members of his family also supported Colette's reforms: in 1421, his brother Jean II of Bourbon and sister-in-law Marie of Berry founded the convent of reformed Poor Clares in Moulins; and in 1423, his nephew Charles, count of Clermont, founded an institution of the same type in Aigueperse, in the diocese of Clermont. Finally, Jacques' sister, Charlotte of Bourbon, queen of Cyprus since her marriage to Janus II of Lusignan in 1409, contributed written evidence to the inquest in 1414 about the life and virtue of Jeanne-Marie of Maillé. A canon of Saint-Martin of Tours, Jean Robert, produced a letter, dated 1412, from the rulers of Cyprus, in which they begged the recluse of Tours to intercede on behalf of their kingdom, which had fallen prey to various calamities, including an invasion of grasshoppers which were destroying the entire harvest; in addition, Queen Charlotte asked Jeanne-Marie to send a jar of her homemade ointment, which was highly effective against disease.[22]

The second aristocratic network whose ties to the Franciscan movement emerged from the Tours inquest was composed of the Angevin dynasty, or, more precisely, what is commonly called the Second House of Anjou and the families connected to it. On several occasions, in the *vita* as well as in the proceedings, mention is made of the material aid provided to Jeanne-Marie in periods of difficulty by Queen Marie, that is to say Marie of Châtillon or Brittany (†1404), wife of Louis I of Anjou. Between 1360 and 1386 Queen Marie frequently resided in Tours in the palace of the king of Sicily, and she later returned there after Touraine came under the rule of Louis of Orléans.[23] She held Jeanne-Marie in such esteem that she asked her to be the godmother of one of her sons, either Louis II, who was born in 1377, or, more likely,

Charles, duke of Calabria.[24] This Marie of Brittany or Anjou was none other than the daughter of Charles of Blois, the pious duke of Brittany who was killed at the battle of Auray in 1364 and buried in the Franciscan monastery at Guingamp. Miracles soon began to occur at his tomb, and in 1369 a fresco representing him kneeling before St. Francis in the Franciscan church in Dinan began to bleed, enflaming the general hatred for the Montforts and their English protectors. A popular cult, orchestrated by the Franciscans, sprang up all over Brittany, and it was no coincidence that the canonization proceedings of Charles of Blois took place in 1371 in the Franciscan monastery of Angers and at the instigation of Louis I of Anjou, his son-in-law, who paid all of the expenses of the inquest.[25] Now, Jeanne-Marie of Maillé was a devout follower of Charles of Blois and, moreover, of St. Yves, whose canonization the duke of Brittany had obtained from Clement VI in 1347, and who was believed to have been a Franciscan tertiary.[26] A witness stated that Jeanne-Marie brought a piece of the hair shirt of Charles of Blois from Angers to Tours, and treasured it as a relic.[27] All of these devotions and cults reveal the close ties between the Franciscan movement and the house of the counts of Blois-Châtillon. And this family acted as patrons of the convent of the Poor Clares of La Guiche, near Blois, which they chose as their burial place. That tradition was continued by Charles of Orléans when he became count of Blois, and especially by his sister Margaret, the future mother of François II—a significant choice of name—of Brittany.

Moreover, one of the principal witnesses at the 1414 inquest, Jean Tennegot or Tenengot, canon of Tours, declared that while he was studying civil law at Angers, he often went to the Franciscan friary, where he met certain saintly women: Jeanne-Marie of Maillé and the "lady of Mayenne, countess of Thouars" who lived there and devoted themselves to prayer and good works.[28] The "lady of Mayenne" was no other than Isabelle of Avaugour (†1399 or 1400), an aunt of Charles of Blois and founder of the Franciscan convent in Dinan. Her second husband was the viscount of Thouars, whom she married in 1370; three years later she had Louis of Anjou grant her the baronage of Mayenne for life. She renounced it in 1385 to retire to the Franciscan convent in Angers, to which she was very generous in her will of 1393; the Franciscans of Dinan were also included in her bequest.[29]

The close ties between the house of Anjou, lineages related to it, and Franciscan circles were maintained after 1400; and Jeanne-Marie's exceptional longevity enables us to follow their evolution over the next generation. For instance, the witnesses at the 1414 inquest included the wife of Louis II of Anjou, Yolanda of Aragon (1380–1442), who testified to the esteem in which she held the holy woman who had cured her of a serious ailment called "le horion," or whooping cough.[30] Yolanda of Aragon, who was deeply influenced by the Franciscans, also had an important political role: in 1413, her daughter Marie had married the count of Ponthieu, the future Charles VII. We know that her chaplain was a Franciscan, Brother Raphaël, who helped promote the cult of St. Michael the Archangel in France at the time when the resistance of Mont-Saint-Michel to the besieging English army inspired the enthusiasm of the Armagnacs. Moreover, this monk was one of the examiners of Joan of Arc at Chinon and Poitiers in 1429; and both Yolanda and Marie actively supported the Maid of Orléans and urged the Dauphin to override the objections of the "politicians" in his entourage. Finally, it was the future queen Marie who in 1429 solemnly welcomed to Orléans Brother Richard, the famous Franciscan preacher who was spreading the devotion to the Holy Name of Jesus from town to town while at the same time announcing the imminent coming of France's liberator. The importance of the encounter between Joan of Arc and Brother Richard, which took place in Orléans itself in 1429, is so well known that we need not belabor this point.[31] On the other hand, it is less certain that Joan of Arc actually spoke with St. Colette at Moulins: the traditional account of this meeting is not at all implausible, but it remains to be proven. Whatever the case may be, there is a striking congruence between the aristocratic milieux frequented by Jeanne-Marie of Maillé and the groups that welcomed Joan of Arc in 1429. A final example will convince us of the reality of these connections: during the inquest of 1414, one of the most important pieces of evidence in favor of Jeanne-Marie's sanctity was the letter addressed to the commission by Marie of Montfort-Laval, countess of Alençon and of the Perche by her marriage to Jean I of Alençon (†1415). Her father, Jean V of Montfort, would bring the Dominican Vincent Ferrer to Brittany in 1418–1419; her son, Jean II of Alençon, was to be one of Joan of Arc's closest comrades.[32]

Jeanne-Marie of Maillé thus constitutes an essential link in the network of solidarity that connected a good part of the aristocracy of western France to the Franciscan order. From the Penthièvre to the Mayenne, from Vendée to Anjou, the Blois region and the far-off Bourbonnais, numerous families of the upper and middle aristocracy were influenced by the Franciscans and the Poor Clares and supported them in return. In this regard it is significant that lineages with the exalted status of princely or even royal houses—such at least were their titles and their ambitions—like those of Anjou, Bourbon, and Blois-Châtillon, as well as more modest houses like those of Thouars, Alençon and Clisson, were all intent on promoting movements of reform, whether it be the Observance or the reform advocated by Colette, by founding new monasteries or restoring declining ones at a time when the economic and political situation was not at all favorable to these activities. This simple observation in itself testifies to the closeness of the ties linking the aristocracy of the Center-West region with the followers of St. Francis.[33] It is striking too that these same milieux, in the next generation, often welcomed and supported Joan of Arc. If no one still claims today that Joan of Arc was a Franciscan tertiary, it nevertheless seems obvious that she was influenced by the Franciscans in Lorraine, and that, through Brother Richard and other religious she met in Orléans, she came into contact with the Observance, as her devotion to the Holy Name of Jesus and the sign IHS on her flag attest. For this reason, it is not surprising that the people in the Dauphin's entourage who evinced the same kind of spirituality should recognize in her a woman who was authentically inspired by God.[34]

⸺◈⸺

In this study, we have concentrated exclusively on the aristocratic component of the Franciscans' network of sympathizers and supporters in central-western France in the late fourteenth and early fifteenth centuries, since these are the milieux which appear most clearly in the documents concerning Jeanne-Marie of Maillé, because of her social origins and the quality of the people with whom she associated.[35] The inquest at Tours demonstrated, however, that her personal influence and that of the Franciscans of her city extended to other social groups. In addition to great ladies like Yolanda of Aragon and the countess of Alençon, several money-changers from Tours, a judge, a royal sergeant, and various women of the bourgeoisie and the lower classes also took part in the inquest. These are shadowy figures, to be sure—we often know nothing about them but their names—but their presence demonstrates that the influence of Jeanne-Marie and her Franciscan associates reached far beyond the world of palaces and châteaux.[36]

Thus, the documents assembled in 1414–1415 to establish the sanctity of a penitent woman of Tours provide a picture of the Franciscan presence in western France that is, on the whole, less bleak than that usually painted for the period of the Hundred Years' War. To be sure, between 1330 and 1390, the foundation of new monasteries ceased, and severe crises weakened or ruined existing communities. But that does not seem to have prevented the deep penetration of Franciscan influence within the various social classes, thanks to the presence of Franciscans in noble households, the rise of the Third Order among the urban laity, and the rapid diffusion of popular cults such as those of St. Yves and Charles of Blois—not to mention that of Jeanne-Marie of Maillé herself, which remained alive in this region until the Protestants destroyed her tomb in 1562. In any case, the revival was early and rapid, and, at the beginning of the fifteenth century, the Franciscan spirit was thriving in the Loire region which, far more than Paris, at that time constituted the living heart of France.

PART IV

THE INSPIRED WORD

FEMALE PROPHETS, VISIONARIES, AND MYSTICS IN MEDIEVAL EUROPE

ALTHOUGH THE CONCEPT of the Middle Ages has come into general currency and its use has resolved more problems than it has created, beneath the apparent unity of this term lurk shifts and discontinuities to which historians have become increasingly sensitive in recent years. This is particularly evident in the sphere of religion, where it is impossible to ignore the differences that separate, for example, the simple unpolished faith of the eleventh-century Crusaders from that of the fourteenth-century Beguines, infinitely more subtle and complex in its expressions. Migne had already sensed this in his own day, when he settled on the year 1200 as the end-point for his renowned *Patrologia Latina*. As debatable as that date may seem in some respects, it might not have been such a bad choice after all, because it was indeed between the end of the twelfth century and the first decades of the thirteenth that matters in this domain took a new turn, as is illustrated by the spiritual experience of St. Francis of Assisi and the relative decline of the religious orders of Benedictine or Augustinian orientation, soon to be supplanted by the mendicant friars. Among the fundamental changes that took place during these decisive decades, one of the most important—even if it long remained unnoticed—was the appearance of a new spirituality, based not on monkish contemplation but on the search for conformity to Christ, which would result in the divinization of man *hic et nunc*, in his body and his soul. In this perspective, the ultimate objective of a Christian was no longer the veneration of the King of Heavens in his magnificence but rather the imitation of the God who had come to earth in his humanity. Thus religious life tended to come forth from the cloister to become accessible to all of the faithful and in particular to women, who, for the first time in centuries, were again poised to play an important role in the Church.

Among those who made a mark on their times, the earliest was surely St. Hildegard of Bingen (†1179) who, from her convent on the Disibodenberg, did not hesitate to launch menacing warnings at the emperor, the pope, and the bishops and abbots of the Germanic world. But she was a thoroughly exceptional person, a nun who combined her prophetic gifts with a strong interest in physics and medicine.[1] Moreover, her example was little emulated after her death, for convent life in the twelfth and thirteenth centuries encouraged instead the blossoming and development of an affective or speculative sort of mysticism that cared little about attracting the attention of the faithful or the Church hierarchy. In fact, only in the middle of the fourteenth century did a stream of female prophets and visionaries appear. Its fountainhead was St. Bridget of Sweden (†1373), who in 1343 began to receive and transmit visions concerning the urgent need to return the papacy to Rome, reform the ecclesiastical hierarchy and religious orders, and convert those faithful who were accused of wallowing in sin. Bridget, founder of the monastery of Vadstena, opened the way to a whole series of women who, from this period until the middle of the fifteenth century, claimed to speak in God's name and thereby to exercise some authority in the Church. Some, like Bridget herself and her contemporary, St. Catherine of Siena (†1380), became famous; but most of them remained obscure or had only limited influence. Nevertheless, this phenomenon was so novel and so important that it deserves closer examination, whatever the impact of the messages delivered by these female visionaries may actually have been.[2]

The rise of this phenomenon is obviously related to the increasingly marked administrative and political character of the ecclesiastical hierarchy at the time of the Avignon papacy. Faced with the emerging national monarchies, the Roman Church reacted by extreme centralization, taking from the bishops a large share of their prerogatives and prestige, and by developing statelike structures, particularly in the area of finances. Jurists had the upper hand everywhere, and religious movements that did not display absolute obedience were harshly suppressed, as was clearly illustrated by the repressive measures used against the Franciscan Spirituals and the Beguines, especially beginning with the papacy of John XXII. But more than anything else, it was the Great Schism that made possible the efflorescence of visionary prophesying and its emergence to public view.[3] The Great Schism caused conflict between—and thus the weakening of—competing hierarchies and, as it continued, awakened grave doubts among the faithful. Each obedience put most of its efforts into securing the political support of temporal lords, but it is significant that both Rome and Avignon were aware of the assistance that could be offered by mystics or prophets who rallied to their cause or who could raise their prestige. Thus, Clement VII tried to turn the renown of the young cardinal Peter of Luxemburg (†1387) to his advantage, as did Benedict XIII that of the visionary Marie Robine, who had moved from Béarn, her native village, to live near the papal palace. Similarly, the cause of Urban VI was passionately supported by Catherine of Siena in Italy and, at a more modest level, by Constance of Rabastens in the Toulouse region. Somewhat later, at the time of the Council of Pisa, Jeanne-Marie of Maillé rallied to Alexander V, the Franciscan pope whose election she had foretold. Institutional crises and spiritual unrest between 1378 and 1430 created a climate that encouraged women everywhere to speak out. In general, these were simple lay women who were deeply troubled by the miseries of their times, who did not hesitate to claim that the revelations they transmitted were divine. The best known and most significant example was, of course, Joan of Arc.[4]

Among the characteristics shared by these women, the first and most important was consciousness of their divine election. God had chosen them for a particular mission, despite their personal unworthiness, or rather *because* of it. "I am your God who wishes to speak to you; I speak not only for you but for the salvation of others. You will be my channel."[5] But this simultaneously humble and imposing vocation—the task of being God's intermediary among men—was only accepted after He had reassured the seer and told her exactly what to expect. The voice which spoke to Constance of Rabastens in 1384 was similarly insistent:

> "Fear nothing and seek neither advice nor human aid, for none will be granted you; but divine aid will never abandon you." She drew a breath and said, "Lord, how can this come about, since I am a sinful woman?" The voice answered: "Do not doubt what I say, for I repeat that it is time for the Son of Man to demonstrate his power, and it will be demonstrated through you, because you are a woman. By woman the faith was preserved and by woman it shall be revealed, and this woman is you."[6]

Thus, through revelations or visions, power was transferred from Christ to these women, who were with a single stroke promoted to the role of heralds and spokesmen of God. Trying to escape their destiny, those to whom this mission was entrusted reminded God of their ignorance of theology and the risk of error that resulted from it. But their divine interlocutor reassured them by promising to grant them true wisdom, which is far beyond anything that theologians and learned men can achieve; and the reference to the biblical and evangelical theme that God preferred to reveal His message to the humble and to children was usually enough to overcome their hesitations.

However much their temperaments and sensibilities may have differed, once they were convinced of the importance of their mission and the authenticity of their election, the visionaries of that time all took the same measures. Rather than addressing themselves to the people, they tried to promote Church reform from the top down, as if to them the *reformatio in capite* [reform of the head] would command the *reformatio in membris* [reform of the members]. In most cases, the visionaries did not question the hierarchical structures of the Church: even if they criticized clerics for their deficiencies, they merely sought to induce them to play their proper roles. For example, the seventh book of St. Bridget's *Revelations* contains a series of visions concerning the papacy: Christ confirms to her that, even if certain popes have been great sinners and even if one of them—John XXII—

is certainly in Hell, their decisions on matters of faith are still entirely valid, except in cases of manifest heresy. And even John XXII was not in error when he stated that Christ had possessed something of his own because he wore a tunic that his mother had given him.[7] In Catherine of Siena's case, this attitude is even more apparent, since she refers to the Roman pontiff as a "true Christ on earth" when she calls on the Florentines to submit to the will of Gregory XI; and after his death she prays for the coming of an angelic and evangelical pope to restore the Church, a pope whom she believes—at least for a time—to have found in the person of Urban VI.[8] Far from being heterodox or promoting the subversion of the established order, the visionary prophecy of this era seems, rather, to be the place of refuge for a kind of evangelism which no longer was welcomed by ecclesiastical institutions, and the expression of a desire for reform that sought to reach its goals by persuading the highest levels of the hierarchy. But the next generation, from 1385 to 1400, was less deferential. The tones of Constance of Rabastens (around 1385-1386) and Marie Robine (whose prophesies date from about 1390-1398) became increasingly apocalyptic and threatening as time went by and the Church, like society at large, remained indifferent to their injunctions and calls to order. Thus Constance, after comparing the Avignon cardinals to false prophets and Avignon to Nineveh, heard a voice telling her: "Few are they who wish to drink from my chalice, but those who drink from it I will preserve and defend. No one should be greater than his Lord, but many prefer to be counted among the destroyers of the faith."[9] The incomprehension and outright hostility of their contemporaries, and the rejection of their messages by the clerics for whom they were primarily intended, caused the messengers to become discouraged and angry. When Constance of Rabastens' spiritual director refused to put her revelations in writing out of fear of his superiors and of the archbishop of Toulouse, Constance claimed that the voice sent her a message whose content bordered on heresy, according to the standards of the day: "Tell your confessor to write them [i.e., the revelations] down, because he owes more allegiance to God than to men." In fact, it took a "miracle"—in this case, an illness that almost killed him—to make him agree to take up his pen.[10] Moreover, to fortify Constance in the face of the accusations of possession

or satanism that she was sure to confront, the voice declared to
her on another occasion:

> I repeat to you that all this can only come about through
> miracles, and it is a great miracle that a sinful woman such
> as you can proclaim to them the Holy Scriptures, which you
> have never studied. But you have proclaimed the Holy Trinity,
> the holy Incarnation, and the holy Sacrament of the altar—
> that is to say, things which are all hidden from the Devil and
> which he would never dare nor be able to confess.[11]

But the most obvious consequence of the prolongation of the
schism was surely the politicization of these women's visions and
revelations, and the accentuation of their messianic character. In
effect, a situation had been created in which neither side could
impose its will on the other by reason or by force, since this was
not a conflict between orthodoxy and heresy but rather a struggle
between rival obediences. This fatal rupture of the religious unity
of Christendom meant that the State gradually became the point of
reference. From this time on, beliefs and hopes confronted one another in the political arena, which was itself becoming increasingly
centered on the sovereign. St. Bridget still looked to the emperor,
whom she saw return to Rome with the pope to restore peace and
harmony among Christians. More often, it was the King of France,
the sacred personage whose mission was not only to govern well
but also to protect the Church and ensure the salvation of his
subjects, as St. Catherine of Siena declared in her letters to Charles
V.[12] We have thus progressed from the criticism of ecclesiastical
institutions—Bridget often said that the rectors of the Church
should not be emulated, since most of them were wicked—to
the conviction that nothing more could be expected from this
hierarchy, and that the salvation of Christendom would come in
the person of a great prince. And when the latter disappointed
them, as was the case with Charles VI, the visionaries did not
mince their threatening words: Marie Robine announced that Paris
would be destroyed if France did not return to the obedience of
Benedict XIII.[13] In the same way, Constance of Rabastens, several
years earlier, had ordered Gaston Phoebus, the count of Foix, to
set the king back on the right track and to organize with him

the "Great Crossing," that eschatological crusade dear to all of these women, from Catherine of Siena on, which would reunite the energies of Christendom, divided by war and by the Great Schism, and boost spiritual vitality.[14] Their ultimate ambition was a return to Christian radicalism that would bring on the reform of the Church in its head and members and a campaign against clerical vices, especially in matters of sexuality and poverty.

To achieve these ambitious and unrealistic goals, the visionaries knew that they had only two weapons at their disposal: threats of God's wrath and reminders of His infinite mercy. They used them alternately and in varying proportions, depending on their temperaments: Catherine of Siena preferred to emphasize the infinite love of the Sacrificial Lamb, while Marie Robine did not hesitate to announce the imminent end of the world, if her appeals went unheeded.[15]

The other innovative spiritual movement which developed in Western Christendom between the thirteenth and fifteenth centuries, often in conjunction with the one we have just discussed, was mysticism. It originated in the Low Countries—in the widest sense of the term—and in Germany, among such figures as Marie of Oignies, Hadewijch of Antwerp and Mechtilde of Magdeburg. After 1250 it spread to Italy and Provence, with Margaret of Cortona, Angela of Foligno and Douceline of Aix. By the fifteenth century numbers of female mystics were to be found in France and England, and even as far off as western Prussia, where Dorothy of Montau lived.[16] We are thus dealing with a pan-European phenomenon, the extent of which has only recently begun to be appreciated. Since scholars and editors of texts long focussed their attention exclusively on the Rhineland and Flemish group, many very interesting personalities were left unexamined. These figures all sought to attain union with God by exploring their personal spirituality. Their experiences were thus different from monastic spirituality, which was essentially communal and bookish—even though some female mystics did live in convents. For these women, the love of God, defined and experienced as a desire, constituted the human subject. For this reason, they did not hesitate to affirm, contrary to St. Bernard, that our world is not a *regio dissimilitudinis*, a realm of estrangement, but rather that the soul while still here on earth is able to merge with God. In fact, they molded their entire existence around the effort to reach Jesus by imitating His suffering, an effort sometimes climaxing in a state of ecstasy that was described in terms of erotic or sexual pleasure, in which the soul unites with its creator, or rather loses itself in Him.[17] For if God's love is a free gift and is complete in itself, human love is both desire and awareness of a lack. The essential task is to create a vacuum in oneself to make space for the divine Husband and to reach a state of annihilation in which the subject is able to discern only Life communicated and shared. This is the true meaning of the exchange of hearts, which first appeared in St. Clare of Montefalco (†1308) and is found again in Catherine of Siena and Dorothy of Montau.

At first sight, the rise of mysticism, particularly characteristic of feminine milieux, would not seem to be a phenomenon that should disturb the ecclesiastical authorities, since the women who gave themselves over to these experiences led retiring lives—as either cloistered nuns or solitary recluses—and were not interested in claiming any kind of power. Nevertheless, the clergy quickly perceived the growth in their numbers as a threat. As early as the 1250s, Lamprecht of Regensburg, a Franciscan preacher, wrote the following verses about female mysticism:

> This art arose only yesterday
> Among the women of Brabant and Bavaria.
> What kind of art can it be, Lord God,
> if old women are more skilled in it
> than wise and learned men?[18]

When the clerics attempted to define the grounds for their concern, several reasons emerged. They certainly feared that they would be ousted from their role as indispensable intermediaries between God and humankind, but they also worried that the faithful would turn away from practicing Christian virtue in order to chase after extraordinary states of consciousness. After all, many of these women, especially the Beguines, went so far as to claim that works were of no help in achieving union with God, and that beatific visions were not reserved to the hereafter. Moreover, some of these women were lightning rods for very strange phenomena. Transposing the whole vocabulary of church reform into their own experiences and even their own bodies, they in effect replicated on the physiological level the wounds and infirmities that afflicted ecclesiastical institutions. Their bloody wounds, whether self-inflicted or received as stigmata, constituted a mute protest against the abuses and vices of a Christianity which had betrayed all of its ideals. These experiences rendered them suspect in the eyes of the Franciscan Gilbert of Tournai, who in his treatise *De scandalis Ecclesiae*, written in 1274, criticized the Beguines "for being taken by subtleties and welcoming extravagances." He singled out one of them—undoubtedly Elisabeth of Spalbeek—who was said to have received the stigmata of Christ: "If this is true," he wrote, "then we should remove her from the shadows and spread her repute! If, however, this is false, let us strike down her hypocrisy and fakery."[19]

In the final analysis, these weak women, isolated and devoid of any kind of power, constituted a far more serious danger for the clergy than did the female visionaries who, whether or not they were genuinely inspired, all claimed to deliver messages from God. In effect, the mystics offered a new, purely existential definition of religious life, which was presented as a loving relationship and as sensual enjoyment (*fruitio*). Their vocabulary itself bears witness to this, as it describes ecstasy as a state in which the soul experiences ineffable sweetness and suavity. Thus, well before this idea was applied in the sciences, knowledge of religious matters was defined in terms of direct experience. Moreover, mysticism developed and diffused an individualistic conception of religious life. God was felt to be the object of human desire, and the very source of *my* desire. God was sought within the framework of a unique and solitary relationship, separate from the crowd and usually apart from any liturgical ceremony. Of course, far from disparaging the sacraments, women like Catherine of Siena and Dorothy of Montau yearned to receive the Eucharist as often as possible. But it mattered little to them whether they received it during mass or not, because the only thing that counted was to unite themselves with God by ingesting the body and blood of Christ.[20]

In the end, the female mysticism of the late Middle Ages proved profoundly subversive, insofar as it emphasized the divorce between love and intellectual knowledge. By so doing, despite its

perfectly orthodox appearance, it undermined one of the fundamental postulates of medieval Christianity: the harmonious synthesis of faith and reason so resolutely pursued by theologians
from St. Anselm to St. Thomas Aquinas, including Abelard, Peter
Lombard, and Albertus Magnus. To be sure, by the end of the
fourteenth century, the beautiful edifice of scholastic theology
was already beginning to crack under the influence of William
of Ockham and nominalism. But as yet this had affected only a
small number of clerics and scholars. The mystical current likewise
involved only a small number of people, but their outlook revealed,
by accentuating it, that a far deeper evolution was in progress,
because these mystics, who generally were simply laywomen, were
in this respect utterly typical.

Apart from some rare and exceptional figures like Marguerite
Porète, who was burned in Paris in 1310 for having defended
heretical theses in her *Mirror of Simple Souls*, and certain Beguines who espoused the theses of the *fraticelli* or the Brethren
of the Free Spirit, most of the mystics of this era were not violently
persecuted by the Church, to which they remained faithful.[21] But
an aura of suspicion surrounded them because they tended to live
on the fringes of the institutions to which they were tenuously
linked by the clerics who served as their directors of conscience
and recorded their visions and states of mind. We must also note
that it was not uncommon for the director and his charge to
establish an ambivalent relationship that could even result in a
complete reversal of roles, as the churchman, fascinated by the
mystic, became her apologist and the publicist of her revelations.

It would be a gross oversimplification, and as such historically
unacceptable, to claim that there was a direct relationship between the visionary and mystical currents that characterized the
late Middle Ages and the Reformation of the sixteenth century.
Obviously, it would be an oversimplification to isolate one element
from the whole—for example, religious individualism—and label
it a harbinger of the events of 1517 and successive years. The
movements that we have briefly presented were themselves full
of contradictions, and their heritage is ambiguous. As we have
seen, the female prophets of the fourteenth and early fifteenth
centuries dreamed of a regenerate clergy and a holy papacy, even
as they discounted the importance of the ecclesiastical institution

by privileging their direct relationships with God. For their part, female mystics promoted contemplation and the search for ecstatic rapture, but some among them continued to devote a large part of their energies to the most traditional and commonplace devotions of medieval piety, such as pilgrimages, crusades, or the accumulation of indulgences. Nevertheless, it would not be unfair to call them precursors of the religion of the future, to the extent that their devotion was a painful and sometimes tragic effort to overcome the sadness of being in the world and living in a society that was a slave to sin. This was what inspired their withdrawal into interiority and their impassioned quest for unity, which arose from the acute consciousness that something was lacking. As Michel de Certeau has observed about the seventeenth century—but the same could be said of the female mystics of the Middle Ages—"they were heartsick from absence because they were heartsick for the One and Only."[22] There is no gap between the unity of the Church and union with God; it is still the same harrowing obsession. Finally, by affirming that Christians of all stations and of both sexes could arrive at the fullness of religious life, since God bestows Himself through grace alone, female visionaries and mystics of the late Middle Ages called into question the traditional hierarchy of the states of perfection, which placed monks and clerics at the top of the ladder and relegated the simple faithful to the bottom rung. It would make no sense to call this an anticipation of the Reformation. But it is not immaterial to realize that, as early as the fourteenth century, men and especially women passionately desired the reform of the Church, so much so that they were willing to risk their existence on this hope.

NINETEEN

MYSTICAL SANCTITY AT THE TIME OF THE AVIGNON PAPACY AND THE GREAT SCHISM

THE DEVELOPMENT OF female mysticism can be considered one of the major spiritual innovations of the thirteenth century. Its rise was felt earlier in the Netherlands and the Germanic countries than in Mediterranean Europe, where the first great female mystics were Douceline (†1274), sister of Hugues of Digne, in Provence, and, more importantly, Margaret of Cortona (†1297), Clare of Montefalco (†1308), and Angela of Foligno (†1309), in Italy.[1] But only in the fourteenth century did the Roman Church begin to give serious consideration to the sanctity of these female ecstatics, whose extraordinary gifts ranged from clairvoyance to levitation.[2] One cannot help but be struck by the fact that, with the exception of St. Clare of Montefalco, all of these saints were laywomen whose spiritual experiences took place outside of convent walls.[3] This paradoxical situation was surely related to the laxity of many convents at the end of the thirteenth century, which rendered them unattractive to a spiritual elite enamored of perfection. But it can also be explained by the evolution of mentalities, as religious life came to be perceived as a solitary quest for union with God, something ill suited to the demands of communal living.[4]

The Church's ratification of mystical sanctity was an important event, for almost all of the exemplars of this spirituality were women. Indeed, until that time, apart from rare exceptions, female religious could only pursue their spiritual vocations within the framework of a masculine community with its prescribed rules and structures.[5] Even as late as the beginning of the thirteenth century, someone like Elisabeth of Thuringia was strictly subordinated to her director of conscience, who sometimes imposed his own ideas on her when he saw fit and would even go so far as to strike her. A few decades later, the relationships between the female saints and their masculine entourages had shifted. To be sure, from Margaret of Cortona to Dorothy of Montau, pious laywomen continued to be surrounded by clerics as in the past, but in many cases these clerics were now disciples rather than spiritual guides.[6] The best known and most spectacular case is that of St. Catherine of Siena, whose *brigata* included churchmen of very different backgrounds (even if most were Dominicans), united in their common admiration of the *Mamma*.[7] But there is nothing exceptional here; we find the same thing in the cases of Delphine of Puimichel and Bridget of Sweden. Delphine's sphere of influence extended from her convent at Cabrières and her *oustau* [hostel] at Apt to many clerics, both secular and regular, in Provence and the Comtat Venassin.[8] St. Bridget was surrounded by religious like Peter Olafsson and Alfonso of Jaen, who hastened to collect and write down the revelations which her divine Husband dictated to her.[9] Thus, by virtue of their mystical experiences, women of the later Middle Ages managed to break the tie of dependence subordinating them to men and to turn it to their advantage. Excluded until then from the ministry of the Word, they became the mouthpiece used by the Spirit to speak directly to the Christian people.

As we know, the saintly female mystics of the fourteenth century did not hesitate to approach popes and prelates in order to reveal God's will to them, sometimes in vehement terms. For example, the records of her canonization proceedings show that Delphine of Puimichel spoke with Clement VI in Avignon. Although the contents have not survived, the conversation must have had a certain importance. She also received several visits from Cardinal Anglic Grimoard, brother of Urban V, who testified at length about her.[10] Better known are the virulent criticism of the condition of the Church and the suggestions for reform that St. Bridget addressed to Gregory XI; in her eyes the return of the pope to Rome was only a prelude to profound transformations of the hierarchy and the clergy. These urgent warnings to the princes and great ones of this world were accompanied by accusations and threats.[11] As for Catherine of Siena, her precise role in the events of 1376-1378 has been much discussed by historians in recent decades.[12] For their part, the witnesses who testified at the proceedings in Venice (1406-1411) were convinced that it was considerable.[13] From our perspective, their conviction is more important than the objective historical reality: it shows that in the opinion of certain ecclesiastical circles, including the papacy itself, the intervention of a woman in Church affairs was considered to be at least admissible, if not normal, when the authenticity of her message was certified by her extraordinary talents and her indisputable orthodoxy. Thus, through a total reversal of perspective, members of the sex which was the incarnation of physical and moral weakness in the religious literature of the feudal era were considered by the end of the fourteenth century to have a privileged place in the history of salvation.

The causes of this spectacular reversal merit investigation. Certain signs lead us to interpret the mystical movement of the late fourteenth century as a resurgence of the penitential ideals of the thirteenth, which had lain dormant during the Avignon papacy. In fact, in the canonization proceedings of the holy women who participated in the movement, one cannot help but be struck by the renewed potency of certain virtues and behaviors traditionally associated with the most rigorous kinds of ascetic spirituality.[14] For example, the proceedings emphasize the suffering these women voluntarily inflicted upon themselves, representing a sort of mute protest against the laxity of the clergy and the tendencies toward secularization that were apparent within the heart of the ecclesiastical hierarchy.[15] Furthermore, most of them held fast to the ideal of poverty: Clare of Montefalco, Delphine of Puimichel, and Dorothy of Montau even engaged in begging, moved less by necessity than by a desire to submit to humiliation, which they received with great joy.[16] If we add to this the fact that some of them claimed to be following direct orders from the Holy Spirit and to be answerable to no one except Christ, we can understand why these women were all targets of persecution before their sanctity was recognized by the Church.[17]

It would be misleading, however, to accord excessive importance to these aspects of the sanctity of the female mystics, since
these were not what attracted the most attention from their contemporaries or from the papacy when it had to pronounce on their
cases. Even if their religious ideals resembled those of the thirteenth century, their emphasis was different from that of St. Francis or St. Elisabeth. To be sure, all female mystics conceived of
Christian perfection as the imitation of Christ. But—except in the
case of Delphine of Puimichel, who belonged to the Franciscan
movement—it was no longer a question of "following nude the
nude Christ" by coming to the aid of the destitute and sharing the
life of the poor. "It is more perfect to imitate Christ in his suffering
than in his actions," said John Marienwerder tellingly of Dorothy
of Montau, his spiritual charge.[18] This skepticism about the value
of action not only called into question the importance of works
of mercy as compared with the contemplation of the sorrowful
mysteries; it also resulted in a new concept of sanctity, defined
as "the perfect knowledge of God, resulting from direct vision."[19]
This process was the complete antithesis of the voluntarist search
for perfection which characterized someone like, for example,
St. Margaret of Hungary in the thirteenth century. In her *Revelations* and in conversations reported by witnesses, St. Bridget
never missed a chance to emphasize that the prophetic function
she exercised was independent of her personal merits. Neither
one's birth, nor station, nor level of culture bore any weight in
the eyes of God, who sent his Spirit and his messages to those
who showed themselves to be receptive to his call.[20] Thus the
mystical movement went far beyond penitential ideals in that it
totally spiritualized religious life, declaring its domain to be the
inner life and its goal to be the identification of the human soul
with God in a loving fusion of wills.[21] It represented the end point
and climax of the evolution which, since the thirteenth century,
had tended to make of religious matters an autonomous universe.

Far from being popular, late medieval mystical sanctity was, on
the contrary, highly elitist. It reached for the summits and was
comfortable there. It flourished in small circles of devout people,
groups of "friends of God" where clergy and laity enamored of perfection came to seek the "spiritual consolations" that their parish
or convent communities were unable to offer.[22] Female mystics

were not indifferent to the salvation of the populace, but they addressed themselves exclusively to political and religious leaders: to kings, popes, at the very least to bishops and heads of orders. The masses, with whom they had very little contact, aroused nothing but their suspicion: didn't they clamor for wonders and miracles, while the only thing that mattered to these women was the conversion of the heart?[23] For a long time, this purified conception of religious life was unpopular and even distrusted. But the Great Schism and the conciliar crisis, by unsettling the certainties of the clerics and shaking the people's confidence in ecclesiastical institutions, brought to the forefront the ideals of the reformers. In their view, both Church and society were so corrupted by sin that grace and salvation could no longer be communicated to humanity through the usual channels, and instead would come via a few exceptional beings designated by their extraordinary gifts. From this perspective, their visions, revelations, and prophetic denunciations constituted an extension of the fervent and intimate dialogue that these sanctified souls were carrying on with the Creator, its prolongation in the direction of the sinful and faithless world. This was not just a matter of a new language: in fact the ability to proclaim the divine will among men soon became the pre-eminent criterion of perfection.[24] Mystical discourse, having rushed to the aid of imperiled hierarchies, received from them in return the legitimacy and consideration that it had long been denied.

Nevertheless, the success of female mystics was ambiguous, and it would be excessive to interpret it as a sign of any lasting improvement in the condition of women in the Church. If the clergy had come to look favorably on them, it was because they managed to escape most of the temptations that threatened human beings. Their perfection was defined by a total abandonment of the self to the divine will in exchange for which they received their exceptional gifts: clairvoyance, prophecy, visions, revelations, and so on. Their ignorance enabled them to receive the infusion of knowledge; their ardent devotion to the body of Christ enabled them to forgo material nourishment; their voluntary association with Christ's suffering enabled them to reach a state of physical insensitivity during the rapture of the perfect union. But it is not enough to recognize the growing place of women among the saints. We must also ask ourselves which aspects of femininity attracted the attention of the clergy. As it happens, they were fascinated not by their wifely or motherly qualities, but by the affective, irrational, and sometimes even pathological aspects of their personalities. The saintly women became the last resort of the Church in the crisis that was shaking theological systems and institutions. Their prestige was momentarily reinforced as a result. But in the end, the lay condition was devalued by this evolution toward a conception of Christian perfection that was increasingly alien to temporal realities and life in society.

TWENTY

EUCHARISTIC DEVOTION AND MYSTICAL UNION IN LATE-MEDIEVAL FEMALE SAINTS

THE OBJECT OF this study is to investigate the role of eucharistic devotion both in the lives of female mystic saints during the late Middle Ages and in others' perception of their sanctity, by drawing on the evidence of canonization proceedings and various hagiographic or iconographic documents. We must state at the outset that this role was considerable; and this phenomenon was as remarkable as it was novel. Indeed, until the fourteenth century, references to the eucharistic piety of the servants of God were few and limited. Of the thirteenth century bishops who became saints, it is simply noted that they celebrated the sacrifice of the Mass in a dignified manner and that they shed abundant tears at the moment of the consecration of the host. In the case of members of mendicant orders, we learn that they recited the Mass every day with pleasure. But in the end, all this is only an unimportant surface manifestation of the pastoral zeal which animated them and which at that time constituted one of the fundamental criteria of perfection for clerics.[1] The same can be said for lay saints of the same period, *mutatis mutandi*. If the inquests inquired into their sacramental practice, it was above all to demonstrate their penitential spirit: they confessed often and prayed regularly, but seldom took communion. There is nothing surprising in this, since we know from other sources that the clergy were concerned more with the risk that the faithful, all of whom presumed to be sinners, would profane the sacrament of the altar, than with encouraging them to develop the habit of receiving the eucharist more frequently than the annual communion mandated by the Fourth Lateran Council.[2]

Beginning with the fourteenth century, and especially after 1350, there was a noticeable shift in this domain. It was then that mystical sanctity, an essentially female phenomenon, sprang into prominence and won ecclesiastical recognition. Eucharistic piety played a crucial role for these holy women, since their ecstasies or raptures often appear to have been brought about by receiving the eucharist or by the desire to receive it. Not satisfied with weeping abundantly at the moment of communion, they seemed to have actually been transformed by the sacrament. For example, "when she received the body of Christ," Jeanne-Marie of Maillé "would become like a rose in May and her face would blush crimson."[3] The descriptions of Catherine of Siena are even more precise. Here the connection between the devotion to the body of Christ and the sacrifice of the mass is severed: the saint sought and ardently desired communion because it gave her direct contact with Jesus through the consecrated host. This meeting, which resulted in the loving fusion of wills—those of Christ and his handmaiden/spouse—would give rise in Catherine to an intoxicating sense of divinization. Comparable accounts were given in the case of Catherine's contemporary, Dorothy of Montau (†1394), a Prussian mystic. The terms describing her experiences came from the vocabulary of sensual delight: *delectatio, consolatio, gaudium*, and so on. An exchange of words of love accompanied these effusions, leading her to a veritable orgasm (*"copula intima peracta"*), which was followed by "pleas and very sweet and delectable thanksgivings to God."[4]

In Dorothy's case everything points to the idea of physical possession. According to a witness, before taking communion one day Dorothy heard the voice of Christ saying to her, "Today you shall have me sacramentally," and in fact she received him in the Eucharist "like the comeliest bridegroom of all the sons of men, like an all-powerful king with his splendid army and train."[5] The theme of the most sublime nuptial mysticism thus emerged from the realm of intimate experience or private confidences to become demonstrative arguments intended to establish and develop reputations for sanctity. From this perspective, eucharistic concerns appeared in an entirely new light and assumed in canonization proceedings and hagiographic literature an importance that they had never had before.

Among these eucharistic themes, the one most commonly found in the lives of holy women in the fourteenth and fifteenth centuries was the opposition between earthly and heavenly nourishment. Once the mystic received the body of her Spouse, she had such a sensation of sweetness (*suavitas, dulcedo*) that all food seemed flavorless by comparison. For this reason, she refused to eat—as in the case of Dorothy of Montau, who undertook fasts that her confessor deemed excessive—or to keep her food down. Witnesses at the proceedings in Venice (1411-1417) testified that Catherine of Siena used a twig to make herself vomit at the end of even very frugal meals, after eating only a bit of bread and some vegetables. As the Carthusian Stefano Maconi clearly stated, these phenomena of anorexia were not unrelated to the origin of Catherine's reputation for sanctity. In fact, it was rumored in Siena that she subsisted solely on the Holy Sacrament, which was held by all to be a great marvel.[6] Here we find a very popular theme: the saint who engaged in such extreme alimentary asceticism that his or her survival could only be the result of a miracle, as divine intervention mysteriously ensured the nourishment of the body. Clerics were suspicious of such exploits: in one of his treatises on the discernment of spirits, Jean Gerson boasted of having unmasked the imposture of a woman in Arras who had acquired a reputation for sanctity because of her alimentary privations but who in fact ate secretly.[7]

The refusal of these female mystic saints to eat normal food represented the mirror image or the counterpart of their intense desire to receive the body of Christ in the form of bread and wine as often as possible. These manifestations of "eucharistic starvation" (*esuries*) ran up against the censure of the Church, which was opposed to frequent communion for the laity. The sources all agree on this subject. Dorothy of Montau, born in 1347, had made her first communion at the age of eleven or twelve. After that, she would have liked to receive the body of Christ seven times a year, but she was only allowed this favor twice a year (during Advent and at the end of Lent). Once she was a married adult, she could take communion seven times a year, and even every Sunday, when she became a widow and a recluse. But this was not enough for her, because she confessed daily and would have liked to be united with God every time that she was freed of her sins. Her profound dissatisfaction revealed itself in her insomnia during the nights preceding her Sunday communions and in her sadness at being separated from God for such a long time. When the moment came, as witnesses at her canonization proceedings stated, "she was as agitated as boiling water" and "if she had been allowed, she would gladly have snatched the host from the hands of the priest and crammed it in her mouth." After receiving the sacrament, she had (we are told) the sensation of carrying a fetus in her belly.[8]

Tommaso Caffarini reported identical phenomena concerning St. Catherine of Siena in his *Libellus de supplemento*, which devoted an entire section to her wonders and eucharistic miracles.[9] Among these was the occasion when Christ came in person to give her communion since she had not received the *licentia communicandi* from her prioress or from the priest who watched over her. Before obtaining this celestial intervention, St. Catherine had addressed a supplication to her mystical Spouse: "Lord, did you not say 'If you do not eat my flesh . . . ?' Yet I do wish to eat this flesh, and they will not give it to me!" Similarly, communion was sometimes offered to her miraculously, when she herself did not dare approach it because of her feelings of unworthiness.[10]

One final subject merits our attention, because it sheds light not only on the mystics' eucharistic devotion but also on their spirituality. It concerns the tangible forms that Jesus assumed in order to give himself eucharistically to his servants in the Sacrament. These images were neither simple nor univocal. First, there was that of the child: Catherine of Siena often saw Christ appear in the host with the features of a child who offered himself to her like a son and whom she received like a mother. She experienced visions of blood even more frequently: during the elevation, she would see the blood of Christ trickling down on the altar. Her profound awareness of the role of this blood as the instrument of our redemption made her a cultivator and propagator of the devotion to the Holy Blood. For this reason, she loved to drink vinegar and any other liquid that had the color of blood, which evoked for her the memory of the Blessed Passion. Similarly, when the host was broken in front of her, she saw it become bloody.[11] Sometimes the female mystics superimposed the two images of the child and the victim of Calvary. At the end of the fourteenth century, Jeanne-Marie of Maillé saw Christ at the elevation of the host "in the form of a very small child running with blood, wounded on the side, hands, and feet so severely that blood flowed copiously."[12] In the case of Catherine of Siena, this "eucharistic realism" reached the point of bloodthirstiness: biting into the host gave her the impression of "chewing the flesh of Jesus, with drops of his blood in her mouth" and "ingesting a tiny, bloody Christ."[13] In any case, the wine of the Eucharist was more important to her than the bread, because wine especially called to mind the slaughter of the Sacrificial Lamb. Thus, like the Bohemian Utraquists in the fifteenth century, she insisted on the fact that it was necessary to drink it to be saved, and be steeped in it to be sanctified. This conviction sometimes gave rise to paroxystic behavior: one day she bit the chalice offered to her with such fervor and force that the imprint of her teeth was left in the metal, and the priest had trouble extracting it from her mouth.[14]

From these few examples, which could easily be multiplied by studying other saints of the same period, two main conclusions emerge: the first concerns the growing importance of eucharistic devotion in religious life and as a criterion of sanctity. In this era, when the mystical model dominated all others, Christian perfection tended to be identified with direct contact with God. Going beyond the traditional kinds of mediation—charity, asceticism, pious works—a small number of elite souls chose to explore the path of intimate union. Accordingly, it is not surprising that the Eucharist, the pre-eminent point of encounter of the divine and the human, took on greater importance. We must note, however, that this devotion to the body and blood of Christ was to a great extent detached from the liturgical celebration within whose framework it had hitherto been situated. The frequent communion so ardently desired by these female saints was seen as an opportunity to enjoy God and his presence totally and intensely. More than just the climax of the sacrifice of the mass, it represented the meeting of the soul and its Spouse and the consummation of a union during which the rest of the world ceased to exist.

The clerics who organized their canonization proceedings, wrote their *vitae*, and celebrated their miracles also emphasized the eucharist, but from another perspective. This was the period, in fact, when sacramental marvels tended to eclipse miraculous cures, whose ambiguity had been denounced by the papacy since the time of Innocent III. Catherine of Siena, to take but a single example, did not do much healing during her lifetime. On the occasion of one of the few healing miracles that is clearly attributable to her, when the beneficiary of the miracle tried to thank her, she replied: "Do not receive this gift from me, but from the venerable sacrament of the body of Jesus Christ which I, despite my unworthiness, have received today."[15] And if we consider the wonders which her Dominican biographers ascribed to her, we see that they consisted of such things as miraculously detecting unconsecrated wafers that had been mixed up with the consecrated ones. More than anything else, it was the visions, revelations, and other "spiritual consolations" which constituted for her entourage the surest proofs of the state of sanctity she had attained. In the final analysis, the Church's recognition of mystical sanctity marks a stage in the history of mentalities because it was accompanied by an effort to define and circumscribe the area of a newly purified supernatural.

TWENTY ONE

The Reaction of the Church to Late-Medieval Mysticism and Prophecy

IT IS NOT THE PURPOSE of this study to add to or to revise our knowledge of the behavior or the teachings of the two great fourteenth-century mystics, St. Bridget (†1373) and St. Catherine (†1380). Many scholars—including theologians, historians, and psychoanalysts—have taken on this task in recent years, in Sweden for St. Bridget, and in Italy for St. Catherine, who has been the object of major studies on the occasion of the six hundredth anniversary of her death. For my part, I would simply like to use the large corpus of sources on the two saints recently made available in good critical editions to underscore the novelty of the experiences of these exceptional women and investigate whether the official recognition of their sanctity insured that mystical and prophetic discourse would have a well-defined status in the late medieval Church.[1] With this goal in mind, I will not be concerned with the minor differences between the Scandinavian princess from the northern mists and the Sienese *mantellata*, the product of an urban civilization that was already bathed in humanist currents. My attention will be focused instead on the essential characteristics that the two had in common and that distinguished them from other female mystics of the Middle Ages.

The outburst of prophecy and visionary mysticism which characterized the fourteenth century could not help but create new problems for the Church, and we even find echoes of these problems in the lives of St. Bridget and St. Catherine, who both found it difficult to make themselves heard. To succeed in finding an audience, they first had to overcome the double handicap of their femininity and their "lack of culture." Indeed, like almost all women of their day, they were *illiteratae*, meaning that they had not received a formal education. Bridget struggled to learn Latin in Rome, and Catherine had only a vague understanding of it. In any case, their cultural formation was more scriptural than theological. Both had a good knowledge of the Bible; Bridget even had it translated into Swedish, along with the important commentary of Master Matthias, which gave great prominence to apocalyptic themes.[2] What Catherine read is less well known, but her correspondence reveals the preponderant influence of the letters of St. Paul and the Johannine writings.[3] In both cases, certain twelfth-century spiritual works must be added, such as the *Speculum virginum* and the *Liber de modo bene vivendi*, attributed at that time to St. Bernard, which the Swedish saint always carried with her, and the *Confessions* of St. Augustine, with which St. Catherine seems to have been familiar.[4] But more than by treatises, which they understood only with difficulty, these pious laywomen seem to have been influenced by manuals of devotions, by saints' lives—Bridget had a certain number translated into Swedish—and especially by the liturgy, from which they drew many of their images, such as the Fountain of Life.[5] For all this, however, they did not become speculative mystics, like so many women in the Germanic world several decades earlier.[6] Bridget even showed great scorn for the learned culture of her day, which she accused of encouraging conceit while doing little or nothing for the salvation of the soul.[7] Catherine, with her ties to the Dominicans, was more respectful of scholars, and the key role that intellect plays in her conception of the mystical life is well known. But she did not make much concrete use of a theology whose rudiments she barely knew: rather than with Thomism, she associated herself, as Louis Canet has shown, with a current of Augustinian thought which, though followed by a minority within the Dominican Order, still retained its vigor.[8] Our saints' relative indifference to doctrinal authority caused them some problems, as we know: when she stopped in Cyprus on her way back from a pilgrimage to the Holy Land,

Bridget was "persecuted" by a Dominican, Brother Simon, who called her mad and would not rest until she had left the island.[9] For her part, Catherine was the target of the hostility of various religious, especially Franciscans, and in 1374 her orthodoxy was examined by a commission of theologians during the chapter general of the Dominicans in Florence.[10] The saints emerged from these tests with their standing enhanced; but the very fact that they ran up against the opposition of certain clerics proves that their right to speak out was not self-evident.

Moreover, their ideas about the role of ordinary believers within the Church ran counter to clerical conceptions. For example, for Bridget perfection consisted of obedience to the divine will and receptivity to the Holy Spirit, which was present in the heart of each of the faithful. One day, as she was meditating on a passage of the *Speculum virginum* concerning the hierarchy of the states of perfection and the graduated rewards that human beings could expect in the other world, depending on whether here on earth they had been virgins, chaste, or married, she fell into a "rapture," at the end of which she declared: "I just heard a voice in my spirit tell me that virginity deserves a crown, widowhood is close to God, marriage is not excluded from heaven, but it is obedience that ushers all people into glory."[11] This point is fundamental because the mission of these laywomen and their role in the Church could only be justified by the equality of all of the baptized in the eyes of God that entitled all those whom He elected, no matter who they were, to speak out. Catherine's ideas were hardly different. In her opinion, God did not care about one's worldly status, but only about the sanctity of one's desires. Any person of any station could love Him because it is not our status that separates us from him, but only bad will.[12]

The fidelity of these great female mystics to their lay condition deserves our full attention. They were not the first women to seek union with God outside the cloister: other women, both orthodox and not, had preceded them. But St. Bridget was one of the rare wives and mothers whose sanctity was recognized by the Church in the Middle Ages, and her example was followed by other married women whose destinies were similar: Dorothy of Montau in eastern Prussia (†1394) and St. Francesca Romana in the city of Rome itself (†1440). St. Bridget marks the end of what may be called the "sexual taboo" in matters of sanctity.[13] The case of St. Catherine seems more conventional, since she lived a celibate life and consecrated her virginity to God, but we will discuss below her exceptional dealings with the opposite sex. Both St. Bridget and St. Catherine were fascinated by the religious life: we know how much energy Bridget put into creating and winning recognition for the Order of the Most Holy Savior of Vadstena, and how enthusiastically Catherine set about establishing the monastery of her dreams at Belcaro, near Siena.[14] But they chose to remain in the world in order to render more effective the message they were assigned to transmit. Living in the world offered them the opportunity to reach a proper balance between action and contemplation. Far from closing out the rest of the world, their mystical experiences thus led directly to a commitment to the salvation of souls. For Bridget, this pastoral dimension was an integral part of her vocation itself; when Christ appeared to her in her great vision of 1345, he declared: "I am your God who wishes to speak with you. . . . I speak not only for you but for the salvation of others."[15]

From the start, Bridget's prophetic mission was directed at the reform of the Church, beginning with that of the papacy, which was conditioned on its return to Rome. Bridget, like Catherine, believed firmly in the apostolic see; both were convinced that the *reformatio in membris* could not be accomplished without the *reformatio in capite*. A slight difference of emphasis can nevertheless be discerned between them: the Swedish saint had a profound, almost visceral attachment to the Church of Rome, from which her country had received the faith and towards which she felt a debt of gratitude and love. Her Rome was that of the martyrs, which Christ had showed her in her vision of 1349: "Go to Rome, where the *piazze* are covered with gold and run red with the blood of the saints."[16] While she lived there, between 1349 and 1373, she spent most of her time visiting the basilicas, the catacombs, and the Coliseum, and diligently following the stational liturgy. Her personal drama, as we find it expressed in the *Revelations*, was that of the tension between her ideal Rome—the Rome of the apostles and martyrs, the holy city where one could earn the jubilee indulgences—and the reality of Rome, with its buildings tumbling in ruin, its unworthy and greedy prelates, and its restless populace always ready to riot. All of Bridget's actions were directed toward making the reality of Rome conform to her ideal, and she considered her success to depend on the papacy's return to the place where it belonged.[17] It was symptomatic in this regard that, to her mind, Rome was synonymous with the entire Church. Her attitude attested indirectly to the irreversible force of the movement of centralization that, since the time of Gregory VII, had tended to identify the Church of Rome ever more closely with the universal Church. Catherine of Siena's inclinations, on the other hand, were perhaps less strictly Roman and more "papalist" in character. It is true that she was every bit as eager as Bridget to see the supreme pontiff return to the banks of the Tiber; but for her, the pontifical office counted more than the city. For this reason, the reproaches she addressed to Gregory XI were less virulent than those of the Swedish prophetess. Despite his faults and vacillations, he remained for her "sweet Christ on earth." As she wrote to the governing council of Florence, at that time engaged in a war with the Holy See,

> Whoever wrongs the pope wrongs God, [and] even if the clergy, including the pope, were devils incarnate rather than good and tender fathers, it would still be fitting to be submissive and obedient to them, not for their sake as individuals but as Christ's vicars, in order to obey God.[18]

However, in her eyes as well as in Bridget's, the Church was above all the mystical body of Christ. As she stated many times, its true wealth lay in souls, not in cities and worldly goods.[19] More than the politics of reconquest of the Papal State, the cause of reform and the prospect of a crusade justified her militant commitment to the return of Peter's successor to Rome.[20] Her ideal was a papacy that would use its immense authority and the eminent prestige of its function to further the good of souls. She was to make this clear in the time of Urban VI, when she tried to assemble a religious elite in Rome that would encircle with its counsels a pope she hoped would be angelic and evangelical. But her efforts in 1379 to realize this old dream of the Spirituals were unavailing. Most of the people whom she summoned to this "council of saints" did not want to leave their convents or their hermitages, and it was not long before the pope himself dashed the saint's hopes.[21]

A final characteristic brought Bridget and Catherine together and distinguished them from the female mystics who had preceded them. This had to do with the kind of relationships that they had with their clerical entourages. These pious laywomen spent all or nearly all of their lives surrounded by priests and, even more often, monks or friars; and they could not fail to come under their influence. We need only think of the roles that the monk Matthias or the hermit Alfonso of Jaen played in the life of St. Bridget. But here, the relationships between the spiritual directors and their charges were utterly different from the ties of dependence and submission which bound St. Elisabeth of Thuringia (†1234) to Conrad of Marburg, or even Dorothy of Montau to John Marienwerder.[22] In the *Revelations*, the former bishop of Jaen was sometimes designated by the title of "*evangelista tuus*," Bridget's evangelist. It was he who, along with the two Peter Olafssons, took down what Bridget reported about her visions and put into good Latin the messages that God had transmitted. His role, as we know, was not that of a simple secretary, and his personal contribution to the composition and presentation of the Bridgettine corpus was certainly not negligible.[23] Nevertheless, he remained in the shadow of the authority of the inspired woman, acting more as her collaborator than her director; and it was to her that everyone referred in praising the *Revelations*. The situation is even clearer in St. Catherine's case, because the clerics in her *famiglia*, of whom the Dominicans were the most numerous, played more the part of disciples than that of spiritual masters. Even Raymond of Capua, whom the Dominicans had placed at her side to be her guide, occasionally received terrible reprimands from the *mamma*, who had no patience for his pusillanimity.[24] Her many secretaries drafted her correspondence and she dictated the *Dialogue* to them, but their influence on her writings was almost exclusively stylistic. In any case, such interference would not have been tolerated by this woman who set herself up as judge of all consciences and whose sentences so often began with the words "*Io voglio . . . ,*" I want. Thus, by claiming for themselves a prophetic function and by presenting themselves as the organs through which God made his will known to the Christian people,

Bridget and Catherine posed the problem of the access of women to the ministry of the Word—something that hitherto had always been denied them—as well as the entirely new question of the authenticity of private revelations and the faith that they should be accorded.

Given these circumstances, it is easy to understand why the Church found it so hard to acknowledge the sanctity of certain female mystics. The popes of the Middle Ages instituted canonization proceedings for various women who belonged to this category, but, apart from St. Bridget's and St. Catherine's, none of these cases came to a successful conclusion at the time.[25] Even for those two whom we are accustomed to considering the greatest female saints of the late Middle Ages, things did not proceed without difficulty. Bridget had the singular privilege of being canonized three separate times: by Boniface IX in 1391, John XXIII in 1415, and Martin V in 1419. Even so, her opponents did not give up the fight: at the Council of Constance, the merits of the Swedish prophetess were publicly contested. Some churchmen, offended by the use that the the Roman obedience and its partisans had made of the *Revelations,* did not hesitate to call her orthodoxy into question; but the pressure brought to bear by the representatives from Scandinavian states prevented the debate from going any further, and the dossier was temporarily closed.[26] At the Council of Basel some years later, the attacks against St. Bridget started up again with renewed vigor. This time they were concentrated on the content of certain revelations, where the churchmen gathered in council discovered 123 heretical propositions![27] Condemnation was avoided, however, thanks to the solid and impassioned intervention of the Dominican Juan de Torquemada, who in his *Defensorium* argued for the orthodoxy of the disputed texts. In the end, the council limited itself to condemning the unwarranted pretensions of Bridgettines, who likened the *Revelations* of the Swedish saint to the Gospels, and to declaring that certain obscure passages should be clarified and revised by competent persons, which was done in 1436.

The case of St. Catherine of Siena does not seem to have aroused the same level of passion, but we should note that her canonization (in 1461) was somewhat belated, and that it was due more to the actions of her illustrious fellow-Sienese, Pope Pius II (Aeneas

Silvius Piccolomini) and of the Dominican Observants (Raymond of Capua, Giovanni Dominici, Tommaso Caffarini), who had made Catherine their emblem, than to her own gifts as a mystic. When the Dominicans wanted to have the reality of her stigmata officially recognized, they met with the resolute opposition of the Franciscans, who were intent on reserving for their founder the privilege of this act of grace, which they considered unique and unrepeatable. The result was a violent conflict between the two orders, which reached its climax during the pontificate of the Franciscan pope Sixtus IV. In a series of bulls issued between 1472 and 1478, he prohibited the representation of the stigmatization of St. Catherine on church walls and forbade all mention of it to the faithful.[28] This decision was not revised until the seventeenth century, when the papacy declared itself in favor of the reality of St. Catherine's stigmata.[29]

The writings of Jean Gerson (1363–1429) provide us with superb evidence about the problems that the rise of female prophecy presented for late medieval clerics. Gerson, himself a fervently spiritual person who was influenced both by Augustinian thought and St. Bonaventure, cannot be considered an opponent of mystical tendencies, even if he did attack Ruysbroek over some ambiguities he had discovered in the *De ornatu nuptiarum spiritualium*.[30] Gerson was deeply troubled by the question of the authenticity of the visions and revelations that had been attributed to many women of his day, and he dedicated several treatises to this problem. The first was *De distinctione verarum visionum a falsis*, written in 1401.[31] In it he voiced his distrust of private revelations and asserted that the Church must have them examined by theologians before making official pronouncements about them. He was also skeptical about extreme asceticism (*abstinentia nimia*), which in his opinion was almost always a cloak for deception and in any case ran the risk of promoting hallucinations. As an example, he told the story of a woman in Arras who had aroused the admiration of the townspeople by not eating for several days in a row. He sought her out and was able to unmask her imposture and shatter her pretensions to sanctity.[32] In the same context he spoke in unflattering terms of another unnamed woman whom some have wished to identify as Catherine of Siena: "In our own time there was a woman who was celebrated for such revelations, whose delirious character is demonstrated, if I am not mistaken, by this symptom." Although it cannot be verified, the hypothesis is entirely plausible, because we know that the Sienese mystic indulged in prolonged fasts and her biographers extolled her physical incapacity to eat solid food.[33] In the same work, Gerson emphasized the need to verify that the love of which these women spoke was actually *divinus amor* and not some ambiguous *humanus amor*—as was the case with a certain Marie of Valenciennes, who, to his mind, expressed herself in terms that were much too passionate and carnal to have been inspired by the Holy Spirit. According to Gerson, this fault was common to many Beguines of his time, both male and female, whose pronouncements and visions should be received with extreme caution.[34]

In his 1415 treatise *De probatione spirituum*, the chancellor of the University of Paris returned to the question of private revelations during the debates of the Council of Constance on St. Bridget.[35] Without taking a position on the specific case of the Swedish saint, he provided a basis for evaluating the merits of religious messages transmitted by devout Christians who were neither theologians nor clerics, while still respecting the spontaneity of their inspiration. A few years later (in May of 1423, according to Palémon Glorieux), he gave the same question more thorough treatment in his *De examinatione doctrinarum*, where he emphasized the importance of criteria of authority for the discernment of spirits.[36] In his opinion, only those who have either an official function in the Church, doctrinal authority, direct experience, or special charisma had the right to make pronouncements on these subjects. But it was also important to ascertain whether their revelations conformed to the Scriptures and to ecclesiastical tradition, and to investigate the station, qualities, morals, and goals of those who claimed to speak in the name of God. At the end of the treatise, he summarized his ideas in the following lines:

Concilium, Papa, Praesul, Doctor bene doctus,
Discretor quoque spirituum de dogmate censent.
Qualis sit doctrina, docens quis quique sodales,
Si finis sit fastus quaestusque sive libido.

> Let Council, Pope, Leader, learned Master,
> Discerning person, too, judge the inspiration
>   of the teaching:
> What kind of doctrine it is, who the teacher
>   and who the associates,
> Whether the purpose be pomp and profit
>   or debauchery.

For our purposes, this work is all the more important in that Gerson made explicit reference to the deathbed statement of Gregory XI, who advised his followers to be suspicious of the *mulierculae* and other visionaries, and regretted having been too attentive to them in making the decision to return to Rome, which was to be the origin of the Great Schism.[37]

———— ❧ ————

Thus, despite the favorable impression that might follow from the canonizations of St. Bridget and St. Catherine of Siena, we can affirm without exaggeration that mystical discourse in its visionary and prophetic forms did not find a place in the late medieval Church. Attacked by some who considered it usurpation or abuse, it was exploited by others only in order to restore some luster to an obedience or a pontifical monarchy that had been badly tarnished. Once the Schism and the conciliar crisis passed, the simple faithful who had believed themselves to be authorized to speak on behalf of God would be asked to return to the ranks and leave the positions of leadership to the learned, who had yielded them only temporarily and unwillingly. There are various reasons for this lack of comprehension. The first—unacknowledged but obvious—had to do with the fact that most of the mystics were women. To the clerics, convinced of the intrinsic weakness of the female sex, it was obvious that these women, if left to their own devices, were very likely to fall into excess or error. Moreover, the academics and masters of theology who then held sway in the Church were suspicious of these uneducated laywomen who dared to stand up to them and even to take them to task. To the extent that it seemed to call into question the role of the clergy in the transmission of the Word, female prophecy could not help but provoke the hostility of those who considered themselves to be the indispensable intermediaries between God and men. For this reason, it is not surprising that some of these women, from Marguerite Porète to Joan of Arc, to mention only the best known, ended by being burned at the stake. It was not until the sixteenth and especially the seventeenth centuries—with Teresa of Avila, Jeanne of Chantal, Marguerite-Marie Alacoque, and so many others—that the inspired word was admitted into the Church and awarded the place of honor that the medieval clergy had denied it. But this new mysticism which took a leading role with the support of the ecclesiastical hierarchy no longer had any prophetic overtones. While Bridget of Sweden and Catherine of Siena had tried to shape the history of their times by direct recourse to the supernatural and by acting upon institutions, the saints of the following centuries were heirs of the other current of medieval mysticism: that which, far from the world and from men, considered the intimate union of the Creator with his creature the only experience worth desiring.

TWENTY TWO

Joan of Arc and Female Prophecy in the Fourteenth and Fifteenth Centuries

THE TRADITIONAL IMAGE of Joan of Arc, as schoolbooks have transmitted it for generations, has so accustomed us to see her as a sort of meteor, an exceptional being who stepped out from the shadows without warning and attained tremendous fame in just a few months, that we have come to accept that her career had the same logic as fairy tales or hagiographic literature. The fact that a humble peasant woman from Lorraine, who had come to see the Dauphin with a few men-at-arms, managed to be received by him and, what is more, convinced him to entrust her with an army, seems so "normal" to us, after hearing the story told so many times, that we have ceased to be surprised by it. But let us imagine for a moment what would happen today if a female visionary from a provincial town asked to be admitted to the presence of the head of state in order to give him warnings and advice. The odds are that she would have little success getting past the entrance gate to the presidential palace, even if she had a letter of recommendation from the prefect of the Department of the Vosges. Should we conclude that medieval authorities did not react in the same way as modern ones to such spontaneous initiatives, and that the king of France paid more heed to his subjects than the president does to his fellow citizens? That is hardly likely, and we would soon be tangled in contradictions if we pursued that line of reasoning. Therefore, I believe that we should seek a different kind of answer to this question, which looms large as soon as we attempt to disengage the history of the Maid of Orleans from the clichés that encumber it. In fact, it seems to me that her adventures were less unusual than we have been led to believe, and that they can be elucidated if we place her in a larger context. Perhaps we could even simply call her one member of a distinctive group, the female prophets of the late Middle Ages. Far from minimizing her merits or questioning her greatness, my interpretation aims to show that it was not her times that made her an extraordinary personage, but rather the richness of her personality and the impression she left on the collective memory of the French.

During the second half of the fourteenth century, there developed a current of female prophecy whose leading representatives came from the laity. The rash of visions and revelations which marked the century between 1350 and 1450 was evidently related to the crisis which was then agitating the Church. The transfer of the papal seat from Rome to Avignon, the abortive return of Urban V, the tribulations of the Great Schism after 1378, and, finally, the conflicts that for decades set the popes against the great councils of Constance and especially Basel: all of these helped to create a climate of disarray and, before long, an institutional crisis that made a profound impression on devout spirits. Thus the conditions encouraged people—almost all of them women—to speak out, people who up to that time had lacked the opportunity and the ability to make their voices heard in a Church in which the weight of clerical structures had become overwhelming.[1] Most displays of prophetic inspiration took a stereotypical form: one day an ordinary laywoman, generally a very pious person, would hear God summon her to the ministry of the Word and would receive visions and revelations. She would then seek to communicate them in the form of messages addressed to the pope and the rulers, since the object of the messages was the good of the Church and the salvation of the Christian people, a responsibility which rested primarily on the shoulders of the leaders. Not content with writing them letters, the inspired woman would try to meet them in person to persuade them of the authenticity of her mission and provide them with unmistakable signs of her divine election.

In France, the first of these female prophets was a widow named Constance, from Rabastens, in the region of Albi. Her revelations, which must have originally been in Latin or Provençal, have been preserved in a Catalan translation. They were written down by her confessor, Raymond of Sabanac, and published by the great historian of the Western Schism, Noël Valois, at the end of the nineteenth century.[2] This woman, who (like all the female mystics of her times) called herself the "bride of Christ," seems to have discovered her prophetic vocation during a vision in 1384. In her revelations, Constance of Rabastens expressed the kind of doubts about the legitimacy of the Avignonese pope that must have been widespread in southern France. She claimed that Christ had declared to her: "The cardinals have crucified me a second time; they have done worse things than Pontius Pilate. I had created one pope; they have appointed another."[3] As an opponent of Clement VII, she considered Urban VI to be the authentic successor to the throne of St. Peter and hoped that France would side with him. It is in this connection that the political dimension of her prophecies becomes clear. In fact, the Hundred Years' War was raging at the time, and southwestern France was not spared by the conflicts of 1384-1386, when these messages were recorded. Constance reacted patriotically, as Joan of Arc was to do some decades later. She appealed to Gaston Phoebus, the count of Foix, who was loyal to King Charles VI, to take up arms against John II of Armagnac, who at the time had sided with the English in the Albi region. Moreover, she assigned Gaston Phoebus a mission which went far beyond the local context: he was to save France from foundering in the abyss, reestablish the legitimate pope—the pope of Rome—on his throne, and lead Charles VI to the conquest of the Holy Land.[4] This yearning for peace between the principal sovereigns of Christendom in order that they might make the "great crossing" together under the aegis of a regenerated papacy was a typically medieval preoccupation, and one that had been present in St. Bridget and St. Catherine of Siena. But it does not seem that her passionate appeals met with much success. We do know that starting in 1385 Constance of Rabastens ran afoul of the Inquisitor of Toulouse, who forbade her to publish her visions, and that she spent some time in prison.[5] After that, she disappeared without a trace.

A few years later, another woman, Jeanne-Marie of Maillé (1331–1414), had similar experiences; but we are much better informed about them, thanks to the records of the inquest held in Tours in 1415 to promote her canonization.[6] In this case, we are dealing with a woman of the upper aristocracy of the Loire valley, who was related by blood or friendship with the most powerful lineages of the day: she was the godmother of one of the sons of Louis I of Anjou and Marie of Brittany, and a friend of Yolanda of Aragon, wife of Louis II of Anjou (who would later be a supporter of Joan of Arc), as well as of Charlotte, Queen of Cyprus, the sister of Jacques II de Bourbon, count de la Marche.[7] Widowed by Robert of Sillé in 1362, she went to Tours, where she lived in reclusion next to the Franciscan convent under the direction of one of their number, Father Martin of Boisgaultier. She too was profoundly disturbed by the prolongation of the Great Schism; in 1396, she predicted the election of a Franciscan pope who would put an end to the rift in the Church, and this prophecy was not forgotten when the Franciscan Alexander V was elected by the Council of Pisa in 1409.[8] Nor was Jeanne-Marie indifferent to the calamities of her own country. As early as 1395, she announced to her entourage "many things which would come to pass in the kingdom of France." She had also predicted that Charles VI would come to Tours that same year, an event which took place as foretold. On that occasion she was presented to the sovereign by his nephew, Louis II of Anjou, and had the opportunity to converse with him "in private and at length." Unfortunately, we know nothing of the substance of their discussions, apart from the fact that she persuaded the king to liberate a certain number of prisoners. In 1398 she went to Paris and had another meeting with Charles VI in the Church of the Celestines, whose tenor is also unknown.[9] She next spent a week as the guest of Isabelle of Bavaria. She took this occasion to reproach the queen and her courtiers for their luxury, singling out the pointed shoes then in fashion at the court of France for special criticism, and took them to task for their misrule, lecturing them about the suffering of the masses who were crushed by taxes and poverty. Having received no satisfaction there (as was only to be expected), she returned to Tours to finish her days in prayer and penitence.[10]

A third and final figure deserves our attention: a simple peasant, Marie Robine or Marie the Gascon (†1399).[11] Born in Héchac

(Department of the Hautes-Pyrénées) in the diocese of Auch, she was suffering from a supposedly incurable illness in 1387. Attracted by the young cardinal Peter of Luxemburg's reputation as a miracle worker, she went to his tomb in Avignon, the site of many of his miracles. There she was cured in the presence of Clement VII, and she remained thereafter in the city of the popes, living as a recluse within the walls of the cemetery of Saint Michael, supported by the alms that the pontiffs instructed the Celestines to provide her.[12] After a few months, she too began to have visions and to dictate the revelations that God was transmitting to her. From the outset they were directed toward two problems: the settlement of the schism, and the attitude of the French monarchy in this matter. Marie Robine's second vision, dated February 22, 1398, was quite explicit about this:

> "Go see the king," said the voice to her, "tell him to achieve the unity of the Church through the means that I have indicated and to see to it that he does not withdraw from the obedience of Benedict XIII. Such a ploy is rooted in pride, envy and avarice . . . Tell the king also to bring about reform in the Church."[13]

Faithful to God's instructions, she wrote to Charles VI but received no response. After another vision, which took place in April 1398 in the presence of Marie of Brittany, she went to Paris, arriving on June 2, and tried in vain to have an audience with the French prelates, who were holding a national council to discuss the very question of the subtraction of obedience.[14] Unable to meet with the king, she nevertheless managed to be admitted to the presence of Isabelle of Bavaria, who entrusted her with a message for Benedict XIII, calling on him to resign. Back in Avignon, she had more visions in 1399, visions whose content was increasingly pessimistic and apocalyptic: they presented the spectacle of France ravaged by the Antichrist, and even evoked a popular revolt which would destroy the monarchy and its capital:

> "We asked the King of France to restore the Church militant to its rightful state, yet he will do nothing for us," said the voice; "we will cast him from his throne by the hands of his own subjects, and some will die in great rivers of blood, and

our followers will be true martyrs . . . and people will say: here stood Paris."[15]

With the figure of Marie Robine, we approach that of Joan of Arc. As Noël Valois already noted early this century, the theologian Jean Erault in fact invoked Marie's testimony during the inquest conducted in Poitiers in March, 1429 by a commission of prelates and doctors assembled at the Dauphin's request to scrutinize Joan of Arc's orthodoxy.[16] If we can believe Jean Barbin, who mentioned this episode at the time of Joan's rehabilitation proceedings, Erault noted in her favor the prophecy of a certain "Marie of Avignon," who can only have been our Marie Robine. She was quoted as saying: "I had many visions of this sort: many weapons appeared to me; I was afraid for a moment that I would have to use them myself. I was told not to worry, for they were not meant for me, but for a maiden who would come after me and would rescue the kingdom."[17] The prophetic announcement cited by Jean Barbin does not appear in the text of the *Livre des révélations et visions de Marie Robine*, but this book is not necessarily a compendium of everything that the recluse of Avignon ever said. It could also be an apocryphal tradition, invented after the fact to help the cause. In either case, all the evidence leads us to believe that the prophecies of Marie Robine were more widely known than the survival of one unique manuscript might indicate.

From the study of these individual cases, which all date from France in the years 1380–1400 and are certainly not anomalous, a pattern of female prophetic intervention emerges. The process consists essentially of going to court to communicate God's warnings and signals to the king. The same action is one of the central elements of the story of Joan of Arc, and it is not unreasonable to think that if she was received by the "King of Bourges," and rather effortlessly at that, it was because other prophetesses had preceded her to the palace steps, thereby rendering her request less unusual.

At first sight, however, Joan of Arc seems very different from the women we have been discussing, who belonged to the generation before hers. Joan left us neither prophecies nor revelations, and although she sent many letters (to the English, the Hussites, and others), she is known for her military exploits rather than her correspondence. Nevertheless, the differences should not be pushed too far, because we cannot forget that, like Constance of Rabastens or Marie Robine, Joan claimed to be inspired by "voices"—those of St. Catherine, St. Margaret, or St. Michael—that incited her to work for the salvation of the kingdom. This turned out to be one of the principal charges lodged against her by the judges of Rouen. In addition, it is very important to note that from the start, Joan was considered a prophetess by her contemporaries. As evidence we need only mention the first reference to Joan in the notes of an anonymous Parisian chronicler known as the "Burgher of Paris," when he described the events of 1429 in Orleans:

> "Item, at that time there was a Maid, as she was called, in the valley of the Loire, who called herself a prophet and said: 'Such and such a thing will really take place.' And she was entirely opposed to the regent of France and his men."[18]

Indeed, Joan's military actions need to be placed in their religious as well as their political context. In the very year that she freed Orleans, the Parisian masses had been thrown into upheaval by the preaching of Brother Richard, a Franciscan Observant who seems to have created around himself an atmosphere of exaltation based on prophetic announcements and apocalyptic predictions. This aroused the suspicions of the Parisian authorities, who accused him of collusion with the Armagnacs and soon put an end to his sermons. It is not surprising to find this same person in Orleans in 1430, where he preached during the Lenten season with equal success. We know that Joan met him at that time, and that he accompanied Queen Marie of Anjou when she made her entrance into the city in May. According to the chronicle of the notary of La Rochelle, the monk convinced the residents of Troyes that Joan was capable of enabling the French army to pass right over their ramparts.[19] Whatever the accuracy of this report and the nature of the relationship—still insufficiently studied—between Joan of Arc and the great popular preacher, it seems clear that her military exploits were related in some way to the religious atmosphere of the times, an atmosphere deeply marked by eschatological tensions and messianic expectations of which women were increasingly the beneficiaries, not just the mouthpieces. Indeed, in an *exemplum* at the end of his *De examinatione doctrinarum*, the great Parisian scholar Jean Gerson tells of the arrest in Bourg-en-Bresse in 1424 of a devout woman who claimed to work miracles and who affirmed "that she was one of five women sent by God in his compassion to redeem innumerable souls from Hell."[20] Joan of Arc's message was certainly more political, and we know that she cared more for the salvation of France than for that of Christendom. But the passion that drove her was not in any way nationalistic, and the fact that she wrote a "letter to the Hussites" proves that she was not indifferent to the fate of the Church.[21]

In fact, Joan of Arc was not the only woman of her era to take up arms for a worthy cause. Another "holy woman," Piéronne the Breton, a penitent under the direction of Brother Richard, fought on the side of the Armagnacs with a female friend. They were captured by the Anglo-Burgundians near Corbeil and tried in Paris in 1430. According to the account of the Burgher of Paris, Piéronne affirmed that "God often appeared to her in his humanity," a statement which was enough to get her burned at the stake in front of the church of Notre Dame.[22] Even more unusual was the story of the "false maiden Claudia," reported by the same chronicler and by the German inquisitor Johannes Nider. Nider spoke of her in his famous treatise *Formicarius*, written between 1430 and 1438, which was dedicated to the multifarious evil deeds of the Devil. He made particular mention of the cases of women "appearing to be men who said that they had been sent by God"—a formulation which in itself demonstrated that these women constituted a well-defined category and were not just isolated cases.[23] He discussed Joan of Arc and two other women, one of whom was burned at the stake in Paris (undoubtedly Piéronne the Breton), but gave special attention to a "maiden" from the diocese of Cologne, whom he had heard about from one of his colleagues, the Dominican Heinrich Kalteisen. This unnamed woman dressed as a man and led the existence of a military commander;[24] she even boasted that she could guarantee the victory of one of the two candidates vying to be archbishop of Trier. Summoned by the inquisitor of Cologne, she managed to flee to France under the protection of Count Ulrich of Württemberg. There she revealed her "true nature," becoming the concubine of a priest in Metz, after having married a knight. For Nider, her affirmation that Joan of Arc had indeed been sent by God was merely another reason to doubt that this was so. We would know nothing more about her if the Burgher of Paris had not written at length, under the year 1440, about the fantastic adventures of the person he called the false maid Claudia, who was thought by many of her contemporaries to be Joan of Arc: persuaded that Joan had not died in Rouen, they believed she had now mysteriously returned to life or come out of hiding.[25] The false Joan herself fostered this ambiguity by calling herself Joan of Lily. Arrested and tried in Paris in 1440, she admitted having come from the region of Cologne and having married a knight in Lorraine named Robert des Armoises, to whom she had borne two sons. Having gone to see the pope in Italy to expiate a grave sin, she became a "soldier in the war of the Holy Father Eugene"; then she came to France and participated in military operations in the region of Poitiers in 1439.[26] The verdict in her trial has not survived, and we have no further trace of her.

Faced with these manifestations of female prophecy in their most authentic and most equivocal forms, the great majority of clerics in the first half of the fifteenth century were profoundly suspicious: their reactions waver between skepticism and outright rejection, extending even to the execution of women who claimed—improperly, in their opinion—to be messengers of the Almighty. Moreover, Gerson was one of the very few theologians of his time to admit, despite his prejudice against mysticism and female revelations, that Joan of Arc might have been sent by God.[27] On this point Gerson, alone among all his colleagues, concurred with popular sentiment, which rallied unreservedly to the Maid. After so many decades of trouble, during which the men who governed the Church and France had proven incapable of finding cures for the ills afflicting their institutions, the times were ripe for the public to transfer its continually frustrated hopes for victory and peace to the figure of a woman. Others had preceded her on this path, but without obtaining the same results. Joan's success was undoubtedly due to her gift of prophecy—the sign of her divine election—and even more so to the authenticity of her spiritual life, to which the trial at Rouen bore moving witness.[28] Considered from this perspective, the condemnation and execution of the "good woman from Lorraine" take on a special meaning, one which has been obscured by an exclusively patriotic interpretation of the "Joan of Arc phenomenon." Her death at the stake was not only the result of the dynastic Anglo-French conflict, nor even of the political struggle between the Armagnacs and Burgundians. It demonstrated, rather, the exasperation felt by the university scholars and the great clerics, masters of the Church during the years of the Council of Basel, when confronted with the religion of the simple folk and the pretensions of these women who claimed the right to speak freely in the name of the Holy Spirit, which they had received through the grace of baptism.

CONCLUSION

AT THE END OF this volume, which has focused on particular moments and settings, it would surely not be inappropriate to step back somewhat from the facts and attempt to trace some general patterns. This attempt at recapitulation is all the more appropriate because, without overlooking the importance of popular religious movements—which is fundamental, but difficult to define because of their exceptional and spasmodic character—we have concentrated on more stable groups, like confraternities, and the individual destinies of a small number of late medieval men and women, each one of which is by definition a particular case.

First of all, our analysis has revealed the existence of major differences between the actual religious practices of the laity and what was prescribed for them. Many laypeople did less than what the Church required, as we know from the endless complaints about negligent or disobedient parishioners, repeated everywhere in the synodal statutes and on the occasion of pastoral visits. Some, on the other hand, asked more of the Church: mystics who desired frequent communion, for example, or the Bohemian Hussites, one of whose basic demands was permission to receive the Eucharist in both forms, a privilege that was in principle reserved to the clergy. But it is not enough, as too often has been done in the past, to consider these differences only in the light of their distance from the ecclesiastical norms which are taken to be absolutes or ideals.

One of the novel characteristics of the period we have studied was the ability of laypeople to create autonomous forms of piety which, while generally avoiding clashes with orthodoxy, succeeded in reshaping the religious message disseminated by the clergy to meet their feelings and specific needs. This is particularly obvious in the case of devotions to the saints: in establishing the cults of "martyred children," presented as victims of the accursed Jews, or in that of St. Roch, which incarnated the anguished yearning of the people of the fifteenth century for protection against the plague, it was the common people who led the way, with the clergy doing their best later on to channel or "salvage" devotions which it felt more ready to tolerate than approve. This process was repeated in other, even more important areas, like civic religion, so lively in the Italian communcs and city-states, and monarchic religion, which flourished north of the Alps, particularly in France, at the time of the Hundred Years' War. Far from being minor or residual phenomena, these were fundamental forms of lay religiosity, intent on linking religious affairs with political, economic, and social concerns, and placing the power of the sacred, the source of fertility and harmony, at the service of the human communities in which it was rooted.

At the same time, but in the opposite direction, a current of mystical inspiration was attempting to establish a purely spiritual conception of religious life based on a personal and intimate relationship with God. To be sure, the lay groups actually affected by these new tendencies were small, since the masses remained attached to their far more conventional ideas of the supernatural, by virtue of which a certain number of efficacious rites were supposed to guarantee bountiful harvests and protect the populace against natural calamities and enemy attacks. If these beliefs cannot necessarily be interpreted as superstitions or magical practices, we have to admit nonetheless that beginning with the fourteenth century it becomes difficult to consider the lay world a homogeneous unity. An ever-deeper rift was opening up between a devout minority, in search of "spiritual consolations," and the masses, who remained quite attached to their individual and collective practices, the aims of which were purely utilitarian. In the end, this contrast was to lead to the lacerations of the Reformation, which would attempt at the same time to reestablish God in His transcendence, to free the religious from the ascendency of the social, and to liberate civic society from clerical interference.

It is appropriate, finally, to return to the notion of the rise of the laity, in order to remove any misunderstandings. We have observed the incontestable rehabilitation of the lay status in the twelfth and thirteenth centuries. This period marked the collapse of a set of obstacles and restrictions that had blocked the access of the faithful to an authentic religious life. The first of these was war: the Church first held it in check, then sanctified it through the Crusades. The second was manual labor, whose ascetic value and, above all, social utility were increasingly valued by the clergy. Indeed, all kinds of work were acceptable: that of peasants, artisans, and even merchants, for at the beginning of the fourteenth century, some hagiographers and theologians, generally with ties to the mendicant orders, went so far as to affirm that merchants could sanctify themselves in the exercise of their professions. Moreover, the practice of charity through works of mercy gave all of these men (and women as well) an opportunity to work out their own salvation, while penitential spirituality attached value to humility, asceticism and poverty. This was the time when the canonists confirmed the existence of a new type of Christian, the "lay religious" (*laicus religiosus*), who was neither worldly nor withdrawn from the world but attempted to carry on his professional and familial life in conformity with the requirements of the Gospel. Even the fundamental obstacle of sexuality, which had prevented married people and especially women from attaining sanctity, seemed to crumble around the edges in the thirteenth century, with the development of the new concept of conjugal chastity. This notion made it possible to define a Christian practice of marriage, justified by procreation and the spiritual progress of the couple, who were called upon to vanquish their libido by periodically observing continence. Thus all of the major problems that had for so long kept the laity from reaching Christian perfection seem to have been solved—at least in principle—at the beginning of the fourteenth century.

Nevertheless, in just a few decades all of these achievements were abruptly called back into question, and, especially after 1348, spirituality of the most traditional kind returned with a vengeance. Under the influence of the *Lives of the Desert Fathers*, translated and amply discussed by the preachers, and of St. Jerome, who, as Daniel Russo has ably demonstrated in the case of Italy, then reached the zenith of his popularity, a new climate took hold, exalting eremitism and reclusion, rigorous asceticism and the most classic forms of flight from the world.[1]   The evangelism of the thirteenth century, Franciscan in inspiration, was now replaced by a religion of pain and sorrow, dominated by the problem of death and last things and full of eschatological tensions. In this context, a value as significant as poverty became spiritualized, with emphasis now placed on the annihilation of the soul and the renunciation of all individual will, rather than on relationships with one's fellow men and women. Moreover, the poor began to be regarded with suspicion: they were considered imposters or loafers who avoided work. Individual charity on their behalf seemed more dangerous than useful. On all fronts, the efforts of the previous century to provide the laity with an autonomous form of spirituality lost ground. Following the lead of the Franciscan Peter John Olivi, some theologians openly doubted whether marriage was fully sacramental; military functions and royal power became increasingly secularized; and, after St. Louis, the synthesis of good government and Christian perfection no longer seemed possible. Most significantly, at the time of the Council of Vienne and during the pontificate of John XXII, the ecclesiastical hierarchy and the secular clergy turned against the lay men and women who had tried to lead an intense religious life while remaining in the world. The condemnations of Beguines and Beghards between 1316 and 1323 signalled a decisive change in this regard. The clergy, anxious to retain their role as indispensable mediators in the religious domain, opposed the translation of the Scriptures into the vernacular and, at best, offered the faithful nothing more than second-rate "moral lessons," or programs for spiritual life that were totally unsuited to the concrete conditions of lay existence. All efforts were directed toward bringing the laity back into line, turning them back into docile sheep.

This reversion was especially marked in the area that had already posed the greatest problem in the preceding era: sexuality. In fact, although many spiritual writers and preachers of the fourteenth and fifteenth centuries denounced the fundamentally perverse nature of sexuality, it would be unfair to attribute this conviction to the clergy alone. If the affirmation of the primacy of virginity was rooted in a venerable Christian tradition, it was also echoed in general belief, which saw it as a source of magical powers. Theologians and ordinary faithful alike considered sexual life, even in marriage, to be a kind of defilement or stain: one sign of this is the liturgical ceremony of churching, intended to reintegrate women into the community after childbirth. In a society where the weight of sexual taboos remained considerable, and in which rape was considered not so much an attack on charity as a sacrilege, it is hardly surprising that the only women who received the honor of sainthood were unmarried or widowed.

Must we end this volume with a recognition of failure, as if, after a period of opening and thaw, the situation had simply returned to its starting point? That would certainly be excessive, for it must be emphasized that the "mystical invasion" of the late Middle Ages, in which women played an essential role, left in ruins the traditional monastic framework that placed monks and nuns at the vertex, with the secular clergy below them and the simple faithful on the bottom. As St. Bridget of Sweden stated in one of her revelations on women: "Virginity deserves a crown, widowhood is close to God, marriage is not excluded from heaven, but it is obedience that ushers all people into glory." By making admission to heaven depend on performing God's will rather than belonging to a given spiritual order, the Swedish prophetess ratified one of the fundamental conquests of lay spirituality. But we must recognize that, torn as it was between a Church in the process of clericalization and a society just beginning to become secularized, late medieval culture proved unable to define a peculiarly Christian usage of the world for those living in it. The problem in all of its complexity was not even posed until the seventeenth century, with St. Francis of Sales and his *Introduction to the Devout Life*. It is not clear, moreover, that it has been satisfactorily resolved even now, and that the questions that we have raised in this book have lost all their immediacy.

NOTES

Preface

1. "The Saint," in *Medieval Callings*, ed. Jacques Le Goff, trans. Lydia G. Cochrane (Chicago: University of Chicago Press, 1990), 313-345.

2. *Les laïcs au Moyen Age. Pratiques et expériences religieuses* (Paris: Les Editions du Cerf, 1987); *I laici nel Medioevo: Pratiche ed esperienze religiose*, trans. Francesco Sircana (Milan: Mondadori, 1989).

3. The essays not included in this translation are chapters 5, 6, and 10 of the original: "Les chrétiens face à la guerre, de l'Antiquité à la Renaissance," "Homebon de Crémone (†1197), marchand et saint," and "Les confréries au Moyen Age: esquisse d'un bilan historiographique." In rearranging the essays, the present chapter 5 took the place of the original chapters 5 and 6, and parts II and III of the original were re-ordered and combined to form the present part II. The present chapter 5 originally appeared as "Une nouveauté du XIIe siècle: Les saints laïcs de l'Italie communale," in *L'Europa dei secoli XI e XII fra novità e tradizione: Sviluppi di una cultura*, Atti della X Settimana internazionale di studio. Mendola, 25-29 August 1986 (Milan: Vita e Pensiero, 1989), 57-80.

4. "Une campagne de pacification en Lombardie autour de 1233: L'action politique des Ordres Mendiants d'après la réforme des statuts communaux et les accords de paix," *Mélanges d'Archéologie et d'Histoire*, 78 (1966): 503-549; and "Les stigmates de saint François et leurs détracteurs dans les derniers siècles du Moyen Age," *Mélanges d'Archéologie et d'Histoire*, 80 (1968): 595-625. These essays, like most of the others mentioned in this introduction, were collected in the volume *Religion et société dans l'Occident médiéval* (Turin: Bottega d'Erasmo, 1980).

5. "Charité et pauvreté chez Ste Elisabeth de Thuringe d'après les actes du procès de canonisation," in *Etudes sur l'histoire de la pauvreté (Moyen Age-XVIe siècle)*, ed. Michel Mollat (Paris: Publications de la Sorbonne, 1974), vol. 1, 163-173.

6. "L'idéal de sainteté dans le mouvement féminin franciscain aux XIIIe et XIVe siècles," in *Movimento religioso femminile e Frances-*

canesimo nel secolo XIII, Atti del VII Convegno internazionale di Studi francescani, Assisi, 11-13 October 1979 (Assisi: Società internazionale di Studi francescani, 1980), 317-337 (chapter 14 of this volume).

7. *La Spiritualité du Moyen Age occidental, VIIIe-XIIe siècles* (Paris: Presses Universitaires de France, 1975)

8. Gabriel Le Bras, *Les institutions ecclésiastiques de la Chrétienté médiévale,* vol. 12 of *Histoire de l'Eglise depuis les origines jusqu'à nos jours,* ed. Augustin Fliche and Victor Martin (Paris: Bloud & Gay, 1959 and 1964); *Etudes de sociologie religieuse* (Paris: Presses Universitaires de France, 1955 and 1956); *Introduction à l'histoire de la pratique religieuse en France* (Paris: Presses Universitaires de France, 1942 and 1945); *L'église et le village* (Paris: Flammarion, 1976).

9. Introduction to Etienne Delaruelle, *La piété populaire au Moyen Age* (Turin: Bottega d'Erasmo, 1980), xix and xv. In addition to this introduction, Vauchez contributed a bibliography of Delaruelle's publications to this collection of his essays. Herbert Grundmann's *Religiöse Bewegungen im Mittelalter* (Berlin, 1935; second edition Darmstadt: Wissenschaftliche Buchgesellschaft, 1961), though not often cited by Vauchez, is nonetheless a decisive influence on his treatment of the religious movements of the twelfth and thirteenth centuries—as it is on any discussion of that subject.

10. Etienne Delaruelle, E.-R. Labande, and Paul Ourliac, *L'Eglise au temps du Grande Schisme et de la crise conciliaire (1378-1449),* vol. 14 of *Histoire de l'Eglise depuis les origines jusqu'à nos jours,* ed. Augustin Fliche and Victor Martin (Paris: Bloud & Gay, 1964).

11. Gilles Gérard Meersseman, *Ordo Fraternitatis: Confraternite e pietà dei laici nel medioevo,* Italia Sacra, 24-26 (Rome: Herder, 1977).

12. I am thinking in particular of Jean Delumeau, who has written both works of fundamental importance for early modern religious history and deeply personal meditations on the present condition and the future of Christianity. Delumeau traces his trajectory from history to active engagement in the preface to *Un chemin d'histoire. Chrétienté et christianisation* (Paris: Fayard, 1981).

13. Personal communication from André Vauchez; May 21, 1991.

14. For an excellent review of the literature and analysis of current debates, see John Van Engen, "The Christian Middle Ages as an Historiographical Problem," *American Historical Review,* 91 (1986): 519-552.

15. The range of Vauchez's current inquiries is indicated by the "Questionnaire d'orientation" appended to his essay on "Les pouvoirs informels dans l'Eglise aux derniers siècles du Moyen Age: visionnaires, prophètes et mystiques," *Melanges de l'École Française de Rome, Moyen*

Age-Temps Modernes, 96 (1984): 292–293. The bulk of the essay itself has been incorporated in chapter 18 of this volume.

Introduction

1. [Michel Mollat, *The Poor in the Middle Ages: An Essay in Social History*, trans. Arthur Goldhammer (New Haven and London: Yale University Press, 1986); Bronislaw Geremek, *The Margins of Society in Late Medieval Paris*, trans. Jean Birrell (New York: Cambridge University Press, 1987); Georges Duby, *William Marshal: The Flower of Chivalry*, trans. Richard Howard (New York: Pantheon Books, 1985). Of course, William Marshal was hardly an unknown figure before Duby's work: see, for instance, Sidney Painter, *William Marshall: Knight-Errant, Baron, and Regent of England* (Baltimore: Johns Hopkins University Press, 1933; reprint Toronto: University of Toronto Press, 1982).]

2. [As quoted in Brian Tierney, *The Crisis of Church and State* (Englewood Cliffs, NJ: Prentice-Hall, 1964), 175.]

3. [Emile Amann and Auguste Dumas, *L'Eglise au pouvoir des laïcs (888–1057)*, vol. 7 of *Histoire de l'Eglise depuis les origines jusqu'à nos jours*, ed. Augustin Fliche and Victor Martin (Paris: Bloud & Gay, 1943).]

4. [Cinzio Violante, *La pataria milanese e la riforma ecclesiastica, I: Le premesse (1045–1087)* (Rome: Istituto storico italiano per il Medio Evo, 1955); Violante, "I laici nel movimento patarino," in his *Studi sulla cristianità medioevale* (Milan: Vita e Pensiero, 1975), 145–246; Giovanni Miccoli, "Per la storia della pataria milanese," in his *Chiesa gregoriana* (Florence: La Nuova Italia, 1966), 101–160.]

5. [Etienne Delaruelle, *La piété populaire au moyen âge* (Turin: Bottega d'Erasmo, 1980), and his contribution to Etienne Delaruelle, E.-R. Labande, and Paul Ourliac, *L'Eglise au temps du Grand Schisme et de la crise conciliaire (1378–1449)*, vol. 14 of *Histoire de l'Eglise depuis les origines jusqu'à nos jours*, ed. Augustin Fliche and Victor Martin (Paris: Bloud & Gay, 1962); Raoul Manselli, *La religion populaire au moyen âge. Problèmes de méthode et d'histoire* (Paris: Vrin, 1975); Gilles Gérard Meersseman, *Ordo Fraternitatis. Confraternite e pietà dei laici nel medioevo*, Italia Sacra, 24–26 (Rome: Herder, 1977). For an appreciation of Meersseman's work, see chapter 9 of this volume.]

1. The Idea of God

1. [M.-D. Chenu, *Nature, Man, and Society in the Twelfth Century: Essays on New Theological Perspectives in the Latin West*, trans. Jerome

Taylor and Lester K. Little (Chicago: University of Chicago Press, 1968), 230-238.]

2. *The Middle Ages of "The People"*

1. See Dominique Barthélemy, *L'ordre seigneurial, XI-XII siècle* (Paris: Seuil, 1990), 90-100.

2. Pierre Toubert, *Les Structures du Latium médiéval: Le Latium méridional et la Sabine du IXe au XIIe siècle* (Rome: École Française de Rome, 1973).

3. Georges Duby, *Guerriers et paysans (VII-XII siècle): Premier essor de l'économie européenne* (Paris: Gallimard, 1973) [*The Early Growth of the European Economy: Warriors and Peasants from the Seventh to the Twelfth Century*, trans. Howard B. Clarke (Ithaca: Cornell University Press, 1974)].

4. "Raoul s'emporta tellement qu'il ne fit pas de jugement, / les fit tous tristes et dolents. A plusieurs arracher les dents / et les autres fit empaler, arracher les yeux, poings couper; / à tous fit les jarrets rôtir, même s'ils en devaient mourir; / d'autres furent brûlés vivants ou plongés dans le plomb bouillant." Wace, *Roman de Rou*, ed. A.-J. Holden, vol. 1 (Paris: A. & J. Picard, 1970), 191-196.

5. Robert Fossier, *La Terre et les Hommes en Picardie jusqu'au XIIIe siècle*, Publications de la Faculté des lettres et sciences humaines de Paris-Sorbonne, Série Recherches 48-49 (Paris-Louvain: B. Nauwelaerts, 1968).

6. Robert Fossier, *Histoire sociale de l'Occident médiéval* (Paris: A. Colin, 1970).

7. Claude Carozzi, *Le Carmen ad Rotbertum regem d'Adalbéron de Laon: Edition, traduction et essai d'explication* (Doctoral diss., University of Paris IV, 1973). See also, by the same author, "La tripartition fonctionnelle et l'idée de paix au XIe siècle," in the *Actes du 101e congrès des sociétés savantes (Lille, 1976)* (Paris: 1978), 9-22.

8. Georges Duby, *Les Trois Ordres ou l'Imaginaire du féodalisme* (Paris: Gallimard, 1978) [*The Three Orders: Feudal Society Imagined*, trans. Arthur Goldhammer (Chicago: University of Chicago Press, 1980)]. See also Jacques Le Goff, "Note sur société tripartie, idéologie monarchique et renouveau économique du IXe au XIIe siècle," in his *Pour un autre Moyen Age: Temps, travail et culture en Occident: 18 essais* (Paris: Gallimard, 1977), 80-90 ["A Note on Tripartite Society, Monarchical Ideology, and Economic Renewal in Ninth- to Twelfth-Century Christendom," in his *Time, Work, and Culture in the Middle Ages*, trans. Arthur Goldhammer (Chicago: University of Chicago Press, 1980), 53-57].

9. Georges Dumézil, *Mythe et Epopée*, vol. 1, *L'idéologie des trois fonctions dans les épopées des peuples indoeuropéens* (Paris: Gallimard, 1968).

10. See on this subject the valuable analysis of Claude Carozzi in his study on "Les fondements de la tripartition sociale chez Adalbéron de Laon," *Annales: Economies, Sociétés, Civilisations* 33 (1978): 683-702.

11. In addition to Duby's work, *Les Trois Ordres*, see Jean Batany, "Des 'trois fonctions' aux 'trois états'?" *Annales: Economies, Sociétés, Civilisations* 18 (1963): 933-938.

12. Georges Duby, "Les laïcs et le paix de Dieu," in his *Hommes et Structures du Moyen Age* (Paris-The Hague: Mouton/DeGruyter, 1973), 227-240 ["Laity and the Peace of God," in *The Chivalrous Society*, trans. Cynthia Postan (Berkeley and Los Angeles: University of California Press, 1977), 123-133].

13. Robert Fossier, "Les mouvements populaires en Occident au XIe siècle," in *Comptes rendus de l'Académie des inscriptions et belles-lettres* (1971), 257-269.

14. Cinzio Violante, "I laici nel movimento patarino," in his *Studi sulla cristianità medioevale* (Milan: Vita e Pensiero, 1975), 145-246, and Etienne Delaruelle, *La Piété populaire au Moyen Age* (Turin: Bottega d'Erasmo, 1975).

15. Jean Rémy Palanque and Etienne Delaruelle, *Des origines à la chrétienté médiévale (IIe-fin du XIIe siècle)*, vol. I of *Histoire du catholicisme en France*, ed. André Latreille, Etienne Delaruelle and Jean Rémy Palanque (Paris: Editions Spes, 1957), 229.

16. On these topics, see André Vauchez, *La Spiritualité de l'Occident médiéval, VIIIe- XIIe siècle* (Paris: Presses Universitaires de France, 1975).

17. Georges Duby, *L'Economie rurale et la vie des campagnes dans l'Occident médiéval* (Paris: Aubier, 1962) [*Rural Economy and Country Life in the Medieval West*, trans. Cynthia Postan (Columbia, SC: University of South Carolina Press, 1968)].

18. Tadeusz Manteuffel, *Naissance d'une hérésie: les adeptes de la pauvreté volontaire au Moyen Age* (Paris and The Hague: Mouton, 1970).

19. Jacques Le Goff, "Le vocabulaire des catégories sociales chez saint François d'Assise et ses biographes du XIIIe siècle," in *Ordres et Classes: Colloque d'histoire sociale, Saint-Cloud, 24-25 mai 1967*, ed. D. Roche (Paris: Mouton, 1973), 93-123.

20. See on this subject *Etudes sur l'histoire de la pauvreté (Moyen Age-XVIe siècle)*, ed. Michel Mollat (Paris: Publications de la Sorbonne, 1974) and Michel Mollat, *Les Pauvres au Moyen Age. Etude sociale* (Paris: Hachette, 1978) [*The Poor in the Middle Ages: An Essay in*

Social History, trans. Arthur Goldhammer (New Haven and London: Yale University Press, 1986)].

21. Michel Mollat and Philippe Wolff, *Ongles bleus, Jacques et Ciompi: Les révolutions populaires en Europe aux XIVe et XVe siècles* (Paris: Calmann-Lévy, 1970) [*The Popular Revolutions of the Late Middle Ages* (London: Allen & Unwin, 1973)].

22. Charles de La Roncière ably demonstrated this in his important study on "Pauvres et pauvreté à Florence au XIVe siècle," in *Etudes sur l'histoire de la pauvreté*, vol. II, 661-746.

23. See on this topic Emmanuel Le Roy Ladurie, *Montaillou village occitan de 1294 à 1324* (Paris: Gallimard, 1975) [*Montaillou: The Promised Land of Error*, trans. Barbara Bray (New York: George Braziller, 1978)] and Jean-Claude Schmitt, *Le Saint Lévrier: Guinefort guérisseur d'enfants depuis le XIIIe siècle* (Paris: Flammarion, 1979) [*The Holy Greyhound: Guinefort, Healer of Children Since the Thirteenth Century*, trans. Martin Thom (Cambridge: Cambridge University Press, 1983)].

3. The Laity in the Feudal Church

1. [Abbo of Fleury, *Apologeticus ad Hugonem et Rodbertum reges Francorum*, J. P. Migne, ed., *Patriologia Latina*, vol. 139, 463.]

2. ["Adversus Simoniacos," *Monumenta Germaniae Historica, Libelli de lite*, vol. 1, 208 and 235.]

4. The Crusades: The Masses Appear on the Scene

1. [See *Juifs et chrétiens dans le monde occidental, 430-1096* (Paris and The Hague: Mouton, 1960), 384-391.]

2. [Le Goff makes this statement in *La civilisation de l'Occident médiéval* (Paris: Arthaud, 1964), 98.]

5. A Twelfth-Century Novelty: The Lay Saints of Urban Italy

1. On the obstacles which long impeded laymen from attaining sanctity, see André Vauchez, *La spiritualité de l'Occident médiéval, VIIIe-XIIe siècles* (Paris: Presses Universitaires de France, 1975), 105-145 and the other essays in the present collection.

[In this essay, the word "saint" is used for anyone regarded as a saint during the Middle Ages, whether or not the Church eventually sanctioned the cult through official canonization.]

2. The most recent are those of Robert Folz, *Les saints rois du Moyen Age en Occident, 6e-13e siècles*, Subsidia Hagiographica 68

(Brussels: Société des Bollandistes, 1984) and Gabor Klaniczay, "From Sacral Kingship to Self-Representation: Hungarian and European Royal Saints in the 11th-13th Centuries," in *Continuity and Change: Political Institutions and Literary Monuments in the Middle Ages. Proceedings of the Tenth International Symposium*, ed. Elisabeth Vestergaard (Odense: Odense University Press, 1986), 61-86. [See also Susan J. Ridyard, *The Royal Saints of Anglo-Saxon England: A Study of West Saxon and East Anglian Cults* (New York: Cambridge University Press, 1988)].

3. See Marc Bloch, *Les rois thaumaturges*, 3rd ed. (Paris: Gallimard, 1983) (with an important preface by Jacques Le Goff). [*The Royal Touch: Sacred Monarchy and Scrofula in England and France*, trans. J.E. Anderson (London: Routledge and Kegan Paul, 1973)].

4. See Percy Ernst Schramm, *Der König von Frankreich. Das Wesen der Monarchie vom 9. zum 16. Jahrhundert, ein Kapitel aus der Geschichte des abendländischen Stadtes* (Weimar: H. Böhlaus Nachfolger, 1939).

5. In particular, Joseph Claude Poulain, *L'idéal de sainteté dans l'Aquitaine carolingienne d'après les sources hagiographiques (750-950)*, Travaux du Laboratoire d'histoire religieuse de l'Université Laval 1 (Québec: Presses de l'Université Laval, 1975), 88-144, and Vito Fumagalli, "Note sulla *Vita Geraldi* d'Oddone di Cluny," *Bullettino dell'Istituto storico italiano per il Medio Evo* 76 (1964), 217-240.

6. As Patrick Corbet has shown in *Les saints ottoniens: Sainteté dynastique, sainteté royale et sainteté féminine autour de l'an Mil.* (Sigmaringen: J. Thorbecke, 1986).

7. Michel Parisse, "La conscience chrétienne des nobles," in *La cristianità dei secoli XI e XII in Occidente: Coscienza e strutture di una società. Atti della ottava Settimana internazionale di studio (Mendola 1980)* (Milan: Vita e Pensiero, 1983), 259-280.

8. On the medieval iconography of the heroes of the *chansons de geste*, see Rita Lejeune and Jacques Stiennon, *La légende de Roland dans l'art du Moyen Age* (Brussels: Arcade, 1967) [*The Legend of Roland in the Middle Ages* (New York: Phaidon, 1971)] and Rita Lejeune, "L'esprit de croisade dans l'épopée occitane," in *Paix de Dieu et guerre sainte en Languedoc*, Cahiers de Fanjeaux 4 (Toulouse: Privat, 1969), 174-183.

9. See on this subject André Vauchez, *La Sainteté en occident aux derniers siècles du Moyen Age, d'après les procès de canonisation et les documents hagiographiques*, Bibliothèque des Ecoles françaises d'Athènes et de Rome 241 (Rome: Ecole Française de Rome, 1981), 410-426.

10. On St. Domingo de la Calzada, see his *Vita* (*Bibliotheca hagiographica latina antiquae et mediae aetatis* [henceforth *BHL*] 2234),

published in the *Acta Sanctorum*, May, vol. 3, col. 167-168, and Luis Vazquez de Parga, Jose M. Lacarra and Juan Uria Riu, *Las peregrinaciones a Santiago de Compostella* (Madrid: Consejo Superior de Investigaciones Cientificas. Escuela de Estudios Medievales, 1949), vol. 2, 162-173; on St. Bénézet, whose relics worked numerous miracles in Avignon in the years between 1230 and 1250, see *Acta Sanctorum*, April, vol. 2, col. 255-264, and François Lefort, "La légende de saint Bénézet," *Revue des questions historiques* 23 (1878), 555-570.

11. His *Vita* (*BHL* 8789), published in the *Acta Sanctorum*, April, vol. 3, col. 837-840, can not be dated with certainty but, according to its Bollandist editors, was composed no more than a few decades after his death. See *Acta Sanctorum*, April, vol. 3, col. 828.

12. On Allucio, see *Allucio da Pescia: (1070-ca. 1134): Religione e società nei territori di Lucca e della Valdinievole* (Rome: Jouvence, 1991). These conference proceedings supplement the short notice about him in *Acta Sanctorum*, October, vol. 10, col. 235-236, which includes the undated *Vita* (*BHL* 303), found in his reliquary in 1344.

13. This dossier, which Papebroch could not obtain in the seventeenth century, contains a group of miracles that took place at Teobaldo's tomb between 1285 and 1354, and a *Vita* which was probably composed before the end of the thirteenth century. This group of texts was published by Luigi Giordano, *Il rotolo di S. Teobaldo Roggeri* (Alba: 1929), following a manuscript preserved in the Archivio Capitolare of Alba. The same author is responsible for a biography of Teobaldo that unfortunately lacks historical rigor: *Storia di S. Teobaldo Roggeri, il santo dell'antico comune e delle corporazioni* (Alba: 1929). See also Niccolò del Re, entry "Teobaldo Roggeri," in *Bibliotheca Sanctorum*, vol. 12 (Rome: Città Nuova, 1969), col. 201-203.

14. See Giordano, *Il rotolo*, 35.

15. *Vita auctore Benincasa* (*BHL* 7084), edited in *Acta Sanctorum*, June, vol. 4, col. 345-381. On Ranieri and his cult, see Natale Caturegli, entry "Ranieri di Pisa," in *Bibliotheca Sanctorum*, vol. 11 (Rome: 1968), col. 37-44. On the medieval iconography of Ranieri, see George Kaftal, *Iconography of the Saints in Tuscan Painting* (Florence: Sansoni, 1952), col. 874-884.

16. On St. Omobono see Vauchez, *La sainteté en Occident*, 412-417.

17. A description of the hagiographic documents can be found in André Vauchez, "Le trafiquant céleste: saint Homebon de Crémone (†1197), marchand et père des pauvres," in *Horizons marins, itinéraires spirituels (Ve-XVIIIe siècles)*, ed. Henri Dubois, Jean-Claude Hocquet, and

André Vauchez, *Histoire ancienne et médiévale* 20 (Paris: Publications de la Sorbonne, 1987) vol. 1: *Mentalités et sociétés*, 115-122.

18. Innocent III, *Quia pietas* (12.1.1199), ed. Othmar Hageneder, Anton Haidacher and Herta Eberstaller, *Die Register Innozenz III*, vol. 1 (Cologne-Graz: Böhlaus Nachfolger, 1964), 761-764.

19. This is true of the *Vita* known as *Labentibus annis* (*BHL* 3971), edited by Francesco Gatta, "Un antico codice reggiano su Omobono, il 'santo popolare' di Cremona," *Bollettino storico cremonese* 12 (1942), 111-115.

20. Master Rufino's *Vita* of Raimondo was published in *Acta Sanctorum*, July, vol. 6, col. 644-657. The original text has been lost, and what the Bollandists published is a retroversion in Latin from a sixteenth-century Italian translation. On the biography and cult of Raimondo Palmerio, see André Vauchez, entry "Raimondo Zanfogni", in *Bibliotheca Sanctorum*, vol. 11, col. 26-29.

21. *Miracula* (*BHL* 7068 and 7069), in *Acta Sanctorum*, July, vol. 6, col. 657-663.

22. On Obizio da Niardo, see *Acta Sanctorum*, February, vol. 1, col. 578-579 for accounts of a few miracles, and *Chronicon* of Jacobus Malvecius, in *Rerum Italicarum Scriptores* 14 (Milan: 1729) col. 883-886. See also E. Camisani, entry "Obizio," in *Bibliotheca Sanctorum* 9 (Rome: Citta Nuova, 1967), col. 1085-1086.

23. Bonincontro Morigia, *Chronicon Modoetiense*, in *Rerum Italicarum Scriptores* 12, col. 1085-1088. Many of the primarily cult-related documents gathered at the 1582 inquest have been published in the *Acta Sanctorum*, June, vol. 1, col. 754-763. Gerardo's historical existence is beyond doubt, since he is mentioned in contemporary records: see Giuliano Riva, "Due documenti di S. Gherardo," *Archivio storico lombardo* (1906), 45-66, and Ezio Franceschini, "Un documento inedito del 1198 su S. Gerardo Tintori," in *Festschrift Bernhard Bischoff zu seinem 65. Geburtstag*, ed. Johanne Autenrieth and Franz Brunhölzl (Stuttgart: A. Hiersemann, 1971), 322-324.

24. The latest research on the subject is found in the proceedings of the conference *Gerardo Tintori, il santo di Monza* (Monza: 1979), in particular in the contributions of Jean Leclercq, "La figura di San Gerardo," 45-55, and Giovanni Spinelli on his cult and iconography, "L'iconografia del B. Gerardo," 119-177.

25. The Bollandists' article on Gualtero of Lodi (*Acta Sanctorum*, July, vol. 5, col. 323) contains little specific information about him. Today he is better known thanks to the publication of his *Vita* by Alessandro Caretta in the *Archivio storico lodigiano* (1969) 3-27, and the article by Luigi Samarati, entry "Gualtero," in *Bibliotheca Sanctorum*, vol. 7

(Rome: 1966) col. 421-423. See also the collection of essays, *S. Gualtero confessore lodigiano (1184-1224)* (Milan: Tipografia M.E., 1960).

26. On Ubaldesca of Pisa, see *Acta Sanctorum*, May, vol. 6, col. 845-846, and Natale Caturegli, entry "Ubaldesca," in *Bibliotheca Sanctorum*, vol. 12, col. 731-732.

27. See Vauchez, *La sainteté en Occident*, 427-435.

28. His lone medieval biographer describes him as a "*vir bellicosus et summae prudentiae*," and says that after his conversion he devoted himself to penitence "*sepultis illecebris militaris curae.*" See Jacobus Malvechius *Chronicon*, col. 885-886.

29. Benincasa of Pisa, Ranieri's confessor and biographer, wrote that he was born "*ex clarissimis parentibus.*" See *Acta Sanctorum*, June, vol. 4, col. 347.

30. On the founding of this hospital, which took place in 1174, see Luigi Modorati, *Dell'Ospedale di S. Gerardo* (Monza: 1924) and Anton Francesco Frisi, *Memorie storiche di Monza e sua corte*, vol. 1 (Milano: Tipografia sociale, 1794) [reprinted Biblioteca istorica della antica e nuova Italia 119 (Bologna: Forni, 1970)], 263-272.

31. See Luigi Salamina, "S. Gualtero (Lodi, 1184-1224), *Archivio storico lodigiano* 61 (1942), 100.

32. On Gualfardo's membership in the merchant-artisan milieu, see his *Vita*, in *Acta Sanctorum*, April, vol. 3, col. 828: "*In eodem vero loco* [i.e. Verona] *beatissimus Gualfardus in sellarum exercitio (nam optimus sellator erat) parvo tempore moratus. . .* " He had come there "with some journeyman merchants" and had at first taken residence in the city with a journeyman. In the early sixteenth century, he was venerated as the patron saint of the confraternity of harness-makers in Verona.

33. Medieval hagiographic sources explicitly designate St. Omobono as a *sartor* and indicate that he possessed a vineyard and some fields in the outskirts of Cremona that were worked by laborers.

34. *Vita* of Teobaldo of Alba, 29-30: "*didicit suere subtellares et tota sua adholescentia cerdonum offitio fungebatur.*" After refusing to marry his master's daughter and succeed him, "*equavit se asinis et mulis onera deportantibus.*"

35. *Vita* of Raimondo Palmerio, 646.

36. See Eugenio Dupré Theseider, "L'eresia a Bologna nei tempi di Dante," in *Studi storici in onore di Gioacchino Volpe per il suo 80°compleanno*, vol. I (Florence: Sansoni, 1958), now reproduced in Theseider, *Mondo cittadino e movimenti ereticali nel Medio Evo* (Bologna: Patron, 1978), 261-315, especially 280-281.

37. The author of the *Vita* of St. Omobono, *Labentius annis*, says explicitly that he was "*mediocris status popularis*" (111).

38. *Vita* of Raimondo Palmerio, 646. ["His kin were neither extremely illustrious nor extremely base, but were private citizens and, as for their domestic possessions, neither poor nor wealthy."]

39. Otto of Freising, *The Deeds of Frederick Barbarossa*, trans. and ed. Charles Christopher Mierow and Richard Emery (New York: Columbia University Press), 128.

40. *Acta Sanctorum*, April, vol. 3, col. 829.

41. *Acta Sanctorum*, June, vol. 4, col. 348, 351-357, 359.

42. On the importance of pilgrimage in lay piety, see Pierre-André Sigal, *Les marcheurs de Dieu: pèlerinages et pèlerins au Moyen Age* (Paris: A. Colin, 1974) and Francis Rapp, "Les pèlerinages dans la vie religieuse de l'Occident médiéval," in *Les pèlerinages dans l'Antiquité classique et l'Occident médiéval*, ed. Marc Philonenko and Marcel Simon (Paris: P. Geuthner, 1974), 117-160.

43. *Acta Sanctorum*, July, vol. 6, col. 648-649. On the principal itineraries followed by pilgrims in Northern Italy, see Giacomo C. Bascapè, "Le vie dei pellegrinaggi medievali attraverso le Alpi centrali e la pianura lombarda," *Archivio storico per la Svizzera italiana* (1936), 5-45.

44. Vauchez, *La sainteté en Occident*, 234-241 and 450-455.

45. On the material problems facing medieval travelers or pilgrims in their journeys, see *Gastfreundschaft, Taverne und Gasthaus im Mittelalter*, ed. Hans Conrad Peyer, Schriften des historischen Kollegs 3 (Munich/Vienna: R. Oldenbourg, 1983).

46. Benincontro Morigia, *Chronicon Modoetiense*, col. 1085: "[Gerardo Tintori] *leprosos manu sua tegebat; omnes infirmos quos hospitabatur cum osculo pacis recipiebat illosque in omni hora debita personaliter ministrabat et cuiuslibet servitium necessitatis sine indignatione eis faciebat.*" The title of *pater pauperum* was given to St. Omobono in the *Vita "Labentibus annis,"* 112.

47. *Acta Sanctorum*, July, vol. 6, col. 651f.

48. Benincontro Morigia, *Chronicon Modoetiense*, col. 1016: Gerardo Tintori supposedly crossed the swelling river Lambro on his cloak when he saw his hospice threatened with flooding "*sine alio cogitatu nisi cum magno fervore ad pauperes infirmos qui repraesentant personam Christi.*"

49. *Vita* of Ranieri of Pisa, 349: "*non possum pauperes videre necessitudinem pati et quae apud me sunt non tribuendo non misereri.*"

50. *Vita* of Raimondo Palmerio, 651-652.

51. At least according to the account in the fourteenth-century Italian *Vita* entitled *Della cripta di Cremona*, ed. Giulio Bertoni, "Di una *Vita* di S. Omobono del secolo XIV," *Bollettino storico cremonese* 3 (1938), 164: "venne molto exoso al'infernali demoni in tanto che un'volta

pre le altre fo si gravamente percosso e battuto che fo contrecto con voce lacrimosa chiamar a Dio." According to the context, it seems that the "devils" who administered the beating were heretics, who at that time were numerous and influential in Cremona.

52. According to Ranieri's biographer, Christ appeared to him immediately after he had given food to the poor near the Holy Sepulchre in Jerusalem, saying: *"Ego hodie te feci similem mei"* (*Vita* of Ranieri of Pisa, 356).

53. On the difficult birth of medieval lay spirituality, see Yves Congar, entry "Laïcat au Moyen Age," in *Dictionnaire de Spiritualité*, vol. 9 (Paris: Beauchesne, 1976), col. 79-83.

54. Ranieri's biographer, after noting his divine election, justified the *regale sacerdotium* which made him "the leader and prince of his people" in these terms: *Et est sacerdos mortificatione carnis. Unde beatus Apostolus ait: "Obsecro vos per misericordiam Dei ut exhibeatis corpora vestra hostiam viventem sanctam Deo placentem." Quicumque Deo hostiam offert, sacerdos est secundum hunc modum, et bonae mulieres corpore me crucifigentes sacerdotis nomine censentur... Unde et Petrus ait: "Vos estis ergo genus electum, regale sacerdotium." Ideo mulieres et viri chrismate fronte et vertice unguuntur ut adversus Diabolum simus reges et sacerdotes pugnantes semper et orantes. Et Joannes in Apocalypsi sua: "Et fecit nos Deo nostro regnum et sacerdotes." Vita* of Ranieri of Pisa, 355.

55. *Vita* of Ranieri of Pisa, 356.

56. See on this subject Giovanni Miccoli, "Limiti e contraddizioni della restaurazione postgregoriana," in *Storia d'Italia*, vol. 2, part 1: *Dalla caduta dell'Impero romano al secolo XVIII* (Turin: Einaudi, 1974), 516-608.

57. On this important problem, see the fundamental study by Rolf Zerfass, *Der Streit um die Laienpredigt: Eine pastoralgeschichtliche Untersuchung zum Verständnis des Predigtamtes und zu seiner Entwicklung im 12. und 13. Jahrhundert* (Freiburg im Breisgau, Basel, Vienna: Herder, 1974).

58. *Vita* of Ranieri of Pisa, 348.

59. *Vita* of Raimondo Palmerio, 651.

60. *Vita* of Raimondo Palmerio, 648.

61. See Zerfass, *Der Streit um die Laienpredigt*, and Etienne Delaruelle, "Saint François d'Assise et la piété populaire," in *La piété populaire au Moyen Age* (Turin: Bottega d'Erasmo, 1975), 261-264.

62. Innocent III, *Quia pietas* (see note 18). On the notion of *laicus religiosus* and its institutional implications, see Daniela Rando,

"Laicus religiosus. Tra strutture civili ed ecclesiastiche: l'Ospedale di Ogni Santi in Treviso (sec. XIII)," *Studi medievali*, 3rd ser., 24 (1983), 617-656.

63. See on this subject the proceedings of the colloquium *Lavorare nel Medio Evo: rappresentazioni ed esempi dall'Italia dei secc. X–XVI* (Todi: Centro di studi sulla spiritualità medievale, Università degli studi di Perugia, 1983).

64. *Vita* of Teobaldo of Alba, ed. Giordano, 29-30.

65. *Vita* "*Labentibus annis*," 111: "*Hic Homobonus parentum artibus vacans in mercature arte doctus evasit ita tamen, quod raro fieri solet, [ut] fidem et equalitatem in permutandis rebus pro posse servaret.*" See on this subject Vauchez, "Le trafiquant céleste: saint Homebon de Crémone," 119.

66. See on this subject the well-balanced synthesis of Diana M. Webb, "A Saint and his Money: Perception of Urban Wealth in the Lives of Italian Saints," in *The Church and Wealth: Papers Read at the 1986 Summer Meeting and the 1987 Winter Meeting of the Ecclesiastical History Society*, ed. W. J. Sheils and Diana Wood, Studies in Church History 24 (Oxford: Basil Blackwell, 1987), 61-73.

67. *Vita* "*Labentibus annis*," 112-113.

68. *Vita* of Raimondo Palmerio, 648.

69. *Vita* of Raimondo Palmerio, 648-649.

70. See chapter 15 in this book.

71. *Vita* of Teobaldo of Alba, 30.

72. On the origin of the notion of an *Ordo conjugatorum*, see Gilles Gerard Meersseman, "I penitenti nei secoli XI e XII," in *Ordo Fraternitatis: Confraternite e pietà dei laici nel Medio Evo* (Rome: Herder, 1977), vol. I, 265-304.

73. Obizio (†1204) supposedly spent his final days at the abbey Santa Giulia in Brescia, where he was buried. See Jacobus Malvecius, *Chronicon Brixianum, ab origine urbis ad annum usque MCCXXXII*, in *Rerum Italicarum Scriptores*, ed. Ludovico Muratori, vol. 14 (Milan: 1729), col. 886. Ranieri of Pisa had ties with both the monks of San Vito and the canons of the cathedral of Pisa: see the *Vita* of Ranieri of Pisa, 359-360.

74. *Vita* of Ranieri of Pisa, 370-371.

75. The dedication of the *Vita* of Raimondo Palmerio leaves no doubt on this subject: "*Humilibus Jesu Christi pauperibus xenodochii sanctissimi patris nostri Raymundi Palmerii, ego Rufinus magister minimus in canonica XII apostolorum*," *Vita*, 646. The author of the *Vita* of Gualtero of Lodi introduces himself in these terms: "*Ego frater*

Bonus Joannes canonicus, fratris Gualterii consanguineus, notus et fidelis amicus, qui predicta didici, vidi ac manifeste cognovi" (26).

76. As we hope to be able to demonstrate soon, this is the *Vita* entitled *Cum orbita solis,* which seems to have preceded the canonization of St. Omobono since it makes no mention of it.

77. *Vita* of Teobaldo of Alba, 32-33 and 47.

78. The charter of the foundation of the hospital of Monza that Gerardo founded in 1174 stated that it would make an annual offering of two one-pound candles to the altar of the collegiate church of San Giovanni of Monza. See Luigi Modorati, *Dell'Ospedale di S. Gerardo* (Monza: Tipografia sociale, 1924), 86-88.

79. *Acta Sanctorum,* July, vol. 6, col. 656-657.

80. The text can be found in *Acta Sanctorum,* October, vol. 10, col. 226-234. It was on this occasion that they found *"legendam de vita et quibusdam miraculis dicti sancti Allucii in cartula pecuria scriptam."*

81. Giordano, *Il rotolo,* 50-52.

82. Vauchez, *La sainteté en Occident,* 150.

83. Vauchez, *La sainteté en Occident,* 131-162.

84. On the importance of the cults of saints in late medieval civic religion, see chapter 13 of this volume.

85. *Vita* of Teobaldo of Alba, 33: *"Igitur ex oblacionibus per populos concurrentes exhibitas in honorem sancti gloriosi Theobaldi nutu et voluntate dei facta sunt in civitate quatuor sublimia opera, videlicet ecclesia, campanile, revolutiones sive volte et hospitale pauperum. Eddificavit ecclesiam quae conjunxit alias duas simul ut se inde civitatis et pacis copulam demonstraret; in factione campanilis potest intelligi civitatis custos [ut] ipsam protegat et deffendat; in revolutionibus faciendis intelligitur civitati consulere et bonis ipsius consiliis interesse; in ordinatione hospitalis se esse procuratorem pauperum demonstravit et ipsos super totam possessionem substituit in heredes."*

86. *Miracula,* in *Acta Sanctorum,* June, vol. 4, col. 363.

87. See André Vauchez, "Conclusion" of the volume *Allucio da Pescia: Religione e società nei territori di Lucca e della Valdinievole,* pp. 325-328.

88. The popularity of pilgrimages to Alba is attested to by Luigi Giordano, *Storia di S. Teobaldo Roggeri* (Alba: 1929), 111-143.

89. See Vauchez, "Le trafiquant céleste: saint Homebon de Crémone," 120-122.

90. A separate study should be consecrated to the cult of St. Isidore the farmer († circa 1130), a peasant from the area of Madrid who was widely venerated in Spain beginning in the thirteenth century, and whose cult then found great success in South America.

91. See on this subject Brenda M. Bolton, "*Vitae Matrum*: A Further Aspect of the *Frauenfrage*," in *Medieval Women*, ed. Derek Baker (Oxford: Basil Blackwell, 1978), 253-273.

92. On this evolution of lay sanctity as it is reflected in hagiography, see Vauchez, *La sainteté en Occident*, 446-448.

93. Adolf Von Harnack, *Lehrbuch der Dogmengeschichte*, vol. 3 (Leipzig: Mohr, 1897), 385.

6. Two Laypersons in Search of Perfection: Elzéar of Sabran and Delphine of Puimichel

1. This biographical data comes from fourteenth-century sources: for Elzéar, canonized in 1369 but whose canonization proceedings are lost, a *vita* in Latin, written around 1370 and published in *Acta Sanctorum*, September, vol. 7, col. 576-592, and a *vita* in Provençal dating from the 1390s, published in *Vies occitanes de saint Auzias et de sainte Delphine, avec traduction française, introduction et notes*, ed. Jacques Cambell (Rome: Pontificium Athenaeum Antonianum, 1963), 41-127; for Delphine, the canonization proceedings of 1363, *Enquête pour le procès de canonisation de Dauphine de Puimichel, comtesse d'Ariano* (†26.XI.1360) (*Apt et Avignon: 14 mai-30 octobre 1363*), ed. Jacques Cambell (Turin: Erasmo, 1978) and a *vita* in Provençal contemporary to that of Elzéar, ed. Jacques Cambell, *Vies occitanes*, 128-245. There is no satisfactory modern biography of this saintly couple, but some useful elements can be found in Roselyne de Forbin d'Oppède, *La bienheureuse Delphine de Sabran et les saints de Provence au XIVe siècle* (Paris: Plon, 1883), and the *Armorial général de France: généalogie historique de la maison de Sabran-Pontevès* (Paris: Firmin-Didot, 1897).

2. On this aspect of Elzéar and Delphine's behavior, see chapter 16 of this volume.

3. Besides St. Francis of Sales, who speaks of him in chapter 12 of his *Introduction to the Devout Life*, trans. John Kenneth Ryan (New York: Harper and Row, 1966; Image Books, 1989), we cite also the Jesuit Étienne Binet, *La vie et les éminentes vertus de saint Elzéar de Sabran et de la bienheureuse Delphine, vierges et mariez, deux phénix de la France* (Paris: 1622) [*The Lives and Singular Virtues of Saint Elzear, Count of Sabran, and of his Wife, the Blessed Countesse Delphina, Both Virgins and Married*, trans. Thomas Hawkins (Paris: J. Cousturier, 1638)] and Jean-Marie de Vernon, *Histoire générale et particulière du tiers ordre de saint François d'Assize*, vol. I (Paris: 1667), 510ff. According to the *Vie occitane*, Elzéar, exasperated by efforts to obtain favors from him,

cried out "How perverse the people of this country are! They try to corrupt me and to pervert me with their gifts."

4. *Vie occitane de saint Elzéar*, 103-107.

5. On these religious movements, the best work remains Raoul Manselli, *Spirituali e Beghini in Provenza* (Rome: Istituto storico italiano per il Medio Evo, 1959).

6. On François of Meyronnes, see the fundamental work of Bartholomäus Roth, *Franz von Mayronis O.F.M.: Seine Leben, seine Werke, seine Lehre vom Formalunterschied in Gott* (Werl: Franziskus-druckerei, 1936), which can be usefully integrated with the study of Jacques de Lagarde-Sclafer, "La participation de François de Meyronnes, théologien franciscain, à la querelle de la pauvreté," in *Etudes franciscaines* 10 (1960), 53-73.

7. *Vie occitane de saint Elzéar*, 113.

8. *Vita latina*, in *Acta Sanctorum*, September, vol. 7, 553.

9. *Vie occitane de sainte Delphine*, 143-145.

10. According to the chronology established by Jacques Cambell, *Enquête*, 32-37.

11. The first condemnation of the Beguines of Languedoc and their Franciscan spiritual directors was promulgated by the council of Béziers in 1299, presided by Gilles Aycelin, the archbishop of Narbonne: see Edmond Martène and Ursin Durand, *Thesaurus novus anecdotorum*, IV (Paris: Lutetiae Parisiorum, 1717), 226-227.

12. John XXII, *"Quia interdum filia"* (to Sancha), published in Odorico Rinaldi, *Annales ecclesiastici ab anno quo card. Baronius MCX-CVIII desinit usque ad annum MDXXXIV continuati*, vol. 5, XXVI (Rome: 1646-1647), 59. On the spiritualist currents at the Angevin court in Naples, see Mercedes van Heuckelum, *Spiritualistische Strömungen an den Höfen von Aragon und Anjou während der Höhe des Armutsstreites* (Berlin-Leipzig, W. Rothschild, 1912).

13. Elzéar's will was published in Forbin d'Oppède, *La bienheureuse Delphine*, 412-425.

14. *Vie occitane de sainte Delphine*, 185-191.

15. On Philip of Majorca, see Jean Marie Vidal, "Un ascète de sang royal, Philippe de Majorque," in *Revue de questions historiques* 88 (1910), 361-403.

16. On Andrea da Galiano, see Franz Ehrle, "Zur Vorgeschichte des Concils von Vienne," *Archiv für Literatur und Kirchengeschichte des Mittelalters* 4 (1888), 82-96, and the studies of Edith Pàsztor, "Il processo di F. Andrea da Galiano," in *Archivum Franciscanum Historicum* 48 (1955), 252-297, and Andrea Chiarini, "Il processo di F. Andrea da Galiano," in *Bollettino della Deputazione Abruzzese di Storia*

Patria 6 (1953-1956), 56ff. On the accusations of Adhémar de Mosset, see the study of Jean Marie Vidal, "Procès contre Adhémar de Mosset," in *Revue d'Histoire de l'Eglise de France* 1 (1910), 555-589, 682-699, and 711-724.

17. This letter, dating from March 1332, was published by Rinaldi, *Annales ecclesiastici*, vol. 5, XX, 535-536.

18. Guillaume Espitalier is little known to historians. Of Catalan or Aragonese origins (see José-María Pou y Martì, *Visionarios, beguinos y fraticelos catalanes. Siglos XIII-XV* [Vich: Editorial Seráfica, 1930], 251), he was in Provence with Elzéar in 1317 and in Naples around 1330 (*Bullarium Franciscanum* 6, 608). On the accusations made against him by Adhémar de Mosset, see the study by Jean Marie Vidal, "Procès contre Adhémar de Mosset," 685-686.

19. In a sermon he gave in Naples, Guillaume Espitalier had mentioned a miracle accomplished by Elzéar that he had heard about from Philip of Majorca: *Vie occitane de Elzéar*, 124-125 and *Enquête*, 175, n. 7.

20. His *Vita* was inserted in the *Chronica XXIV generalium*, a compilation of Franciscan hagiography composed around 1374 by Arnaldo di Samatan and published in *Analecta franciscana* 3 (Quaracchi: Collegium S. Bonaventurae, 1897), 564-572. See also Bartolomeo of Pisa, *De conformitate vitae beati Francisci ad vitam Domini*, published in *Analecta franciscana* 4 (Quaracchi: Collegium S. Bonaventurae, 1906), 290-292.

21. Lydia von Auw, *Angelo Clareno et les spirituels italiens* (Rome: Storia e Letteratura, 1979) and her edition *Angeli Clareni opera*, vol. 1, *"Epistole"* (Rome: Istituto storico italiano per il Medio Evo, 1980).

22. In his *Apologia pro vita sua*, published in *Archivium Franciscanum Historicum* 39 (1946), 63-200, Angelo defends himself against the charge of disobedience to the Church and recalls his condemnation of the rebellion of the Italian *fraticelli* against the authority of the pope.

23. Angelo Clareno, *"Epistole,"* letter 43, 206.

24. Clareno, Letter 29, 154. On Robert's fluctuating positions vis-à-vis Pope John XXII, see Emile Léonard, *Les Angevins de Naples* (Paris: Presses Universitaires de France, 1954), 256-257.

25. Angelo Clareno, *"Epistole,"* 289-290.

26. *"Povertate è nulla avere e nulla cosa poi volere."* Iacopone da Todi, *Laude*, ed. Franco Mancini (Roma-Bari: Laterza, 1980), 102 [Jacopone da Todi, *The Lauds*, trans. Serge and Elizabeth Hughes (New York: Paulist Press, 1982), 186].

27. According to the *Vie occitane* (189), Delphine justified her vow of poverty of 1333 in these terms: "Since my lord the sainted count

left this life, God has often strongly urged me to renounce the world and all of my possessions; however, led by my sensuality to follow the advice of some carnal people, I have neglected to follow his counsel and repeatedly put off the execution of my plan, since I had become lax and lukewarm in doing good deeds, and was beginning to lose all good will through God's righteous judgment. But the Lord who is kindly and merciful and of infinite goodness . . . looked upon me with a favorable eye, again ignited and warmed my heart and placed me in a condition of great peace and complete tranquility. This is why I feel obliged to put into action this good will that he has restored to me. As a result I have given away every material thing and put my trust in Providence alone."

28. Clareno, *"Epistole,"* letter 62, 286-87.

29. *Enquête,* 326. The episode took place in January, 1343.

30. On these movements and their repression, see Clément Schmitt, article "Fraticelles," in *Dictionnaire d'histoire et de géographie ecclésiastique,* vol. 18, fasc. 106 (Paris: Letouzey et Ane, 1977), col. 1063-1108.

31. On Philippe Cabassole, see Michel Hayez, article "Cabassole (Philippe)" in *Dizionario biografico degli Italiani,* vol. 15 (Rome: Istituto Enciclopedia Italiana, 1972), 678-681. On his "conversion" at Delphine's hands, see his deposition in *Enquête,* 539.

32. *Enquête,* 253.

33. *Vie occitane de sainte Delphine,* 160-163.

34. *Enquête,* 225.

8. The Pastoral Transformation of the Thirteenth Century

1. Pierre Riché, "La pastorale populaire en Occident (VIe-XIe siècle)," in *Histoire vécue du peuple chrétien,* ed. Jean Delumeau, vol. 1 (Toulouse: Privat, 1979), 195-224.

2. See André Vauchez, *La spiritualité du Moyen Age occidental (VIIIe-XIIe siècle)* (Paris: Presses Universitaires de France, 1975).

3. The source of these citations is the French translation of the records of the canonization proceedings published by Father Marie-Humbert Vicaire, in *Saint Dominique: La vie apostolique,* Chrétiens de tous les temps 10 (Paris: Editions du Cerf, 1965), 75-91.

4. See on this subject Jacques Le Goff and Jean-Claude Schmitt, "Au XIIIe siècle. Une parole nouvelle," in *Histoire vécue du peuple chrétien,* ed. Jean Delumeau, vol. 1 (Toulouse: Privat, 1979), 257-280.

5. See Vicaire, *Saint Dominique,* 75-91.

6. [The description of St. Francis comes from Thomas of Spalato, *Historia Salonitarum,* ed. Leonhard Lemmens, *Testimonia minora*

saeculi XIII de S. Francisco Assisiensi (Quaracchi: Ex Typ. Collegii S. Bonaventurae, 1926), 10.]

7. [See *De rebus alsaticis in euntis saeculi XIII*, ed. Philipp Jaffé, *Monumenta Germaniae Historica: Scriptores*, vol. 17, ed. Georg Heinrich Pertz (Hanover, 1861; reprint, Stuttgart: Anton Hiersemann, 1963), 232.]

8. See in particular *La Religion populaire en Languedoc du XIIIe siècle à la moitié du XIVe siècle*, Cahiers de Fanjeaux 11 (Toulouse: Privat, 1976), and the study by Jean-Claude Schmitt, *Le Saint Lévrier: Guinefort guérisseur d'enfants depuis le XIIIe siècle* (Paris: Flammarion, 1979) [*The Holy Greyhound: Guinefort, Healer of Children since the Thirteenth Century*, trans. Martin Thom (Cambridge: Cambridge University Press, 1983)].

9. See the proceedings of the colloquium *Faire croire. Modalités de la diffusion et de la réception des messages religieux du XIIe au XVe siècle* (Rome: Ecole Française de Rome, 1981).

10. Michel Zink, *La Prédication en langue romane avant 1300* (Paris: Champion, 1976).

11. See in particular Jacques Le Goff, "Métiers et professions d'après les manuels de confesseurs du Moyen Age," in *Pour un autre Moyen Age. Temps, travail et culture en Occident. 18 essais* (Paris: Gallimard, 1977), 162-180. ["Trades and Professions as Represented in Medieval Confessors' Manuals," *Time, Work, and Culture in the Middle Ages*, trans. Arthur Goldhammer (Chicago: University of Chicago Press, 1980), 107-121.]

12. Claude Carozzi, "Le ministère de la confession chez les prêcheurs de la province de Provence," in *Les Mendiants en pays d'Oc au XIIIe siècle*, Cahiers de Fanjeaux 8 (Toulouse: Privat, 1973), 325-354. See also the proceedings of the colloquium "Les ordres mendiants et la ville en Italie centrale (v.1220-v.1350)," published in the *Mélanges de l'Ecole Française de Rome, Moyen Age-Temps Modernes* 89 (1977), 555-773.

9. "Ordo Fraternitatis": Confraternities and Lay Piety in the Middle Ages

* This tribute to Father Meersseman was presented in Rome on the occasion of the publication of a three-volume collection of his studies on medieval confraternities entitled *Ordo Fraternitatis: Confraternite e pietà dei laici nel medioevo*, Italia Sacra 24-26 (Rome: Herder, 1977).

1. [In the course of this essay, reference is made to various essays by Gilles Gérard Meersseman, all of which have now been published in *Ordo*

Fraternitatis: "Les confréries de Saint-Dominique," *Archivum Fratrum Praedicatorum* 20 (1950), 5-113, now in *Ordo Fraternitatis*, vol. 2, 578-697, as "Le confraternite di san Domenico"; "Les confréries de Saint Pierre Martyr," in *Archivum Fratrum Praedicatorum* 21 (1951), 51-196, now in *Ordo Fraternitatis*, vol. 2, 754-920, as "Le confraternite di san Pietro Martire"; "Les congrégations de la Vierge," *Archivum Fratrum Praedicatorum* 22 (1952), 5-176, now in *Ordo Fraternitatis*, vol. 2, 921-1117, as "Le congregazioni della Vergine"; "Les Milices de Jésus-Christ, *Archivum Fratrum Praedicatorum* 23 (1953), 275-308, now in *Ordo Fraternitatis*, vol. 3, 1233-1270, with the title "Le milizie di Gesù."]

2. [Yves Congar, *Jalons pour une théologie du laïcat*, Unam sanctam 23 (Paris: Editions du Cerf, 1953). Translated by Donald Attwater, under the title *Lay People in the Church: A Study for a Theology of the Laity* (Westminster, Md.: Newman Press, 1957). In addition to the studies collected in *Ordo fraternitatis*, see Meersseman, *Dossier de l'ordre de la Pénitence au XIIIe siècle*, Spicilegium Friburgense 7 (Fribourg: Editions Universitaires, 1961).]

3. [*La vita comune del clero nei secoli XI e XII: Atti della prima Settimana di Studio. Mendola, 4-10 settembre 1959*, Pubblicazioni dell'Università Cattolica del Sacro Cuore 3.2 and 3, Miscellanea del Centro di Studi Medioevali 3 (Milan: Vita e pensiero, 1962).]

4. [Pierre Michaud-Quantin, *Universitas. Expressions du mouvement communautaire dans le Moyen Age latin*, L'Église et l'État au Moyen Age, vol. 13 (Paris: J. Vrin, 1970).]

5. [On the Confraternity of the Capuciati, see "La confraternita della Madonna di Le Puy, in *Ordo Fraternitatis*, vol. 1, 196-201.]

6. [Cyrille Vogel, *Le pécheur et la pénitence au Moyen Age*. Chrétiens de tous les temps 30 (Paris: Éditions du Cerf, 1969).]

7. [This paper, presented at the "III Settimana internazionale di studio della Mendola" (August 21-27, 1965) and published in the volume of the proceedings, *I laici nella "società christiana" dei secoli XI e XII* (Milan: Vita e Pensiero, 1968), 306-339, has now appeared in a revised and enlarged version entitled "I penitenti nei secoli XI e XII," in *Ordo fraternitatis*, vol. 1, 265-304.]

8. *Summa aurea*, book 3 (Venice: 1570), 193.

9. [Giovanna Casagrande, "Devozione e municipalità. La compagnia del S. Anello/S. Giuseppe di Perugia (1487-1542)," in *Le mouvement confraternel au Moyen Age: France, Italie, Suisse*, Collection de l'Ecole Française de Rome 97 (Rome: Ecole Française de Rome, 1987), 155-183; and Charles de La Roncière, "La place des confréries dans l'encadrement religieux du contado florentin: l'exemple de la Val d'Elsa," *Mélanges*

de l'Ecole Française de Rome, Moyen Age-Temps Modernes, 85 (1973), 31-77, 633-671.]
  10. [Ida Magli, *Gli uomini della penitenza. Lineamenti antropologici del medioevo italiano* (Milan: Garzanti, 1977).]

10. Medieval Penitents

  1. [Jacques de Vitry, *The Life of Marie d'Oignies*, trans. Margot H. King, Peregrina Translations Series 3 (Toronto: Peregrina, 1989).]
  2. [See *Ex Chronico universali anonymi Laudunensis*, ed. Georg Waitz, in *Monumenta Germaniae Historica: Scriptores*, vol. 26 (Hanover, 1882; reprint Stuttgart: Anton Hiersemann, 1964), 449.]
  3. [On this figure, see chapter 5 of this volume.]
  4. [Gilles Gérard Meersseman, *Dossier de l'ordre de la Pénitence au XIIIe siècle*, Spicilegium Friburgense, vol. 7 (Fribourg: Éditions Universitaires, 1961; 2nd ed. 1982), 92-112.]
  5. [Giunta Bevignate, *Legenda de vita et miraculis beatae Margaritae de Cortona*, in *Acta Sanctorum*, February, vol. 3 (Antwerp: 1658), col. 298-357.]

11. Liturgy and Folk Culture in the Golden Legend

  1. Jacobus de Voragine, *The Golden Legend*, trans. and adap. Granger Ryan and Helmut Ripperger (New York, London, Toronto: Longmans, Green, 1941), 278-280.
  2. Jean Beleth, *Rationale divinorum officiorum*, ch. 122, "De litaniis," ch. 123, "De institutione et modo litaniarum," in Jacques-Paul Migne, *Patrologia latina*, 202, col. 128-130.
  3. *The Golden Legend*, 278.
  4. *The Golden Legend*, 280.
  5. Under the feast day of Gregory the Great, March 12: *The Golden Legend*, 179-180.
  6. *The Golden Legend*, 280.
  7. On this problem, see Fernand Cabrol, entry "Litanies," in *Dictionnaire d'archéologie et de liturgie chrétienne*, vol. 9, col. 1740-1771.
  8. *The Golden Legend*, 243-244; see Henri Leclercq, entry "Processions de Saint-Marc," in *Dictionnaire d'archéologie et de liturgie chrétienne*, vol. 10, col. 1740-1741.
  9. Michel Andrieu, "Ordo Romanus L," in *Les Ordines Romani du haut moyen âge*, vol. 5, *Les textes*, Spicilegium Sacrum Lovaniense,

Etudes et documents 29 (Louvain: Spicilegium Sacrum Lovaniense Administration, 1961), 314-341.

10. Michel Andrieu, "Ordo Romanus L," 314.

11. In fact, as Evelyne Patlagean has shown in "Les armes et la cité à Rome du VIIe au IXe siècle et le modèle européen des trois fonctions sociales," in *Mélanges de l'Ecole Française de Rome, Moyen Age-Temps Modernes* 86 (1974), 25-62, esp. 36, the seven groups in question are the following: clerics, *possessores* (or *nobiles*), and *plebs* for the men; nuns and deaconesses, noble matrons and *universae feminae* for women. The pilgrims must be added: they were not members of the city, but were granted a place in the processions, like that which welcomed Charlemagne at the Milvian Bridge in 800.

12. Michel Andrieu, "Ordo Romanus L," 316.

13. *The Golden Legend*, 278.

*[Their name arises from the fact that the weather in Europe on these particular days is notoriously cold.]

14. Arnold Van Gennep, *Manuel de folklore français contemporain*, vol. 1.4, "Les cérémonies périodiques cycliques et saisonnières," part 2: "Cycle de mai, le Saint-Jean" (Paris: A. Picard, 1949), 1625-2092.

15. Henri Leclercq, entry "Rogations," in *Dictionnaire d'archéologie et de liturgie chrétienne*, 14.2, col. 2459-2461.

16. St. Avitus, "Homilia de rogationibus," in Migne, 59, col. 289-294.

17. "Ordo romanus L," 316.

18. "Ordo romanus L," 317. "Arise, saints, from your dwelling-places. Sanctify these places, protect the people and preserve us in peace, we who are sinners. Hallelujah."

19. *The Golden Legend*, 279.

20. *The Golden Legend*, 280. "Holy God, strong and holy, strong and everlasting One, have pity on us."

21. Francesc Llop y Bayo has shown this quite well in "Toques de campanas y otros rituales colectivos para alejar las tormentas," in the proceedings of the colloquium *Fêtes et Liturgie* (Madrid: Casa de Velazquez, 1988), 121-134.

22. *The Golden Legend*, 280.

23. Van Gennep, vol. 1.4, 1637ff.

24. *The Golden Legend*, 280.

25. Louis Dumont, *La Tarasque: Essai de description d'un fait local du point de vue ethnographique*, L'Espèce humaine 8 (Paris: Gallimard, 1951); Van Gennep, vol. 1.4, 1668-1669; Jacques Le Goff, "Culture ecclésiastique et culture folklorique au Moyen Age: saint Marcel de Paris et le dragon," in *Pour un autre Moyen Age: Temps, travail et culture en Occident: 18 essais* (Paris: Gallimard, 1977), 236-279 ["Ecclesiastical

Culture and Folklore in the Middle Ages: Saint Marcellus of Paris and the Dragon," *Time, Work, and Culture in the Middle Ages*, trans. Arthur Goldhammer (Chicago: University of Chicago Press, 1980), 159-188]; Marie-France Gueusquin, *Le Mois des dragons* (Paris: Berger-Levrault, 1981).

26. Gueusquin, Le Mois des dragons, 125.

27. Henri Leclercq, entry "Dragon," in *Dictionnaire d'archéologie et de liturgie chrétienne*, vol. 4.2, col. 1537-1540.

28. *The Golden Legend*, 280.

29. *Rationale*, col. 129-130.

30. *The Golden Legend*, 280.

31. *The Golden Legend*, 278-280.

32. Gueusquin, Le Mois des dragons, 127-130.

33. See Odette Pontal, "Les statuts de Paris et le synodal de l'Ouest," vol. 1, *Les Statuts synodaux français du XIIIe siècle: Précédés de l'historique du synode diocésain depuis ses origines* (Paris: Bibliothèque nationale, 1971), 89, ¶99.

34. "Ordo romanus L," 316, and "Les Statuts de Paris," 87, ¶88.

35. See on this subject the proceedings of the colloquium *Le Charivari: Actes de la table ronde organisée à Paris (25-27 avril 1977) par l'Ecole des Hautes Etudes en Sciences Sociales et le Centre National de la Recherche Scientifique*, ed. Jacques Le Goff and Jean-Claude Schmitt (Paris: Mouton, 1981).

36. See André Vauchez, "Jacques de Voragine et les saints du XIIIè siècle dans la *Légende dorée*," in *Legenda aurea: sept siècles de diffusion: Actes du Colloque international sur la Legenda aurea: texte latin et branches vernaculaires, à l'Université de Québec à Montréal, 11-12 mai 1983* (Paris: Vrin and Montreal: Bellarmin, 1986), 27-56.

12. Anti-Semitism and Popular Canonization:
The Cult of St. Werner

1. MS. 1139, Municipal Library of Trier, and MS. 858, Palat. lat., Vatican Library. The Bollandists' edition, which does not follow the text of the inquest but instead reconstitutes it on the basis of certain themes, is found in *Acta Sanctorum*, April, vol. 2, col. 714-734.

2. This text, translated from the Flemish, is cited by Jean Stengers, *Les Juifs dans les Pays-Bas au Moyen Age*, Académie royale de Belgique. Classe de lettres et des sciences morales et politiques. Mémoires, vol. 45, 2 (Brussels: Palais des académies, 1950), 56-57. [For a recent study of similar stories in sixteenth-century Germany, see R. Po-chia Hsia, *The Myth of Ritual Murder* (New Haven: Yale University Press, 1988).]

3. F. Pauly, "Zur Vita des Werner von Oberwesel. Légende und Wirklichkeit," *Archiv für Mittelrheinische Kirchengeschichte* 16 (1964), 94-109.

4. Henri de Grèzes, *Saint Vernier (Verny, Werner, Garnier), martyr, patron des vignerons en Auvergne, en Bourgogne et en Franche-Comté* (Clermont-Ferrand, 1889).

5. Joseph Desaymard and Emile Desforge, "Note sur la dévotion à Saint Verny, patron des vignerons d'Auvergne," in *L'Art populaire en France*, ed. Adolphe Riff (Strasbourg: Librairie Istra, 1930), 35-39.

6. Prosper Lambertini [Pope Benedict XIV], *De servorum Dei beatificatione et beatorum canonizatione*, vol. 5 (Prato: 1840), 404 (*"ex immemorabili consuetudine uti martyr colitur"*).

*13. Patronage of Saints and Civic
Religion in the Italy of the Communes*

*[To avoid cumbersome turns of phrase, the masculine form of singular pronouns is used throughout this essay. The reader should bear in mind that saintly women are included here as well.]

1. Archivio di Stato, Orvieto, Libri di riformanze del Consiglio, *ad annum* 1350, ff. 540v-543.

2. Libri di riformanze del Consiglio, f. 121.

3. See the documents published by Martino Bertagna, "Note e documenti attorno a S. Lucchese," *Archivum Franciscanum Historicum* 62 (1969), 19-42. Another ceremony of the same type is described in an article of the statutes of Padua, enacted in 1269, two years after the death of the Blessed Anthony the Pilgrim (†1267), as reported in Andrea Gloria, *Statuti del comune di Padova dal secolo XII all'anno 1285* (Padua: F. Sacchetto, 1873), 181: "...*potestas Padue et antiani* [...] *et officiales cum cereis pro comuni Padue persolvendis et gastaldiones frataliarum honorabilis populi paduani debeant ire omni anno in processione in festo beati Antonii peregrini cum cereis et candelis.*" [For a more detailed study of this figure, see Antonio Rigon, "Dévotion et patriotisme communal dans la genèse et la diffusion d'un culte: le bienheureux Antoine de Padoue surnommé le 'Pellegrino' (†1267)," in *Faire croire: Modalités de la diffusion et de la réception des messages religieux du XIIe au XVe siècle* (Rome: Ecole Française de Rome, 1981), 259-278.]

4. See Bertagna, "Note e documenti," 20-21.

5. Bertagna, "Note e documenti," 32-33.

6. Bertagna, "Note e documenti," 34-35.

7. Lodovico Zdekauer, *Il Constituto del Comune di Siena dell'anno 1262*, book I, III (Milan: Hoepli, 1897), 54-55.

8. *Statuta Communis et Civitatis Tarvisii, Additiones ad annum 1313*, rubr. CXXV, ff. 28-30.

9. Angelo Marchesan, *Treviso medievale: Istituzioni, usi, costumi, aneddoti, curiosità, studio storico documentato* (Treviso: Tipografia Funzionari Comunali, 1923), 186-187.

10. *Statuta Communis et Civitatis Tarvisii, Additiones ad annum 1314*, rubr. XXX, f. 156. The event referred to in this passage is the insurrection of August 15, 1312, against Guecellone da Camino and his followers.

11. Francesco Lanzoni, *Storia ecclesiastica e agiografica faentina dal XI al XV secolo*, Studi e testi 252 (Vatican City: Biblioteca Apostolica Vaticana, 1969), 422.

12. L. Baldiserri, "Degli Antichi Statuti della città d'Imola," *La Romagna* 9 (1912), 241-245.

13. Bertagna, "Note e documenti," 28-30.

14. See the statutes of Spello (Umbria), Book IV, c. XLIII ("De faculis fiendis"), cited in the canonization proceedings of the blessed Andrea Caccioli, O.F.M. (†1254) Spoleto, 1730-1734; Archivio Segreto, Vatican, Riti, Processi 2912, f. 570.

15. See for example the petition addressed to the council of Montesanto, a small town in the Marches, by a musician from Assisi: *"Si vobis placet, ipse intendit ac velit cum sui instrumenti sonitu vestrum commune honorare in festo Nativitatis Domini, in festo Resurrectionis eiusdem, in festivitatibus sancti Angeli, sancti Gerii et sancti Stephani."* (Canonization process of the blessed Gerio [†1270], Archivio Segreto, Vatican, Riti, Processi, f. 145.)

16. See Agnolo di Tura, *Cronache senesi*, ed. Alessandro Lisini and Fabio Iacometti, *Rerum Italicarum Scriptores*, 2nd ed., vol. 15, part 6 (Bologna: Nicola Zanichelli, 1939), 306. In 1354 the distribution of sweets or *biricuscoli* on three saints' days cost the commune of Siena 174 lire. On the custom of running a palio in honor of saints, see Giovanni Cecchini and Dario Neri, *Il Palio di Siena* (Siena: Monte dei Paschi, 1958).

17. See the documents cited on this subject by E. Castaldi, *Santo Bartolo, il Giob della Toscana* (Florence: Giannini, 1928), 72.

18. See Fabio Alberti, *Notizie antiche e moderne riguardanti Bevagna città dell'Umbria* (Venice: Stamp. Coleti, 1791), 175.

19. Johannes Meier, *Liber de viris illustribus ordinis Praedicatorum*, ed. Paulus von Loë, Quellen und Forschungen zur Geschichte der Domenikanerordens in Deutschland 12 (Leipzig: O. Harrassowitz, 1918), 71.

20. On these ceremonies in honor of saints and on how they took place in urban settings, see Daniel Arasse, *"Fervebat pietate populus.* Art, dévotion et société autour de la glorification de saint Bernardin de

Sienne," in *Mélanges de l'Ecole Française de Rome, Moyen Age-Temps Modernes* 79 (1977), 189-263.

21. Text published by Ludovico Bargigli da Pelago, *Antica leggenda della vita e dei miracoli di Santa Margherita di Cortona* (Lucca: F. Bonsignori, 1793), 183. (Reprint, ed. Emilio Crivelli [Siena: Tipografia editrice S. Bernardino, 1897].)

22. On St. Bevignate, whom we discuss below, see Léon Kern, "Saint Bevignate de Pérouse," in *Etudes d'histoire ecclésiastique et diplomatique*, Mémoires et documents publiés par la Société d'histoire de la Suisse romande, ser. 3, vol. 9 (Lausanne: Payot, 1973), 1-15.

23. Rambaldo degli Azzoni Avogari, *De B. Henrico qui Tarvisii decessit anno Christi MCCCXV commentariorum pars altera* (Venice: P. Valvasense, 1760), 65-68.

24. Statutes of Cortona, Book IV, f. 75, *ad annum* 1318, cited by Girolamo Mancini, *Cortona nel Medio Evo* (Florence: 1897; reprint Rome: Multigrafia Editrice, 1969), 78.

25. The lack of evidence is obvious in the case of Bevignate, about whom there was almost no surviving historical record by the end of the thirteenth century. On the financial aspects of the problem, we need only cite the example of the city of Osimo, in the Marches, which had to consider the possibility of selling a house it owned in order to cover the expenses of an embassy sent to the Curia to solicit the canonization of its late bishop Benvenuto Scotivoli (†1282). See the documents published by Filippo Vecchietti and P. Compagnoni, *Memorie istorico-critiche di Osimo* (Rome: 1782), 103-110.

26. In 1316 the commune of Treviso instructed the ambassadors it was sending to the Curia to request the canonization of the Blessed Rigo (†1315) to put themselves in contact *"cum aliquibus de curia qui sciant mores curiae et qualiter possint introduci ad summum pontificum et quo modo et ordine sit in ipso negotio procedendum."* (Deliberations of the Council of 20 October 1316, in Rambaldo degli Azzoni Avogari, *De B. Henrico*, 66.)

27. On these developments, see André Vauchez, *La Sainteté en Occident aux derniers siècles du Moyen Age*, Bibliothèque des Ecoles Françaises d'Athènes et de Rome 241 (Rome: Ecole Française de Rome, 1981), 75-78.

28. Thus the statutes of Cremona include the rubric *"De sententiis tempore feriato et non feriato quo agi potest"* which was updated between 1349 and 1356. A long list of feast days is accompanied by a list of days *"quibus fiunt oblaciones per Commune nostrum,"* which includes local saints like St. Omobono (†1197) and the Blesseds Facio (†1271) and Alberto (†1279). See *Statuta et ordinamenta communis Cremonae facta*

et compilata currente anno Domini MCCCXXXIX, in *Corpus statuto-rum*, ed. Ugo Gualazzini, vol. 1 (Milan: A. Giuffré, 1952) 92-94. In Faenza, in the statutes of 1414, the rubric *"De feriis et diebus feriatis"* also makes a distinction between the major holidays of universal nature and those which are celebrated locally by the clergy and the commune. *"Et intel-ligatur populos celebrare quanto maior pars artificum laborantium iuxta plateam sanctorum et sanctarum sub quorum vocabulo ecclesia que capella nuncupatur et teneatur constructa fuerit in civitate Faven-tie vel aliquo de burgis dicte civitatis."* Lanzoni, *Storia ecclesiastica e agiografica*, 418.

29. The statutes of Padua in 1269 make this statement concerning the feast day of Blessed Anthony the Pilgrim: *"Et in die festivitatis eius clausae teneantur stationes quaecumque que circa palatium et plateas communis sunt."* (see Gloria, *Statuti del comune di Padova*, 181). Fines were imposed on those who worked on feast days: see Mancini, *Cortona nel Medio Evo*, 177.

30. See the deliberations of the Council of the commune of Treviso of 26 November 1316, in degli Azzoni Avogari, *De B. Henrico*, 61: *"Ad bonorem et reverentiam Dei omnipotentis et Beatissime Marie semper Virginis et Beatorum Petri et Pauli et beatorum Liberalis et Henrici confessorum."*

31. Bertagna, "Note e documenti," 21 and 27.

32. Kern, "Saint Bevignate," 8.

33. See the writ of cession of 1392, in da Pelago, *Antica leggenda*, 176: *"Corpus pretiosum collocatum fuit et est in oratorio seu ecclesia sancti Basilii quod est dicti communis et populi civitatis Cortone et per ipsum commune et populum extitit fabricatum in summitate civitatis Cortone, quod oratorium vulgariter nominatur ecclesia sancti Basilii et sancte Margarite de Cortona."*

34. Bertagna, "Note e documenti," 34-35.

35. In 1447 the Dominican prior requested authorization from the council of Cividale del Friuli to open the tomb *"di una certa signora Ben-venuta sepolta nel cimitero dei Domenicani, che ha la reputazione di essere Beata"* (Archivio comunale, Cividale, vol. 1262, *ad annum* 1447).

36. This happened for example in Cremona, at the bishop's au-thentication of the relics of St. Omobono in 1356. See Pellegrino Merula, *Santuario di Cremona* (Cremona: 1627), 290.

37. Bertagna, "Note e documenti," 8.

38. See Vauchez, *La Sainteté*, 277-280.

39. Archivio di Stato, Siena, Deliberazioni del Consiglio Generale, vol. 140, ff. 42-43. Among the reasons listed there entitling the saint

to a public cult was the fact that he was "*tam de nobili stirpe natus*" ["born of such noble blood"].

40. Archivio di Stato, Orvieto, Libri di riformanze del Consiglio (4 June 1347), rubr. LXV, f. 38.

41. Michele Maccarrone, *Studi su Innocenzo III*, (Padua: Antenore, 1972) and especially V. Natalini, "San Pietro Parenzo (†1199)," *Lateranum*, n.s. 2.2 (Rome: 1936), 118ff.

42. See Elizabeth Carpentier, *Une ville devant la peste: Orvieto et la peste noire de 1348* (Paris: S.E.V.P.E.N., 1962), 34-41.

43. *Libri di riformanze del comune di Amandola*, cited in the canonization proceedings of the blessed Anthony of Amandola of the order of the Hermits of St. Augustine (Fermo: 1756), Archivio Segreto, Vatican, Riti, Processi 744, ff. 231-267.

44. *Libri di riformanze del comune di Amandola*, ff. 231-233. *[That is, the annual offering was quadrupled, since 50 soldi is the equivalent of 2 1/2 pounds.]

45. See the documents published by L. Fausti, "Di un episodio religioso-politico della fine del XIV secolo a Spoleto," *Archivio per la storia ecclesiastica dell'Umbria* 5 (1921) 57-66.

46. See André Vauchez, "La commune de Sienne, les ordres mendiants et le culte des saints: histoire et enseignements d'une crise (novembre 1328-avril 1329)," in *Mélanges de l'Ecole Française de Rome, Moyen Age-Temps Modernes* 89 (1977), 757-767, reprinted in Vauchez, *Religion et Société dans l'Occident médiéval* (Turin: Bottega d'Erasmo, 1981), 125-135.

47. Text published by F. Cristofani, "Memorie del beato Pietro Pettignano," in *Miscellanea Francescana* 5 (1890), 38.

48. A. Riccieri, "Indice degli Annali ecclesiastici perugini tratto dalla cancelleria decemvirale," in *Archivio per la storia ecclesiastica dell'Umbria* 5 (1921), 394.

49. Lanzoni, *Storia ecclesiastica e agiografica*, 102-104.

50. See Francesco Filippini, *S. Petronio, vescovo di Bologna* (Bologna: 1948) and especially Alba Maria Orselli, "Spirito cittadino e temi politico-culturali nel culto di San Petronio," in *La Coscienza cittadina dei comuni italiani del Duecento (Todi 1970)*, Convegni del Centro di studi sulla spiritualità medioevale 11 (Todi: 1972), 283-344.

51. *Acta Sanctorum*, March, vol. 3, 243.

52. *Acta Sanctorum*, March, vol. 3, 243.

53. Archivio di Stato, Siena, Deliberazioni del Consiglio Generale, Libro 107, f. 33v, and Cristofani, "Memorie del Beato Pietro Pettignano," 33.

54. Riccieri, "Indice degli Annali ecclesiastici perugini," *ad annum* 1453.

55. On the popular cult of the blessed Alberto of Villa d'Ogna in Cremona and Parma in 1279, see Salimbene de Adam, *Cronica*, ed. Gianni Scalia, vol. 2, Scrittori d'Italia 233 (Bari: Laterza, 1977), 733-736 [Eng. trans., *The Chronicle of Salimbene de Adam*, ed. Joseph L. Baird, Giuseppe Baglivi and John Robert Kane (Binghamton, NY: Medieval and Renaissance Texts and Studies, 1986)]; on new *beati* venerated in Tuscany at the end of the fourteenth century, see Franco Sacchetti, *Opere*, ed. Aldo Borlenghi (Milan: Rizzoli, 1957), 1113-1119.

56. See, for example, Arnold van Gennep, *Le Culte populaire des saints en Savoie*, 2nd ed., Archives françaises d'ethnologie 3 (Paris: Maisonneuve, 1973) and Schmitt, *Le Saint Lévrier*.

57. See on this subject the interesting perspectives for the sixteenth century opened by Luigi Donvito, "La 'religione cittadina' et le nuove prospettive sul cinquecento religioso italiano," in *Rivista di storia e letteratura religiosa* 19 (1983), 434-474.

58. On this movement of after-the-fact regularization of local cults which had existed "from time immemorial," see Vauchez, *La Sainteté*, 488-489.

59. See Hans Conrad Peyer, *Stadt und Stadtpatron im mittelalterlichen Italien*, Zürcher Studien zur allgemeinen Geschichte 13 (Zürich: Europa, 1955).

60. On the crisis of the communal form of government at the end of the Middle Ages, see Philip J. Jones, "Communes and Despots: The City-State in Late Medieval Italy," *Transactions of the Royal Historical Society*, ser. 5, 15 (1965): 71-96.

14. Female Sanctity in the Franciscan Movement

1. The various elements that constitute the canonization proceedings of St. Elisabeth of Thuringia were published by Albert Huyskens, *Quellenstudien zur Geschichte de hl. Elisabeth, Landgräfin von Thüringen* (Marburg: N.G. Elwert, 1908). On Rose of Viterbo, see Giuseppe Abate, *S. Rosa di Viterbo, Terziaria francescana: Fonti storiche della vita e loro revisione critica* (Rome: Editrice "Miscellanea Francescana," 1952), which includes some chapters of the thirteenth-century *Vita prima*; the transactions of the canonization process of 1457, preserved in the archives of the monastery of Santa Rosa at Viterbo, were partially published in the *Acta Sanctorum*, Sept., vol. 2, col. 442-479 [=*Bibliotheca hagiographica latina*, 7346-7348]. The inquest held in Assisi in 1253 on the life and miracles of St. Clare is known to us through a fifteenth-century translation in the Umbrian dialect, ed. Zeffirino Lazzeri, "Il processo di canonizzazione di S. Chiara d'Assisi," *Archivum franciscanum*

historicum 13 (1920), 439-493. The proceedings of the inquest of St. Clare of Montefalco, held in 1318-1319, have been edited by Claudio Leonardi and Enrico Menestò, *Il Processo di canonizzazione di Chiara da Montefalco* (Florence: La Nuova Italia, 1984). Finally, an excellent critical edition of Delphine's canonization proceedings, which took place in Apt and Avignon in 1363, has recently been published by Jacques Cambell, *Enquête pour le procès de canonisation de Dauphine de Puimichel, comtesse d'Ariano (†26.XI.1360) (Apt et Avignon, 14 mai-30 octobre 1363)* (Turin: Bottega d'Erasmo, 1978).

2. On this point, we recapitulate the conclusions of the article by Jane Tibbetts Schulenburg, "Sexism and the Celestial Gynaeceum from 500 to 1200," *Journal of Medieval History* 4 (1978), 117-133.

3. For more information on these statistical data, see André Vauchez, *La Sainteté en Occident aux derniers siècles du Moyen Age d'après les procès de canonisation et les documents hagiographiques* (Rome: Ecole Française de Rome, 1981).

4. See on this subject Philippe Delhaye, "Le dossier antimatrimonial de l'*Adversus Jovinianum* et son influence sur quelques écrits latins du XIIe siècle," *Mediaeval Studies* 13 (1951), 65-86 as well as the work by Marie Louise Portmann, *Die Darstellung der Frau in der Geschichtschreibung des früheren Mittelalters*, Basler Beiträge zur Geschichtswissenschaft 69 (Basel-Stuttgart, Helbig & Lichtenhahn, 1958). The latter work has given rise to an interesting polemic about the condition of women in the Middle Ages: see especially the reviews of Simone Roisin, in *Revue belge de philologie et d'histoire* 38 (1960), and Baudouin de Gaiffier, in *Analecta bollandiana* 78 (1960).

5. See the texts cited by Robert Bultot in his numerous publications on the *contemptus mundi*, especially *Christianisme et valeurs humaines: La doctrine du mépris du monde en Occident, de saint Ambroise à Innocent III*. Vol. 4, *Le XIe siècle* (Louvain/Paris: Editions Nauwelaerts, 1963-1964).

6. Like, for example, the countess Mathilda of Canossa, whose close relations with Gregory VII are well known, or Ermengard, the countess of the Maine, whose "spiritual director" was Robert of Arbrissel.

7. The monasteries still adopted the rules and constitutions of masculine orders, without adapting them to the specific needs and problems of women. See on this subject Micheline de Fontette, *Les Religieuses à l'âge classique du droit canon: Recherches sur les structures juridiques des branches féminines des ordres* (Paris: J. Vrin, 1967).

8. J. P. Migne, *Patriologia Latina*, 200, col. 1024.

9. [*"Nam cum uiro concessum non sit quod sit uel dicatur pater Dei, hoc tamen prestitum est mulieri ut sit parens Dei."*] Adam of

Eynsham, *The Life of St. Hugh of Lincoln*, ed. Decima Douie and Hugh Farmer, vol. 2 (London: Nelson, 1961), 48.

10. We refer the reader on this point to the paper by Giovanni Gonnet, "La donna nei movimenti pauperistico-evangelici," in *Movimento religioso femminile e francescanesimo nel secolo XIII: Atti del VII Congresso internazionale, Assisi, 11-13 ottobre* 1979 (Assisi: Società Internazionale di Studi Francescani, 1980), 103-129. See also Gottfried Koch, *Frauenfrage und Ketzertum im Mittelalter: Die Frauenbewegung im Rahmen des Katharismus und des Waldensertums und ihre sozialen Wurzeln* (12.-14. *Jahrhundert*) (Berlin: Akademie-Verlag, 1962), a work that has been criticized by Etienne Delaruelle, *Revue d'histoire ecclésiastique* 60 (1965), 159-161 and Raffaello Morghen, *Cahiers de civilisation médiévale* 9 (1966), 239-243.

11. See Alcantara Mens, *Oorsprong en Betekenis van de Nederlandse Begijnenen-begardenbeweging: Vergelijkende studie: XIIde-XIIIde euw* (Antwerp: Vitgeversmij N.V. Standaard-Boekhandel, 1947) and Ernest W. McDonnell, *The Beguines and Beghards in Medieval Culture, with Special Emphasis on the Belgian Scene* (New Brunswick: Rutgers University Press, 1954).

12. The fundamental study in this area remains that of Herbert Grundmann, *Religiöse Bewegungen im Mittelalter: Untersuchungen über die geschichtlichen Zusammenhänge zwischen der Ketzerei, den Bettelorden und der religiösen Frauenbewegung im 12. und 13. Jahrhundert und über die geschichtlichen Grundlagen der deutschen Mystik* (Hildesheim: Olms, 1961).

13. For these complex problems, we refer the reader both to the works of Father Gilles Gérard Meersseman, collected under the title *Ordo fraternitatis: Confraternite e pietà de laici nel Medioevo* (Rome: Herder, 1977), and to the proceedings of the conferences on this theme organized by Father Mariano d'Alatri, *L'Ordine della Penitenza di San Francesco d'Assisi nel secolo XIII. Atti del convegno di studi francescani. Assisi, 3-4-5 luglio 1972* (Rome: Istituto storico dei Cappuccini, 1973) and *I Frati penitenti di San Francesco nella società del Due e del Trecento. Atti del 2° convegno di studi francescani. Roma, 12-13-14 ottobre 1976* (Rome, Istituto storico dei Cappuccini, 1977). [On the work of Father Meersseman, see also chapter 9 of this volume.]

14. The way of life of these female penitents was studied in great detail by Giuseppe Garampi, in his *Memorie ecclesiastiche appartenenti all'istoria e al culto della B. Chiara di Rimini* (Rome: Niccolò e Marco Pagliarini, 1755), 79-150. See also the important article by Mario Sensi, "Incarcerate e Penitenti a Foligno nella prima metà del Trecento," in *I Frati penitenti di San Francesco*, 291-308.

302 Notes to Pages 174-176

15. Gilles Gérard Meersseman, ed. *Dossier de l'ordre de la Pénitence au XIIIe siècle*, Spicilegium Friburgense 7 (Fribourg: Editions universitaires, 1961).

16. We need only think of *fabliaux* such as *Les Braies du cordelier* or *Frère Denise*, whose virulence is equalled only by their ingenuity.

17. On the concrete conditions of life of the first Clarisses, see Engelbert Grau, "Die Klausur im Kloster S. Damiano zu Lebzeiten der heiligen Klara," in Isaac Vazquez, ed., *Studia historico-ecclesiastica. Festgabe für Prof. Luchesius G. Spätling, O.F.M.* (Rome: Pontificium Athenaeum Antonianum, 1977), 311-346.

18. "Il processo di canonizzazione di S. Chiara," 463 and 473.

19. On the importance of the "privilege of poverty" in the life and spirituality of St. Clare, see Paul Sabatier, "Le privilège de la pauvreté," in *Revue d'histoire franciscaine* 1 (1924), 1-54 and 469-482, and Engelbert Grau, "Das 'Privilegium pauperitatis' der hl. Klara. Geschichte und Bedeutung," in *Wissenschaft und Weisheit* 38 (1975), 17-25. [See also Clara Gennaro, "Chiara, Agnese e le prime consorelle: Dalle 'Pauperes Dominae' di S. Damiano alle Clarisse," in *Movimento religioso femminile e francescanesimo*, 169-191.]

20. "Il processo di canonizzazione di S. Chiara," 457-458 and 476-477. On the importance of this theme in Franciscan piety, see Ottaviano Schmucki, "Das Leiden Christi im Leben des hl. Franziskus von Assisi. Eine Quellenvergleichende Untersuchung im Lichte der zeitgenössischen Passionfrömmigkeit," *Collectanea Franciscana* 30 (1960), 5-30, 129-145, 241-263, and 353-397.

21. "Il processo di canonizzazione di S. Chiara," 465 and 476.

22. "Il processo di canonizzazione di S. Chiara," 469-470. One nun declared that St. Clare's life had been astonishing "per la molta abstinentia, la quale non pareva se dovesse potere fare da uomo [for her great abstinence, of which a man would not seem capable]." See also 448 and 475.

23. "Voleva sostenere el martirio per amore del Signore [She wanted to undergo martyrdom out of love for the Lord]," "Il processo di canonizzazione di S. Chiara," 465.

24. This observation is valid not only for the Poor Clares, strictly speaking, but also for a whole series of sainted nuns, who introduced Franciscan-inspired practices and customs into their communities and their rules for living. Examples include the blessed Beatrice II of Este (†1262), who pronounced her monastic vows in the presence of Salimbene and founded the monastery of Santo Stefano della Rotta, near Ferrara, and the blessed Margherita Colonna (†1280), in the region of

Rome. Beatrice has been studied by F. Mostardi, *La Beata Beatrice II d'Este* (Venice: 1963) [and by Antonio Rigon, "La santa nobile: Beatrice d'Este (†1226) e il suo primo biografo" in *Viridarium Floridum: Studi di storia veneta offerti dagli allievi a Paolo Sambin,* ed. Maria Chiara Billanovich, Giorgio Cracco, and Antonio Rigon (Padua: Antenore, 1984), 61-87]. On Margherita, see Livario Oliger, *B. Margherita Colonna: Le due vite scritte dal fratello Giovanni Colonna Senatore di Roma e da Stefania Monaca di S. Silvestro in Capite...* (Rome: Istituto Grafico Tiberino, 1935).

25. Good summaries on the spirituality of St. Elisabeth can be found in the book by Jeanne Ancelet-Hustache, *Sainte Elisabeth de Hongrie* (Paris: Editions franciscaines, 1947) and, especially, in the article "Elisabetta d'Ungheria," by Edith Pàsztor, in *Bibliotheca Sanctorum* 4 (Rome: 1964), 1110-1121.

26. There is much testimony to this effect in the canonization proceedings, *Quellenstudien,* 135-148. See also the rigorous and well-documented study of Wilhelm Maurer, "Die heilige Elisabeth und ihr Marburger Hospital," *Jahrbuch d. Hessische Kirchengeschichte Vereinigung* 7 (1956), 36-69.

27. *Quellenstudien,* 136.

28. *Quellenstudien,* 120, 125, 157.

29. See André Vauchez, "Charité et pauvreté chez sainte Elisabeth de Thuringe d'après les actes du procès de canonisation," in Michel Mollat, ed., *Etudes sur l'histoire de la pauvreté, Moyen Age-XVIe siècle,* vol. 1 (Paris: Publications de la Sorbonne, 1974), 163-173.

30. Joy was an extremely important element in the spirituality of St. Elisabeth, both the joy which she felt when performing charitable acts and lowly tasks (*Quellenstudien,* 119) and that which she tried to provide for others (*Quellenstudien,* 133): after the distribution of the alms she had given them "*ceperunt cantare pauperes et bene se habere, quo audito dicebat beata Elizabeth: ecce dixi vobis quod letos deberemus facere homines... et ipsa gaudens erat cum gaudentibus.*"

31. In the absence of a comprehensive work on Delphine and her milieu, useful information can be found in the work of Father Jacques Cambell, *Vies occitanes de saint Auzias et de sainte Dauphine* (Rome: Pontificium Athenaeum Antonianum, 1963), and in the introduction to the edition of her canonization proceedings cited in note 1 above. [See also chapter 6 of this volume.]

32. As attested to by the mention of her relationship with Ubertino da Casale in the canonization proceedings of 1363 and by the fact that her name figures in the correspondence of Angelo Clareno, edited in 1980

by Lydia von Auw [*Epistole* (Rome: Istituto Storico Italiano per il Medio Evo, 1980)]. In Naples she certainly knew and spent time with Philip of Majorca.

33. [On this aspect of Delphine's spirituality, see chapter 16 of this volume.]

34. *Vita auctore Vito de Cortona,* [=*Biblioteca hagiographica latina* 4041] published in *Acta Sanctorum,* May, vol. 4, col. 385-418. On the historical personage, see the extremely critical judgment of Robert Davidsohn, in his *Storia di Firenze* (Italian trans. Florence: Sansoni, 1956), 2:180-188. [See also Anna Benvenuti Papi, "Umiliana dei Cerchi: Nascita di un culto nella Firenze del Dugento," *Studi Francescani* 77 (1980), 87-117.]

35. *Vita auctore Vito de Cortona,* col. 386.

36. This was not only a theme of hagiography, as it may be tempting to think. Depositions of the witnesses at the canonization proceedings abound with statements on this point. For more information on this subject, see my book *La Sainteté en Occident* [and chapter 15 of this volume].

37. The juridical and economic problems she faced at this moment have been clearly reconstructed by Ancelet-Hustache, *Sainte Elisabeth,* 251-256, on the basis of information provided by Ernst Heymann, "Zum Ehegütterrecht der hl. Elisabeth," in *Zeitschrift der Vereins für thüringischen Geschichte* N.S. 19 (1909).

38. The reference is to the attack on the monastery of Sant'Angelo in Panzo, which was led by their uncle Monaldo, 2 April 1212. Thomas of Celano, *The Legend of St. Clare of Assisi,* in *The Legend and Writings of St. Clare of Assisi* (New York: St. Bonaventure Press, 1953) part 1, ch. 5 and 6.

39. See R. Toso D'Arenzano, entry "Mareri Filippa," in *Bibliotheca Sanctorum,* 8 (Rome: 1967), 754-756, and A. Chiappini, "S. Filippa Mareri e il suo monastero di Borgo S. Pietro de Molito nel Cicolano," in *Miscellanea francescana* 22 (1921), 65-119. [See also *Santa Filippa Mareri e il monastero di Borgo S. Pietro nella storia del Cicolano, Atti del Convegno di Studi di Borgo S. Pietro del 24-26 ottobre 1986* (Borgo S. Pietro di Petrella Salto: Istituto delle Suore Clarisse di Santa Filippa Mareri, 1989).]

40. There are many depositions regarding this in her canonization process, conducted in Hungary in 1276, and edited by Vilmos Fraknói, *Monumenta Romana episcopatus vesprimiensis (1103-1526),* vol. 1 (Budapest: Collegium historicorum hungarorum romanorum, 1896), in particular 184, 194, 254, and 264. The saint was said to have affirmed before her companions (202): "Michi est melius esse sine labris in paradiso

quam ire in infernum cum labris et naso." On her spirituality, see Astrik Gabriel, "The Spirituality of St. Margaret of Hungary," in *Cross and Crown* 3 (1951), 298-309.

41. *Vita auctore Vito de Cortona*, 388.

42. *Vita auctore Vito de Cortona*, 388-389.

43. On the complex and as yet insufficiently understood relationship between Rose of Viterbo and the Franciscan movement, see the contradictory opinions of Stanislao da Campagnola and Mariano D'Alatri in the volume *L'Ordine della penitenza di San Francesco d'Assisi nel secolo XIII*, 157-179 and 194-196.

44. *Vita auctore Vito de Cortona*, col. 389: "misit [Deus] et hanc novae vitae et sanctae conversationis mirabilem fundatricem."

45. This meeting took place sometime between 1221 and 1225. St. Francis placed her under the direction of Brother Ruggero of Todi, who pronounced the eulogy after her death in 1236. Cf. *Acta Sanctorum*, March, vol. 1, col. 417-418. [The historical accuracy of this supposed encounter has been vigorously challenged by Robert Brentano, "Santa Filippa Mareri nel movimento religioso femminile del secolo XIII," in *Santa Filippa Mareri*, 36-37.]

46. *Vita auctore Vito de Cortona*, col. 395: *"Desiderabat esse in arduis montibus et in desertis et solitudinis, in locis inaccessibilibus, ut solum haberet pro victu herbas et de Deo libere cogitaret."*

47. Her biographer mentions the "diabolical" temptation which tormented her friend Gisla (*Vita auctore Vito de Cortona*, col. 392): *"Ita ut omnino sola existere cuperet in desertis, cum periculosum sit mulieribus solitudo."* The danger threatening lone women was obviously a sexual one, but not exclusively sexual: as the fifteenth-century Dominican Johannes Nider was to say in his *Formicarius*, *"Mulier cum sola sit, mala cogitat!"*

48. *Vita auctore Vito de Cortona*, col. 392: *"Domum reputa solitudinem nemoris et familiam silvestres feras et inter eas eris sicut in nemore."*

49. *Vita auctore Vito de Cortona*, col. 389: *"Qualiter Minorum Fratrum vitam plenius tenere potuit quae Christi evangelium tam perfecte servavit?"*

50. He calls them effeminate (*"non filii sed filiae nominantur"*) and responds to their arguments with a defense of the contemplative life. *Vita auctore Vito de Cortona*, col. 389-390.

51. *Vita auctore Vito de Cortona*, col. 390-391.

52. We refer to the *Miracula intra triennium ab obitu patrata* [=*Bibliotheca hagiographica latina* 4043] and the story of the *Appari-*

tiones, written in 1239 and published in *Acta Sanctorum*, May, vol. 4, col. 401-407.

53. Vito of Cortona said on this subject "*Erat quippe hortus conclusus et multa magna quae habuit non aperiebat nisi urgente ipsam gratia Spiritus Sancti.*" *Vita auctore Vito de Cortona*, col. 397.

54. The *Vida de la benaurada sancta Douceline*, composed around 1300 by Philippine de Porcellet, who had succeeded her in 1274 as head of the Dames de Roubaud, has been published in French translation by Raoul Gout, *La vie de sainte Douceline. Texte provençal du 14e siècle* (Paris: Bloud et Gay, 1927); see also Baudouin de Gaiffier, entry "Douceline," in *Dictionnaire de spiritualité*, vol. 3 (Paris: 1957) col. 1672-73, and Claude Carozzi, "Douceline et les autres," in *La Religion populaire en Languedoc*, Cahiers de Fanjeaux 11 (Toulouse: Privat, 1976), 251-267.

15. Conjugal Chastity: A New Ideal in the Thirteenth Century

1. See André Vauchez, *La Sainteté en Occident aux derniers siècles du Moyen Age d'après les procès de canonisation et les documents hagiographiques* (Rome: Ecole Française de Rome, 1981), 410-420.

2. Vauchez, *La Sainteté en Occident*, 413-414.

3. It is worth mentioning that the compiler of the *Libellus de dictis IV ancillarum*, ed. Albert Huyskens (Kempten-Munich: 1911), 7-8, was already trying to present St. Elisabeth as an example for married women. See on this subject the remarks of Edith Pàsztor, "Sant'Elisabetta d'Ungheria nella religiosità femminile," in *Annali della Facoltà di Lettere e Filosofia* 5 (1984), 83-99. On the positive view of her marriage which could be derived from the testimony of her servants, see Raoul Manselli, "Santità principesca e vita quotidiana in Elisabetta d'Ungheria: la testimonianza delle ancelle," in *Analecta Tertii Ordinis Regularis* 18 (1985), 24-45.

4. Second sermon of Boniface VIII, ed. François du Chesne, *Historiae Francorum Scriptores*, vol. 5, 483: "*Iste numquam carnem suam divisit in plures nec cum aliqua peccatum commisit, ita quod excepta uxore propria virgo ab aliis permansit.*"

5. A good summary of the sources and bibliography about St. Hedwig can be found in Romuald Gustaw, entry "Jadwiga Slaska," in *Hagiografia Polska*, vol. I, (Lublin: Ksiegarnia Sw. Wojciecha, 1971), 457-485, which is far superior to the corresponding article in the *Bibliotheca Sanctorum*.

6. The bull of canonization of St. Hedwig (*Exultat cunctorum*), dated 26 March 1267, was published in *Acta Sanctorum*, Oct., vol. 8,

col. 200-223. The text is preserved in ms. Lat. 3278, Paris, Bibliothèque Nationale, ff. 378-383, under the title of *Libellus de vita, miraculis et canonizatione beate Hadevigis de Polonia*. The sermon given in Viterbo on the day of the canonization has been published by Joseph Gottschalk, "Die Hedwigspredikt des Papstes Klemens IV vom Jahre 1267," in *Archiv für schlesische Kirchengeschichte* 15 (1957), 17-30. The *Legenda maior* and the *Legenda minor* [=*Bibliotheca hagiographica latina* 3766 and 3767] were published in the *Acta Sanctorum*, Oct., vol. 8, col. 224-264 and 200-202 respectively. This edition is quite reliable, but has the drawback of dividing the original text into new sections and introducing new titles. For the original section divisions and titles, it is preferable to refer to ms. Palatino Lat. 857 of the Vatican Library, ff. 3-70, which in any case has not attracted the attention of the editors of these hagiographic texts in the *Monumenta Poloniae Historica. Pomniki dziejowe Polski*, vol. 4 (Krakow: Nakl. Akademii Umiejetno'sci, 1884), 501-665. Currently, the best biography of St. Hedwig is Joseph Gottschalk's *Die heilige Hedwig Herzogin von Schlesien* (Graz-Cologne: Bohlau Verlag, 1964). For the medieval iconography of St. Hedwig, it is sufficient to consult the works of Teresa Dunin-Wasowicz, particularly her edition of the *Legenda Slaska* (Warsaw: Zaklad Narodowy im. Ossolinskich, 1967). An excellent description of medieval sources on St. Hedwig can be found in the work of Ortrud Reber, *Die Gestaltung des Kultes weiblicher Heiliger im Spätmittelalter; die Verehrung der Heiligren Elisabeth, Klara, Hedwig und Birgitta* (Hersbruck: Kommissionsverlag K. Pfeiffer, 1963), particularly 19-21 and 53-56. On their contents, see Vauchez, *La Sainteté en Occident*, 431-433.

7. Bull *Exultat cunctorum*, 200: "*Cum clarae memoriae Henrico duce Poloniae matrimonium duxit legitime contrahendum, in quo impartitum bonum conjugii salubriter conservando sic prudenter se gessit quod thori fidem inviolatam custodiens, prolem in Dei timore susceptam erudiens, ab ipso duce cui non praecipiti voluptatis affectu sed discreto semper inhaesisse judicio creditur rationis quousque sorte fatali est assumptus de medio, per separationis injuriam non divertit, licet ut orationi et contemplationi vacarent devotius, thorum ex pari voto et consensu unanimi per multa annorum curricula habuerunt sequestratum.*"

8. Gottschalk, "Die Hedwigspredikt," 20-21: "*Elegit [. . .] flagellum asperitatis in libertate et licentia maritalium amplexum sanctimoniam castitatis.*"

9. Gottschalk, "Die Hedwigspredikt," 22: "*Voluptatum ignibus per totum tempus predictum estuata non fuit.*"

10. Gottschalk, "Die Hedwigspredikt," 20: "*Quinymmo ex pari voto et consensu unanimi, tamen Hedwige principaliter inducente, thorum habuerunt sequestratum.*"

11. For the editions of this text, see note 6 above. Our citations follow the edition of the Bollandists in the *Acta Sanctorum*.

12. *Legenda maior*, 225: "*Per filiorum quippe generationem aeternam salutem consequi sperans.*"

13. *Legenda maior*, 225.

14. On medieval marriage, see Dominikus Lindner, *De usu matrimonii. Eine Untersuchung über seine sittliche Bewertung in der katholischen Moraltheologie alter und neuer Zeit* (Munich: 1929); John Thomas Noonan, *Contraception: A History of Its Treatment by the Catholic Theologians and Canonists* (Cambridge: Belknap Press of Harvard University Press, 1965); and Jean-Louis Flandrin, *Le Sexe et l'Occident. Evolution des attitudes et des comportements* (Paris: Seuil, 1981).

15. *Legenda maior*, 225.

16. See A. Vauchez, "Pénitents au Moyen Age," in *Dictionnaire de spiritualité*, vol. 12, 1 (Paris: Beauchesne, 1984) col. 1010–1023.

17. *Legenda maior*, 225.

18. Gilles Gérard Meersseman, *Dossier de l'ordre de la Pénitence au XIIIe siècle*, 2nd ed. (Fribourg: Editions universitaires, 1982), 92–112.

19. "*Diebus jejuniorum a propriis uxoribus abstinere opportet.*" Gratian, *Decretum*, III, 33 (*De Poen.*) q. 4–5, in *Corpus iuris canonici*, ed. Emil Albert Friedberg (Leipzig: B. Tachnitz, 1879–1881); reprint Graz: Akademische Druck-und Verlaganstalt, 1955), col. 1247–50.

20. A. Vauchez, *La Spiritualité du Moyen Age occidental: VIIIe-XIIe siècles* (Paris: Presses Universitaires de France, 1975), 105–145.

21. See the rule of the Militia of the Virgin (Bologna, 1261), edited by G.G. Meersseman, *Dossier*, 302: "*De vita fratrum in matrimonio existentium: vivant sub oboedientia prelatorum suorum, salvo iure matrimonii contracti aut etiam contrahendi, et in conjugali vel perpetua castitate.*"

22. Ivo of Chartres, *Decretum*, XV (*Patrologia latina*, 161, 893): "*In tribus quadragesimis anni et in die dominico et in feria quarta conjugales se continere debent.*" On the problem in general, see Jean-Louis Flandrin, *Un temps pour embrasser: Aux origines de la morale sexuelle occidentale (VIe-Xe siècle)* (Paris: Seuil, 1983). [The Ember Days are the three days of fasting prescribed on the Wednesday, Friday, and Saturday of the first week of Lent, the Octave of Pentecost, the third week of September, and the third week of Advent.]

23. *Legenda maior*, p. 225.

24. *Legenda maior*, p. 226.

25. *Legenda maior*, p. 226.
26. See Vauchez, *La sainteté en Occident*, 442-445.

16. The Virginal Marriage of Elzéar and Delphine

1. On the role and importance of the *articuli interrogatorii* in medieval canonization proceedings, see André Vauchez, *La Sainteté en Occident aux derniers siècles du Moyen Age d'après les procès de canonisation et les documents hagiographiques* (Rome: Ecole Française de Rome, 1981), esp. 54-60. The 91 articles of Delphine's canonization proceedings have been published by Jacques Cambell, *Enquête pour le procès de canonisation de Dauphine de Puimichel, comtesse d'Ariano* (†26.XI.1360) *(Apt et Avignon: 14 mai-30 octobre 1363)* (Turin: Bottega d'Erasmo, 1978). The first article, cited here, is on page 31. On the careers of Elzéar of Sabran (†1323) and Delphine of Puimichel (†1360), see chapter 6 of this volume.

2. *Enquête*, art 14, p. 40: "*Quod ipsa domina Dalphina et ipsius domine conversacio fuit principium et causa virginitatis ac honestatis eiusdem mariti.*"

3. This seigniorial code, formerly preserved in the Franciscan archives of Apt, was published in French by Abbé Boze, *Histoire de saint Elzéar et de sainte Delphine* (Avignon: 1821); the passage cited is found on page 40.

4. "Vie occitane de saint Elzéar," ed. Jacques Cambell, *Vies occitanes de saint Auzias et de sainte Delphine avec traduction française, introduction et notes* (Rome: Pontificium Athenaeum Antonianum, 1963), 76-77. According to Father Cambell, the Latin *vita* of St. Elzéar was probably composed by a Franciscan around 1370 on the basis of earlier hagiographic texts. It was published by the Bollandists in the *Acta Sanctorum*, Sept., vol. 7, col. 576-593. The Latin *vita* of Delphine, which was undoubtedly written at the same time, is lost. The *Vies occitanes* of the two saints were written between 1380 and 1390 in the region of Albi, or at least by a Franciscan native to the area. This is not, as we can demonstrate in the case of Elzéar, simply a translation of the Latin *vita*, because the author was familiar with certain oral traditions which enabled him to make some interesting additions to the Latin texts on which he drew. On these questions, see Cambell, *Vies occitanes*, 12-26.

5. "Vie occitane de saint Elzéar," 101. Delphine, while separated from her husband who was waging war in Italy, had initially pronounced a vow of chastity alone and in secret in 1312 or 1313. See "Vie occitane de sainte Delphine," 165-167.

6. "Vie occitane de saint Elzéar," 81.

7. On this essentially Neapolitan period in Delphine's life, see André Vauchez, "Entre la Provence et l'Italie du Sud: Elzéar et Delphine de Sabran," in *Actes du colloque franco-italien d'histoire religieuse de Chambéry (septembre 1984)*, ed. Michele Maccarrone and André Vauchez (Geneva: 1987), 89–100.

8. This will was published by the Marchioness Roselyne de Forbin d'Oppède in *La Bienheureuse Delphine de Sabran et les saints de Provence au XIVe siècle* (Paris: Plon, 1883), 412–425, a work which remains of interest on many points.

9. *Enquête*, 193.

10. *Enquête*, 384–385 and 431.

11. *Enquête*, 484 and 539.

12. *Enquête*, 73–74 and 498.

13. *Enquête*, 411 and 470.

14. "*Libellus supplex*," published in *Acta Sanctorum*, Sept., vol. 7, col. 558. The number of twenty-seven years is incorrect: their marriage in fact lasted twenty-four years.

15. Urban V canonized St. Elzéar on April 14, 1369, but the bull of canonization was promulgated by his successor Gregory XI on January 5, 1371. The text of the bull was published in *Acta Sanctorum*, Sept., vol. 7, col. 526–527.

16. In addition to St. Francis of Sales, who speaks of him in the *Introduction à la vie dévote* (chap. 12), we must mention the Jesuit Etienne Binet, *La vie et les éminentes vertus de saint Elzéar de Sabran et de la bienheureuse comtesse Delphine, vierges et mariez, deux phénix de la France* (Paris: 1622) [(*The Lives and Singular Virtues of Saint Elzéar, Count of Sabran, and of his Wife, the Blessed Countesse Delphina, Both Virgins and Married*. Trans. Sr. Thomas Hawkins (Paris: J. Cousturier, 1638)] and Jean-Marie de Vernon, *Histoire générale et particulière du tiers ordre de saint François d'Assize*, vol. I (Paris: G. Josse, 1667), 510–545.

17. *Vie occitane de sainte Delphine*, 149.

18. *Enquête*, 364.

19. *Vie occitane de sainte Delphine*, 139.

20. René Nelli, "La continence chez les cathares," in *Mystique et Continence: Travaux scientifiques du VIIe Congrès international d'Avon. Congrès international de psychologie religieuse* (Bruges: Desclée, De Brouwer, 1952), 139–151. Let us not forget that for the Cathars, procreation meant putting a damned creature into the world, and procreation was evil because it repeats the satanic operation of the incarnation of spirit in matter. Jean-Louis Biget has provided a good description of

the convergence between the Cathars and the Beguines, both in their social recruitment and in some of their beliefs, in his study "Autour de Bernard Délicieux: franciscanisme et société entre 1295 et 1300," in *Revue d'histoire de l'Eglise de France* 70 (1984), 75-93, esp. 83-88.

21. Nowadays, certainly, no one believes any more that the troubadours were propagandizers of and adherents to the doctrine of nonphysical love. But some themes in their poetry, such as "love from afar" and their tendency to maintain a certain distance with respect to spontaneous desire, may have encouraged rigorous self-control. See on this subject Diego Zorzi, *Valori religiosi nella letteratura provenzale: la spiritualità trinitaria* (Milan: Vita e pensiero, 1954) and Francisco J. Oroz Arizcuren, *La lérica religiosa en la literatura provenzal antigua. Edición crítica, traducción, notas y glosario* (Pamplona: Excma. Diputación Foral de Navarra, Institución Principe de Viana, 1972).

22. *Vie occitane de sainte Delphine*, 149.

23. *Vie occitane de sainte Delphine*, 135.

24. *The Golden Legend of Jacobus de Voragine*, trans. and ed. Granger Ryan and Helmut Ripperger (New York, London, Toronto: Longmans, Green, 1941), 282.

25. St. Jerome, "*Adversus Jovinianum*," I, *Patrologia latina*, vol. 23, 246 and 252. On the diffusion and influence of this work in the Middle Ages, see Philippe Delhaye, "Le dossier antimatrimonial de *l'Adversus Jovinianum* et son influence sur quelques écrits latins au XIIe siècle," in *Mediaeval Studies* 13 (1951), 65-86.

26. On Melania the Younger and Pinian, see Georges Goyau, *Sainte Mélanie* (383-439) (Paris: V. Lecoffre, 1908). Delphine may have had access to the writings of St. Jerome through anthologies of ascetic literature in Provençal such as those published by Diego Zorzi, "Testi inediti francescani in lingua provenzale," in *Miscellanea del Centro di studi medievale dell'Università Cattolica del Sacro Cuore*, vol. 1 (Milan: Vita e pensiero, 1956), 249-324.

27. Statutes of the council of Béziers (1299) in Edmond Martène and Ursin Durand, *Thesaurus novus anecdotorum*, vol. 4 (Paris: Sumptibus F. Delaulne, etc., 1717; reprinted Farnborough, Hants: Gregg, 1968-1969), col. 226-227.

28. On this subject, see the fundamental work of Raoul Manselli, *Spirituali e Beghini in Provenza*, Studi storici, fasc. 31-34 (Rome: Istituto Storico Italiano per il Medio Evo, 1959).

29. Manselli, *Spirituali e Beghini*, 221: "*Matrimonium est lupanar privatum [. . .] Homo cognoscendo carnaliter propriam uxorem peccat mortaliter.*"

30. On Olivi's ideas and works, see the summary by Pierre Peano, entry "Olieu," in the *Dictionnaire de spiritualité*, vol. 11 (Paris: 1982), 751-762.

31. Aquilin Emmen, "Virginità e matrimonio nella valutazione dell' Olivi," in *Studi Francescani* 64 (1967), 11-57 (with an edition of chapters 6-11 of the *De perfectione evangelica*).

32. [On the controversy surrounding Olivi and his work, see David Burr, *The Persecution of Peter Olivi* (Philadelphia: American Philosophical Society, 1976) and Burr, *Olivi and Franciscan Poverty: The Origins of the "Usus Pauper" Controversy* (Philadelphia: University of Pennsylvania Press, 1989).]

33. "Vie occitane de saint Elzéar," 78-79.

34. *"Que son voluptuoses e carnals del vil plasers d'aquest mon et amix de leur carn."* Mathieu de Bouzigues, "Considération sur la mort," in Zorzi, "Testi inediti francescani," 282-283. On this personage, see P. Ferdinand M. Delorme, "La *Confessio fidei* du frère Mathieu de Bouzigues," in *Etudes franciscaines* 49 (1937), 224-239.

35. *Vie occitane de sainte Delphine*, 146-147 and "Vie occitane de saint Elzéar," 52-53.

36. "Vie occitane de saint Elzéar," 111-112.

37. *Vie occitane de sainte Delphine*, 160-161. Arnold stated that for many physiological reasons they would be unable to have children before the age of twenty-five, and that it was therefore useless to bother them about this for the time being.

38. On Arnold of Villanova and his eschatological conceptions, see Raoul Manselli, *La "Lectura super Apocalypsim" di Pietro di Giovanni Olivi: Ricerche sull'escatologismo medievale*, Studi storici 19-21 (Rome: Istituto Storico Italiano per il Medio Evo, 1965), and Raoul Manselli, Columba Battle, and Georg Jüttner, entry "Arnald von Villanova," in *Lexikon des Mittelalters*, vol. I (Munich: Artemis Verlag, 1980) col. 994-996. [See also Francesco Santi, *Arnau de Vilanova: L'obra espiritual*, Història i Societat 5 (València: Diputació Provincial de València, 1987).]

39. This text has been edited by Franz Pelzer, "Ein Elogium Joachims von Fiore auf Kaiser Heinrich II und ihre Gemahlin Kunegunde," in *Liber Floridus Paul Lehmann* (Saint-Odile: 1950), 328-354, according to Ms. Vat. Lat. 3819. Raoul Manselli has edited and discussed Arnold's text (*Magistri Arnaldi de Villanova introductio in librum Joachim "De semine scripturarum"*) in his study "La religiosità d'Arnaldo di Villanova," *Bulletino dell'Istituto Storico Italiano per il Medio Evo* 63 (1951), 1-100. According to Marjorie Reeves, *The Influence of Prophecy in the Later Middle Ages: A Study in Joachimism* (Oxford: Clarendon Press, 1969), this commentary was written in 1292.

40. See Norman R. Cohn, *Les fanatiques de l'Apocalypse* (Paris: Julliard, 1962), 179–188. (Trans. of *The Pursuit of the Millenium* [Fairlawn, N.J.: Essential Books, 1957; New York: Harper, 1961].)

41. See on this subject the texts cited by Georges Peyronnet, "Une série de traditions sur Jeanne d'Arc," in *Mélanges de science/histoire religieuse* 38 (1981), 195–206.

42. *Enquête*, 244.

17. A Holy Woman During the Hundred Years' War: Jeanne-Marie of Maillé

1. See Henri Lemaître, "Géographie historique des établissements de l'ordre de saint François en Touraine (Ouest de la France) du XIIIe au XVe siècle," in *Revue d'histoire franciscaine* 6 (1929), 299–353.

2. Hervé Martin, *Les Ordres mendiants en Bretagne (vers 1230–vers 1530): Pauvreté volontaire et prédication à la fin du Moyen-Age* (Rennes/Paris: C. Klincksieck, 1975).

3. See on this subject Jean Mauzaize's thought-provoking synthesis, "Franciscains et ordres mendiants du XIIIe au XVe siècle," in *Histoire religieuse de la Touraine*, ed. Guy Marie Oury (Chambray-lès-Tours: C.L.D., 1975), 109–120, which also contains an ample bibliography on the convents of the region.

4. The inquest, begun on 11 April 1414, was concluded on 20 March 1415. The dossier published by the Bollandists in the *Acta Sanctorum*, March, vol. 3, col. 734–762, includes the *Vita* of Jeanne-Marie of Maillé written by her confessor Martin of Boisgaultier and the depositions of sixteen witnesses (two in writing), both clerical and lay. On their content, see the article of Thérèse Griguer, "La vie et le procès de canonisation de J.-M. de Maillé," in *Annales de Bretagne et des pays de l'Ouest* 91 (1984), 27–37. The only worthwhile biography of Jeanne-Marie was written by Father Léopold de Chérancé, *La Bienheureuse Jeanne-Marie de Maillé* (Paris: 1905). The canonization proceedings begun in Tours in 1414–1415 produced no result, surely because of the troubled situation created by the Great Schism; and it was not until the nineteenth century that the Holy See, after an inquest in 1869, officially recognized her cult in 1871.

5. On Jeanne-Marie's family, see Ambroise Ledru and Louis J. Denis, *Histoire de la maison de Maillé* (Paris: A. Lemerre, 1905), particularly vol. 1, 380–431. All of the information that follows comes from this well-documented work, which uses and cites many contemporary sources.

6. *Vita* in *Acta Sanctorum*, col. 735.

7. *Vita* in *Acta Sanctorum*, col. 735: *"Et factum est ut ambo, relictis nuptiarum copulationibus spretoque liberorum propagine, Sponso qui in caelo est perpetim se disposuerint applicare."* Jeanne-Marie's virginity was acknowledged by witnesses at her death: cf. the inquest of 1414-1415, in *Acta Sanctorum*, col. 760.

8. On these problems, see André Vauchez, *La Sainteté en Occident aux derniers siècles du Moyen Age d'après les procès de canonisation et les documents hagiographiques* (Rome: Ecole Française de Rome, 1981), 442-445. [On the virginal marriage of Delphine and Elzéar, see chapter 16 of this volume.]

9. *Vita* in *Acta Sanctorum*, col. 735. All of the biographical indications that follow come from this text. In the Middle Ages, St. Yves was held to have been a Franciscan tertiary, and the Franciscans propagated his cult throughout Christendom.

10. Inquest of 1414-1415, in *Acta Sanctorum*, col. 739: *"Supplicavit [Minores] quod amore Christi ipsam ut pauperem in aliquo tugurio sui conventus recolligere dignarentur. Qui ministro provinciali annuente piae petitioni praebuerunt assensum."*

11. Inquest of 1414-1415 in *Acta Sanctorum*, col. 754-755. This was the blessed Bonincontro of San Miniato.

12. *Vita* in *Acta Sanctorum*, col. 740.

13. Inquest of 1414-1415, in *Acta Sanctorum*, col. 756.

14. Inquest of 1414-1415, in *Acta Sanctorum*, col. 748 and 750.

15. On the reform efforts of St. Colette and her spiritual director Henri de la Baume, until research currently underway is completed, we can refer the reader only to the articles by Father Ubald d'Alençon published in the *Archivum Franciscanum Historicum* between 1909 and 1911. See also Mariano d'Alatri, entry "Coletta di Corbie" in *Bibliotheca Sanctorum*, vol. 4 (Rome: 1964), col. 76-81.

16. It was in 1410 that St. Colette reformed the convent of the Poor Clares in Besançon. Research on the history of the Franciscan Observance in France is still in its infancy, with the exception of Brittany. We will therefore have to rely on the old but still useful article by Father Gratien de Paris, "Les débuts de la réforme des Cordeliers en France et Guillaume Josseaume," in *Etudes franciscaines* 31 (1914), 415-439.

17. Inquest of 1414-1415, in *Acta Sanctorum*, col. 756.

18. The violence, in truth, was not unilateral. Under the pontificate of Benedict XIII, the Conventuals had been expelled from the Convent of Loches *manu militari* at the instigation of the Observants; see the article by Jean Mauzaize cited in note 3 above.

19. The first chapter general of the Franciscan Observance was held at Bressuire in 1416. By annulling the decisions of Alexander V,

the Council of Constance had in effect recognized the autonomy of the twelve reformed houses in the province, such as Mirebeau, whose foundation had been authorized in 1388 by Jean Philippe, provincial of Touraine. However, it was not until the period of the Council of Basel that the Observants won complete freedom to organize themselves independently of the Conventuals.

20. *Vita* in *Acta Sanctorum*, col. 744.

21. On this personage and his story, see Arthur Huart, *Jacques de Bourbon roi de Sicile, frère mineur, cordelier à Besançon (1370-1438)* (Couvin: Maison Saint-Roch, 1909), which was corrected on certain points (particularly the erroneous assertion that he became a Franciscan friar, whereas actually he died as a tertiary) by the article of Ferdinand M. Delorme, "Jacques de Bourbon fut-il mineur cordelier?" in *La France franciscaine* 8 (1925), 455-459.

22. Inquest of 1414-1415, in *Acta Sanctorum*, col. 750-751.

23. Louis I of Anjou (†1384) was the son of John the Good and Bonne of Luxemburg. Count of the Maine and Anjou, in 1360 he married the heiress to the duchy of Britanny, Marie of Châtillon, and became duke of Touraine in 1370 after he was granted an increase in appanage by his brother Charles V. Queen Joanna I of Naples adopted him in 1380 and designated him her heir, and his claim to the throne was supported by the Avignonese pope Clement VII; despite this, he was not able to take possession of his kingdom.

24. *Vita* in *Acta Sanctorum*, col. 739. Marie of Anjou gave Jeanne-Marie a Bible (*Vita*, col. 737) and had her treated by her doctor when a woman threw a rock at her while she was praying and broke her spine (*Vita*, col. 756).

25. On this subject, see Martin, *Les Ordres mendiants*, 366-371, and Vauchez, *La Sainteté en Occident*, 269-271.

26. *Vita* in *Acta Sanctorum*, col. 740.

27. Inquest of 1414-1415, in *Acta Sanctorum*, col. 752.

28. Inquest of 1414-1415, in *Acta Sanctorum*, col. 747.

29. For the sake of completeness, we must add to the list of Jeanne-Marie of Maillé's aristocratic contacts the names of at least three women who played a role in her life or appeared at the inquest of 1414-1415. Jeanne of Bauçay (†1401), the countess of Longueville, donated the head of one of the Eleven Thousand Virgins given to her by a Dominican bishop to the Franciscan church of Loudun; Jeanne-Marie was invited to the ceremony, but, after praying before the relic in the chapel of the château of Bauçay, declared that it was a man's head, not a woman's (Inquest of 1414-1415, *Acta Sanctorum*, col. 755). Isabelle of Clisson, wife of Renaud of Ancenis, was related to Olivier of Clisson, who established

at Clisson the first Observant convent in Brittany; together with Jeanne-Marie, she founded a chapel in honor of St. Stephen in the Church of Saint Martin in Tours. Finally, the lady of the Hunaudaye—whose precise identity is unknown to us—let the Blessed Jeanne-Marie use her carriage and horses to transfer some precious relics from Angers to Tours in 1388 (Inquest of 1414-1415, in *Acta Sanctorum*, col. 752).

30. Inquest of 1414-1415, *Acta Sanctorum*, col. 758. Yolanda of Aragon had married Louis II of Anjou in 1400. Born in 1377, he became king of Sicily in 1389, but had to yield to his rival Ladislaus of Durazzo in 1399. It is worth mentioning that he supported Pope Alexander V— whose coming Jeanne-Marie had foretold—while his adversary sided with Gregory XII. He tried in vain to regain his kingdom in 1411.

31. Siméon Luce, "Deux documents inédits relatifs à frère Richard et Jeanne d'Arc," in *Revue bleue* (1922), 201-204.

32. Marie of Brittany, daughter of Jean V of Montfort, was born in 1391. She had five children, one of whom was Jean II. Her testimony at the inquest of 1414-1415 appears in *Acta Sanctorum*, col. 762.

33. [In Italy, too, princely families supported the Observant movement and other currents of religious reform. See Gabriella Zarri, "Aspetti dello sviluppo degli Ordini religiosi in Italia tra Quattro e Cinquecento: Studi e problemi," in *Strutture ecclesiastiche in Italia e in Germania prima della Riforma*, ed. Paolo Prodi and Peter Johanek (Bologna: Il Mulino, 1984), 207-257.]

34. On the "Franciscanism" of Joan of Arc, we refer the reader to the precise and well-balanced summary of Étienne Delaruelle, "La spiritualité de Jeanne d'Arc," in *La Piété populaire au Moyen Age* (Turin: Bottega d'Erasmo, 1975), 362-363.

35. Some revealing passages concerning the close ties between Jeanne-Marie of Maillé and the highest nobility can be found in the inquest of 1414: see *Acta Sanctorum*, col. 747: "*Reges, principes, duces et barones qui veniebant causa devotionis visitare limina B. Martini dictae dominae magnum honorem exhibebant et more nobilium ad osculum recipiebant, ut rex Siciliae, comes de Marchia et plures alii qui eam parentem et consanguineam vocabant.*" We know that on various occasions, both in Paris and in Tours, she had conversed with Charles VI and Isabelle of Bavaria.

36. Among the personages who at the time of the inquest seem to have been closely linked with the Franciscans of Tours were Jean of Pontlevoy, a money changer who was one of the leading citizens of the city, and Jean Gobin, son of a superintendent of the mint. On these commercial milieux in Tours at the beginning of the fifteenth century, see Bernard Chevalier, *La ville de Tours et la société tourangelle*

(1356-1520) (Lille: Service de reproduction des thèses, Université de Lille, 1974), 220-234.

18. Female Prophets, Visionaries, and Mystics in Medieval Europe

1. [On Hildegard, see the recent studies by Peter Dronke, *Women Writers of the Middle Ages: A Critical Study of Texts from Perpetua (†203) to Marguerite Porete (†1310)* (Cambridge: Cambridge University Press, 1984), 144-201, and Barbara Newman, *Sister of Wisdom: St. Hildegard's Theology of the Feminine* (Berkeley and Los Angeles: University of California Press, 1987).]

2. For the "mystical invasion" which marks the final centuries of the Middle Ages, see chapter 19 in this volume.

3. [On the general prophetic climate, not limited to female visionaries, see Roberto Rusconi, *L'attesa della fine: Crisi della società, profezia ed Apocalisse in Italia al tempo del grande scisma d'Occidente (1378-1417)* (Rome: Istituto Storico Italiano per il Medio Evo, 1979).]

4. [For these personages, see chapter 22 in this volume.]

5. Bridget of Sweden, *Revelaciones extravagantes*, 47, ed. Lennart Hollman, Svenska Fornskrifts ällskapet. samlingar. 2nd ser., Latinskaskrifter 5 (Uppsala: Almqvist & Wiksellsboktryckeri, 1956).

6. A French translation of the *Revelations* of Constance of Rabastens, by Jean-Pierre Hiver-Bérenguier, was published in 1984 [*Constance de Rabastens: mystique de Dieu ou de Gaston Fébus* (Toulouse: Privat)]. The original Provençal text was edited by A. Pagès and Noël Valois, "Les prophéties de Constance de Rabastens," in *Annales du Midi* 8 (1896), 241-278.

7. Bridget of Sweden, *Revelaciones*, Book VII, c. 7, ed. Birger Bergh (Uppsala: Almqvist & Wiksellsboktryckeri, 1967), 133-134. [For an English translation, see *The Revelations of Saint Birgitta*, ed. William Patterson Cumming (London: Oxford University Press, 1929).]

8. On this subject, see Robert Fawtier and Louis Canet, *La Double Expérience de Catherine Benincasa (sainte Catherine de Sienne)* (Paris, Gallimard, 1948).

9. Constance de Rabastens, *Révélations*, 32.

10. Constance de Rabastens, *Révélations*, 21.

11. Constance de Rabastens, *Révélations*, 63.

12. Paul Ourliac, "Les lettres à Charles V," in *Atti del simposio internazionale Cateriniano-Bernardiniano: Siena, 17-20 Aprile 1980*, ed. Domenico Maffei and Paolo Nardi (Siena: Accademia Senese degli Intronati, 1982), 173-180.

13. See the passages from ms. 520 of the municipal library of Tours (ff. 115-128) published by Noël Valois, "Jeanne d'Arc et les prophéties de Marie Robine" in *Mélanges Paul Fabre: Etudes d'histoire du moyen âge* (Paris: A. Picard, 1902), 452-467. [See also Matthew Tobin, "Le 'Livre des révélations' de Marie Robine (†1399): Etude et édition," *Mélanges de l'Ecole Française de Rome, Moyen Age-Temps Modernes* 98 (1986), 229-264.]

14. Constance de Rabastens, *Révélations*, 26. In another revelation (37) she announces that the world only will last seven more years if it does not convert.

15. Marie Robine, ms. 520 of the municipal library of Tours, ff. 126-127.

16. [See chapter 19 in this volume. Translations of works by or about many of these women are available in Emilie Zum Brunn and Georgette Epiney-Burgard, *Women Mystics in Medieval Europe*, trans. Sheila Hughes (New York: Paragon Press, 1989), which is limited to the Rhineland and Flemish mystics, and in *Medieval Women's Visionary Literature*, ed. Elizabeth Avilda Petroff (Oxford: Oxford University Press, 1986), which effectively illustrates the temporal and geographical range of the movement.]

17. On these aspects of medieval mysticism, see the interesting study by Jacques Maitre, "Entre femmes: Notes sur un filon du mysticisme catholique" in *Archives de sciences sociales des religions* 55 (1983), 105-137, which proposes a psychoanalytic interpretation of the relation between the soul and its creator as it is described in the writings of that era.

18. Text edited by Karl Weinhold, *Lamprecht von Regensburg: Sanct Francisken Leben und Tochter Syon* (Paderborn: F. Schöningh, 1880), 341.

19. Gilbert de Tournai, "*Collectio de scandalis Ecclesiae*," ed. Autbert Stroick, in *Archivum Franciscanum Historicum* 24 (1931), 61-62.

20. See chapter 20 in this volume.

21. For the relations between the female mystics and ecclesiastical authorities, see the hypotheses advanced by Maitre, "Entre femmes," 127-132, and chapter 21 in this volume.

22. Michel de Certeau, *La Fable mystique, XVIe- XVIIe siècle* (Paris: Gallimard, 1982).

19. Mystical Sanctity at the Time of the
Avignon Papacy and the Great Schism

1. Mystical states are described in great detail in the life of St. Douceline, first composed in 1297: Raoul Gout, ed., *La Vie de sainte Douceline:*

Texte provençal du XIVe siècle (Paris: Bloud et Gay, 1927). On this Beguine and her circle, see Alessandra Sisto, *Figure del primo francescanesimo in Provenza: Ugo e Douceline di Digne* (Florence: Olschki, 1971), and Claude Carozzi, "Une béguine joachimite: Douceline, soeur d'Hugues de Digne," in *Franciscains d'Oc: Les Spirituels (ca. 1280-1324)*, Cahiers de Fanjeaux 10 (Toulouse: Privat, 1975), 169-201. Central Italian mystical movements at the end of the thirteenth century are the subject of an excellent synthesis by Giorgio Petrocchi, "Correnti e linee della spiritualità umbra ed italiana del Duecento," in *Atti del IV Convegno di studi umbri (Gubbio, 1966)* (Perugia: 1967), 133-176, which includes a rich bibliography. [On Angela of Foligno, see *Il Libro della beata Angela da Foligno*, ed. Ludger Thier and Abele Calufetti (Grottaferrata: Editiones Collegii S. Bonaventurae ad Claras Aquas, 1985).]

2. Female mystics who were objects of canonization proceedings in the fourteenth century were:

—St. Clare of Montefalco: a partial copy of her canonization proceeding, dating from 1318-1319, is in the Vatican Archives; [the full text is now available in print: *Il processo di canonizzazione di Chiara da Montefalco*, ed. Enrico Menestò, Quaderni del Centro per il Collegamento degli studi medievali e umanistici nell'Università di Perugia 14 (Florence: La Nuova Italia, 1984). On this personage, see *S. Chiara da Montefalco e il suo tempo: Atti del quarto Convegno di studi storico-ecclesiastici. Spoleto, 28-30 dicembre 1981*, ed. Claudio Leonardi and Enrico Menestò (Florence: La Nuova Italia, 1985).]

—Delphine of Puimichel (or of Sabran): the transactions of her 1363 canonization proceedings in Apt have been published by Jacques Cambell, *Enquête pour le procès de canonisation de Dauphine de Puimichel, comtesse d'Ariano († 26.XI.1360) (Apt et Avignon: 14 mai-30 octobre 1363)* (Turin: Bottega d'Erasmo, 1978).

—St. Bridget: the proceedings of the inquests into her life and miracles, held in Sweden and Italy between 1376 and 1380, have been published by Isak Gustaf Alfred Collijn, *Acta et processus canonizacionis beate Brigitte, efter cod. A14 Holm., Cod. Ottob. lat. 90 o. cod. Harl. 612* (Stockholm: Almqvist & Wiksells, 1924-1931).

—Dorothy of Montau: a critical edition of the inquest conducted at Marienwerder (eastern Prussia) between 1404 and 1406 has been published by Richard Stachnik, Anneliese Triller and Hans Westpfahl, *Die Akten des Kanonisationsprozess Dorotheas von Montau von 1394 bis 1521*, Forschungen und Quellen zur Kirchen- und Kulturgeschichte Ostdeutschlands 15 (Cologne/Vienna: Böhlau, 1978). [See also Johannes Marienwerder, *The Life of Dorothea of Montau*, trans. Ute Stargardt (Toronto: Peregrina, 1991).]

—St. Catherine of Siena: the diocesan proceedings that took place in Venice between 1411 and 1416 on the orders of the bishop of Castello and served as the basis of her canonization in 1461 were published by Marie Hyacinthe Laurent, *Il processo castellano*, Fontes Vitae S. Catherinae Senensis historici 9 (Milan: Bocca, 1942).

3. Delphine of Puimichel, Bridget of Sweden, Dorothy of Montau, and Jeanne-Marie of Maillé were widows. Catherine of Siena had rejected marriage at a very young age.

4. The lives of fourteenth-century laywomen who were the objects of canonization proceedings invariably ended in reclusion, with the exception of St. Bridget, who lived in Rome with her daughter, her sons, and her confessors in a house open to all.

5. Cf. Micheline de Fontette, *Les Religieuses à l'âge classique du droit canon. Recherches sur les structures juridiques des branches féminines des ordres* (Paris: J. Vrin, 1967).

6. This phenomenon appeared most clearly in the Mediterranean regions, where the fascination exercised by the saintly women was attested as early as the beginning of the fourteenth century. The canonization proceedings of Clare of Montefalco state, for example, that Cardinal Pietro Colonna visited her several times. He was also interested in the revelations of Angela of Foligno, and approved their content in 1309. Another cardinal, Napoleone Orsini, also played a major role in Clare's canonization proceeding, and presented a very favorable report about her to the consistory. [See the recent study by John Coakley, "Friars as Confidants of Holy Women in Medieval Dominican Hagiography," in *Images of Sainthood: Medieval Europe*, ed. Renate Blumenfeld-Kosinski and Timea Szell (Ithaca: Cornell University Press, 1991).]

7. On this subject, see Robert Fawtier and Louis Canet, *La Double Expérience de Catherine Benincasa (sainte Catherine de Sienne)* (Paris: Gallimard, 1948), and Gilles Gérard Meersseman, "Gli Amici spirituali di S. Caterina a Roma nel 1378, alla luce del primo manifesto urbanista," *Bollettino senese di storia patria* 69 (1962), 83–123 [=*Symposium Catherinianum nel Vê centenario della canonizzazione di S. Caterina da Siena* (Siena, 1962)].

8. From depositions at the canonization proceedings of 1363, we know that she "converted" Bertrand, bishop of Apt to a better life, along with several canons, and she brought back to the right path Franciscans who supported heretical theses about poverty and the Roman church. [See chapter 6 in this volume.]

9. Of course Bridget, like all of the other female mystics of her day, clearly did come under the influence of her counselors; and they put their own stamp on the messages whose recording she entrusted to them, if only by translating those messages from the vernacular to Latin.

But the fundamental fact remains that this mystic was the one who took the initiative and that her entourage acted simply as her instruments and spokesmen, even if their role was actually more important than it seems.

10. The direct approach to sovereigns—whether popes or kings— is typical of feminine sanctity between the mid-fourteenth and mid-fifteenth centuries. In addition to Joan of Arc, who immediately comes to mind, two other similar cases are worthy of mention. The blessed Jeanne-Marie of Maillé went to Tours in 1395 and to Paris in 1398 to transmit messages and warnings from God to Charles VI; see her *Vita* [=*Bibliotheca hagiographica latina*, 5515], in *Acta Sanctorum*, Oct., vol. 8, col. 740-741. In Italy, the blessed Ursulina of Parma (1375-1408) went to Rome and Avignon to ask Boniface IX and Clement VII to end the schism; see her *Vita* [=*Bibliotheca hagiographica latina*, 8452], in *Acta Sanctorum*, Apr., vol. 1, col. 723-739.

11. *Acta et Processus*, 519: "*Quod statim postquam veniret* [the Pope to Rome], *inciperet reformare sanctam Dei Ecclesiam et omnes status ecclesiasticos et reducere eos ad pristinum statum sanctitatis primevorum patrum sanctorum et quod extirparet certa vicia de Curia Romana et mutaret consiliarios et mores suos.*" See also 525-526.

12. In particular by Fawtier and Canet, *La double expérience*, 150-165, which downplays it.

13. *Il Processo castellano*, 430-442.

14. For example, pilgrimages played an important role in the religious experiences of fourteenth-century saints connected with the mystical movement: St. Bridget went to Rome, Santiago di Compostela, Cologne (the Magi and the Eleven Thousand Virgins), the shrine of St. Michael at Monte Gargano, Saint-Maximin (St. Mary Magdalen), Ortona (St. Thomas), Assisi and Jerusalem. See *Acta et processus*, art. 13, p. 14. Dorothy of Montau also went to Rome for the Jubilee of 1390.

15. Delphine searched for "new ways to do penance" in the *Vitae Patrum*, and flagellated herself every time she thought she had offended God. St. Catherine of Siena did penance with iron hooks and fasted for as long as fifty days. See *Il Processo castellano*, 33 and 267.

16. Delphine wished to be poor and no longer called countess nor honored by the people. See her *Vita* in Jacques Cambell, ed., *Vies occitanes de saint Auzias et de sainte Delphine avec traduction française, introduction et notes* (Rome: Pontificium Athenaeum Antonianum, 1963), 187-189. During Dorothy of Montau's canonization proceedings, her confessor stated: "*In tantum diligebat paupertatem quod cupiebat esse pauper toto spiritu et nonnunquam in despecto et simulato habitu sedit inter mendicos*" (*Die Akten*, 201).

17. The orthodoxy of mystics was doubtful *a priori*, and during their lifetimes the clergy was often hesitant about it. For example, at

the insistence of her confessor, Delphine of Puimichel had to make a profession of faith to the Church on her deathbed, the necessity of which she does not seem to have understood. Catherine of Siena had to undergo a severe examination by three prelates, one of whom, a Franciscan archbishop, remained hostile to her (*Il processo castellano*, 269–270). In addition, she was persecuted in Siena by a popular theologian and preacher, the Franciscan Lazzarino of Pisa, who eventually admitted that he had acted wrongly towards her, however, and placed himself under her direction (330). To be sure, some of the statements these saints made were sure to arouse the suspicion of the clerics. For example, Dorothy of Montau did not hesitate to claim: *"Ego non erro nec possum errare quia habeo unum doctorem et magistrum qui me et omnes homines diligenter informat"* (*Die Akten*, 109).

18. *Die Akten*, 260, *"Ut esset perfecta Christi imitatrix in passionibus arduis, cum perfectius esset Christum imitari in passionibus quam in actibus."*

19. This definition was provided by a witness questioned about the sanctity of Catherine of Siena: *"Perfecta Dei dilectio ex clara visione procedens"* (*Il processo castellano*, 152).

20. This attitude was so new that it was not always understood by her contemporaries. For this reason, bishop Heming of Åbo, visiting St. Bridget in Rome, was scandalized when he saw her eating *"de cibis sibi appositis,"* with a hearty appetite (*Acta et processus*, 521).

21. This concept was vigorously expressed by Clare of Montefalco in a statement repeated in her canonization proceedings: *"Tanta est amicitia Dei ad animam et anime ad Deum quod quicquid Deus vult, vult anima et quicquid vult talis anima, vult etiam Deus ipse."* See Menestò, ed., *Il processo di canonizzazione di Chiara da Montefalco*, 274.

22. Clare of Montefalco, for example, was in contact with a whole network of spiritual friends, extending from Spoleto to Perugia and Rome. On the circles of devout people in which mysticism flourished in Germanic countries, see Francis Rapp, "Les groupes informels à la fin du Moyen Age: types rhénans," in *Les Groupes informels dans l'Eglise, 2e Colloque du CERDIC [Centre de recherche et de documentation des institutions chrétiennes] Strasbourg, 13-15 mai, 1971*, ed. René Metz and Jean Schlick (Strasbourg: CERDIC-publications, 1971), 180–193. [*Informal Groups in the Church: Papers of the Second Cerdic-Colloquium, Strasbourg, May 13-15, 1971*, trans. Matthew J. O'Connell, Pittsburg Theological Monograph Series 7 (Pittsburgh: Pickwick Press, 1975).] The cult of St. Catherine of Siena did not arise in the city where she lived but rather radiated from Venice, the principal center of the Dominican Observants.

23. The attitude of Delphine of Sabran, who refused to receive pilgrims who had come to her convent to obtain healing, is quite revealing in this regard. Female mystics generally were hostile to popular religion, which they considered a pile of superstitions. The canonization proceedings of St. Bridget have preserved some of her diatribes against the magic practiced by Swedish peasants and against the cult of King Eric the Saint, who, as she had seen in a vision, was not in Heaven, but rather in Purgatory or perhaps even in Hell: *Acta et processus*, 387.

24. At the end of the fourteenth century there was an attempt to transform into mystics certain saints who do not seem to have been mystics in their lifetimes. For example, in the canonization proceedings of Peter of Luxemburg, who was a contemplative and a restless spirit but not at all an ecstatic or a prophet, one article affirms that "it is probable that he had numerous and important communications and consolations from God, although this has remained unknown to men." To corroborate this statement, which aimed to make the young cardinal conform to the prevailing model of sanctity, only one witness could be found to state that Christ on the cross had appeared to Peter while he was praying at Châteauneuf-du-Pape. In the depositions of witnesses at his canonization proceedings in 1417, Nicholas of Linköping—a bishop—was presented as a great prophet whose redoubtable predictions were later born out. [For insightful discussions of Peter of Luxemburg, Nicholas of Linköping, and other figures who appear in this essay, see Richard Kieckhefer, *Unquiet Souls: Fourteenth-Century Saints and their Religious Milieu* (Chicago: University of Chicago Press, 1984).]

20. Eucharistic Devotion and Mystical Union in Late-Medieval Female Saints

1. On these subjects, see André Vauchez, *La Sainteté en Occident aux derniers siècles du Moyen Age d'après les procès de canonisation et les documents hagiographiques* (Rome: Ecole Française de Rome, 1981).

2. [For a contrary argument, that eucharistic piety was a distinctive concern of female mystics from the start of the thirteenth century, see Caroline Walker Bynum, "Women Mystics and Eucharistic Devotion in the Thirteenth Century," *Women's Studies* 11 (1984), 179-214.]

3. Her *Vita*, written soon after her death by the Franciscan Martin de Boisgaultier, was published in the *Acta Sanctorum*, March, vol. 3, col. 735-744. The citation comes from col. 740.

4. Most of these citations come from the *Septililium*, a treatise on the mystical gifts of Dorothy of Montau composed by her confessor Johannes Marienwerder, and published by Franz Hipler in the *Analecta*

bollandiana 4 (1885), 121-161 (in particular *Tractatus III: De eucharistia*). See also Johannes Marienwerder, *The Life of Dorothea of Montau*, trans. Ute Stargardt (Toronto: Peregrina, 1991).

5. *"Tu hodie sacramentaliter habebis me...sicut sponsus prae filiis hominum speciosissimus et tamquam rex prepotens cum magnifico exercitu et apparatu."* The texts of these canonization proceedings (1404-1406) can be found in the edition by Richard Stachnik, Anneliese Triller and Hans Westpfahl, *Die Akten des Kanonisationsprozess Dorotheas von Montau von 1394 bis 1521*, Forschungen und Quellen zur Kirchen- und Kulturgeschichte Ostdeutschlands 15 (Cologne/Vienna: Böhlau, 1978).

6. *Il processo castellano*, ed. Marie Hyacinthe Laurent, Fontes Vitae S. Catherinae Senensis historici 9 (Milan: Bocca, 1942), 267-268. [This characterization of Catherine's behavior as anorexic, first presented at a conference in 1980 and then published in 1982, has since been developed by Rudolph M. Bell, *Holy Anorexia* (Chicago: University of Chicago Press, 1985). For a wider ranging analysis of the cultural meaning of eating and not eating, see Caroline Walker Bynum, *Holy Feast and Holy Fast: The Religious Significance of Food to Medieval Women* (Berkeley and Los Angeles: University of California Press, 1987).]

7. Jean Gerson, *De distinctione verarum visionum a falsis*, in *Opera omnia*, ed. Lud. Ellies du Pin, vol. 1 (Antwerp: Sumptibus Societatis, 1706) col. 46.

8. See the canonization proceedings cited above and the *Septililium*, 125.

9. *Libellus de supplemento: Legende prolixe virginis Beate Catherine de Senis (auctore Thomaso Antonii de Senis "Caffarini")*, ed. Giuliana Cavallini and Imelda Foralosso (Rome: Edizioni Cateriniane, 1974), especially 75-120.

10. *Libellus*, 78-81 and 94.

11. *Libellus*, 76 and 79.

12. Canonization proceedings of Jeanne-Marie of Maillé (diocesan inquest conducted at Tours in 1414-1415), published in *Acta Sanctorum*, March, vol. 3, col. 755.

13. *Libellus*, 79.

14. *Il processo castellano*, 50.

15. *Libellus*, 116.

*21. The Reaction of the Church to
Late-Medieval Mysticism and Prophecy*

1. The canonization proceedings of St. Bridget have been edited by Isak Collijn, *Acta et processus canonizacionis beate Brigitte, efter*

cod. A14 Holm., Cod. Ottob. lat. 90 o. cod. Harl. 612 (Stockholm: Almqvist & Wiksells, 1924-1931). A critical edition of *Les Revelaciones* (hereafter cited as *Rev.*) is currently being prepared. Book I, *Sancta Birgitta; with Magister Mathias' Prologue*, ed. Carl-Gustaf Undhagen (Stockholm: Almqvist & Wiksell International, 1977), Book V, *Liber Questionum*, ed. Birger Bergh (Uppsala: Almqvist & Wiksellsboktryckeri, 1971), and book VII, ed. Birger Bergh (Uppsala: Almqvist & Wiksellsboktryckeri, 1967) have already been published, as well as the *Revelaciones extravagantes* (hereafter cited as *Extr.*), which was published in 1956 by Lennart Hollman (Svenska Fornskrifts ällskapet. samlingar, 2nd ser., Latinskaskrifter 5 [Uppsala: Almqvist & Wiksellsboktryckeri]). For the other books, we will have to make do with the old, very imperfect Roman edition, *Revelationes sanctae Brigittae*, 2 vols. (Rome, 1628). [An English translation of the Latin translation of the Swedish *Revelaciones* has been published by the Early English Text Society, ed. William Patterson Cumming (London: Oxford University Press, 1929). In addition, a translation of two chapters of the *Revelations* can be found in Birgitta of Sweden, *Life and Selected Revelations*, ed. Marguerite Tjader Harris, trans. Albert Ryle Kezel (New York: Paulist Press, 1990).]

The canonization proceedings of St. Catherine of Siena were edited by Father Marie Hyacinthe Laurent, *Il processo castellano*, Fontes Vitae S. Catherinae Senensis historici 9 (Milan: Bocca, 1942). There is an excellent critical edition of part of Catherine's correspondence by the late Eugenio Dupré Theseider, *Epistolario di S. Caterina da Siena*, Fonti per la storia d'Italia 82 (Rome: Istituto Storico Italiano per il Medio Evo, 1940). Numerous modern editions of the *Dialogo della divina Provvidenza* exist: we refer preferably to the edition of Innocenzo Taurisano (Rome: F. Ferrari, 1947). [Catherine of Siena, *The Dialogue*, trans. Suzanne Noffke (New York: Paulist Press, 1980). A complete English edition of Catherine's letters is in preparation, and the first volume has already appeared: *Letters of Catherine of Siena, Vol. One: Letters 1-88*, trans. Suzanne Noffke, Medieval and Renaissance Texts and Studies 52 (Binghamton: SUNY Press, 1988).]

On the present state of scholarship on Bridget and Catherine, see Igino Cecchetti, entry "Brigida di Svezia," *Bibliotheca Sanctorum*, vol. 3 (Rome: Città Nuova, 1963) col. 439-530, Adriana Oddasso Cartotti, entry "Caterina Benincasa," *Bibliotheca Sanctorum*, col. 996-1044, and *Atti del simposio internazionale Cateriniano-Bernardiniano, Siena, 17-20 aprile 1980*, ed. Domenico Maffei and Paolo Nardi (Siena: Accademia Senese degli Intronati, 1982).

2. *Rev.* I, 3 and VI, 89. On the difficulties encountered by the saint in learning Latin, see *Rev.* IV, 74 and VI, 105.

3. On this subject, see Robert Fawtier and Louis Canet, *La Double Expérience de Catherine Benincasa (sainte Catherine de Sienne)* (Paris: Gallimard, 1948), 274-275.

4. The *Liber de modo bene vivendi*, which purports to be a letter of spiritual direction from St. Bernard to his sister, was published in *Patrologia latina*, vol. 184, col. 1199-1306. The influence of Cistercian spirituality on St. Catherine is well illustrated in Fawtier and Canet, *La double expérience*, 259-68.

5. On St. Bridget and the hagiographic texts, see *Acta et processus*, 66. On the influence of the liturgy, especially Dominican, see *Rev.* III, 14-18; IV, 31-35. For the same influences on St. Catherine, see Fawtier and Canet, *La double expérience*, 63-64.

6. See the proceedings of the colloquium *La Mystique rhénane, Colloque de Strasbourg, 16-19 mai 1961* (Paris: Presses Universitaires de France, 1963).

7. See *Rev.* I, 33; IV, 129; VI, 116. The core of her thinking on this point is summarized in this statement attributed to Christ (*Extr.* XXIII): "*Nam mater mea carissima simplicissima fuit, Petrus idiota, Franciscus rusticus; et tamen plus profecerunt animabus quam magis eloquentes quia perfectam caritatem ad animas habuerunt.*"

8. On the influence of Augustinian thought on Catherine, see Fawtier and Canet, *La double expérience*, 247-251 and 268-271.

9. *Acta et processus*, 429-431. See *Rev.* IV, 24; VI, 90 and 102; VII, 16-19. Other attacks during the saint's lifetime are mentioned in *Acta Sanctorum*, Oct., vol. 4, 532-535.

10. On the hostility of the Franciscan Lazzarino of Pisa and the persecutions that she had to suffer before winning him over to her side, see *Il processo castellano*, 331-333. On the examination of Catherine by the general chapter of the Preachers, see Fawtier and Canet, *La double expérience*, 95-96.

11. *Extr.* XCVI; see also *Rev.* VI, 30.

12. See letter 224, to Lorenzo del Pino: "*Sicche vedete che in ogni stato potete avere Dio, perocché lo stato non è che cel tolle ma solo la mala volontà*" [Thus you see that you can have God in any station, since your station is not what keeps you from Him, but only bad will]. See also letters 52 and 299, cited by Fawtier and Canet, *La double expérience*, 313-314.

13. See André Vauchez, *La Sainteté en Occident aux derniers siècles du Moyen Age d'après les procès de canonisation et les documents hagiographiques* (Rome: Ecole Française de Rome, 1981).

14. Bridget herself composed the rule of the Order of the Holy Savior, and Christ was said to have dictated the architectural plans for

Vadstena to her; see *Extr.* XXVIII. On St. Catherine and her monastery at Belcaro, see Fawtier and Canet, *La double expérience*, 159-161.

15. *Extr.* XLVII, and *Acta et processus*, 80-81.

16. *Rev.* IV, 142 and VI, 63. Cf. also *Extr.* VIII and *Acta et processus*, 94 and 515-516.

17. *Rev.* III, 27; IV, 81-85; VI, 102; VII, 29.

18. Letter 198. See Fawtier and Canet, *La double expérience*, 337-339.

19. Letters 2 (to Gregory XI) and 41.

20. Letters 10, 52 and 312. See Fawtier and Canet, *La double expérience*, 347-353.

21. Fawtier and Canet, *La double expérience*, 201-206.

22. We know that Conrad of Marburg did not hesitate to strike St. Elisabeth when she disobeyed him or acted without consulting him. Similarly, the canonization proceedings of Dorothy of Montau record a revelation during which God supposedly told her: "*Tu et confessor tuus unam debetis habere voluntatem, et illam debet habere non tu sed ille*" (*Procès*, partial edition (Vatican City, 1971), 422. [A complete edition of the canonization proceeding has now been published: see chapter 19, note 2.]

23. On the role of Alfonso of Jaen, see *Extr.* XLVIII-XLIX and CIX.

24. Letter 101. See Fawtier and Canet, *La double expérience*, 240-241.

25. This is true of the proceedings of St. Hildegard of Bingen (1233-1243), St. Clare of Montefalco (†1308, inquest in 1318-1319), Delphine of Puimichel (†1360, inquest in 1363), Dorothy of Montau (†1394, inquest in 1404-1406). The cases of Douceline of Aix (†1274), Margaret of Cortona (†1297) and Angela of Foligno (†1309) were not even considered during the Middle Ages.

26. See the report of the discussion on this question in Hermann von der Hardt, *Magnum Oecumenicum Constantiense Concilium de universali ecclesiae reformatione, unione, et fido*, vol. 3 (Frankfurt, 1968), Part 2, 28-38; Part 4, 39-40 [=*De rebus Brigittae*]. The vicissitudes of her canonization are mentioned by Martin V in the prologue to the final bull, whose text can be found in the *Acta Sanctorum*, Oct., vol. 4, col. 476-478.

27. One of the main adversaries of the *Revelations* of St. Bridget was the theologian Matthias Doering, who claimed that they were the work of Master Matthias of Linköping. On this argument, see Giovan Domenico Mansi, *Sacrorum Conciliorum nova et amplissima collectio*, vol. 30, 697-814.

28. See Luke Wadding, *Annales Minorum, seu trium ordinum a*

S. Francisco institutorum, vol. 15 (Florence: Ad Aquas Claras, 1931), ch. 70-74.

29. In 1630, Urban VIII recognized their existence, but emphasized that they had been luminous, not bloody. The liturgical feast day of the Holy Stigmata of Catherine was instituted in 1727 by Benedict XIII. [Of course, the stigmata of St. Francis had themselves aroused considerable debate, and clerical skepticism about them lasted for decades. See André Vauchez, "Les stigmates de Saint François et leurs détracteurs dans les derniers siècles du Moyen Age," *Mélanges de l'Ecole Française de Rome* 80 (1968), 595-625.]

30. See André Combes, *Essai sur la critique de Ruysbroek par Gerson* (Paris: J. Vrin, 1945-1972).

31. Jean Gerson, *De distinctione verarum visionum a falsis*, in *Opera omnia*, ed. Lud. Ellies du Pin, vol. 1 (Antwerp: Sumptibus Societatis, 1706), col. 43-58.

32. Gerson, col. 48.

33. Gerson, col. 54. On Catherine's alimentary asceticism, see *Il processo castellano*, 267-268.

34. Gerson, col. 55. We might wonder whether this Marie is actually Marguerite Porète, who came from Valenciennes.

35. Jean Gerson, "De probatione spirituum," *Opera omnia*, v. 1, col. 37-42. On this subject, see also the study of Paschal Boland, *The Concept of "Discretio spirituum" in John Gerson's "De probatione spirituum" and "De distinctione verarum visionum a falsis"*, The Catholic University of America Studies in Sacred Theology 2nd ser. 112 (Washington: Catholic University of America Press, 1959).

36. Jean Gerson, "De examinatione doctrinarum," in Palémon Glorieux, ed., *Oeuvres complètes de Gerson*, vol. 9 (Paris: Desclée, 1973), 458-475. The date is given on p. xiv.

37. "*Hic positus in extremis [. . .] protestatus est coram omnibus, ut caverunt ab hominibus, tam viris quam mulieribus, sub specie religionis visiones loquentibus sui capitis; quia per tales ipse seductus esset [. . .] ut se et Ecclesiam ad discrimen schismatis tunc imminentis traxerit. . . ,*" (Gerson, "De examinatione doctrinarum," 469-470).

22. Joan of Arc and Female Prophecy In the Fourteenth and Fifteenth Centuries

1. On the situation of the laity in the Church at that time, see Etienne Delaruelle, Edmond-René Labande, Paul Ourliac, *L'Eglise au temps du Grand Schisme de la crise conciliaire (1378-1449)*, Histoire de l'Eglise depuis les origines à nos jours 14 (Paris: Bloud et Gay, 1964),

esp. vol. 2, 493–518. A few men did participate in this prophetic movement, as they note on p. 510. For Italy, we should mention the lay preacher Tommasuccio of Foligno, who travelled through Umbria and Tuscany in the second half of the fourteenth century announcing great catastrophes; see Michele Faloci Pulignani, *Le Profezie del beato Tommasuccio da Foligno del Terz'ordine di S. Francesco* (Foligno: Feliciano Campitelli, 1887). [See most recently *Il b. Tomasuccio da Foligno terziario francescano ed i movimenti religiosi popolari umbri nel Trecento, Analecta T.O.R.* 131 (1979).] But the great majority of the "prophets" of the time were women.

2. André Pagès and Noël Valois, "Les prophéties de Constance de Rabastens," *Annales du Midi* 8 (1896), 241–278, based on Bibliothèque Nationale, Paris, ms. Lat. 5055, ff. 35–38. A French translation of the Provençal text was published by Jean Pierre Hiver-Bérenguier, *Constance de Rabastens, mystique de Dieu ou de Gaston Phébus?* (Toulouse: Privat, 1984), 171–206.

3. Pagès and Valois, "Les prophéties," 245.

4. Pagès and Valois, "Les prophéties," 246.

5. Pagès and Valois, "Les prophéties," 248.

6. Canonization proceedings of 1414–1415, published in *Acta sanctorum*, March, Vol. 3, col. 744–762. [On Jeanne-Marie of Maillé, see chapter 17 of this volume.]

7. Yolanda of Aragon was a witness at her canonization proceedings; see *Acta Sanctorum*, col. 758.

8. *Acta Sanctorum*, col. 758.

9. These details are found in the saint's *vita* (*Bibliotheca hagiographica latina* 5515), composed by her Franciscan confessor, Martin of Boisgaultier, and published in *Acta sanctorum*, March, vol. 3, col. 733–744. See in particular col. 740.

10. *Acta Sanctorum*, col. 741–742.

11. Only one manuscript of *Le Livre des révélations et visions de Marie Robine* is known: ms. 520 of the municipal library of Tours, ff. 115–128. Noël Valois, who had the merit of identifying it, limited himself to analyzing it and publishing brief extracts in "Jeanne d'Arc et la prophétie de Marie Robine," *Mélanges Paul Fabre: Etudes d'histoire du moyen âge* (Paris: A. Picard, 1902), 452–467. The Latin text of the prophecies has been published by Matthew Tobin, "Le 'Livre des révélations' de Marie Robine (†1399). Etude et édition," *Mélanges de l'Ecole Française de Rome, Moyen Age-Temps Modernes* 98 (1986), 229–264.

12. This, at least, is what Philippe de Mézières recounts in *Le Songe du vieil pèlerin*, Bibliothèque Nationale, Paris, ms. français 22542, f. 108. His testimony is confirmed by that of Robert Gervais, bishop of Senez at

the end of the fourteenth century, who, in his *Myrrha electa*, mentions her miraculous cures and prophecies (see Bibliothèque Nationale, Paris, ms. lat. 1467, f. 52).

13. *Livre des révélations*, f.115.

14. *Livre des révélations*, f.118.

15. *Livre des révélations*, f.126-127v.

16. Valois, "Jeanne d'Arc," 462-463.

17. *Procès en nullité de la condamnation de Jeanne d'Arc*, ed. Pierre Duparc, Société de l'histoire de France 491, vol. I (Paris: Klincksieck, 1977), 375.

18. *Journal d'un Bourgeois de Paris, 1405-1449*, ed. Alexandre Tuetey (Paris: Champion, 1881), 236-237; see also 268. [A new edition has just been published: *Journal d'un Bourgeois de Paris de 1405 à 1449*, ed. Colette Beaune (Paris: Livre de Poche, 1990), 257; see also 291-297. For an English translation, see *A Parisian Journal 1405-1449*, trans. Janet Shirley (Oxford: Clarendon Press, 1968).]

19. On this somewhat enigmatic monk and his relationship with Joan of Arc, see the material presented by Etienne Delaruelle in his study "L'Antéchrist chez saint Vincent Ferrier, saint Bernardin de Sienne et autour de Jeanne d'Arc," in *L'Attesa dell'età nuova nella spiritualità della fine del Medio Evo, 16-19 ottobre 1960* (Todi: Accademia tudertina, 1962), 39-64, now reprinted in *La Piété populaire au Moyen Age* (Turin: Bottega d'Erasmo, 1975), 329-354.

20. Jean Gerson, *Opera omnia*, ed. Lud. Ellies du Pin, vol. 1 (Antwerp: Sumptibus Societatis, 1706), col. 19-20: "*Haec mulier sub pallio devotionis et revelationum fingebat miracula. Astruebat enim se esse de quinque foeminibus missis a Deo compassive pro redimendis innumeris animabus de inferno.*" After being tortured in Lyons, this woman confessed her "deception"; but, since she did not seem to be a heretic, she was allowed to do penance.

21. The attribution of the "letter to the Hussites" to Joan of Arc has often been debated. Whatever the truth of the matter, her contemporaries were convinced that she was its author; thus, the inquisitor Johannes Nider in his *Formicarius*, written before 1438 (Douai 1602), 387, considered this letter a sign of Joan's presumptuousness. I am grateful to Pierrette Paravy of the University of Grenoble for calling this work to my attention.

22. *Journal d'un Bourgeois de Paris*, 259 [=new ed. p. 282]. In a different passage the author mentioned yet another woman, Catherine of La Rochelle, who also fought in the ranks of the Armagnacs. A Parisian inquisitor declared in 1431 "that there were four of them, of which three were taken prisoner, that is to say this Maid [Joan of Arc] and Péronne and

her companion; and one who was with the Armagnacs named Catherine of La Rochelle . . . and he said that all four women had been directed by Brother Richard the Franciscan because he was their spiritual father" (271) [=new ed. 299-300].

23. Johannes Nider, *Formicarius*, 383-391.

24. *Formicarius*, 385. "*Arma deferebat et vestimenta dissoluta velut unus de nobilium stipendiariis, choreas cum viris ducebat et potibus ac epulis [. . .] insistebat.*" We will not dwell here on the importance of the theme of women dressed as men, whose anthropological implications have been illuminated by Marie Delcourt, "Le complexe de Diane dans l'hagiographie chrétienne," in *Revue de l'histoire des religions* 153 (1958), 1-33, and more recently by Evelyne Patlagean, "L'histoire de la femme déguisée en moine et l'évolution de la sainteté féminine à Byzance," *Studi Medievali*, 3rd ser., 17 (1976), 597-623.

25. *Journal d'un Bourgeois de Paris*, 354 [=new ed. p. 397]: "When she was near Paris, there resurfaced the great error of firmly believing that she was the Maid."

26. *Journal d'un Bourgeois de Paris*, 355 [=new ed. p. 398].

27. See the French translation of the *Traité de Jean Gerson sur la Pucelle*, ed. Jean-Baptiste Monnoyeur (Paris: A. Picard, 1930). The Latin text is found in Gerson's *Opera Omnia*, vol. 4, col. 859-868. It was one of Gerson's final works.

28. On this point, see the splendid essay by Etienne Delaruelle, "La spiritualité de Jeanne d'Arc," *Bulletin de littérature ecclésiastique* 65 (1964), 17-33 and 81-98, now reprinted in his *La Piété populaire au Moyen Age*, 355-388.

Conclusion

1. [Daniel Russo, *Saint Jérôme en Italie: Etude d'iconographie et de spiritualité (XIIIe-XVe siècle)* (Rome: Ecole Française de Rome, 1987). For a more wide ranging study, see Eugene F. Rice, Jr., *Saint Jerome in the Renaissance* (Baltimore: Johns Hopkins University Press, 1985).]

INDEX

Abate, Giuseppe, 299 n 1
Abbo of Fleury, 41, 276 n 1
Abelard, Peter, 17, 228
Abruzzi, 78, 79
Abruzzo Citra, 74
Achilles, Saint, 197
Adalbert of Laon, Bishop, 30-31
Adam of Eynsham, 300 n 9
Adelaide, Empress, 52
Adhémar de Mosset, 78, 287 n 16,
   287 n 18
Adige, river, 54, 60
Agatha, Saint, 197
Agnes, Saint, 197
Agnes, daughter of Hedwig of Silesia,
   187
Agnes, sister of Clare of Assisi, 179
Agnes of Bohemia or Prague, 172
Agnolo di Tura, 295 n 16
Agostino Novello, 164
Aigueperse, 211
Aimon of Bourges, Archbishop, 32
Alacoque, Marguerite-Marie, 253
Alain de Lille, 17
Alayette, half-sister of Delphine of
   Puimichel, 77, 193, 196
Alba, 55, 58, 66, 69, 278 n 13,
   284 n 88
Alberico da Romano, 155
Alberti, Fabio, 295 n 18
Alberto, hermit, 55, 60
Alberto of Villa d'Ogna, 296 n 28,
   299 n 55
Albertus Magnus, 228
Albi, 257, 309 n 4
Albigensians, 20
Alençon, house of, 213, 214

Alerino dei Rembaudi, Bishop, 68
Alexander II, Pope, 15
Alexander III, Pope, 173
Alexander V, Pope, 208, 209, 221,
   258, 314 n 19, 316 n 30
Alexandria, 47
Alexis, Saint, 195, 197
Alfonso of Jaen, 232, 248, 327 n 23
Allucio of Pescia, 54, 58, 68, 70,
   278 n 12, 284 n 80
Alphant, Gersende, 74, 76, 193, 198,
   201
Alps, 59, 266
Alquier de Riez, Philippe, 76, 78, 82,
   193, 198
Alsace and Alsatians, 101, 125
Amalfi, 47
Amandola, 162, 163, 298 n 43
Amann, Emile, xvi, 273 n 1
Ambillou, 207
Amboise, monastery of, 209
Ambrogio of Massa, 154
Ambrose, Saint, 165, 168
Amiens, cathedral of, 23
Anatolia, 46
Ancelet-Hustache, Jeanne, 303 n 25,
   304 n 37
Andrea da Galiano, 78, 286 n 16
Andrieu, Michel, 132, 291 n 9,
   292 n 10, 292 n 12
Angela of Foligno, 72, 172, 225, 231,
   319 n 1, 320 n 6, 327 n 25
Angelo Clareno, 78-80, 81, 82, 193,
   287 n 22, 287 n 23, 287 n 24,
   287 n 25, 288 n 28, 303 n 32
Angers, 207, 212, 316 n 29
Angevins, 74, 75

Angoulême, 32
Anjou, 205, 214
Anjou, house of, 211–213, 214
Anne, daughter-in-law of Hedwig of
    Silesia, 190
Anselm of Bec, 16, 17, 228
Ansouis, code of, 192
Anthony of Amandola, 162–163,
    298 n 43
Anthony of Padua, 100, 156, 174,
    294 n 3, 297 n 29
Antoniola, 165
Antonio Veneziano, 55
Apt, 74, 126, 177, 191, 193, 194, 232,
    300 n 1, 309 n 3, 319 n 2
Apulia, 132
Aquitaine, 3, 13, 20
Arasse, Daniel, 295 n 20
Arbois, 152
Arezzo, 163
Ariano, 74, 75
Armagnacs, 213, 261, 262, 264,
    330 n 22
Armenia and Armenians, 46
Arnoldo di Samatan, 287 n 20
Arnold of Villanova, 82, 201–202,
    312 n 37, 312 n 38, 312 n 39
Arras, 13, 250
Assisi, 78, 295 n 15, 299 n 1, 321 n 14
Asti, 55
Auch, 259
Aude, 199
Augsburg, 54
Augustine of Hippo, 61, 244
Augustinians, 154, 162, 219, 250,
    326 n 8
Auray, 212
Autenrieth, Johanne, 279 n 23
Autun, 5
Auvergne, 6, 110, 151
Auxerre, 5, 151
Avignon, 53, 78, 79, 82, 191, 223,
    259, 278 n 10, 300 n 1, 321 n 10
Avitus, Saint, 134, 292 n 16
Aycelin, Gilles, Archbishop, 198–199,
    286 n 11

Bacharach, 142, 143, 144, 146, 148,
    149, 150, 151
Bagnols-sur-Cèze, 73
Baker, Derek, 285 n 91
Baldiserri, L., 295 n 12
Baldwin of Luxemburg, 143, 144
Barbin, Jean, 260
Bargigli da Pelago, Ludovico,
    296 n 21, 297 n 33
Barthélemy, Dominique, 274 n 1
Barthélemy of Montbazon, 206
Barthélemy of Provence, 81
Bartolo, Blessed, 156
Bartolomeo of Pisa, 287 n 20
Bascapé, Carlo, Bishop, 57
Bascapé, Giacomo C., 281 n 43
Basel, Council of, 249, 256, 264,
    315 n 19
Basilicata, 80
Batany, Jean, 275 n 11
Battle, Columba, 312 n 38
Béarn, 221
Beatrice II of Este, 302 n 24
Beaune, Colette, 330 n 18
Beauvais, 32
Becket, Thomas, 53
Becquet, Jean, 108
Beghards, xvii, 268
Beguines, xvii, xix, 3, 70, 76, 78, 82,
    119, 120, 174, 177, 180, 199, 200,
    202, 203, 219, 221, 226, 227, 228,
    251, 268, 286 n 11, 311 n 20,
    319 n 1
Bela IV, King, 179
Belcaro, 246
Beleth, Jean, 129, 131, 133, 134, 135,
    136, 291 n 2
Bell, Rudolph M., 324 n 6
Benedict XII, Pope, 80
Benedict XIII, Pope, 209, 221, 224,
    259, 314 n 18, 328 n 29
Benedict XIV, Pope, 152, 294 n 6
Benedictines and Benedictine order,
    11, 79, 175, 219
Bénézet, Saint, 53, 278 n 10

Benincasa of Pisa, Canon, 55, 63, 68, 280 n 29
Benvenuta of Cividale del Friuli, 297 n 35
Benvenuti Papi, Anna, 304 n 34
Bergh, Birger, 317 n 7, 325 n 1
Bernard of Azona, 80
Bernard of Clairvaux, 16, 19, 20, 43, 46, 50, 51, 52, 61, 88, 99, 143, 225, 326 n 4
Berry, 205
Bertagna, Martino, 294 n 3, 294 n 4, 294 n 5, 294 n 6, 295 n 13, 297 n 31, 297 n 34, 297 n 37
Bertoni, Giulio, 281 n 51
Bertrand, bishop of Apt, 320 n 8
Bertrand du Guesclin, 209
Besançon, 151, 208, 211, 314 n 16
Bethlehem, 60
Bevagna, 156-157
Bevignate, Giunta, 126-127, 291 n 5
Bevignate of Perugia, 158, 160, 166, 296 n 22, 296 n 25
Béziers, 199, 311 n 27
Béziers, Council of, 198-199, 286 n 11
Bianchi, 124
Bianconi, Giacomo, 156-157
Biget, Jean-Louis, 310 n 20
Bigois, François, 208-209, 210
Billanovich, Maria Chiara, 303 n 24
Binet, Etienne, 285 n 3, 310 n 16
Black Death, 124, 125, 194
Bloch, Marc, 30, 277 n 3
Blois, 212, 214
Blois-Châtillon, house of, 214
Blumenfeld-Kosinski, Renate, 320 n 6
Blumenkranz, Bernhard, 45
Bodeken, abbey, 147
Boland, Paschal, 328 n 35
Boleslas, son of Hedwig of Silesia, 187
Bollandists, x, 55, 56, 142, 206, 278 n 11, 279 n 20, 279 n 25, 293 n 1, 308 n 11, 309 n 4, 313 n 4
Bologna, 59, 99, 156, 165
Bolton, Brenda M., 285 n 91
Bonaventure, Saint, 34, 250

BonGiovanni of Lodi, Canon, 58, 68
Boniface VIII, Pope, xv, 186, 306 n 4
Boniface IX, Pope, 249, 321 n 10
Bonincontro of San Miniato, 208, 314 n 11
Bonne of Armagnac, 211
Bonne of Luxemburg, 315 n 23
Boppard, 142, 144
Borlenghi, Aldo, 299 n 55
Borromeo, Carlo, Bishop, 57
Bot, Raymond, Bishop, 194
Bourbon, house of, 214
Bourbonnais, 214
Bourg-en-Bresse, 262
Boze, Abbé, 309 n 3
Brabant, 119
Breno, 57
Brentano, Robert, 305 n 45
Brescia, 56, 57, 58, 283 n 73
Bressuire, monastery of, 209, 314 n 19
Brice of Tours, 156
Bridget of Sweden, xix, 105, 220, 222, 224, 232, 234, 243-249, 257, 269, 317 n 5, 317 n 7, 319 n 2, 320 n 2, 320 n 4, 320 n 9, 321 n 14, 322 n 20, 323 n 23, 324 n 1, 326 n 5, 326 n 14, 327 n 27
Bridgettines, 249
Brioude, 7
Brittany and Bretons, 8, 101, 205, 212, 314 n 16, 316 n 29
Brunhölzl, Franz, 279 n 23
Bultot, Robert, 300 n 5
Burgundian kingdom, 134
Burgundy and Burgundians, 5, 11, 149, 151, 262, 264
Burr, David, 312 n 32
Bynum, Caroline Walker, 323 n 2, 324 n 6
Byzantine Empire, 46, 48, 69

Cabassole, Philippe, Cardinal, 81, 288 n 31
Cabrières, 126, 177, 232
Cabrol, Fernand, 291 n 7
Caccioli, Andrea, 295 n 14

Caen, 11
Caffarini, Tommaso, 240, 250
Cahors, 5
Calufetti, Abele, 319 n 1
Camaldolese, 180
Cambell, Jacques, 285 n 1, 286 n 10,
    300 n 1, 303 n 31, 309 n 1,
    309 n 4, 319 n 2, 321 n 16
Camisani, E., 279 n 22
Campigliano, 54
Canet, Louis, 317 n 8, 320 n 7,
    321 n 12, 326 n 3, 326 n 4,
    326 n 5, 326 n 8, 326 n 10,
    326 n 12, 327 n 14, 327 n 18,
    327 n 20, 327 n 21, 327 n 24
Capuciati, confraternity of the, 110,
    290 n 5
Carcassonne, 199
Caretta, Alessandro, 279 n 25
Carolingian dynasty, 95, 96
Carozzi, Claude, 274 n 7, 275 n 10,
    289 n 12, 306 n 54, 319 n 1
Carpentier, Elizabeth, 298 n 42
Carthusians, 173, 208, 239
Cartotti, Adriana Oddasso, 325 n 1
Casagrande, Giovanna, 290 n 9
Casasana, or Quisisana, 77, 193
Castaldi, E., 295 n 17
Castello, bishop of, 320 n 2
Castiglione, Branda, Cardinal, 146
Castillon, 198
Catalonia and Catalans, 28, 76, 82,
    201
Catharism and Cathars, 20, 21, 33, 44,
    99, 104, 162, 196, 199, 310 n 20
Catherine of Alexandria, 261
Catherine of Austria, 74
Catherine of La Rochelle, 330 n 22
Catherine of Siena, xix, 72, 105, 115,
    220, 221, 223, 224, 225, 226, 227,
    232, 233, 238, 239, 240-241, 242,
    243-253, 257, 320 n 2, 320 n 3,
    321 n 15, 322 n 17, 322 n 19,
    322 n 22, 324 n 6, 325 n 1,
    326 n 4, 326 n 8, 326 n 10,
    327 n 14, 328 n 29, 328 n 33

Caturegli, Natale, 280 n 26
Cavaillon, 81
Cavallini, Giuliana, 324 n 9
Cecchetti, Igino, 325 n 1
Cecchini, Giovanni, 295 n 16
Cecilia, Saint, 195, 197
Celestines, 259
Certeau, Michel de, 229, 318 n 22
Chalcedon, 137
Chalcedon, Council of, 130
Champagne, 13
Champchevrier, 206
Charlemagne, 292 n 11
Charles IV the Fair, King, 74
Charles V, King, 224, 315 n 23
Charles VI, King, 224, 257, 258, 259,
    316 n 35, 321 n 10
Charles VII, King, 213, 256
Charles II of Anjou, 73, 74
Charles of Blois, Duke, 212, 215
Charles of Calabria, Duke, 74, 75,
    200, 212
Charles of Clermont, Count, 211
Charles of Orléans, 212
Charles of Valois, 74
Charlotte of Bourbon, Queen, 211,
    258
Châteauneuf-du-Pape, 323 n 24
Châteauroux, 208
Chenu, Marie-Dominique, 18,
    273 n 1
Chérancé, Léopold de, 313 n 4
Chevalier, Bernard, 316 n 36
Chiappini, A., 304 n 39
Chiarini, Andrea, 286 n 16
Chinon, 209, 213
Cholet, monastery of, 209
Chuppin, Jean, 151
Ciompi, 35
Cistercians, 43, 87, 102, 119, 189,
    326 n 4
Cîteaux, 18
Cividale del Friuli, 297 n 35
Clare of Assisi, 22, 122, 171, 175-176,
    179, 182, 299 n 1, 302 n 19,
    302 n 22

Clare of Montefalco, 115, 171, 183, 226, 231, 233, 319 n 2, 320 n 6, 322 n 21, 327 n 25
Claudia, the "false maiden," 262, 263
Clement, Saint, 136
Clement VI, Pope, 117, 186-187, 190, 212, 232
Clement VII, Pope, 221, 257, 259, 315 n 23, 321 n 10
Clement of Osimo, 154
Clermont, 14, 46, 151, 211
Clisson, 316 n 29
Clisson, house of, 214
Clovis, 4, 5
Cluny and Cluniacs, xvi, 11, 12, 13, 15, 31, 41, 48, 87
Coakley, John, 320 n 6
Cohn, Norman R., 313 n 40
Colette, or Nicolette, of Corbie, 208-209, 211, 213, 214, 314 n 15, 314 n 16
Collijn, Isak Gustaf Alfred, 319 n 2, 324 n 1
Cologne, 143, 145, 262, 263, 321 n 14
Colonna, Margherita, 302 n 24
Colonna, Pietro, 320 n 6
Columbanus, Saint, 8
Combes, André, 328 n 30
Compagnoni, P., 296 n 25
Comtat Venassin, 196, 232
Congar, Yves, xiii, 107, 282 n 53, 290 n 2
Conques, 89
Conrad, son of Hedwig of Silesia, 187
Conrad of Marburg, 177, 248, 327 n 22
Consortium sancti Homoboni, 68
Constance, Council of, 249, 251, 256, 315 n 19
Constance of Rabastens, 221, 222, 223-224, 257, 261, 317 n 6, 317 n 9, 317 n 10, 317 n 11, 318 n 14
Constantine, 39
Constantinople, 46, 90, 130, 131, 137
Corbeil, 262

Corbet, Patrick, 277 n 6
Corbie, 32
Cortona, 126, 158, 160, 168, 296 n 24
Cracco, Giorgio, 303 n 24
Cremona and the Cremonese, 56, 57, 58, 68, 70, 280 n 33, 282 n 51, 296 n 28, 297 n 36, 299 n 55
Cristofani, F., 298 n 47, 298 n 53
Crusades, xvii, 15-16, 17, 22, 25, 27, 34, 43, 45-50, 85, 88, 90, 92, 99, 143, 210, 219, 225, 267
Cumming, William Patterson, 325 n 1
Cunegund, Empress, 52, 202
Cyprus, 211, 244

d'Alençon, Ubald, 314 n 15
Dames de Robaud, 306 n 54
Dauphin, the, 213, 255, 260
Dauphiné, 21
Davidsohn, Robert, 304 n 34
de Fontette, Micheline, 300 n 7, 320 n 5
degli Azzoni Avogari, Rambaldo, 296 n 23, 296 n 26, 297 n 30
Delaruelle, Etienne, xii, xvii, 10, 32, 33, 99, 107, 272 n 9, 272 n 10, 273 n 5, 275 n 14, 275 n 15, 282 n 61, 301 n 10, 316 n 34, 328 n 1, 330 n 19, 331 n 28
Delcourt, Marie, 331 n 24
Delhaye, Philippe, 300 n 4, 311 n 25
Delorme, Ferdinand M., 312 n 34, 315 n 21
Delphine of Barras, 73
Delphine of Puimichel or Sabran, xi, 73-82, 126, 171, 177, 179, 191-203, 207, 232, 233, 234, 285 n 1, 285 n 2, 288 n 31, 304 n 33, 309 n 4, 309 n 5, 310 n 7, 314 n 8, 319 n 2, 320 n 3, 321 n 15, 321 n 16, 322 n 17, 323 n 23, 327 n 25
del Re, Niccolò, 278 n 13
Delumeau, Jean, 272, 288 n 1, 288 n 4, 300 n 1, 303 n 31, 309 n 1
Denis, Saint, 7

Denis, Louis J., 313 n 5
Dereine, Charles, 108
Desaymard, Joseph, 294 n 5
Desforge, Emile, 294 n 5
Desiderius, Saint, 5
Devotio moderna, 25
Dinan, 212
Disibodenberg, 220
Doering, Matthias, 327 n 27
Dole, monastery of, 211
Domingo de la Calzada, 53, 277 n 10
Dominic, Saint, 99, 100, 108, 114, 154, 175
Dominican Observance and Observants, 322 n 22
Dominicans or Preaching Friars, ix, 21, 22, 71, 100, 103, 108, 115, 122, 124, 125, 147, 154, 156, 157, 163, 164, 165, 173, 176, 179, 182, 186, 232, 242, 244, 245, 248, 249, 250, 297 n 35, 315 n 29, 326 n 5
Dominici, Giovanni, 250
Domitilla, 197
Donatus, Saint, 163
Donvito, Luigi, 299 n 57
Dorothy of Montau, 225, 226, 227, 232, 233, 234, 238-240, 245, 248, 319 n 2, 320 n 2, 321 n 14, 321 n 16, 322 n 17, 323 n 4, 327 n 22
Douai, 136
Douceline of Aix, 23, 182, 225, 231, 318 n 1, 327 n 25
Douceline of Digne, 172
Douie, Decima, 301 n 9
Dronke, Peter, 317 n 1
Dubois, Henri, 278 n 17
Duby, Georges, xv, 30, 31, 273 n 1, 274 n 3, 274 n 8, 275 n 11, 275 n 12, 275 n 17
Du Chesne, François, 306 n 4
Dumas, Auguste, xvi, 273 n 1
Dumézil, Georges, 30, 275 n 9
Dumont, Louis, 136, 292 n 25
Dunin-Wasowicz, 307 n 6
Duparc, Pierre, 330 n 17

Dupré Theseider, Eugenio, 59, 280 n 36, 325 n 1
Durand, Ursin, 286 n 11, 311 n 27
Durand André of Apt, 81
Durandus *de Orto*, 110

Eberstaller, Herta, 279 n 18
Eleven Thousand Virgins, 321 n 14
Elisabeth of Portugal, 172
Elisabeth of Reute, 172
Elisabeth of Spalbeek, 227
Elisabeth of Thuringia or Hungary, x, 58, 171, 176-177, 178, 185, 232, 234, 248, 299 n 1, 303 n 25, 303 n 30, 306 n 3, 327 n 22
Ellies du Pin, L., 324 n 7, 328 n 31
Elzéar of Sabran, xi, 73-82, 177, 179, 192-203, 207, 285 n 1, 285 n 2, 285 n 3, 286 n 13, 287 n 18, 287 n 19, 309 n 1, 309 n 4, 314 n 8
Emery, Richard, 281 n 39
Emmen, Aquilin, 199, 312 n 31
Eon de l'Etoile, 20
Epiney-Burgard, Georgette, 318 n 16
Erault, Jean, 260
Ercolano, Saint, 165
Eric the Saint, King, 323 n 23
Ermengard, Countess, 300 n 6
Ermengaud of Sabran, 74
Escueillens, 199
Espitalier, Guillaume, 78, 287 n 18, 287 n 19

Facio of Cremona, 115, 296 n 28
Faenza, 155-156, 165, 297 n 28
Faloci Pulignani, Michele, 329 n 1
Farmer, Hugh, 301 n 9
Fausti, L., 298 n 45
Fawtier, Robert, 317 n 8, 320 n 7, 321 n 12, 326 n 3, 326 n 4, 326 n 5, 326 n 8, 326 n 10, 326 n 12, 327 n 14, 327 n 18, 327 n 20, 327 n 21, 327 n 24
Fécamp, 11
Ferrara, 302 n 24
Ferrer, Vincent, 213

Filippini, Francesco, 298 n 50
Filippo of Taranto, 74
Flagellants, 123–125, 126
Flanders, 119
Flandrin, Jean-Louis, 308 n 14,
    308 n 22
Fliche, Augustin, xii, xvi, 272 n 8,
    272 n 10, 273 n 3, 273 n 5
Florence and Florentines, 178, 180,
    181, 223, 245, 247
Folz, Robert, 276 n 2
Fonseca, Cosimo Damiano, 108
Fontenay-le-Comte, monastery of, 209
Foralosso, Imelda, 324 n 9
Forbin d'Oppède, Roselyne de,
    285 n 1, 286 n 13, 310 n 8
Fossier, Robert, 29, 32, 274 n 5,
    274 n 6, 275 n 13
Fraknói, Vilmos, 304 n 40
Francesca Romana, Saint, 245
Franceschini, Ezio, 279 n 23
Franche-Comté, 55, 70, 149, 151, 152
Franciscan Conventuals, 200,
    314 n 18, 315 n 19
Franciscan Observance and
    Observants, 205, 209, 214, 261,
    314 n 16, 314 n 18, 314 n 19,
    316 n 29, 316 n 33
Franciscan Order and Franciscans, ix,
    x, 22, 34, 47, 71, 75, 76, 77, 78,
    79, 80, 81, 82, 100, 108, 109, 113,
    115, 122, 123, 126, 154, 155, 160,
    161, 164, 166, 172, 174, 175, 176,
    178, 179, 180, 181, 182, 193,
    199–200, 201, 202, 205–215, 221,
    250, 258, 267, 268, 286 n 11,
    287 n 20, 302 n 20, 302 n 24,
    305 n 43, 309 n 4, 314 n 9,
    315 n 21, 316 n 36, 320 n 8,
    322 n 17
Franciscan Spirituals, 34, 75, 77, 78,
    79, 80, 82, 177, 193, 199, 200,
    201, 221, 245, 247
Francis of Assisi, ix, 22, 34, 62, 71,
    99, 100, 103, 108, 122, 154, 171,
    174, 175, 176, 178, 179, 180, 182,

208, 212, 219, 234, 288 n 6,
    305 n 45, 328 n 29
Francis of Sales, 269, 285 n 3,
    310 n 16
François II of Brittany, 212
François of Meyronnes, 75–76, 194,
    286 n 6
Fraticelli, 78, 82, 202, 228, 287 n 22
Frederick II, Emperor, 123, 143
Free Spirit, brethren of the, 228
Frères Pontifes, confraternity of, 53
Friedberg, Emil Albert, 308 n 19
Frisi, Anton Francesco, 280 n 30
Fulbert of Chartres, 14
Fulcher of Chartres, 47
Fulda, 143
Fulda, confraternity, 112
Fumagalli, Vito, 277 n 5
Fusignano, Church of San Savino, 165

Gabriel, Astrik, 305 n 40
Gaiffier, Baudouin de, 300 n 4,
    306 n 54
Galicia, 89
Gallerani, Andrea, 161
Garampi, Giuseppe, 301 n 14
Gargano, Monte, 321 n 14
Gatta, Francesco, 279 n 19
Gaul, 4, 5, 8, 134
Gennaro, Clara, 302 n 19
George, Saint, 52, 155
Gerardo, son of Raimondo, 66
Geremek, Bronislaw, xv, 273 n 1
Gerio, Saint, 295 n 15
Germanus, Saint, 5
Gerson, Jean, 24, 239, 250–252, 262,
    263, 324 n 7, 328 n 31, 328 n 32,
    328 n 33, 328 n 34, 328 n 35,
    328 n 36, 328 n 37, 330 n 20,
    331 n 27
Gertrude, daughter of Hedwig of
    Silesia, 187
Gervais, Robert, 329 n 12
Ghibellines, 74, 75, 156
Giacomo, Archpriest, 68
Gilbert of Tournai, 227, 318 n 19

Giordano, Luigi, 278 n 13, 278 n 14,
   284 n 81, 284 n 88
Gisla, 305 n 47
Gloria, Andrea, 294 n 3, 297 n 29
Glorieux, Palémon, 251, 328 n 36
Gobin, Jean, 316 n 36
Gonnet, Giovanni, 301 n 10
Gontran, King, 134
Goths, 165
Gottschalk, Joseph, 307 n 6, 307 n 8,
   307 n 9, 308 n 10
Gout, Raoul, 306 n 54, 318 n 1
Goyau, Georges
Grail cycle, 53
Grandmont, 18
Gratian, 188, 189, 308 n 19
Gratien de Paris, 314 n 16
Grau, Engelbert, 302 n 17, 302 n 19
Great Companies, 210
Gréban, Arnoul, 24
Greeks, 90
Gregorian reform, 98
Gregory I the Great, Pope, 130, 131,
   132, 291 n 5
Gregory VII, Pope, 33, 42, 46, 48, 98,
   247, 300 n 6
Gregory VIII, Pope, 88
Gregory XI, Pope, 223, 232, 247, 252,
   310 n 15, 327 n 19
Gregory XII, Pope, 316 n 30
Gregory of Tours, 6
Grèzes, Henri de, 294 n 4
Griguer, Thérèse, 313 n 4
Grimoard, Anglic, Cardinal, 232
Grundmann, Herbert, xii, 272 n 9,
   301 n 12
Gualazzini, Ugo, 297 n 28
Gualfardo of Verona, 54, 59, 60, 61,
   280 n 32
Gualtero of Lodi, 57–58, 59, 68,
   279 n 25, 283 n 75
Guecellone da Camino, 295 n 10
Guelfs, 156, 162, 163, 164
Gueusquin, Marie-France, 293 n 25,
   293 n 26, 293 n 32
Guillaume, Franciscan tertiary, 209

Guillaume de Signe, 73, 196
Guillaume of Sabran, 73, 77, 198
Guingamp, monastery of, 212
Gustaw, Romuald, 306 n 5
Guy XII, Count, 209
Guyenne, 210

Hadewijch of Antwerp, 225
Hageneder, Othmar, 279 n 18
Haidacher, Anton, 279 n 18
Hardouin V of Maillé, 206
Hardouin VI of Maillé, 206
Harris, Marguerite Tjader, 325 n 1
Hattin, 49, 88
Hayez, Michel, 288 n 31
Hebron, 60
Héchac, 258
Hedwig of Silesia, 185, 186–190,
   306 n 5, 306 n 6, 307 n 6
Heming of Abo, 322 n 20
Henri, monk, 20
Henri, Guillaume, 196
Henri de la Baume, 208, 211, 314 n 15
Henry, son of Hedwig of Silesia, 187
Henry II, Emperor, 52, 202
Henry III, Emperor, 41
Henry VII, Emperor, 74
Henry of Susa, Cardinal Hostiensis,
   113
Henry of York, Cardinal, 146
Henry the Bearded, 187
Heuckelum, Mercedes van, 286 n 12
Heymann, Ernst, 304 n 37
Hilary, bishop of Poitiers, 6
Hildegard of Bingen, 220, 317 n 1,
   327 n 25
Hincmar of Rheims, 110
Hipler, Franz, 323 n 4
Hiver-Bérenguier, Jean-Pierre, 317 n 6,
   329 n 2, 329 n 3
Hocquet, Jean-Claude, 278 n 17
Holden, A.-J., 274 n 4
Hollman, Lennart, 317 n 5, 325 n 1
Holy Land, 16, 47, 50, 52, 55, 56, 59,
   60, 61, 64, 66, 89, 90, 93, 244, 257
Hsia, R. Po-chia, 293 n 2

Huart, Arthur, 315 n 21
Hugh of Avallon, 173
Hugh of Lincoln, 141
Hugues of Digne, 172, 231
Humbert of Romans, 103
Humbert of Silva Candida, 42
Hunaudaye, 316 n 29
Hundred Years' War, 205, 215, 257, 266
Hungary and Hungarians, 28, 96, 143, 304 n 40
Hunzrück, 148
Hussites, 146, 241, 260, 262, 265, 330 n 21
Huyskens, Albert, 299 n 1, 306 n 3

Iacometti, Fabio, 295 n 16
Iacopone of Todi, 80, 287 n 26
Imitatio Christi, 25
Imola, 156
Innocent III, 55, 64, 68, 70, 85, 92, 122, 162, 185, 242, 279 n 18, 282 n 62
Innocent IV, 143
Inquisition and Inquisitors, 36, 59, 78, 80, 257, 330 n 22
Investiture Controversy, 33
Ippolito of Florence, 181
Isabeau, daughter of Jacques de la Marche, 211
Isabelle of Avaugour, 212
Isabelle of Bavaria, 258, 259, 316 n 35
Isabelle of Clisson, 315 n 29
Isidore, Saint, 284 n 90
Issoire, 152
Ivo of Chartres, 189, 308 n 22

Jacobus de Voragine, 129-139, 291 n 1
Jacqueries, 35
Jacques II de Bourbon or de la Marche, Count, 210-211, 258
Jacques de Vitry, 70, 119, 291 n 1
Jaffé, Philipp, 289 n 7
James, Saint, 89
Janus II of Lusignan, 211

Javols, bishop of, 6
Jean I of Alençon, 213
Jean II of Alençon, 213, 316 n 32
Jean I of Bourbon, 210
Jean II of Bourbon, 211
Jean V of Montfort, 213, 316 n 32
Jean of Pontlevoy, 210, 316 n 36
Jean Philippe, provincial of Touraine, 315 n 19
Jean Robert, Canon, 211
Jeanne, wife of Guy XII, 209
Jeanne of Bauçay, countess of Longueville, 206, 315 n 29
Jeanne of Chantal, 253
Jeanne of Montbazon, 206
Jeanne-Marie of Maillé, 126, 172, 205-215, 221, 238, 241, 258, 313 n 4, 313 n 5, 314 n 7, 315 n 24, 315 n 29, 316 n 30, 316 n 35, 320 n 3, 321 n 10, 324 n 12, 329 n 6
Jerome, Saint, 160, 173, 198, 267, 311 n 25, 311 n 26
Jerusalem, 16, 46, 48, 49, 50, 60, 61, 63, 88, 89, 282 n 52, 321 n 14
Jews, 3, 45, 48, 85, 90, 141, 142, 143, 144, 146, 147, 148, 149, 150, 152, 265
Joachim of Fiore, 82, 123, 202
Joan of Arc, xix, 24, 203, 213, 214, 221, 253, 255-256, 257, 260-264, 316 n 34, 321 n 10, 330 n 19, 330 n 21
Joan of Lily, 263
Joanna I of Naples, Queen, 210, 315 n 23
Johanek, Peter, 316 n 33
John, Apostle, 244
John XXII, Pope, 24, 75, 76, 77, 78, 79, 80, 81, 160, 193, 194, 199, 202, 205, 221, 222-223, 268, 286 n 12, 287 n 24
John XXIII, Pope, 249
John II of Armagnac, 257
John the Baptist, Saint, 159, 194, 195
John the Good, 315 n 23

Joli, Jean, 76, 201
Jones, Philip J., 299 n 60
Juan de Torquemada, 249
Julian, Saint, 7
Jumièges, 11
Jüttner, Georg, 312 n 38

Kaftal, George, 278 n 15
Kalteisen, Heinrich, 147, 262
Kern, Léon, 296 n 22, 297 n 32
Kieckhefer, Richard, 323 n 24
Kinga, Queen, 172
Kitzingen, 189
Klaniczay, Gabor, 277 n 2
Knights Templar, 52
Knolles, Robert, 207
Koblenz, 147
Koch, Gottfried, 301 n 10
Krak des Chevaliers, 47
Kumans, 99

Labande, E.-R., 272 n 10, 273 n 5,
    328 n 1
Lacarra, Jose M., 278 n 10
Ladislaus of Durazzo, 316 n 30
Lagarde-Sclafer, Jacques de, 286 n 6
La Guiche, 212
Lambro, river, 281 n 48
Lamprecht of Regensburg, 226
Languedoc, 13, 21, 31, 76, 82, 99,
    196, 199, 200, 202, 286 n 11
Lanzoni, Francesco, 295 n 11,
    297 n 28, 298 n 49
La Rochelle, 261
La Roncière, Charles de, 107, 116,
    276 n 22, 290 n 9
Lateran, Third Council, 99
Lateran, Fourth Council, 91, 92, 99,
    104, 122, 238
Latium, 28
Latreille, André, 275
Laurent, Marie Hyacinthe, 320 n 2,
    324 n 6, 325 n 1
Laval, convent of, 209
Lawrence, Saint, 160
Lazzarino of Pisa, 322 n 17, 326 n 10

Lazzeri, Zeffirino, 299 n 1
Le Bras, Gabriel, xii, xiii, 99, 272 n 8
Leclercq, Henri, 291 n 8, 292 n 15,
    293 n 27
Leclercq, Jean, 279 n 24
Ledru, Ambroise, 313 n 5
Lefort, François, 278 n 10
Legniça, 187
Le Goff, Jacques, xii, xv, 47, 136,
    271 n 1, 274 n 8, 275 n 19,
    276 n 2, 277 n 3, 288 n 4,
    289 n 11, 292 n 25, 293 n 35
Lejeune, Rita, 277 n 8
Lemaître, Henri, 313 n 1
Lemmens, Leonhard, 288 n 6
Leo, Pope Saint, 131
Leo X, Pope, 157–158
Leodegar, Saint, 5
Léonard, Emile, 287 n 24
Leonardi, Claudio, 300 n 1, 319 n 2
Le Puy, 32
Le Roy Ladurie, Emmanuel, 276 n 23
Leutard, 13
Liberale of Treviso, 159
Liège, 119
Liget, 208
Limoges, 7
Lindner, Dominikus, 308 n 14
Lisini, Alessandro, 295 n 16
Llop y Bayo, Francesc, 292 n 21
Loches, monastery of, 209, 314 n 18
Lodi, 57, 58, 68
Loire, valley of the, 126, 206, 209,
    210, 215, 258, 261
Lombardy, ix, 54, 56, 57, 58, 120
Lorenzo del Pino, 326 n 12
Lorraine, 42, 214, 255, 263
Loudun, 315 n 29
Louis VI the Fat, 206
Louis IX, King, 17, 22–23, 185–186,
    206, 268
Louis I of Anjou, 211, 212, 258,
    315 n 23
Louis II of Anjou, 211, 213, 258,
    316 n 30
Louis of Orléans, 211

Louis IV of Thuringia, 178, 185
Lucchese of Poggibonsi, 115, 154, 155, 156, 160, 161
Luce, Siméon, 316 n 31
Lucius III, Pope, 21, 120-121
Luçon, 208
Ludwig II the Severe, 144
Ludwig III the Bearded, 144, 146

Mabille of Simiane, 198
Maccarrone, Michele, 107, 298 n 41, 310 n 7
McDonnell, Ernest W., 301 n 11
Maffei, Domenico, 317 n 12, 325 n 1
Magli, Ida, 116, 291 n 10
Mahaut of Châtillon, 74
Mainz, 132, 148
Mainz, archbishop of, 142-143
Maitre, Jacques, 318 n 17, 318 n 21
Malo, Saint, 8
Malvecius, Jacobus, or Giacomo Malvizzi, 56, 279 n 22, 280 n 28, 283 n 73
Mamertus, Saint, 130, 133, 134
Mancini, Franco, 287 n 26
Mancini, Girolamo, 296 n 24, 297 n 29
Manfredi, Astorgio II, 165
Manselli, Raoul, xvii, 199, 200, 273 n 5, 286 n 5, 306 n 3, 311 n 28, 311 n 29, 312 n 38, 312 n 39
Mansi, Giovan Domenico, 327 n 27
Mantellate, 115
Manteuffel, Tadeusz, 275 n 18
Manzikert, Battle of, 46
Marcel, Saint, 136
Marches, 162, 295 n 15, 296 n 25
Marchesan, Angelo, 295 n 9
Marconi, Stefano, 239
Mareri, Filippa, 172, 179, 180
Mareri, Thomas, 179
Margaret, sister of Charles of Orléans, 212
Margaret, virgin and saint, 261
Margaret of Cortona, 72, 126-127,

157-158, 160, 172, 225, 231, 232, 327 n 25
Margaret of Hungary, 179, 234
Margaret of Scotland, Queen, 52
Margherita of Città di Castello, 157
Mariano d'Alatri, 301 n 13, 305 n 43, 314 n 15
Maria of Venice, 115
Marienwerder, John, 234, 248, 319 n 2, 323 n 4
Marie of Anjou, Queen, 213, 261, 315 n 24
Marie of Berry, 211
Marie of Châtillon or Brittany, Queen, 211-212, 258, 259, 315 n 23, 316 n 32
Marie of Montfort-Laval, 213, 215
Marie of Oignies, 70, 119-120, 225
Marie of Valenciennes, 251
Marie Robine, or Marie the Gascon, 221, 223, 224, 225, 258-260, 261, 318 n 5
Mark, Saint, 69, 129, 132, 137, 168
Marseilles, 75, 136, 198, 201, 202
Martène, Edmond, 286 n 11, 311 n 27
Martha, Saint, 136
Martial, Saint, 7
Martin V, Pope, 146, 249, 327 n 26
Martin, Hervé, 205, 313 n 2, 315 n 25
Martin, Victor, xii, xvi, 272 n 8, 272 n 10, 273 n 3, 273 n 5
Martin of Boisgaultier, 205-206, 208, 210, 258, 313 n 4, 323 n 3, 329 n 9
Martin of Tours, Saint, 5, 145
Mathieu of Bouzigues, 201, 312 n 34
Mathilda, Empress, 52
Mathilda of Canossa, 300 n 6
Matthias of Linköping, 244, 248, 327 n 27
Maurer, Wilhelm, 303 n 26
Mauritius, Saint, 5, 52
Mauzaize, Jean, 313 n 3, 314 n 18
Mayenne, 214
Mechtilde of Magdeburg, 225
Meersseman, Gilles Gérard, xii-xiii, xvii, 107-116, 272 n 11, 273 n 5,

283 n 72, 289, 289 n 1, 290 n 2,
291 n 4, 301 n 13, 302 n 15,
308 n 18, 308 n 21, 320 n 7
Meier, Johannes, 157, 295 n 19
Melania the Younger, 198, 311 n 26
*Memoriale propositi fratrum et
sororum de poenitentia*, 113,
121-122, 188
Menestò, Enrico, 300 n 1, 319 n 2,
322 n 22
Mens, Alcantara, 301 n 11
Menthon, 61
Merula, Pellegrino, 297 n 36
Metz, 7, 136, 262
Miccoli, Giovanni, 273 n 4, 282 n 56
Michael, Saint, 6, 213, 261, 321 n 14
Michael of Cesena, 78
Michaud-Quantin, Pierre, 110, 290 n 4
Michele degli Alberti, Friar, 180-181
Michelet, Jules, 27
Micheline of Pesaro, 172
Mierow, Charles Christopher,
281 n 39
Migne, J.-P., 219, 276 n 1, 291 n 2,
292 n 16, 300 n 8
Milan, xvi, 32, 33, 58, 120, 165, 168
Militia of the Virgin, 308 n 21
Milly, 206
Mirebeau, monastery of, 209, 315 n 19
Modorati, Luigi, 280 n 30, 284 n 78
Mollat, Michel, xii, xv, 271 n 5,
273 n 1, 275 n 20, 276 n 21,
303 n 29
Monaldo, 304 n 38
Monnoyeur, Jean-Baptiste, 331 n 27
Montanism, 197
Montaperti, Battle of, 155
Montesanto, 295 n 15
Montfort family, 212
Monticelli, 180
Mont-Saint-Michel, 213
Monza, 57, 58, 61, 68, 284 n 78
Morghen, Raffaello, 301 n 10
Morigia, Bonincontro, 57, 279 n 23,
281 n 46, 281 n 48
Moselle, 149

Moslems and Islam, 11, 15, 45, 47, 48,
49, 88, 90
Mostardi, F., 303 n 24
Most Holy Savior, Order of, 246,
326 n 14
Moulins, 211, 213
Muratori, Ludovico, 283 n 73

Naples, 74, 75, 76, 77, 78, 80, 81,
193, 195, 200, 210, 211, 287 n 18,
301 n 7
Narbonne, 199, 286 n 11
Nardi, Paolo, 317 n 12, 325 n 1
Natalini, V., 298 n 41
Nelli, René, 196, 310 n 20
Nereus, Saint, 197
Neri, Dario, 295 n 16
Newman, Barbara, 317 n 1
Niardo, 57, 58
Nice, 209
Nicholas IV, Pope, 108
Nicholas of Cusa, 146
Nicholas of Linköping, 323 n 24
Nicole, Sister, 208
Nicopolis, Crusade of, 210
Nider, Johannes, 262-263, 305 n 47,
330 n 21, 331 n 23
Nîmes, 73
Nivelles, 119
Noonan, John Thomas, 308 n 14
Norbert, Saint, 18, 51, 175
Normandy and Normans, 11, 28, 96
Notre-Dame of Planche-de-Vaux,
hermitage of, 207

Oberwesel, 142, 144, 145, 147, 148,
149, 150
Obizio of Brescia, 56-57, 58, 59, 60,
65, 67, 279 n 22, 283 n 73
Odon of Cluny, 52
Oglio, river, 57
Oignies-sur-Sambre, 120
Olafsson, Peter, 232, 248
Oliger, Livario, 303 n 24
Olivi, Peter John, 77, 199-200, 202,
268, 312 n 30, 312 n 32

Olivier of Clisson, 315 n 29
Omobono of Cremona, 53, 55-56, 58, 59, 61, 62, 64, 65, 66, 68, 70, 103, 121, 185, 278 n 16, 280 n 33, 280 n 37, 281 n 46, 281 n 51, 283 n 65, 284 n 76, 296 n 28, 297 n 36
Order of Saint James, 173
Ordo poenitentiae, or Order of the Penitents of Saint Francis, 109, 113, 121, 174, 188
Ordo romanus L, 132-133, 134, 135, 138
Orléans, 13, 213, 214, 261
Orléans, Council of, 134
Ornans, 152
Oroz Arizcuren, Francisco J., 311 n 21
Orselli, Alba Maria, 298 n 50
Orsini, Giordano, Cardinal, 146
Orsini, Napoleone, 320 n 6
Ortona, 321 n 14
Orvieto, 153-154, 161-162
Osimo, 296 n 25
Ot, Guiral, 78, 80
Otranto, 185
Otto of Freising, 59-60, 281 n 39
Ouen, Saint, 5
Ourliac, Paul, 272 n 10, 273 n 5, 317 n 12, 328 n 1
Oury, Guy Marie, 313 n 3

Paderborn, 147
Padua, 294 n 3, 297 n 29
Pagès, A., 317 n 6, 329 n 2, 329 n 3, 329 n 4, 329 n 5
Painter, Sidney, 273 n 1
Palanque, Jean Rémy, 275 n 15
Palatinate, Rhenish, 142, 147
Panzo, monastery of Sant'Angelo, 304 n 38
Papebroch, 278 n 13
Paravy, Pierrette, 330 n 21
Parenzo, Pietro, 154, 161-162
Paris and Parisians, 7, 74, 137, 138, 152, 201, 224, 228, 258, 259, 261, 262, 263, 316 n 35, 321 n 10

Paris, "Burgher of," 261, 262, 263
Paris, University of, 251
Parisse, Michel, 52, 277 n 7
Parma, 299 n 55
Pàsztor, Edith, 286 n 16, 303 n 25, 306 n 3
Pataria or Patarines, xvi, 32, 43
Patlagean, Evelyne, 292 n 11, 331 n 24
Paul, Saint 89, 244
Pauly, F., 150, 294 n 3
Pavia, 61
Pazzi, Gaspare, 163
Peano, Pierre, 312 n 30
Peasant War, 35
Pelagius, Pope, 131
Pelzer, Franz, 312 n 39
Penthièvre, 214
Perceval, 53
Perche, 213
Péronne, 330 n 22
Pertz, Georg Heinrich, 289 n 7
Perugia, 116, 123, 158, 160, 165, 166, 322 n 22
Pescia, 54, 68
Peter, Saint, 11, 89
Peter Lombard, 17, 82, 228
Peter Martyr, Saint, 114, 163
Peter of Luxemburg, 221, 259, 323 n 24
Peter the Hermit, 15
Petrarch, Francesco, 81
Petrocchi, Giorgio, 319 n 1
Petroff, Elizabeth Avilda, 318 n 16
Petronio, Saint, 165
Peyer, Hans Conrad, 281 n 45, 299 n 59
Peyronnet, Georges, 313 n 41
Philip III, King, 206
Philip IV the Fair, King, xv
Philip of Majorca, 77, 79, 80, 193, 286 n 15, 287 n 19, 304 n 32
Philippe de Mézières, 329 n 12
Philippe of the Chèze, 207
Philonenko, Marc, 281 n 42
Phoebus, Gaston, Count, 224, 257
Piacenza, 56, 57, 61, 66, 70

Picardy, 8, 29
Piéronne the Breton, 262
Pierre of Bruys, 20
Pietro Pettinaio or Pettignano, 115, 164, 166
Pinian, Valerius, 198, 311 n 26
Pisa and Pisans, 47, 55, 58, 60, 63, 67, 68, 69, 283 n 73
Pisa, Council of, 208, 221, 258
Pius II, Pope, 249
Poggibonsi, 154-155, 156, 160, 161, 168
Poitiers, 5, 136, 208, 209, 213, 260, 263
Poitou, 209
Pontal, Odette, 293 n 33
Poor Clares, Order of (Clarisses), 122, 172, 176, 180, 208, 209, 210, 211, 212, 214, 302 n 24, 314 n 16
Porcellet, Philippine de, 306 n 54
Porète, Marguerite, 228, 253, 328 n 34
Portmann, Marie Louise, 300 n 4
Poulain, Joseph Claude, 277 n 5
Pou y Martì, José-María, 287 n 18
Po Valley, 70
Prémontré and Premonstratensians, 18, 98
Prodi, Paolo 316 n 33
Provence, 3, 21, 73, 74, 76, 78, 82, 126, 136, 172, 177, 193, 194, 196, 198, 200, 202, 203, 207, 225, 231, 232, 287 n 18
Provins, 136
Prussia and Prussians, 225, 245
Puimichel, 192
Pyrenees, 89

Raimondo Palmerio, 56, 57, 58, 59, 60, 61, 62, 64, 65, 66, 68, 70, 279 n 20, 280 n 35, 281 n 38, 281 n 50, 282 n 59, 282 n 60, 283 n 68, 283 n 69, 283 n 75
Rainieri Fasani, 123
Rando, Daniela, 282 n 62
Ranieri of Pisa, 55, 58, 59, 60, 62, 63, 67-68, 69, 278 n 15, 280 n 29,

281 n 49, 282 n 52, 282 n 54, 282 n 55, 282 n 58, 283 n 73, 283 n 74
Raphaël, Friar, 213
Rapp, Francis, 281 n 42, 322 n 22
Raspe, Heinrich, 179
Ravenna, sister-in-law of Umiliana, 181
Raymond of Capua, 248, 250
Raymond of Sabanac, 257
Reber, Ortrud, 307 n 6
Reconquista, Spanish, 45
Reeves, Marjorie, 312 n 39
Reims, 7
Religion, Wars of, 205
Remigius, Saint, 7
Renaud of Ancenis, 315 n 29
Renou, Simon, 207
Rhineland, 28, 143, 146, 149, 150, 151, 174, 225, 318 n 16
Rhine River, 144, 148, 150
Rhône River, 200, 202
Riccieri, A., 298 n 48, 298 n 54
Rice, Eugene F., Jr., 331 n 1
Richard, Friar, 213, 214, 261, 262, 331 n 23
Richard II, duke of Normandy, 29
Richard of Pontoise, 141
Richard of Saint-Victor, 19
Riché, Pierre, 96, 288 n 1
Ridyard, Susan J., 277 n 2
Rieti, 180
Riff, Adolphe, 294 n 5
Rigo, or Enrico, of Bolzano, 158, 159, 161, 296 n 26
Rigon, Antonio, 294 n 3, 303 n 24
Rinaldi, Odorico, 286 n 12, 287 n 17
Ripperger, Helmut, 311 n 24
Risi, Isnardo, 77, 193, 194
Riva, Giuliano, 279 n 23
Robert, king of France, 13
Robert des Armoises, 263
Robert of Abrissel, 15, 300 n 6
Robert of Anjou, King, 74, 77, 78, 80, 177, 193, 287 n 24
Robert of Dreux, 206
Robert of Mileto, 79

Robert of Sillé-le-Guillaume, 206, 207, 258

Roch, Saint, 265

Roche, D., 275 n 19

Roches-Saint-Quentin, 206, 207

Roisin, Simone, 300 n 4

Roland, 53

Romana Fraternitas, 111

Rome and Romans, 46, 56, 61, 74, 75, 89, 124, 130, 131, 132, 137, 233, 244, 246–247, 252, 292 n 11, 303 n 24, 321 n 10, 321 n 14, 322 n 22

Rose of Viterbo, 72, 171, 180, 299 n 1, 305 n 43

Roth, Bartholomäus, 286 n 6

Rouen, 136, 261, 263

Rudolf, Emperor, 142, 144

Rufino of Piacenza, Canon, 56, 68, 279 n 20

Ruggero of Todi, 305 n 45

Rukn ad-Din Baibars, 45

Rusconi, Roberto, 317 n 3

Russo, Daniel, 267, 331 n 1

Ruysbroek, Jan van, 250

Ryan, Granger, 311 n 24

Sabatier, Paul, 302 n 19

Sabran family, 73

Sacchetti, Franco, 299 n 55

Saint-Benoît-sur-Loire, 41

Sainte-Baume, 61

Sainte-Foy of Conques, 14, 89

Saintes-Maries-de-la-Mer, 61

Saint-Jean-d'Angély, monastery of, 209

Saint-Maximin, 321 n 14

Saladin, 45, 87

Salamina, Luigi, 280 n 31

Salimbene de Adam, 166, 299 n 55

Salomea, Queen, 172

Salutati, Coluccio, 166

Samarati, Luigi, 279 n 25

Samson, Saint, 8

Sancha, Queen, 74, 77, 79, 80, 193, 286 n 12

San Gimignano, 156

Sansedoni, Ambrogio, 125, 164, 165–166

Santi, Francesco, 312 n 38

Santiago de Compostela, 14, 53, 55, 56, 60, 61, 89, 321 n 14

Saracens, 11, 28, 92, 96, 99

Sault, 201

Savino, Saint, 165

Saxons, 96

Scalia, Gianni, 299 n 55

Scandinavia and Scandinavians, 96, 97

Schism, Great, xix, 25, 124, 208, 221, 225, 235, 252, 256, 257, 258, 313 n 4

Schmitt, Clément, 288 n 30

Schmitt, Jean-Claude, 276 n 23, 288 n 4, 289 n 8, 293 n 35, 299 n 56

Schmucki, Ottaviano, 302 n 20

Schramm, Percy Ernst, 277 n 4

Schulenburg, Jane Tibbetts, 300 n 2

Scotivoli, Benvenuto, 296 n 25

Sées, monastery, 209

Senez, 329 n 12

Sensi, Mario, 301 n 14

Sheils, W. J., 283 n 66

Sibille of Puget, 197, 198

Sibylle, half-sister of Delphine of Puimichel, 196

Sicardo of Cremona, Bishop, 55, 64, 68

Sicily, 47, 82

Sicily, Kingdom of, 74, 81, 211

Siena, 125, 155, 161, 164, 165–166, 168, 239, 246, 295 n 16, 322 n 17

Sienna, confraternity of the Misericordia, 161

Sigal, Pierre-André, 281 n 42

Sigismund, King, 5

Silesia, 186, 187

Sillé, château of, 207

Simon, Friar, 245

Simon, hermit, 180

Simon, Marcel, 281 n 42

Sisto, Alessandra, 319 n 1

Sixtus IV, Pope, 250

Slavic countries and Slavs, 28, 97, 143
Sophie, daughter of Hedwig of Silesia, 187
Speculum virginum, 244, 245
Spello, 295 n 14
Spinelli, Giovanni, 279 n 24
Spoleto, 163-164, 322 n 22
Stachnik, Richard, 319 n 2, 324 n 5
Stanislao da Campagnola, 305 n 43
Stengers, Jean, 293 n 2
Stephen, Saint, 316 n 29
Stiennon, Jacques, 277 n 8
Strabo, Walafrid, 40
Strasbourg, 199
Stroick, Autbert, 318 n 19
Subiaco, abbey of, 79
Szell, Timea, 320 n 6

Tabor, Mount, 60
Tarascon, 136
Tarasque, the, 136
Taurisano, Innocenzo, 325 n 1
Tennegot, or Tenengot, Jean, 212
Teobaldo of Alba, 54-55, 58, 59, 60, 65, 66, 68, 69, 70, 278 n 13, 280 n 34, 283 n 64, 283 n 71, 284 n 77, 284 n 85
Teresa of Avila, 253
Tête d'Oye, Guillaume, Father, 208
Theban Legion, 5
Theodore, Saint, 52
Thibaut de Rougement, Archbishop, 146, 151
Thier, Ludger, 319 n 1
Thomas Aquinas, 228
Thomas de Cantimpré, 70
Thomas of Celano, 179, 304 n 38
Thomas of Spalato, 288 n 6
Thouars, 212
Thouars, house of, 214
Tiber, 131
Tierney, Brian, 273 n 1
Tintori, Gerardo, 57, 58, 59, 61, 67, 68, 70, 279 n 23, 281 n 46, 281 n 48
Tobin, Matthew, 318 n 13, 329 n 11

Tommaso da Chiavano, 163
Tommasuccio of Foligno, 329 n 1
Toso D'Arenzano, R., 304 n 39
Toubert, Pierre, 29, 274 n 2
Toulon, 77, 193
Toulouse, 5, 99, 221, 223, 257
Touraine, 205, 209
Tours, 5, 126, 205, 206, 207, 208, 210, 211, 212, 214, 215, 258, 313 n 4, 316 n 29, 316 n 35, 316 n 36, 321 n 10, 324 n 12
Tréguier, 101
Treviso, 155, 158, 159, 161, 296 n 26, 297 n 30
Trier, 142, 143, 144, 145, 152, 262
Triller, Anneliese, 319 n 2, 324 n 5
Troyes, 136, 261
Trzebinca, monastery of, 189
Tuetey, Alexandre, 330 n 18
Turks, 46, 210
Tuscany, 54, 58, 126, 154, 156, 165, 179, 329 n 1

Ubaldesca of Pisa, 58, 280 n 26
Ubertino of Casale, 82, 200, 303 n 32
Ugolino, Bishop, 68
Ulrich of Württemberg, 262
Umbria, 156, 329 n 1
Umiliana dei Cerchi, 58, 172, 178, 180-182
Umiliati, 113, 120, 174, 188
Undhagen, Carl-Gustaf, 325 n 1
Urban II, Pope, 14, 43, 46, 49
Urban IV, Pope, 186
Urban V, Pope, 195, 232, 256, 310 n 15
Urban VI, Pope, 221, 223, 247, 257
Urban VIII, Pope, 328 n 29
Uria Riu, Juan, 278 n 10
Ursulina of Parma, 321 n 10
Uzzano, 54, 70

Vadstena, 220, 246, 327 n 14
Valais, 5
Valcamonica, 57, 58
Valdelsa, 116

Valdes, 21
Valdinievole, 54, 58
Valenciennes, 328 n 34
Valerian, Saint, 197
Valois, Noël, 257, 260, 317 n 6,
    318 n 13, 329 n 2, 329 n 3,
    329 n 4, 329 n 5, 329 n 11
Van Engen, John, 272 n 14
Van Gennep, Arnold, 133, 136,
    292 n 14, 292 n 23, 292 n 25,
    299 n 56
Vanna, or Giovanna, of Orvieto, 115,
    154, 157
Vasquez, Isaac, 302 n 17
Vatican, basilica of, 131
Vatican Council, Second, xiii, xvii
Vauchez, André, ix–xiii, 271 n 2,
    272 n 9, 272 n 13, 272 n 15,
    275 n 16, 276 n 1, 277 n 9,
    278 n 16, 278 n 17, 279 n 20,
    280 n 28, 281 n 44, 283 n 65,
    284 n 82, 284 n 83, 284 n 87,
    284 n 89, 285 n 92, 288 n 2,
    293 n 36, 296 n 27, 297 n 38,
    298 n 46, 299 n 58, 300 n 3,
    303 n 29, 304 n 36, 306 n 1,
    306 n 2, 307 n 6, 308 n 16,
    308 n 20, 309 n 1, 309 n 26,
    310 n 7, 314 n 8, 315 n 25,
    323 n 1, 326 n 13, 328 n 29
Vazquez de Parga, Luis, 278 n 11
Vecchietti, Filippo, 296 n 25
Vendée, 209, 214
Venice and Venetians, 46, 47, 69, 168,
    233, 239, 322 n 22
Venturino of Bergamo, 124
Vernier [=Werner], Saint, 151, 152
Vernon, Jean-Marie de, 285 n 3,
    310 n 16
Verny [=Werner], Saint, 151
Verona, 54, 58, 280 n 32
Vertus, 13
Vestergaard, Elisabeth, 277 n 2
Vevey, convent of, 211
Vicaire, Marie-Humbert, 288 n 3,
    288 n 5

Vicoforte d'Asti, 55, 58
Vidal, Jean Marie, 286 n 15, 287 n 16,
    287 n 18
Vienne, 130, 134
Vienne, Council of, 200, 268
Viens, 198
Vie occitane de Delphine, 193,
    285 n 1, 286 n 9, 286 n 14,
    287 n 27, 288 n 33
Vie occitane d'Elzéar, 192, 285 n 1,
    285 n 3, 286 n 4, 286 n 7
Vincent, Saint, 151
Violante, Cinzio, 32, 273 n 4, 275 n 14
Virgin of Puy, confraternity of the, 110
Visconti, Federico, 103
Visigoths, 5
Vital, 81
Vita maior of Saint Hedwig, 186,
    187, 188, 189
Vita minor of Saint Hedwig, 187
Viterbo, 180, 186, 299 n 1, 307 n 6
Vito of Cortona, 178, 180, 181,
    306 n 53
Vogel, Cyrille, 111, 290 n 6
von Auw, Lydia, 78, 287 n 21,
    304 n 32
von der Hardt, Hermann, 327 n 26
von Harnack, Adolf, 72, 285 n 93
von Loë, Paulus, 295 n 19
Vosges, 8
Vouillé, 5

Wace, 29, 274 n 4
Wadding, Luke, 327 n 28
Waitz, Georg, 291 n 2
Waldensians, 21, 44, 64, 110, 113
Wartburg, 179
Webb, Diana M., 283 n 66
Weinhold, Karl, 318 n 18
Werner of Bacharach, 142–152
Westpfahl, Hans, 319 n 2, 324 n 5
William VII, 207
Williamites, 144
William Marshal, xv, 273 n 1
William of Norwich, 141
William of Ockham, 228

Winzbach, 144
Wolff, Philippe, 276 n 21
Womrath, 148
Wroclaw, 189

Yolanda of Aragon, 213, 215, 258, 316 n 30, 329 n 7
Yves Hélory, Saint, 101, 207, 212, 215, 314 n 9

Zambrasi, Tebaldello, 156
Zarri, Gabriella, 316 n 33
Zdekauer, Lodovico, 294 n 7
Zerfass, Rolf, 282 n 57, 282 n 61
Zink, Michel, 102, 289 n 10
Zorzi, Diego, 311 n 20, 311 n 26, 312 n 34
Zum Brunn, Emilie, 318 n 16